Brian Friel's Dramatic Artistry
'The Work Has Value'

Brian Friel during a rehearsal of *Performances* at the Gate Theatre, Dublin. Photograph by kind permission of photographer Tom Lawlor and the Gate Theatre, Dublin

Brian Friel's Dramatic Artistry
'The Work Has Value'

Edited by
Donald E. Morse, Csilla Bertha, and Mária Kurdi

Essays taken from
The Hungarian Journal of English and American Studies

For Máire and Pát,
dear friends and
co-admirers of "the work",
Csila Donald
Dublin, May 2006.

Carysfort Press

A Carysfort Press Book

Brian Friel's Dramatic Artistry
'The Work Has Value'
Edited by Donald E. Morse, Csilla Bertha, and Mária Kurdi

First published in Ireland in 2006 as a paperback original by
Carysfort Press, 58 Woodfield, Scholarstown Road
Dublin 16, Ireland
©2006 Copyright remains with the authors

Typeset by Carysfort Press
Cover design by Alan Bennis

Printed and bound by eprint limited
Unit 35, Coolmine Industrial Estate, Dublin 16, Ireland

This book is published with the financial assistance of
The Arts Council (An Chomhairle Ealaíon), Dublin, Ireland

Contents

Copyright Acknowledgements   x
Preface   xi

1 | Introduction: Transparent, Oblique Voices
Paulo Eduardo Carvalho   1

PORTRAITS OF THE ARTIST

2 | 'Singing of Human Unsuccess':
  Brian Friel's Portraits of the Artist
Csilla Bertha and Donald E. Morse   13

3 | Restless Wanderers and Great Pretenders:
 Fox Melarkey and Frank Hardy
Giovanna Tallone   35

4 | Music and Words in Brian Friel's *Performances*
Csilla Bertha   61

AMBIGUITIES OF LANGUAGE

5 | Interpreting Between Privacies: Brian Friel
       and the Boundaries of Language
Ger FitzGibbon   73

6 | Palimpsest: Two Languages as One in *Translations*
Christopher Murray   93

7 | The Hungarian Translator's View of *Translations* and
       the Problems in Translating it into Hungarian
Márton Mesterházi   109

PSYCHOLOGICAL AND SPIRITUAL TORMENTS

8 | Unveiling the Vice: A Reading of *Faith Healer*
Giovanna Tallone   123

9 | Telling Tales: Narratives of Politics
       and Sexuality in *The Gentle Island*
Michael Parker   141

RITUAL AND CEREMONY

10 | Questing for Ritual and Ceremony in a
        Godforsaken World: *Dancing at Lughnasa*
        and *Wonderful Tennessee*
Richard Allen Cave   181

DISABILITY AND EMPOWERMENT

**11 | Disability as Motif and Meaning
in Brian Friel's Drama**
Ruth Niel   205

**12 | *Molly Sweeney* and its Sources:
A Postmodern Case History**
Christopher Murray   229

POLITICS IN AND OF THE THEATRE

**13 | About Some Healthy Intersections:
Brian Friel and Field Day**
Paulo Eduardo Carvalho   251

**14 | Forms of Redress: Structure and Characterization
in *The Freedom of the City***
Michael Parker   271

**15 | An Interview with Richard Pine
about Brian Friel's Theatre**
Mária Kurdi   301

Contributors   *325*
Index   *331*

Copyright Acknowledgements

Grateful acknowledgement is given to Gallery Press for permission to quote material previously published from Brian Friel's plays: *The Loves of Cass McGuire*, *Crystal and Fox*, *The Enemy Within*, *Faith Healer*, *The Freedom of the City*, *The Gentle Island*, *Give Me Your Answer, Do!*, *Molly Sweeney*, *Wonderful Tennessee*, and *Performances*.

Grateful acknowledgement is given to Faber & Faber Publishers for permission to quote material previously published from Brian Friel's plays: from *Selected Plays of Brian Friel*: *Philadelphia, Here I Come!*, *The Freedom of the City*, *Living Quarters*, *Aristocrats*, *Faith Healer* and *Translations*; from *Dancing at Lughnasa*, and *Making History*.

Grateful acknowledgement is given to The Agency (London) Ltd © Brian Friel for permission to quote material previously published from Brian Friel's *Give Me Your Answer, Do!* first published by Gallery Press and Penguin 1997. All rights reserved and enquiries to The Agency (London) Ltd, 24 Pottery Lane, London W11 4LZ info@theagency.co.uk.

Ten of the essays in this book along with the introduction have appeared in the *Hungarian Journal of English and American Studies* and are reprinted with minor changes with the permission of the editor, Professor Zoltán Abádi-Nagy. The essays 'About Some Healthy Intersections: Brian Friel and Field Day' by Paulo Eduardo Carvalho, and 'Telling Tales: Narratives of Politics and Sexuality in Brian Friel's *The Gentle Island*' by

Michael Parker appeared in the Irish Drama Issue of *HJEAS* (1996), guest edited by Csilla Bertha; the essays '"Singing of Human Unsuccess": Brian Friel's Portraits of the Artist' (originally titled '"Singing of Human Unsuccess": The Artist in Brian Friel's *Give Me Your Answer, Do!*') by Csilla Bertha and Donald E. Morse; 'Restless Wanderers and Great Pretenders: Brian Friel's Fox Melarkey and Frank Hardy' by Giovanna Tallone; 'Interpreting Between Privacies: Brian Friel and the Boundaries of Language' by Gerald FitzGibbon; 'Two Languages as One in *Translations*' by Christopher Murray; 'The Hungarian Translator's View of *Translations* and the Problems in Translating it into Hungarian' by Márton Mesterházi; 'Questing for Ritual and Ceremony in a Godforsaken World: *Dancing at Lughnasa* and *Wonderful Tennessee*' by Richard Allen Cave; 'Disability as Motif and Meaning in Brian Friel's Drama' by Ruth Niel; and 'Forms of Redress: Structure and Characterization in Brian Friel's *The Freedom of the City*' by Michael Parker appeared in the Special Issue of *HJEAS* in Honour of Brian Friel at 70 (1999), guest edited by Mária Kurdi; 'Unveiling the Vice: A Reading of *Faith Healer*' by Giovanna Tallone and 'Introduction: Transparent, Oblique Voices' (originally titled, 'The Real Thing') by Paulo Eduardo Carvalho appeared in the Irish Issue of *HJEAS* (2002), edited by Csilla Bertha and Donald E. Morse.

The essay 'A Post-Modern Case History: *Molly Sweeney* and its Sources' by Christopher Murray is reprinted with minor changes from *Études Irlandaises* by permission of the editor Dr. Bernard Escarbelt. The essay 'Words and Music in *Performances*' by Csilla Bertha is reprinted from *English Literature to New Literatures in English, International Perspectives: A Festschrift in Honour of Wolfgang Zach*, edited by Michael Kenneally and Rhona Richman Kenneally and is reprinted by kind permission of the editors. The interview with Richard Pine about the work of Brian Friel by Mária Kurdi appeared originally in *The AnaChronisT* and is reprinted by permission of the editor, Professor Ágnes Péter.

'The Work Has Value'

Brian Friel, *Give Me Your Answer, Do!*

Preface

The essays gathered in *Brian Friel's Dramatic Artistry* survey the most remarkable playwriting career of Ireland's foremost play-wright – a career that now spans close to five decades. His plays provoke a person into knowledge – to borrow Ralph Waldo Emerson's felicitous phrase – knowledge of Ireland, society, history, individuals, while proving to be vastly entertaining to audiences around the world.

Over the past decade, the *Hungarian Journal of English and American Studies* (HJEAS) published by the University of Debrecen in Hungary has commissioned several issues devoted to Irish Studies from a variety of perspectives: *Irish Drama* (1996), *Myth and History in Twentieth-Century Irish Literature* (2002), *Irish Literature and Culture: Getting into Contact* (2004). In 1999 Mária Kurdi, University of Pécs, guest-edited a *Special Issue in Honour of Brian Friel at 70* and it is that issue which forms the core of this volume. Additional essays have been added from the other special HJEAS Irish Studies issues. *Brian Friel's Dramatic Artistry* also includes an interview with Richard Pine about Friel's work from another Hungarian scholarly journal, *The AnaChronisT* published by Eötvös Lóránt University in Budapest. To round out the collection *Etudes Irlandaises* con-tributed an essay by a long-time friend of Irish Studies in Hungary, Christopher Murray. I am most grateful to Carysfort Press for making these essays by scholars from across Europe originally published in Hungary available now in Ireland and elsewhere.

Donald E. Morse
Hungarian Journal of English and American Studies

1 | Introduction:
Transparent, Oblique Voices

Paulo Eduardo Carvalho

Brian Friel's seventieth birthday in 1999 was celebrated in Ireland with honours only rarely accorded to living authors. In the footsteps of the Gate Theatre's Beckett Festival, in 1991, and the subsequent Pinter Festivals (1997, 2001), a tribute festival was organized with the participation of the Abbey Theatre, the Gate, the Lyric Theatre, and the Royal Shakespeare Company, presenting old and new productions of plays including *The Freedom of the City*, *Dancing at Lughnasa*, *Living Quarters*, *Making History*, *Aristocrats*, *A Month in the Country*, *Give Me Your Answer, Do!*, and *Lovers*. The Festival also held an Academic Conference organized by University College Dublin, as well as an exhibition at the National Gallery, pre-show and post-show talks and discussions and public readings of other plays such as *The Enemy Within* and *The Mundy Scheme*. But one of the more lasting consequences of this initiative was the publication of a special issue of the *Irish University Review* (IUR) dedicated to Brian Friel. Edited by Anthony Roche, this volume gathered sixteen essays, contributed by an almost exclusive Irish-Anglo-American group of scholars, the only exception being Csilla Bertha, from Kossuth University, Debrecen, Hungary.

As I suggested, one of the most positive consequences of these celebrations, at least in more scholarly terms, is precisely that which survives time and travels better, like books and journals. 1999 naturally saw the appearance of a highly significant number of publications dedicated to Friel's *oeuvre*, among which, and besides the already mentioned special issue of the IUR, the long much-needed collection of Friel's *Essays, Diaries, Interviews: 1954-1999*, edited by Christopher Murray and published by Faber (a format which was resumed the following year with *Brian Friel in Conversation*, edited by Paul Delaney and published by the University of Michigan Press); and another monograph dedicated to the playwright, *Brian Friel's (Post)Colonial Drama: Language, Illusion and Politics* by F.C. McGrath, Syracuse University Press, adding to the previous and valuable contributions of D.E.S. Maxwell (1973), Ulf Dantanus (1998), George O'Brien (1989), Richard Pine (1990, 1999), Elmer Andrews (1995), and Martine Pelletier (1997). The proof, if any was needed, that the interest for that Irish playwright's work survived the seventieth birthday celebrations is that new books continued to appear over the following years, such as Nesta Jones's new *Faber Critical Guide* (2000), Tony Corbet's *Brian Friel: Decoding the Language of the Tribe* (Liffey Press, 2002), Richard Harp and Robert C. Evans's (editors) *A Companion to Brian Friel* (Locust Hill Press, 2002), and Tony Coult's *About Friel: The Playwright and His Work* (Faber and Faber, 2003).

This abundance of publications, which should be complemented by a reference to countless chapters and essays in other books and academic journals, could make the publication of another volume of previously published essays dedicated to Brian Friel a rather expected and normal initiative, unworthy of any special consideration. What is not at all usual, however, is when the initiative comes from a non-English-speaking country, like Hungary, a country where there are already sufficient grounds for a study on the reception of Friel's plays, as both Csilla Bertha and Mária Kurdi told us in their informed 'Hungarian Perspectives on Brian Friel's Theatre after *Dancing at Lughnasa*' (published in *Druids, Dudes and Beauty Queens: The Changing Face of Irish Theatre*, edited by Dermot

Bolger, New Island, 2001). The present project proves to be all the more relevant because the editors – Donald E. Morse, Csilla Bertha, and Mária Kurdi – managed to gather the contributions of a broad spectrum of scholars and theatre practitioners, not only from Ireland, England, and the United States, but also from Germany, Italy, Portugal, and, naturally, Hungary, thus opening up possibilities, if not for more varied, at least for more alien perspectives on the work of this deservedly celebrated playwright.

Csilla Bertha was, in 1996, the guest-editor of a special issue on Irish Drama of the *Hungarian Journal of English and American Studies* (*HJEAS*), with a representative international panel of contributors. And in 1999, the same HJEAS gave a renewed demonstration of its commitment and attention to the field of Irish Studies by inviting Mária Kurdi to edit a special issue 'in honour of Brian Friel at 70'. Ten of the fourteen texts collected in *Brian Friel's Dramatic Artistry – 'The Work Has Value'* gather precisely the contributions from those two issues, complemented by another one published in a later issue of HJEAS (8.1.2002) and, finally, another three with different origins.

The editors decided to distribute these fourteen texts under various headings, not only with thematic implications, but also with some more technical or structural considerations, thus creating a provisional cartography for the reader: 'Portraits of the Artist', 'Ambiguities of Language', 'Psychological and Spiritual Torments', 'Ritual and Ceremony', 'Disability and Empowerment', and 'Politics in and of the Theatre'. Taking advantage of the Frielian suggestion that 'confusion is not an ignoble condition', I will follow an alternative route, convinced that this might contribute to the multiplication of dialogues and arguments established by this network of necessarily partial perspectives on the vast, valuable, and complex body of work accumulated by Brian Friel over approximately half a century.

In contrast to the work of many of his fellow playwrights of the same generation, like Tom Murphy or Thomas Kilroy, for instance, Friel's plays have travelled very well among different cultures and theatrical traditions, being studied, translated, and produced in a countless number of languages and countries, and this in spite of the persistent Irish nature of their concerns and cultural references. In Mária Kurdi's interview with Richard Pine at the end of this volume, he suggests that:

> people are attracted to his work for two reasons, which may seem contradictory. One is the transparency … When you pick up a copy of a play, you hold a whole world in your hand. And the contradictory thing is the difficulty of actually trying to describe it, it is a tremendous challenge (318).

Due to this, and perhaps to a more complex set of reasons and circumstances that would be interesting to explore with greater depth, Friel has continued Synge's and O'Casey's international reputation, while also, and most curiously, anticipating some of the attention that is currently being given, deservedly or not, to the work of younger playwrights like Frank McGuinness, Billy Roche, Marina Carr, Conor McPherson, Martin McDonagh, Enda Walsh, and Mark O'Rowe. The appeal of Friel's plays in many non-English-speaking countries, and thus in 'translation', is a fact that surely deserves greater attention than has been accorded to it.

I stressed this dimension not only because of a selfish double personal interest in Friel (in my capacity as both translator and scholar), but also because this volume includes some important contributions on *Translations* (1980), revealing a lasting and promising attention to a varied set of questions involved in everything regarding Friel and translation; and I am referring both to the concept of translation in the playwright's own work and to the varied problems raised by the translation proper of his plays into other languages and cultures. One of the less scholarly, but not less stimulating, essays included in this volume is Márton Mesterházi's testimony on 'the problems of translating' *Translations* into Hungarian. Mesterházi develops the presentation of his view on this task around the problems resulting from the linguistic convention of the play and the fact that history is its basic situation, a fact that forces any translator to bear in mind that most international audiences 'think of Irish history as of something very remote' from them. Another fascinating point raised by the Hungarian translator is the suggestion of a dialogue between Friel's play and Murphy's *Famine* (1968/1977), a play also translated by Mesterházi – a productive perspective to be developed in future testimonies could perhaps imply a comparative study of the translator's own 'discourse' as revealed in the Hungarian versions of these two texts.

Christopher Murray's first essay also chooses *Translations* as its pivotal centre, adequately stressing the complexity and the many reverberations of Friel's notion of translation, something that the author of *Twentieth-Century Drama: Mirror up to Nation* (Manchester, 1997) connects to the notion of 'palimpsest'. The main focus of his argument, he presents palimpsest as a 'form of assimilation' and of 'appropriative refiguration', peculiar to the 'nature of Irish imaginative writing in English'. According to the author, *Translations* 'dramatizes the process of palimpsest itself'. In his second essay, 'A Postmodern Case History: *Molly Sweeney* and its Sources', Murray extends this characterization of Friel's dramatic style and compositional mode as dominated by intertextuality and palimpsest to the identification of the many different sources of *Molly Sweeney* (1994), with particular emphasis accorded to Oliver Sack's case history 'To See and Not See', originally published in 1993, and subsequently also the basis for the movie *At First Sight*, directed by Irwin Winkler and starring Val Kilmer and Mira Sorvino, released in 1999. Although it remains debatable to classify Friel as a postmodernist writer solely on the basis of this process of 'fabrication' and incorporation or creative 'translation' of other texts into his own plays, this essay offers us a detailed account of the playwright's 'alchemical' artistry, suggestively linking that broad notion of translation to the equally productive one of 'performance'.

Ruth Niel's contribution explores the motif and meaning of disability in Friel's plays, identifying the different types of disabilities and the functions they serve. Surprising as it may seem, Niel demonstrates that there is hardly 'a play by Friel in which at least one character is not psychologically handicapped or mentally disabled or disturbed'. The consequences of this demonstration prove to be particularly revealing in a work that has always so skilfully combined the public and private dimensions of experience. Following Niel's suggestion that 'Molly Sweeney is the most complex of Friel's disabled characters', a more 'public' reading of this intimate play becomes an ever-renewed necessity.

Translations and performance are also at the core of Ger FitzGibbon's contribution, the third essay that the editors assembled in the group dedicated to 'Ambiguities of Language', in which a famous tirade from *Philadelphia, Here I Come!* (1964) – 'Isn't this your job – to translate?' – is put into dialogue with the complex handling of the questions of language, culture, and identity, and with the characteristic Frielian 'interpenetration of public and private matters', issues central to that play. FitzGibbon hints perhaps at the reasons for Friel's native and international success when he acknowledges both the fact that he is 'one of the clearest, most articulate, playwrights of our time' and that he has progressively thematized in his plays the contradictions concerning the use of language, exploring the possibilities 'beyond language' itself, namely through the use of music, dance, myth, and ritual.

This concern also relates FitzGibbon's to that of Richard Allen Cave, who chooses two other plays, *Dancing at Lughnasa* (1990) and *Wonderful Tennessee* (1993), to explore what he presents as Friel's 'questing for ritual and ceremony in a Godforsaken world'. Cave's contribution is particularly welcome in this context, not only because it reveals a rare attention to the theatrical dimension of the playwright's endeavour, but also because it manages to articulate his hermeneutic efforts with other current concerns in more recent Irish theatre. Recovering an already agreed view on Friel's dramaturgical contribution as having 'relentlessly pushed at the border of conventional stage realism', Cave shows how the body, and its appearance, posture and movement, was already an object of continuous descriptions in *Faith Healer* and how the bodies of the performers in motion emerge as 'intricate signifiers' in later plays. Friel's use of bodily expressiveness – we might say, of more performative dimensions – enables him to introduce fractures in the naturalistic mode, broadening and widening the expressive resources of the theatre, and thus rewriting the processes of articulation and interpretation.

Faith Healer (1979) is another play that recurs in many of the essays collected in this volume, especially in Giovanna Tallone's two contributions. 'Restless Wanderers and Great Pretenders', a thorough and detailed comparative analysis of that text with *Crystal and Fox* (1968), explores their respective background, themes, structure, and language. Special attention is accorded to the fact that both protagonists are 'prototypes of artists restlessly questioning their own identity and investigating their relationship with art and artifice'. Tallone's close reading and intertextual analysis identifies an important number of cross-references between the plays, due to a careful and useful identification of patterns of speech, including choice of lexis, repetitions of words and structures, pauses, and so forth. 'Unveiling the Vice' again proposes a complementary reading of *Faith Healer*, in terms of its organization, structure, and narrative strategy, applying Christopher Murray's suggestion of the postmodern construction of Friel's plays to the identification of the features and legacies of the medieval miracle and morality plays. Special attention is given to the technical and structural device of listing place names and to the traditional allegorical character of the Vice, offered as a prototype for Frank Hardy, but other subsidiary motifs are also suggestively hinted at, such as the Dance of Death, regarded as a precedent for a play which places dead characters – 'all those dead voices' – on stage.

Tallone's discussion of *Crystal and Fox* and *Faith Healer* links well with Csilla Bertha and Donald E. Morse's reading of *Give Me Your Answer, Do!* (1997), 'Friel's first play to address directly the moral, emotional, and psychological issues of a writer', as both contributions productively explore the different 'Portraits of the Artist' in the playwright's dramatic fictions. Suggestive references are made to previous plays – like *Faith Healer, Crystal and Fox, Aristocrats* (1979), and *Wonderful Tennessee* (1993) – in which we already could find the dramatization of the artist's healing and destroying powers. Yet, again, the authors' most stimulating suggestion concerns the artist's exploration of his expressive possibilities/capabilities, a struggle frequently presented and felt as 'the impossibility of expressing the depth of experience' (133), the famous Beckettian 'I can't go on, I'll go on'.

'Portraits of the Artist' is complemented by a study on the balanced importance of 'Music and Words in Brian Friel's *Performances*', the sole contribution in this volume on the more recent 'non-Irish' short plays that the playwright produced over the last few years up to the premiere of *The Home Place*, in February 2005, his first full-length ('Irish') play since *Give Me Your Answer, Do!* Exploring the pervasive and manifold 'musicality' in Friel's work, Csilla Bertha renews the productive application of the literal and metaphoric – and heuristic, we might say – concept of performance to the textual and theatrical workings of the playwright's fictions. What this contribution rightly emphasizes is that *Performances* – again, a composition that makes a prolific use of other 'texts', among them Janáček's love letters and music, and George Steiner's essays – is a much more complex, sophisticated and daring experiment than the mild critical reception of its first production might have suggested. At the very end of her essay Bertha touches upon the notion of the sublime, a concept with romantic reverberations that also has much to say about Friel's 'divining' quality.

Michael Parker offers us two essays, found under the 'Psychological and Spiritual Torments' and 'Politics in and of the Theatre' headings. Both his contributions are nonetheless primarily concerned with a larger understanding of the political implications of the playwright's fictions. 'Telling Tales: Narratives of Politics and Sexuality in Brian Friel's *The Gentle Island*' is a detailed commentary on that much neglected play, first produced in 1971. Confirming the playwright's strategy of insisting on the 'parish' as a 'valid and validating focus for exploring the prevailing, interconnected concerns of the time', Parker exposes the play as a political metaphor that responded to the contexts of frustration and paralysis of the period, in both Northern and Southern Ireland. The centrality of the sexual issues, perhaps never before so dramatically explored by

Friel, connects that experiment with later contributions by playwrights of the following generations, among whom Frank McGuinness would undoubtedly be one of the first to be mentioned.

'Forms of Redress: Structure and Characterization in *The Freedom of the City*' is also concerned with the playwright's understanding of language as 'a site of conflict in which monologic, authoritarian forces strive to close down meaning and suppress the challenge of dialogic'. Exploring the play's structure and characterization, with the help of an illuminating use of Bakhtin's notions of 'parodic stylization' and 'carnival', and Ricoeur's studies on narrative, Parker develops an almost poststructuralist renewed reading of this much debated play in Friel's canon (first produced in 1972), simultaneously stressing the play's 'problematic intersections of literature and politics' and its use of innovative, non-naturalistic, dramatic strategies to deal with issues of authority and closure.

Parker's approach to these two plays links well with my own discussion of the no less debated connection of Brian Friel to the Field Day Theatre Company, between 1980 and 1994, when he finally resigned from the Board of Directors. Deliberately inverting Conor Cruise O'Brien's famous 1975 critique of the intersection of art and politics as an unhealthy one, shared by many commentators in the English-speaking critical world, what I tried to do – back in 1996, when the essay was first published – was mainly to reconsider, in a more unprejudiced mode, the productive tension between the private and the public in Friel's work. Clearly, my approach goes against the reluctance expressed by Christopher Murray – at the beginning of his essay on *Translations* – to the playwright's engagement in the Field Day project, denouncing what I would regard as a forceful effort of presenting the playwright's work as 'art' and the other Field Day activities as mere 'propaganda'. Even if Friel's disenchantment with the project is undeniable and the pursuit of his artistic vision a most personal affair, the playwright's public commitment to the larger effects and reverberations of his work within this project is no less true, as revealed in the many interviews he gave at the beginning of the

1980s and in *Making History*, a play dismissed by Murray as 'the closest Friel ever came to writing a pamphlet'.

Brian Friel's Dramatic Artistry — 'The Work Has Value' concludes with an extraordinary interview of Richard Pine, responsible for one of the most inspired and arguably one of the most influential studies of Brian Friel's *oeuvre*, conducted by Mária Kurdi. Confirming the value of an informed 'conversation' – a format daringly explored by Carysfort Press in 2001 with *Theatre Talk: Voices of Irish Theatre Practitioners*, edited by Lilian Chambers, Ger FitzGibbon, and Eamonn Jordan – this interview covers in an inspiring way a wide variety of topics, functioning as an adequate closure to this volume. The many dialogues, confluences, and debates that dominate the study of Brian Friel's plays, more or less silently echoed in the relations established between the different essays gathered here, find in this interview a most eloquent and useful expression. Having published *Brian Friel and Ireland's Drama* back in 1990, Pine reissued, updated and expanded that already massive study in 1999, under the title *The Diviner: The Art of Brian Friel*. His is a life-long involvement with the Frielian universe, still expressed in the programme notes he has been invited to write for the productions of more recent plays. In this interview, Kurdi discusses with Pine not only more personal issues regarding that involvement, but also larger questions such as the contribution of postcolonial criticism, musicality, nostalgia, failure, loss, home, memory and growing up, Field Day, Irish contemporary drama, Friel's national and international dimensions, and so forth.

As I hope to have made clear, this volume can be seen as a valuable contribution to the broadening of perspectives on the work of Brian Friel, in particular, and Irish drama, in general. Putting side-by-side Hungarian, Irish, and other internationally reputed academics and younger scholars is a splendid way of giving voice to such an attractive and complex area of study. In the 1999 Spring volume of the *Irish Theatre Magazine*, Brian Singleton dared to question the exclusively English-language nature of the productions scheduled for the Friel Festival of that year, advancing the proposition that 'foreign-language Friel

... should also have a place in this celebration, as our identity is, after all, constructed to a larger degree by others from the outside. What I am suggesting, therefore', Singleton added, 'is a much less realistic and insular approach. Diasporic Friel may be "exotic" or "marginal", but could also be deeply enriching. As for foreign Friel – it, too, can be the real thing'. This Hungarian and international, even if necessarily English-speaking tribute to Brian Friel falls rightly into that category, confirming perspectives and opening up new paths to the study of a body of work whose value as a classic makes it increasingly more open to new interpretations and appropriations.

Having had for many occasions the opportunity, and the immense responsibility, of working as the 'go-between' between Friel's plays and Portuguese theatre artists – directors, designers, actors, and so forth – I can testify to the sheer fascination exercised by both the theatricality and the humanity of his fictions, so miraculously capable of conveying foreign experiences as easily recognizable, but no less haunting predicaments. A crafty combination of memory and imagination is perhaps the key to that miracle: the memory that allows us the impression of identity and continuity, but that also limits us to the sphere of the uncertain and unpredictable meetings that permeate our accumulated experience; and the imagination with which we elaborate that memory, project continuity and determine or aspire to new meetings and new experiences. And a clearly particular use of language, permanently vigilant of its powers and limitations and of the possibilities so uniquely offered by theatre of combining words with other expressions, thus creating ever more transparent, oblique voices and – precisely because of that tension which is not the same as a contradiction – more powerful, radiant voices. So it comes as no surprise that so many people around this world of ours are still, tentatively, trying to get to grips with such a resonant universe, confirming that 'the work', at least Brian Friel's, definitely 'has value'.

PORTRAITS OF THE ARTIST

2 | 'Singing of Human Unsuccess': Brian Friel's Portraits of the Artist

Csilla Bertha and Donald E. Morse

> 'Sing of human unsuccess
> In a rapture of distress.'
> – W.H. Auden, 'Elegy: In Memory of W.B. Yeats'

In the ancient Celtic world the druids had magical power through incantations to mediate between humans and gods. 'In early Ireland, such special form of discourse was known simply as *bélra na bhfiled* (literally "the speech of the seer-poets"' (Ó hÓgáin 13). The shaman-poets through such speech could sanctify the marriage of the king to the goddess or to the sovereignty of the land; that is, symbolically form a marriage with the land itself, or, conversely, they could annihilate a ruler by satirizing him. This long-lived Irish traditional concept continues in the figure of the artist as healer, petitioner, and mediator between the human and supernatural worlds. It survives as well in the unusually high esteem accorded to poets, in the great significance of the *seanchaí* – the storytellers in old communities – and in the idea of the responsibility of the poet/artist for the people/community, as well as in the notion of the magic power of the word:

The 'extraordinary skill in speech should be understood to affect reality, not only to interpret it but also to the extent of altering it. And so it emerges clearly from the many descriptions and studies of shamanism … that the power of speech – in terms of its ability and effectiveness, its referential and imagery – is one of the special features of the person who has insight and supernatural power' (Ó hÓgáin 12).

Brian Friel, in his short story 'The Diviner' (1962) creates a metaphor for the magic power of the artist. Using only a Y-shaped twig, the diviner proves the only person able to discover the body of a drowned man after all other attempts have failed including utilizing fishermen's nets and the elaborate equipment brought in by the English military frogmen. Seamus Heaney emphasizes the mystery of miracle, and how it works exclusively for the dowser and not for others. In his poem, 'The Diviner', after the protagonist reveals where the underground spring is,

> The bystanders would ask to have a try.
> He handed them the rod without a word.
> It lay dead in their grasp till nonchalantly
> He gripped expectant wrists. The hazel stirred (9-12, 24).

Heaney, like Friel, relates the diviner's mysterious gift to that of the artist since both are in touch with something hidden and both share 'a gift for mediating between the latent resource and the community that wants it current and released' (qtd. in Kiberd 109). The very name 'diviner' suggests that his extraordinary abilities relate to the divine, but as a human being, he can never quite account for or gain control over them.

Like the power of the diviner, the talent of the artist may be used to reveal truths, whether pleasant or not and these may, in turn, prove either healing or destructive and self-destructive. Friel's plays dramatize in countless forms the artist's healing and destructive powers, as well as the artist's search for certainties, place, and function. Christopher Murray, for example, asserts that '[t]he characters in *Molly Sweeney* are … three aspects of the artist as divine and thus tragic seer in a form of hypostatic union …' (88). Richard Pine enumerates the various shapes the writer takes in Friel's plays; such as: 'map-makers, translators, historians, do-it-yourself philosophers, priests, politicians, schoolteachers, charlatans – all those whose skill depends on the pre-existence of *the word*, those who live by the book and are lived by the book, all those who submit to the idea of myth, of language, which becomes fabular as soon as it is spoken' ('Love' 183). Although many characters embody elements of the creative or destructive power of the artist, only a few struggle directly and explicitly with issues such as the nature of the gift, the function, and morale of the artist, and only Tom Connolly in *Give Me Your Answer, Do!* (1997) is a professional writer. The shaman artist as healer appeared in *Faith Healer*, while the more settled artist figures faced their failures in the later *Wonderful Tennessee* (1993). Tom Connolly's artistic gifts and powers become more explicitly and more severely challenged – if not over-whelmed – by an unmerited Joban catastrophe.

Frank Hardy, the faith healer, becomes tormented with questions about the nature of, and his own relation to, his gift. He both epitomizes and articulates the unceasing uncertainties, the frequent failures, the many weaknesses he experiences together with the necessity of continuing; the Beckettian 'I can't go on, I must go on' attitude of the twentieth-century artist. Similarly to the diviner in the short story, he also has 'divine' power to heal or to make sick, as he is able to conduct healing forces from the spiritual world towards the wretched people who seek recuperation at his sessions. But his control over those powers proves less than that of the diviner, as it becomes clear that his power to heal has nothing to do with his will or ambition. In fact, he does not even know how to make himself receptive to the gift. On the contrary, he is simply at the mercy of his exceptional talent – indeed, as much at its mercy as his clients are. Once he, somewhat bemusedly, reflects on his gift: 'occasionally it worked – oh yes – occasionally it *did* work' (*Faith Healer* 333). A seedy, alcoholic, impoverished descendant of shamanic druids, Frank Hardy cuts a ridiculous, pitiable figure, yet he proves able at times to work miracles. In one out of ten instances, he does make the hopelessly sick and deformed whole again.

Frank Hardy sacrifices to his talent not only his own life but, most selfishly and destructively, also those of his immediate associates, especially his wife and his manager-friend. Being most concerned about healing others and being ready for self-sacrifice – for people he has never seen before, will never see again, and about whom he knows only that they are in need of help and healing – he becomes most selfish in his private life and relations. He does serve a communal good but at the price of inflicting considerable suffering upon the individuals around him. This situation encapsulates the perennial ethical dilemma of whether such a choice serves a higher form of morality or simply exemplifies ordinary immorality. Hardy does not take into account any one else's interests or sensitivities, nor does he consider any norms or rules of living together with other people. Yet, the service of others and the service of one's own talent become paradoxically at one and the same time an example of utmost unselfishness as well as utmost selfishness. Frank Hardy admits that when he was able to cure seemingly incurable people, he felt 'exultation, consummation' not only from the joy and relief over his ability to help others, but also because in those moments, and only in those moments, the 'questions that undermined my life ... became meaningless ... and I had become whole myself and perfect in myself' (333). In this sense, he exemplifies the curious relationship of the artist to the community that lies in this very circularity, for the artist can achieve wholeness only through helping others towards wholeness. 'His acts of transformation are acts of transference' (McGuinness 62). Only through self-sacrifice can the artist arrive at self-fulfilment. Remaking the world into his 'fiction', 'according to his own private standard of excellence', can only appease his tormenting desire for excellence, for 'perfection' which, as the Faith Healer's wife asserts, was always the 'cause of his restlessness and the focus of it' (346).

If Frank Hardy represents a failed artist, his failure nevertheless becomes a heroic one, for he becomes the prototype of the artist in the total sense as he lives only by and for his talent. 'So, in his last days, as his con man's courage dissolves, he lacerates himself with self-doubt and deliberately seeks out a spectacular failure that will kindly put an end to his own slender surviving hope' (Kiberd 112). All his life he wrestles with his own uncertainties concerning his talent. When his questions and self-doubt appear to be killing that talent, then, rather than wait for its demise, Frank arranges for his own death. He decides, as José Lanters contends, 'that the uncertainty of a life without verdicts is unbearable, and opts to end the questions by ending his life' (174). Yet, Hardy's death becomes more than just the end of his life, it is both his admission of failure and his supreme act of creation. Richard Pine eloquently states that 'Frank Hardy continually hurls himself against the barbed wire of apprehension until, after he has torn himself to shreds, he succeeds in making himself whole for the first time' (*Friel* 96). In his last performance, he ritualizes himself and his own death and through this ritual he achieves his status as a sacrificial offering. Friel's play thus acquires 'the radiance of myth, it carries its protagonist and its audience into a realm *beyond* expectation, and it carries the drama back to ... the sacred, where sacrifice was witnessed and the world renewed by that sacrifice' (Heaney, 'Memory' 237).

In other plays, Friel's artist figures may appear in less mythical roles and in more mundane circumstances, where they have less divine power; still, there remains an absence of negative answers to questions posed about their role, function, or possible healing effect. In general, while Friel propounds such questions, he does not offer answers. However, in their very posing, he continually calls attention to the necessity of taking them seriously. The action of *Faith Healer, Wonderful Tennessee,* and *Give Me Your Answer, Do!* implies, if in varying degrees, the question of the right – even the duty – of the artist to subordinate himself and others to his own gift. The Romantics revived the ancient view that it is the responsibility of the artist to follow his divine inspiration wherever it might take him. In Friel's work, this romantic notion of divine inspiration survives under the surface acquiring even stronger ironic overtones than were present in much of Romantic poetry, such as that of Byron and Shelley. In *Crystal and Fox* (1968), Fox embodied only the destructive and self-destructive instincts without the power of creativity or healing, but the Faith Healer follows the Romantic idea that everything revolves around his talent. Grace, his wife, willingly subjects all her interests to her husband's art. Similarly, Angela, Frank's wife in *Wonderful Tennessee*, makes sacrifices to sustain him, although she believes far less in his gifts. The uninspired, rational writer, Frank – whose contrast with the Faith Healer is emphasized by sharing his given name – admits, with some guilt feelings, that he has failed to support his family as a writer-husband. He has had to accept regular financial support from his brother-in-law as well as allow Angela to earn their living by teaching so that he can pursue his writing. Frank's writing, however, does not even aim at bringing redemption to anyone – individual or community – nor does it provide any saving grace to the dried-out author himself. It comes as no surprise then that his rational, intellectual speculations, intended to demystify the world, cannot heal anyone.

The Faith Healer failed because of his self-consciousness and his analytical mind. His too heavy reliance on his intellect blocked his talent, as Teddy, his friend and manager, observes: 'A bloody fantastic talent that hasn't one ounce of ambition because his bloody brains has him bloody castrated!' (357). The latter Frank, in *Wonderful Tennessee*, on the contrary, shows the most unartist-like attitude towards the phenomena of the world as he tries to explain away the mystery, rationalize the irrational, and so move even further away from grace. Yet, he has enough residual sensitivity to experience an epiphany when given one, to participate in the spontaneously arising rituals, and to be able to accept some kind of redemption.

George, the musician, the real artist in *Wonderful Tennessee*, represents the other extreme and probably the more common case of compromising one's talent. He unselfishly sacrificed his talent for his wife and his love for her, with the result that he lost his artistic career. He obviously regrets that he gave up his life as a concert pianist, but now he has no way of amending his choice, since he is going to die soon. George echoes the frustration of other talented figures in Friel's plays such as Claire in *Aristocrats* (1979), who also had dreams of becoming a concert pianist but was thwarted by circumstances. At the end of that play, she faces a situation as bad as George's approaching death: marriage to an old, unattractive Ballybeg widower with four children. Her highest aspiration now can be to teach children to play the piano. In *Give Me Your Answer, Do!* Daisy, and before her, her father Jack, cherished hopes of a career in music, but each became reduced: Daisy to a housewife and Jack to a cocktail bar-pianist. George, in order to be able to marry and support himself and his wife, compromised his talent by spending his professional life playing in a pop group. He most explicitly expresses the end of his artistic career in his 'story' when he plays – somewhat improbably – a virtuoso version of a Beethoven sonata on his accordion, then stops in mid-phrase and formally bows to his audience on the pier rather than to one in a concert hall.

Friel once noted that contemporary Irish people, rather than becoming West Britons, were, instead, becoming East Americans (qtd. in Hickey and Smith 224), as George's pop group, the 'Dude Ranchers' exemplifies. George, however, through his art and through his still-extant gift, retains strong affinities with his roots and old culture, and so, despite his failed career and terminal illness, he still can function as a healer. In his Dionysiac role – identified for him by Angela, who calls him 'Dionysus' and then wreathes him with dried seaweed (11) – he inspires the others to enjoy and express themselves. Through his music, he opens the way to the mysterious, while evoking in them warm feelings, love, caring, sympathy, and empathy. Preserving love and being loved, George is still able to offer healing to those around him. Both Frank Hardy and George lost themselves in order to save others, with the difference that Hardy did it most selfishly, sacrificing others and George most unselfishly, sacrificing himself.

Dying, George facilitates the spiritual healing of others. Frank Hardy at the moment of his death, similarly, reached fulfilment, 'homecoming', and became reconciled with his talent or the lack of it as well as with his inability to control his own capacity to heal. These instances raise the question of whether talent can be fulfilled only at the price of life – whether that of the artist or of others involved in his plight. That in turn raises the question of whether the centuries-old wisdom still holds that only pain and suffering can fuel art.

If it is true to some extent, as the Latin saying goes, that the palm-tree grows under weight, it is also true that too much weight may kill the palm tree, as apparently happened to Tom Connolly in *Give Me Your Answer, Do!* – Friel's first play to address directly the moral, emotional, and psychological issues of a writer. The pain caused by his daughter's autism and his inability to help her appears to have paralysed Tom as a writer by draining his creative force. In *Give Me Your Answer, Do!*, the dilemma whether to serve a talent or earn a living becomes all the more acute. Tom Connolly, although making ends meet through journalism, suffers from a severe writer's block, having produced no new novel or published no new book in over seven years. He resembles Frank Hardy in his willing acceptance of Daisy, his wife's self-sacrifice, without so much as thanking her. Yet, unlike the unruly, uncivilized Frank Hardy, Tom does at least try to fit in with his immediate society. He is friendly to his parents-in-law and other visitors, including his back-biting rival Garret Fitzmaurice – nevertheless, at some fundamental level of awareness, he remains as lonely, and, perhaps, as selfish as Frank in *Faith Healer* or that other Frank in *Wonderful Tennessee*. And, on balance, Tom fits in with his immediate society about as well as they do.

Although *Give Me Your Answer, Do!* is filled with frustrated artists, the primary figure remains Tom Connolly, the writer. A novelist, who precociously published his first novel when he was still an undergraduate, he now has some twelve or perhaps fifteen novels written and most of them published (16). By his middle-to-late fifties though, he is, like his clothes and briefcase, 'casual-to-shabby' and has an 'abused' appearance (11). He wrestles with serious questions about his vocation and his ability to keep practising it. He devotes most of his time and energy to writing the endless round of journalism that pays

Bridget's hospital bills and has no realistic prospect of any change. His experience parallels that of the Irish writer Brian O'Nolan, who had to sacrifice most of his writing career in order to support through journalism a family of twelve that he inherited the day his father died (see Cronin 88-90). Precious little time or energy remained after completing these urgent immediate tasks for either writer to do his more creative writing. In addition, Tom has lost his agent and quarrelled with his publisher.

Probably the most deeply failed artist among all of Friel's artist-figures, Tom Connolly fails both in everyday life and in his art. He causes his family financial uncertainty, can afford only a cheap institution for his daughter, and deprives his wife of the possibility of pursuing her own talent as a pianist (which appears as an issue only in his fantasizing to Bridget). And yet he is the only one in the family who has the courage to face seeing his daughter, and who tries to bring some variety if not joy into her life. His deep caring sharply distinguishes him from Frank, the Faith Healer, who, instead of at least sharing the grief with his sorrow-smitten wife at the loss of their child, turns his back on her and pretends that he does not know and does not care. Nonetheless, from Frank's obsessive repetition of the village's name where the child was born and died, and from the cumulative effect of the differing yet complementary monologues that make up *Faith Healer*, it becomes abundantly clear that Frank suffers just as terribly as his wife. But Frank hides it in himself, never allowing his public face to show his private feelings. Tom, the more humane and perhaps less blindly dedicated artist, sacrifices his own creative energy when he undertakes the task of immersing himself regularly, again and again, in the pain of seeing his daughter.

In *Give Me Your Answer, Do!*, the writer's response to the impossibility of expressing the depth of experience – here the depth of pain and suffering in particular – is a kind of desperate rebellion or revenge. Tom, in his helplessness at his daughter's incurable illness, stops writing novels and the only thing he is able to write is hard core pornography. The hurt caused by this tragedy cannot find words in any 'normal' form, but neither can it allow for the continuation of a career as if that horror had not happened. Silence or irrational anger appears as the only way of coping with the loss. As Private Gar remained well hidden within Public Gar in *Philadelphia, Here I Come!*, so in *Give Me Your Answer, Do!*, the private Tom, deeply wounded and angry to the depths of his being at having to cope with the Joban affliction of an autistic daughter, has burrowed beneath the façade of the public Tom Connolly. Only once did the private Tom erupt to write in a furious white heat of inspiration those two mysterious novels both unpublished and, until the day of the play, unacknowledged and almost forgotten. It is Daisy who recalls their existence to Tom. Once she does, the 'substantial archive', visible throughout the play as a series of neatly arranged folders, becomes the incomplete archive with the two absent folders in the bedroom 'on top of the wardrobe' (24-25). These missing novels achieve importance because of an archive hunter's possible interest in acquiring all of Tom's manuscripts for a research library in Texas. Not only do they figure in an important way in Tom's *oeuvre*, but they also prove important in the family's history being so intimately linked to the autistic daughter and her institutionalization. When Bridget was committed to the hospital at age twelve, some ten or so years before the time of the play, Tom got down to work and in one highly concentrated year of intensive hard exertion produced both novels – a feat that amazes his writer-friend, Garret:

> **Daisy:** He began the first the day Bridget was committed to the hospital. A glorious first of May, I remember. And he went at it with such a fury that he had it finished by Hallowe'en.
> **Garret:** Wow! Six months?
> **Daisy:** Then he went straight into the second without a break and he finished that in five months. I never ever saw him work with such concentration. For a whole twelve months! ...
> **Tom:** I called the first *Bridget* – a sort of working title. I never got around to naming the second. And for some reason I never showed them to anybody.
> **Garret:** And your agent saw them – you had an agent then, hadn't you? (57)

The power of these novels derives from Tom's perceiving and communicating the deeply-felt obscene quality of the world. A world in which a young girl – through no fault of her own and through no one's doing – becomes so severely autistic that she must be institutionalized to save whatever may be left of her parents' life and their home. Thus far, the novels have had only one reader, Daisy, who describes them both off-handedly as 'Hard-core porn – as they say' (58). Tom, known as 'a writer of integrity ... Literary probity. High-minded' (34), now faces the dilemma of whether to include or not these novels in his archive. Once he decides to let the archive hunter become the first public reader – in the interest of offering a 'complete archive ... [which is] always more valuable' (24) – he then faces an additional decision about whether or not to sell his manuscripts as a complete collection including these novels.

This decision, to sell the manuscripts or not, is, in turn, intimately bound up with the question that he – and every creative artist – wrestles with: does 'the work [have] value?' (79). And, concomitantly, how does a writer know it has value? 'The artist is like the Faith Healer, a man who never knows for certain whether he has been successful in bringing off an effect, a broker in risk who must stand before the audience nightly with no assurance that his magic will rub off on others yet again' (Kiberd 108). Sales of books may be one yardstick but not a particularly pertinent one for Tom and his work. Does then the possible sale of his manuscripts to a Texas archive validate his worth as a writer? The archive in itself is a laying bare of his life as a writer, as an artist: 'My entire goddamn life for Christ's sake! ... please tell me it's not altogether worthless', he pleads (23). Gráinne later taunts Garret that the sale price of his archive equals the full artistic worth of his work: 'So now his [Garret's] real worth is established' (52). But Tom rightly objects 'This isn't about money at all' (25). Is this offer to buy Tom's archive 'the substantial confirmation, the tangible evidence!' that Tom at first believes it is? Can he now celebrate because 'The work *must* be good! I'm not imprisoned in the dark any more! Now I can run again! Now I can *dare* again!' (79). But his reaction to the offer, when it finally comes, is to feel 'pleased – well, flattered, I suppose. No more than that. For some reason suddenly no more than a little bit flattered' (78). Tom's validation lies elsewhere.

Garret Fitzmaurice, in contrast to Tom, appears the popular but questionable artist, 'his work is much more immediate, much more – of today than [Tom's]' (24). He does not have integrity, is not high-minded, but he is prolific and his books do sell (24). His public persona is that of the successful, moderately well-known novelist with an agent, one who publishes fairly popular fiction and leads a relatively in-dependent life. But Garret also appears terribly insecure about his real value as an artist as well as about the actual value of his work. He takes every opportunity to remind Tom of Tom's failures, not so much as a way of lowering Tom's stock but as a means of boosting his own (46-47). He and his wife, Gráinne, are childless but come fitted out with a menagerie of various domestic animals – their surrogate children – who supply them with subjects for their endless small talk. Together, Gráinne and Garret also exemplify failed artists. Having created their roles as Ballybeg's small-time version of George and Martha from Edward Albee's *Who's Afraid of Virginia Woolf?*, their goal becomes to humiliate one another in public (49) but to postpone delivering a mortal wound. Gráinne strikes the hardest when she hurts Garret not as a person but as an artist: 'You aren't at all the writer you might have been ... Too anxious to please. Too fearful of offending. And that has made you very popular: people love your – amiability. But I thought once you were more than that. I think you did, too' (49-50). The public Garret remains silent, but the wounded private Garret retorts 'Jesus, Gráinne, you certainly can deliver that mortal wound' (50). She succeeds in annihilating him just because she touches one of the artist's most sensitive nerves by raising the question of whether Garret is an artist or a performer – or, as the Faith Healer says, a 'con man'. 'The artist', maintains Declan Kiberd, 'always keeps his eye remorselessly on his subject, whereas the performer is always watching his audience. The artist risks the displeasure of his audience as he maintains a congenial relationship with his subject, whereas the performer risks the betrayal of his subject as he seeks a congenial relationship with his audience' (113).

The other performer, Jack Donovan, Daisy's father, the cocktail lounge piano player, accepts his job as the best he can do, given circumstances and talent. He at least is honest about being an entertainer, although, as he remarks wryly, all such pianists had plans to become concert pianists (56). Like everyone else in the play, he believes he has failed in some significant way. His failure lies, however, not in his profession, but in his personal life plagued by kleptomania. Because of his petty thievery, he and his wife have had to change addresses often, to avoid humiliation and to escape the headlines, 'Doctor's Husband Charged with Pilfering' (33). Jack tries to accept the disappointment life brings. 'But', as he says, 'there's always an expectation, isn't there? And they don't always work out, do they?' (74)

In *Give Me Your Answer, Do!*, every character from David, the manuscript buyer, who worries that if he does not close this deal he may lose his job, through Daisy's family, to her and Tom's friends, all eventually reveal their failed expectations, their disappointments. Only Daisy herself appears immune to disappointment or perhaps her serenity is only a gin-sodden veneer with which she faces a hostile world. The considerable pile of bills is often for her but a momentary annoyance. 'May the giving hand never fail' to provide – an attitude often adopted by artists. In the closing moments of the play, she appears to be the person who understands Tom best as she soliloquizes about what he will do and why:

> Oh, no, he mustn't sell. ... to sell for an affirmation, for an answer, to be free of that grinding uncertainty, that would be so wrong for him and so wrong for his work. Because that uncertainty is necessary. He must live with that uncertainty, that necessary uncertainty. Because there can be no verdicts, no answers. Indeed, there *must* be no verdicts. Because being alive is the postponement of verdicts, isn't it? (79-80)

That uncertainty, that existential living on the edge, appears to her a necessary quality for Tom's existence as a writer and a person. She understands the danger of, and encourages Tom to overcome, the 'lust for certainty as the last infirmity of the bourgeois mind' that Kiberd identifies as the Faith Healer's tragic flaw (111). There is no evidence, however, that living on the edge leads Tom to create since he must expend almost all his energy on the journalism that brings the quick cash needed to pay that mountain of bills. Within this most Chekhovian play, we are told what Tom decides – he does not sell the archive – but neither the audience nor he can know if it is the best or the right decision. The audience is left with an ambiguous tableau of Tom and Daisy on either side of the record player with his question about the decision hanging in the air 'on wings of song' between them.

> **Tom:** I hope it's the right decision. Give me your answer, do, Daisy.
> **Daisy:** I don't know. Who's to say? (81)

There is the necessary uncertainty. Whatever the answer given and whatever the subsequent course of action taken, it, perhaps in combination with the confession of the missing two novels, may enable Tom to make a real beginning on his 'new novel'. That would be the first in seven years. Like so much else in the play, this possibility is neither affirmed nor denied. 'Who's to say?' In the final scene with Bridget, Tom in his monologue describes how he has '[r]ead very carefully the twenty-three pages I'd already written. And I can tell you, Madam, let me tell you there just may be something there. I don't want to say any more at this stage. But I did get a little – a little quiver – a whiff – a stirring of a sense that perhaps – maybe –' (83).

In contrast to the first scene with Bridget, where Tom fabricates in glowing detail the completion of his non-existent novel that brings to an end 'five very difficult years … five years of – desperation' (14), in this last scene he discusses actually extant pages. And these few pages could signal the beginning of a new creative period which, while it too may be difficult, could result not in flights of fancy but in new work. Like so much of Tom's genuinely good work, however, those pages he refers to were written not yesterday or today but several years ago. Still, perhaps with these pages in hand he will at last be able to make a real beginning on a new novel, and that is more than he has been able to do in many years.

Tom, like every other character in the play, except Bridget and Daisy, is weighed down by his public image, his public face. Friel returns to this issue of the public face prepared 'to meet the faces that you meet' (Eliot 27) by way of each of the characters. In the course of the play, each confronts the fragility of his or her public image from Garret and Gráinne's most raucous appearance to Daisy's mother, Maggie's steadfast refusal to use more than one cane, the 'two sticks' she knows she needs to walk. Daisy's father, Jack, on the other hand, pays excessive attention to his dress and shoes to ward off public scrutiny of his failures, while David, the archive hunter's workaholic approach to his job barely papers over his very real fear of losing it if he fails to produce. Only Daisy appears immune from this search for an acceptable public image as, gin glass in hand, she meets the world and their friends on her own terms. And, in the end, it is Daisy who encourages Tom not to sell the archive although this refusal brings with it the con-siderable cost of lost income that the family needs simply to meet current bills. Whether this act is a sacrificial one on her part or is in some way self-serving is never made clear.

All the action in *Give Me Your Answer, Do!* occurs bracketed by the two scenes between Tom and Bridget, his in-stitutionalized daughter – 'the powerful non-presence', as Richard Pine perceptively describes her ('Love' 188). Tom's stubborn efforts to reach Bridget prove hopeless. He cannot heal the one wound that he would most like to. Still, he uses his imagination to try and console and/or reach his daughter through using a more colourful language than he employs at any other time or with anyone else. But she – so deeply buried inside herself – probably does not hear him as he creates wildly fanciful stories about their immediate family to entertain her:

> ... your grandmother has decided that she has been small for far too long. So every Wednesday evening, when the clock strikes seven, she makes herself grow two inches taller, so that

she is now about – what? – she must be eleven feet tall at least'
(12).

Through fantastic images, he evokes beauty and comedy as
nowhere else in the play, using more of his creative energy than
he has been able to put into writing for years.

Tom knows his stories are only stories, that his promises to
Bridget to take her in the golden balloon are only fantasies; yet,
they allow him to cope with seeing her in her miserable
condition, which is more than Daisy is able to bring herself to
do. As with everything else except brushing her hair, Bridget
meets his stories with silence, making not the least sign in
response. She is the most difficult because the most
unresponsive of any of Tom's 'readers'. In his heroic yet failing
attempts, Tom reflects his vocation as an artist, but, clearly, all
he does is done in desperation. He does not have any illusion
about the present or the future or about his own talent, nor
does he cherish any nostalgia about the past. Instead, he
escapes into fantasies and the fantastic to bring colour and light
into the life of his daughter who does not seem to have any
light around her. The figure of Tom, as father, persistently
trying, against all odds, to awaken the human within his
daughter, becomes one of Friel's most arresting images of the
true artist who must employ his talent even when he knows
there is no rational possibility of change – that the situation is
truly hopeless. As Hamm says in *Endgame*, 'Use your head, can't
you, use your head, you're on earth, there's no cure for that!'
(Beckett 68) Or as Job discovered – and Tom verifies – being
on earth guarantees encountering unmerited suffering – the
subject of the book of Job, most of Beckett's and several of
Friel's plays, including *Give Me Your Answer, Do!*, *Faith Healer*,
and *Wonderful Tennessee*. Still, there remains the Beckettian
obligation of the artist to attempt to give expression to the
suffering of Job, the distress of Hamm, and the disappointment
and frustration of Tom. '[T]o the destructive element submit
yourself', admonished Stein in Joseph Conrad's *Lord Jim* (200).
Nowhere in Friel's plays is this romantic idea clearer than in
Give Me Your Answer, Do! Tom, thrown into the destructive

element by circumstances or fate, willingly immerses himself and accepts his role. Moreover, the true artist, according to Frank McGuinness, 'must take upon himself the sickness of others' (62). Tom does so, and the fruit of his transference of the sickness of his daughter into himself is the two pornographic novels, the shapes he gives to his emerging despair, frustration, fear, anguish, anger, and evil – his Jungian shadow. But whether renewal will occur after this immersion in evil, darkness, and sickness proves more problematic in this play than it does in *Faith Healer* where Frank was still able to heal people one out of ten times. The ambiguity increases in the final scene where Tom repeats most of what he said at the beginning to Bridget, adding a few words about his new novel moving along after all those years of lack of inspiration. Whether the full realization of the shadow, the evil, leads to death or the renewal of creative energy is left unclarified. So, while McGuinness convincingly asserts that 'Friel's dramatic vision is quintessentially Romantic' (61) and '[h]e, not Yeats, is truly the last Romantic' (62), what must be seen as part of that vision is Friel's perspective of irony, doubt, and uncertainty.

Friel, himself a master of words, struggles in several of his plays with the problem of the inexpressible. Frank Hardy in *Faith Healer* only knows by intuition when he is going to possess the strength to heal, but cannot influence or explain it. Michael, the writer-narrator in *Dancing at Lughnasa* (1990), concludes the play by emphasizing the inadequacy of words alone to express experience, feelings, and atmosphere. 'Dancing as if language had surrendered to movement – as if this ritual, this wordless ceremony, was now the way to speak …, to be in touch with some otherness … Dancing as if language no longer existed because words were no longer necessary' (71). Frank in *Tennessee* finds 'the book without words' the emblem of perfection, which ironically also reflects on his own lack of devotion and creative power and/or on the writer's impotence in general. That book, 'the last book ever written – and the most wonderful!' (41), would indeed contain all the mystery, but would share and communicate nothing.

Out of this world of tragedy and pain comes the stuff of
art. Friel, commenting on the artist's role in society, says,
'perhaps this is an artist's arrogance, but I feel that once the
voice is found in literature then it can move out and become
part of the common currency' (qtd. in Pine, *Friel* 191). But there
is little sign that Tom in *Give Me Your Answer, Do!* has found or
will find his voice. Thus far his work illustrates 'the *lack* of
congruence between the word and the situation' (Welch 240).
Hanna Arendt captured the distinction between great and lesser
art when she described great art as

> Praise that pitches itself against all that is most unsatisfactory in
> man's condition on this earth and sucks its strength out of the
> wound – somehow convinced, as the bards of ancient Greece
> were, that the gods spin unhappiness and evil things to mortals
> so that they may be able to tell the tales and sing the songs.

Tom has his subject; but, unlike Friel, all he appears to have
done with it thus far is record its very obscenity in the most
literal terms through his hard core pornographic novels. Will he
now be able to 'suck … strength out of the wound' and
transmute his and his family's suffering into art? Will he have
the 'strength and courage' to help bring 'redemption of the
human spirit' out of 'confusion and disillusion' as Friel believes
the modern dramatist does when disturbing audiences with 'his
terrible, haunting questions?' (qtd. in Andrews 7). In the words
of W.H. Auden, will Tom become able to 'Sing of human
unsuccess / In a rapture of distress?' (143). Still, with this
possible new beginning comes an additional disquieting note.
Describing that 'stirring' he senses in those twenty-three pages,
Tom repeats his promise to Bridget made in the first scene that
if he successfully completes his new novel then he will return
for her. He says that he will 'fold you in my arms; and you and I
would climb into a golden balloon – just the two of us – only
the two of us – and we would soar above this earth and float
away forever across the face of the "darkly, deeply, beautifully
blue sky" – ' (84). The novel will thus become the means of
escape for both of them from their impossible lives.

Unlike his first monologue with Bridget with which the play opens, here, in the last scene, Tom adds and emphasizes the phrases 'just the two of us – only the two of us' (84). Phrases, which by themselves might have no special significance were it not for Daisy's antiphonal exclamation with which the play ends, ' "Oh Tom! – Tom! – Tom, please? – " *Pause. Quick black*' (84). Her interjection adds inevitable ambiguity to Tom's speech. As the curtain falls, an audience is left with only questions, for there is no immediately obvious or coherent way of putting Tom's and Daisy's two phrases together. Tom's vision of escaping from earth may simply be another expression of a father's wish to take his daughter away from this cruel and unforgiving land. Bridget is in the midst of yet another series of shock treatments, which Daisy cannot bear to face and Tom finds very hard to deal with. Or Tom may be threatening suicide – thus becoming free of this earth. Pine believes that 'Daisy realizes that from her recently rediscovered position of strength as helpmeet she has once more retreated to that of handmaiden ... Daisy's gesture of despair as she witnesses this next betrayal is the most frightening and disturbing moment in a [bleak] play' ('Love' 188). Harry White, on the other hand, places the emphasis in this closing scene on the necessity of art for life. 'Tom would rescue his daughter from her solitary incarceration were he able to write his novel, *but not before*. At the last, and in a play that dramatizes the ruinous consequences of artistic neglect, Friel proposes the necessarily redemptive condition of art as a precondition for life itself' (15). But José Lanters cautions that

> The apparently deliberate exclusion of Daisy is ominous ... Paradoxically, even as, on the level of art, Tom is beginning again, on the level of life, tragedy is imminent ... uncertainty has tragic consequences for the lives of people at the same time that it enables art. The possible end and the possible beginning coincide on stage in the final chaotic, mysterious moments of *Give Me Your Answer, Do!* (174)

Friel has brought to the stage in 'this complex and moving play' (Roche 205) a living portrait of a floundering artist in mid-life beset before and behind by troubles and tragedy, who 'wants an overall assessment of what he has done – a judgement, a final verdict' (Friel letter qtd. in Pine, 'Love' 308). Such a judgement, however, cannot be given until uncertainty ends either with death, as in the case of Frank Hardy in *Faith Healer*, or the cessation of writing, as in *Wonderful Tennessee*. So, like most of Friel's characters and all of Samuel Beckett's, Tom cannot go on but does go on as Friel 'sing[s] of human unsuccess / In a rapture of distress'.

Works Cited

Andrews, Elmer. *The Art of Brian Friel: Neither Reality nor Dreams*. London: Macmillan, 1995.

Auden, W.H. 'Elegy: In Memory of W. B. Yeats'. *Collected Shorter Poems*. London: Faber, 1966. 141-43.

Beckett, Samuel. *Endgame*. New York: Grove, 1958.

Conrad, Joseph. *Lord Jim*. London: Penguin, 1949.

Cronin, Anthony. *No Laughing Matter: the Life and Times of Flann O'Brien*. 1989. London: Paladin, 1990.

Eliot, T.S. 'The Love Song of J. Alfred Prufrock'. *The Collected Poems of T. S. Eliot*. London: Faber, 1961. 11-16.

Friel, Brian. *Aristocrats*. *Selected Plays*. London: Faber, 1984. 247-326.

--- *Crystal and Fox*. *Crystal and Fox* and *The Mundy Scheme: Two Plays by Brian Friel*. New York: Farrar, 1970. 1-147.

--- *Dancing at Lughnasa*. London: Faber, 1990.

--- 'The Diviner'. *The Diviner: The Best Short Stories of Brian Friel*. Dublin: O'Brien, 1983. 19-32.

--- *Faith Healer*. *Selected Plays*. London: Faber, 1984. 327-76.

--- *Give Me Your Answer, Do!* London: Penguin, 1997.

--- *Molly Sweeney*. Louchcrew, Oldcastle: Gallery, 1994.

--- *Philadelphia, Here I Come! Selected Plays*. London: Faber, 1984. 23-99.

--- *Selected Plays of Brian Friel*. Introd. Seamus Deane. London: Faber, 1984.

--- *Wonderful Tennessee*. London: Faber, 1993.

Heaney, Seamus. 'The Diviner'. *Selected Poems 1965-1975*. London: Faber, 1980. 24.

--- 'For Liberation: Brian Friel and the Uses of Memory'. *The Achievement of Brian Friel*. Ed. Alan J. Peacock. Gerrards Cross: Smythe, 1993. 229-40.

Hickey, Des, and Gus Smith, eds. *A Paler Shade of Green*. London: Frewin, 1972.

Ó hÓgáin, Dáithí. 'The Shamanic Image of the Irish Poet'. *That Other World*. Ed. Bruce Stewart. 2 vols. Gerrards Cross: Smythe, 1998. 1: 12-48.

Kiberd, Declan. 'Brian Friel's *Faith Healer*'. *The Writer and Society at Large*. Ed. Masaru Sekine. Gerrards Cross: Smythe, 1985. 106-21.

Lanters, José. 'Brian Friel's Uncertainty Principle'. *Irish University Review* 29.1 (1999): 162-75.

McGuinness, Frank. '*Faith Healer*: All the Dead Voices'. *Irish University Review* 29.1 (1999): 60-63.

Murray, Christopher. 'Brian Friel's *Molly Sweeney* and Its Sources: a Postmodern Case History'. *Etudes Irlandaises* 23.2 (1998): 81-98.

Pine, Richard. 'Love: Brian Friel's *Give Me Your Answer, Do!*' *Irish University Review* 29.1 (1999): 176-88.

--- *Brian Friel and Ireland's Drama*. London: Routledge, 1990.

Roche, Anthony. Rev. of *The State of Play: Irish Theatre in the 'Nineties*. Ed. Eberhard Bort. *Irish University Review* 27.1 (1997): 205-08.

Welch, Robert. 'Brian Friel: "Isn't this your job to translate?"' *Changing States: Transformations in Modern Irish Writing*. London: Routledge, 1993. 224-40.

White, Harry. 'Brian Friel and the Condition of Music'. *Irish University Review* 29.1 (1999): 6-15.

3 | Restless Wanderers and Great Pretenders: Brian Friel's Fox Melarkey and Frank Hardy

Giovanna Tallone

> he had an eye for weather-eyes . . .
> and could don manners
> at a flutter of curtains.
> – Seamus Heaney, *The Last Mummer*

Pre-tensions and Pre-texts

In Seamus Heaney's *The Last Mummer* a marginal character is confined in a limbo between the past of rural life and the present 'culture' – or cult – 'of television' (Corcoran, *Heaney* 76), which has dispossessed him. The mummer belongs to the dying tradition of itinerant artists, and at the opening of the poem he comes out of the fog (l. 3) to approach a country-house. Thus he emerges from the undistinguished and indistinguishable realm of mist (l. 9), to which he is doomed to return. The fog is more than an objective correlative, as it enshrines the mummer and his tradition, deceiving both of them. The stone he casts in anger at the house under the spell of the luminous fog of television (l. 6) is a powerless gesture, like Don Quixote fighting the windmills or Cuchulainn fighting the waves.

Two plays by Brian Friel exploit a similar scenario, as both
Crystal and Fox (1968) and *Faith Healer* (1979) revolve around a
fit-up, or travelling show. The 'last mummers' they feature,
however, are not set against the background of changing times,
but are prototypes of artists restlessly questioning their own
identity and investigating their relationship with art and artifice.
I will focus on a comparative analysis of the two plays in terms
of background, themes, structure, and language, with the aim of
pointing out the similarities, differences, and developments of
two complementary works. *Faith Healer* occupies a more
prominent position in Friel's canon and in contemporary Irish
drama than *Crystal and Fox*. However, this study will attempt to
look into both plays identifying possible sources of departure
and development in Friel's early production.

In *Crystal and Fox* the show belongs to the eponymous Fox
Melarkey and includes a melodrama, a raffle, and a trained dog;
hints are also given of a magic show. The company tours the
towns and villages of Ireland, and is composed of Fox, his wife
Crystal, Papa – Crystal's father – El Cid the magician and his
wife, Tanya, who also act in the melodrama, Pedro and his
trained dog, Gringo. Little by little the company breaks up, as
El Cid and Tanya first, and then Pedro, are compelled to leave,
just as other members – Billy Hercules, the Fritter Twins, and
Fox's own son Gabriel – have left over the years. Fox is the
victim of a sort of disease, he has grown uneasy and has lost his
enthusiasm for 'his role of affable, bantering entertainer'
(Kenneally 273), so that he begins to dismantle his own show, a
process which turns out to be an act of self-destruction.

Eleven years later, Brian Friel returns to a travelling show in
Faith Healer. Here the company is reduced to a minimum and so
is the show, featuring Frank Hardy's faith healing power. In fact
only three characters appear: Frank Hardy, the faith healer, his
wife – or mistress – Grace, and their manager Teddy, who in
the past has also worked with trained dogs. The trio, which in a
way recasts Fox, Crystal, and Pedro, wanders through the
villages of Wales and Scotland, later to return to Ireland. This
decision turns out to be destructive, as it is in Ireland that the
faith healer meets his death. The format of the play is

'intergeneric', as 'the forms of novel and drama meet' (Kiberd 106): the three characters on stage never meet, but each of them recites his/her own monologue.

In different ways *Crystal and Fox* and *Faith Healer* break new ground in the context of the Friel canon and are turning points. *Crystal and Fox* is the most enigmatic of 'Friel's four-part catechism of love', a set composed of *Philadelphia, Here I Come!*, *The Loves of Cass McGuire*, *Lovers*, and *Crystal and Fox* itself. It is centred on 'an unusual and dangerously unpredictable character' (Dantanus 115), whose inscrutable impatience with his present life turns out to be pernicious. From this point of view the play's concern with a central character's darkest shades and motivations 'consolidates Friel's work in the theatre-of-character phase of his career' (O'Brien 54). The position of *Faith Healer* is even more crucial, as the playwright's bold experimentation with form gives the play the status of 'monument to his own dramatic kind' (Dantanus 172), it is a 'masterpiece' and a 'culmination' in Friel's progressive complexity (Roche 8), 'the finest play to have come out of Ireland since J.M. Synge's *The Playboy of the Western World*' (Kiberd 106). The structure of individual monologues is well suited to express the development and deepening in psychological insight the playwright had started with Gar O'Donnell's divided self in *Philadelphia*. Halfway between confession, stream of consciousness, and straightforward narration, the play is rich in the variety of themes and issues it provokes, not least the role of the artist and the mystery of faith.

Crystal and Fox was not well received when it first opened in Dublin. Reviews of its premiere express perplexity and often disappointment (Paine 4) after the expectations raised by *Philadelphia* and *The Loves of Cass McGuire*. The play's 'bittiness' elicited 'bemused indifference' in the audience as 'Fox strikes no responsive cord' (Rushe 3). *Crystal and Fox* was 'flawed' (Carberry 27) because its symbolic overtones were unclear (Kelly 10). The play is 'overplotted' and 'undercharacterized' (Corcoran, 'The Penalties of Retrospect' 22), too many things happen too fast, and often in inexplicable ways, which compresses the full development of the play's motifs. However, to some extent *Crystal and Fox* is to be considered seminal for *Faith Healer*, in spite of obvious divergences, and the pivotal position of *Faith Healer* casts a new light on the earlier play. Both plays are based on marginal characters inside a travelling show, therefore both exploit the theatre metaphor as a structuring principle. Both share a set of characters that comes forward as a triangle. In both, the central character is tormented by different forms of restlessness. Both are based on sacrifice and annihilation. In different ways both reconstruct the past – *Crystal and Fox* in Fox's obsession with his past happiness, *Faith Healer* in the contradictory narratives from which only a vague impression of events can be elicited. In both an undercurrent of violence is evident and takes various forms, from Fox's destruction of the fit-up to Gabriel's attempted manslaughter, from Grace's stillborn child to Frank's murder in Ballybeg. In both the nature of love is questioned, as the relationship between Crystal and Fox and Frank and Grace is both overwhelming and full of cruelty. The naturalistic structure of *Crystal and Fox* contrasts strikingly with the non-realistic technique of *Faith Healer*, and this may be responsible for the considerable neglect of the former play.

The vantage point of retrospection, the distance in time, as well as Friel's more recent efforts, including the Field Day experience, his Russian translations and the ventures taken in the 1990s, including *Dancing at Lughnasa* (1990), *Wonderful Tennessee* (1993), *Molly Sweeney* (1994), and *Give Me Your Answer, Do!* (1997), consolidate the undercurrent of motifs in this prolific writer and highlight *Crystal and Fox* and *Faith Healer* as two different sides of the same coin. In terms of setting, themes, and character development, the plays can be read as a sequence and, as discussed later, references and parallels make *Faith Healer* a sort of ideal sequel to *Crystal and Fox*. If *Faith Healer* holds a prominent place in Friel's production, *Crystal and Fox* can be seen as seminal work in his achievement as a playwright as it 'predicts both the later family plays and the plays of language' (Pine 87). Considering *Crystal and Fox* from the point of view of *Faith Healer*, and *Faith Healer* through the mirror of *Crystal and Fox* may help to provide both plays with a reading key, so that they shed light on each other.

Critical analysis has not ignored this mutual connection. *Faith Healer* has been seen as 'a partial reworking' of *Crystal and Fox* (Harding 20). Fox the travelling showman 'foreshadows in some ways the figure of Frank Hardy in *Faith Healer*' (O'Toole 20), and in both plays Friel investigates 'the self-destructive impulses of the artist obsessed with his own art' (Andrews 160).

The six plays that Friel wrote between *Crystal and Fox* and *Faith Healer* show the range of interests and the development in stagecraft on the part of the playwright. He criticized the present state of Ireland in the farce *The Mundy Scheme* (1969) and in the complex violence of *The Gentle Island* (1970), and started his involvement with history in *The Freedom of the City* (1973) and *Volunteers* (1975). The theme of storytelling is pivotal in *The Gentle Island*, where one of the characters says 'There's ways and ways of telling every story. Every story has seven faces' (57). The impossibility of reaching objective truth is also evident in *The Freedom of the City*, in which Friel also displays technical inventiveness. The device of having on stage characters that are revealed to be dead is a major step forward in Friel's experimentation with time and structure, later developed in *Living Quarters* (1977) and exploited at the utmost degree in *Faith Healer*. In all these plays, and in *Aristocrats* (1979) in particular, memory's deceptions and figments are at odds with verifiable facts. *Translations* (1980), *The Communication Cord* (1982), *Making History* (1988), just to mention the plays of the 1980s, can be hardly thought of without *Faith Healer*, which 'makes us see Friel's earlier plays in a different though still coherent way' (Maxwell 201).

On Restlessness

The most immediate impact derives from the affinity between the two characters, Fox Melarkey and Frank Hardy, and from the setting of the travelling show. Much of the characters' identity is moulded by belonging to a show and its fictive world. On the level of plot and characterization some traits overlap: 'Both men are something of a mountebank, and their wives and

friends do not really understand their way to self-destruction'
(Hogan 130).

They are mountebanks – the very word is used twice by
Grace's father in *Faith Healer* (348); they are quacks, charlatans,
pretenders, who have made wandering a mode of being. Their
travelling shows may be the remnants of a lost tradition, but
they are also the symptom of a deeper disquietude. An endemic
bitterness or an unknown disturbance makes them restless and
changes their lives. In a way, both *Crystal and Fox* and *Faith
Healer* investigate the darkest side of the characters that become
catalysts in ultimate questions. Both Fox and Frank are referred
to with similar expressions, and the adjective 'restless' is
repeated nearly obsessively in both plays.

At the opening of *Crystal and Fox*, in Episode 1, the stage
directions focus on the unseen audience within the play, and so
do Fox's lines highlighting their restlessness (11). The
audience's impatience with the show anticipates Fox's own
tiredness and restlessness; not by chance does Fox himself
mention this in a sort of unconscious unmasking of his deeper
self, as if the audience were his *alter ego*. Even his words of love
betray his deep dissatisfaction, as they are nothing but a polite
formula, an automatic response. Fox and Crystal's exchanges
are based on a sort of singsong – 'My love'/'My Fox' – whose
repetition prevents further speech and emotional exposure. On
the other hand this seems to be a sort of strategy on the part of
Fox, because while trying to hide his impatience, at the same
time he gives it away. The pattern of speech based on vocatives
with all its variations sounds like an automatic use of terms of
endearment which resembles a script, not unlike Papa's
playacting by rote in the fake raffle (18). Likewise, his com-
pliments to his actors after the performance are as tired as the
tired audience (15), and they betray his own tiredness. Fox's
language is exhausted and he cannot find any other word but
'nice' to describe his companions' job. It is however Crystal
who observes and detects Fox's condition describing it in nearly
clinical terms. She sees Fox following a pattern, spoiling the
show when the show begins to prosper: 'And you know it's

coming on him … he goes all sort of quiet. And then you could shout at him and he doesn't even hear you' (22).

At the end of the play Crystal's focus is even clearer when casting a backward look on recent events:

> when things were beginning to go well … you got … restless.
> … then you began to skip the places that were good in the past.
> And when we could have done four nights you left after two (60).

Crystal's insight detects a layer of apathy ('he goes all sort of quiet') as a symptom for Fox's unease, which results in an inexplicable need to perform inexplicable acts ('when we could have done four nights, you left after two'). Fox is not unaware of what he is undergoing. Trying to summarize the last five years for the sake of Gabriel, he says of himself with a streak of truth that he has become 'more perverse and more restless' (34), made a 'savage bugger' (36) by his own restlessness. In these hints of self-analysis Fox focuses on change as an inevitable process. 'Things have changed' (34), he says to Gabriel, later adding: 'You'd be surprised. And a man changes, too. You'd be surprised … But I have my Crystal' (34).

The repetition of such expressions as 'change' and 'surprised' highlights Fox's own realm at a point of disruption, his refusal of change and his attempt to carry the past back into the present. The only element of stability is Crystal ('But I have my Crystal'), who embodies the only antidote to change, the dream he wants to come true, to 'live like a child … to die and wake up in heaven with Crystal. What do I want? … if I knew the answer to that, I might be content with what I have' (36).

This is not the first nor will it be the only time that Fox makes use of conditional sentences, which are evenly interspersed throughout the play following the same pattern. In fact, Episode 1 closes on a similar note: 'If I knew a simple answer to that … I'd go in for telling stories' (20). A similar pattern of speech is used at the end of Episode 5, when a series of misfortunes has affected the Fox Melarkey Show: 'if I weren't a superstitious man, … I'd say that heaven's just round the corner' (55). By using second conditionals, Fox enhances his detachment from his own world and his distance from the real thing to enter the realm of the unreal, the dream he wants to come true. This dream implies escape from the oppressive present into a future which is a new enactment of the past, of the way they were, 'just you and me and the old accordion and the old rickety wheel' (55). Fox's dream expresses a death-wish in order to 'experience a death-rebirth sequence, a death-departure from the onerous circus routine and a life-rebirth entry into a "heaven" with his wife' (Robbins 70). Crystal is an instrument of Fox's self-fulfilment, rather than an end in herself. Throughout the play this obsession is revealed as the reason and source of his restlessness, which is codified by his son Gabriel with the words: 'we're a restless breed' (37).

If Act 1 programmatically verbalizes such unease, Act 2 transforms words into action. Pedro's performing dog is killed and Gabriel is caught by the police. However, disaster magnifies Fox's dream and makes its fulfilment possible, if not real. Only the dream exists for him, a 'dream of Eden' (Robbins 67) obsesses him, which has charmed him (Robbins 71) so as to obliterate whatever else may exist.

A strange compulsion can be seen in Frank Hardy, too, who is the victim of a similar kind of obsession. The 'nagging, tormenting, maddening questions that rotted my life' (334) are the counterpart of Fox's haunting dream. Grace, like Crystal, analyses Frank's impatience and calls it 'restlessness', for which she detects a symptom in each of Frank's refashionings, retellings, fabrications (346).

Frank's restlessness is not so easily definable and identifiable, its reasons and motivations are elusive and cryptic. While Fox's has to do with the privacy of a 'transient moment' (Maxwell 203), but also with the contingency of the tangible world around him, Frank's is rooted in solipsism. His tormenting questions involve his gift of faith healing and his identity as a faith healer, as an artist and a performer: 'Was it all chance? – or skill? – ... what power did I possess? ... Could my healing be effected without faith? But faith in what? – in me? – in the possibility? – faith in faith?' (333–34). They are all the more 'nagging, tormenting, maddening' because they cling to one another, widening the gap between Frank and reality. They act as a torture and are capable of transforming and distorting their victim, so that Frank is often referred to by the adjective 'twisted'. In fact Frank's unease recalls Fox's in the choice of lexis for each protagonist. It is Grace who first uses the adjective 'twisted' talking about the faith healer: 'he was such a twisted man!' (345). This echoes Cid's bitter remark in Episode 1 in *Crystal and Fox*, when he says Fox is 'twisted like a bloody corkscrew!' (19). Grace points out Frank's complications, in behaviour and temperament, describing him as 'convoluted' (346). The word 'twisted' is often used in the play, not least in the reference to Donal's twisted finger (351, 372), which Frank succeeds in healing, and which acts as a co-reference to the healer's twisted mind. Donal's finger can be straightened, but Frank's questions prove no less obsessive. He has no power to soothe or silence them, rather his faith healing power – divine or diabolical (Robinson 224) – magnifies his obsessions. And, as Fox has grown more and more restless, Frank has become 'more frantic and more truculent' (349). Even Teddy seems to be contaminated by Frank's twisted and convoluted ways in the troubled choice of the musical theme for the faith healing performance, probably the result of 'a twisted mind' (354).

In his account of Grace's stillborn child, Teddy loses his usual control of language and defines the faith healer as a 'bastard', whose restlessness has more than unknown motifs: 'to walk away deliberately when your wife's going to have a baby in the middle of bloody nowhere … there really was a killer instinct deep down in that man!' (363) Frank seems to share a 'demonic aspect' (Andrews 107) with Fox Melarkey, whose hatred (48) is one of the various forms in which his unease materializes. Unlike *Crystal and Fox*, where restlessness becomes action, in the format of *Faith Healer* restlessness is turned into words. 'Past and present, narration and what it narrates, are simultaneously co-present'; in the recounting of Frank's restlessness the 'textual word is made flesh' (Roche 113). The narration itself is restless, wavering among details and eluding certainty and objective truth. Restlessness is however the key-motif in Frank's obsession, and even his recounting is restlessly

striving for fixity by eluding it. The truth of the story – or
stories – is 'a matter of complex imagining' (Worth 82). The
monologues on their part contain different stories, the stories
of Teddy's artists, of Grace's stillborn baby, of Frank's father's
death and so forth (Deane 19). The meandering of narration
and the mutually exclusive nature of each monologue, rather
than their complementariness, underlie a sort of 'impatience for
Apocalypse' (Andrews 142); the four monologues tell rather
than show.

If wandering belongs to their identity as itinerant artists,
Fox and Frank are also wanderers in words. In *Crystal and Fox*,
Fox's use of language has a double function: it either gives
orders, casting roles as a stage-manager, or it provides order in
a world on the point of rupture. His language wanders into the
present and the future, but more frequently and obsessively into
the past, so that fragments of memories little by little gain
ground. These are very private territories, in which Fox gives
voice to his own unease and disquietude by resurrecting his
past. In fact, it is the past, or the dream of his past, that
dominates these private interludes. In Act 1 he either sums up
his own weariness (36) or shows contempt for his own
company, for the 'yahoo audiences', for his own show, doing
the same tricks again and again (23), in other words he shows
contempt for himself.

Alternatively, Fox wanders into the past, and his memories
take the form of stories. The account of his first meeting with
Crystal, for example, is recast into a fairy-tale (24-25), which
makes you wonder whether all this ever happened at all. On the
other hand, the memory of the incident at dawn, which closes
Episode 5, takes the form of a dialogue, with Fox and Crystal's
quick exchanges of fragments or segments of memories. Crystal
and Fox reconstruct together a swim which ends in a comic
stepping into fish, yet it is Fox that is directing and orches-
trating his jig-saw puzzle (53-54). The episode closes on Fox's
incursion into the future, which is a restoration of the past: 'I'll
get rid of it. And when I do there'll just be you and me and the
old accordion and the old rickety wheel – all we had thirty years

ago … And we'll laugh again at silly things … And everywhere we go we'll know people and they'll know us' … (55).

The obsessive repetition of the conjunction 'and' which characterizes this account of his dream reveals not only Fox's impatience with the future he wants to come true, but also his lack of control over his own imaginings. Friel uses a similar strategy in *Faith Healer*, not in Frank's monologue, but in Grace's, whose collapse is revealing of the double-edged quality of their emotional relationship, demanding and painful at the same time:

> And, as they say, I've got a lot to be thankful for … And I like living in London. And the bedsitter's small but it's warm and comfortable. … And at night I listen to the radio or I read … And on Thursday afternoons I go to the doctor to get my pills renewed (341–42).

Here the difference is as significant as the similarity. In fact, the repetition of 'and' casts a glimpse into Grace's mental labyrinth, and her obsessive use of language is an attempt to impose order onto her scattered memories, as she too is a wanderer in words as well as in time. In his greater control of psychological insight in *Faith Healer*, Friel exploits the compactness of monologue to emphasize fragmentation. Likewise, Frank's monologues are an attempt to impose order (Kenneally 275) onto his own narrative, as the play tries to impose order onto divergent versions of the truth. Frank's speech begins erratically with his litany of place names and proceeds with no control until he calls himself back to order and gives his identity: 'The Fantastic Francis Hardy, Faith Healer, One Night Only' (332).

The place names Frank recites 'just for the mesmerism, the sedation, of the incantation' (332) have an equivalent function to Fox's dream. By reciting his dream, Fox puts it into words and thus gives it substance and reality. However, the recital of his dream is a private undertaking, which has the effect of soothing his restlessness. The mesmeric power of place names in *Faith Healer* is a counterpart to the utterance of Fox's dream in *Crystal and Fox*, a play in which place names – apart from Dublin, Manchester and Ballybeg – are notably missing.

It may be too far-fetched to say that the occasional monologues by Fox in *Crystal and Fox* anticipate the extended monologues in *Faith Healer*. However, the random quality of Fox's final speech – maybe the only true monologue in the play, with its lack of pauses, and inconsequential juxtaposition of confession, memories, imploring, and ritual sing-song – makes it as digressing as Frank's use of language at the opening of *Faith Healer* (64-65).

On Performing

The setting of the fit-up or travelling show provides a significant pattern of similarities and cross-references in both plays. This scenario works on a double axis: it belongs to the level of plot and therefore contributes to the ambience and characterization of the gypsy-like world it depicts. It is also a sustaining principle on the level of structure, as it gives the plays the modernist format of a play-within-a-play, the melodrama cum raffle in *Crystal and Fox*, the faith healing performance in *Faith Healer*. This draws attention to the medium of drama *per se*, to the 'simulation of reality' (Esslin 19), the 'arena of illusion' (Orr 10) of the conscious fiction of drama. At the heart of both plays is a performance, together with its performers. Each play then is about itself, it is about actors and their roles: in *Crystal and Fox* each protagonist plays a part in the melodrama, and about artists; in *Faith Healer* Teddy's stories about the artists he has met in his life, including performing dogs, are a reflection on the role and complexity of art and artists, epitomized in the protagonist's narration. 'We never see the three narrators except as performers' (Worth 82). Therefore, both plays focus on the conscious fiction of acting on a stage, of performing for the sake of an audience.

Crystal and Fox opens on the final part of the melodrama, *The Doctor's Story*, which is part of the Fox Melarkey Show, 'during a brief interval' of its final episode (11). Each character is introduced according to the role he/she is playing: Crystal-Mother Superior, El Cid-Dr. Giroux, Tanya-Sister Petita Sancta.

Clapping from an unseen audience enhances the distribution of the acting space:

> The acting area is divided into two portions. The portion left … occupies about one third of the area; *the dividing line is a flimsy and transparent framework which runs at an angle upstage.* The portion left of this division is the stage inside Fox's marquee; the portion right is the backstage; *the dividing framework is the back wall of the stage* (8, emphasis added).

The 'dividing framework' separates the world of 'fiction' from the world of 'reality'. Not only is it 'the back wall of the stage', in a way it is also the mirror image of the fourth wall twice removed from the 'audience', the 'unseen audience' clapping off-stage, and the audience happening to be in the theatre. It is a matter of Chinese boxes: *The Doctor's Story* is contained in Fox's show which is contained in Friel's play which is contained in a text – or a performance. The stage device builds up different boxes too, thus evoking the words of the song accompanying the Fox Melarkey Show: 'we'll catch a fox / and put him in a box' (18). Not by chance is the dividing line 'flimsy' and 'transparent'. Both adjectives suggest fragility and imperceptibility, yet this framework has a double power: it is capable of separating the worlds, at the same time co-penetrating them. It acts as a lull, just in the same way as, on the level of plot, the play opens on the interval in the Fox Melarkey Show, a no-man's land between *The Doctor's Story* (the melodrama) and the play. The flimsy framework is a no-man's land, too, where transformations are possible. Crossing that borderline means switching to the world of 'fiction' and in the course of Episode 1 this phenomenon is repeated, which emphasizes the fiction and the illusion of drama and the 'Ersatz' to reality such fiction enacts. The stage directions point out the continuous process of masking and unmasking, which accompanies the crossing of that borderline. In fact, early in Episode 1, Fox is made to entertain the restless audience by telling them a story. His contempt for what he is about to do is followed by the servile and flattering language of 'thank yous' when he turns to the audience. As a great pretender, this change is effected by the wearing of his performer's mask: 'then, *switching on his professional smile*, he swings out on to the stage' (12, emphasis added). Likewise, when Cid and Tanya are called back onto the stage first – and not last as Cid had required – the situation is repeated. Cid mutters 'Bastard' to Fox, but then, 'Cid catches Tanya's hand and *assuming a radiant smile* he runs on' (17, emphasis added).

The play-within-a-play is also emphasized by the opening and closing of curtains – the fourth wall – which occasionally sees Papa, Crystal's father, as 'stage manager' (11) obeying Fox's prompt and hoisting up the curtain (13), which marks the opening of the final scene of *The Doctor's Story*. Likewise, Crystal's 'Goodbye' to Cid and Tanya – that is, Mother Superior's to Dr. Giroux and Sister Petita Sancta – which is also the goodbye to the show and the 'audience', is accompanied by Papa lowering the curtain (15). Such self-references to drama and play-acting are concentrated in two specific moments, which provide a sort of balance to each other. One occurs at the opening of the play and occupies most of Episode 1. The other takes place at the opening of Act 2 (and Episode 3), thus marking the play half-way through its development and '[a] rehearsal is in progress' (39). Fox himself draws attention to the rehearsal complaining that other things are being done meanwhile. The 'fiction' of *The Doctor's Story* is intertwined with the 'reality' of the travelling company's everyday life, as the mission hospital in Zambia (14,39), the setting of the melodrama, is extended or expanded to the hospital where Papa is lying and where Crystal is anxious to go. From this point onwards the presence of theatre leaves metaphor and returns to plot. In fact, for financial reasons, the Show is sold to the rival company of Dick Prospects. What remains is the accordion, the rickety wheel, and the primus stove, with which Crystal and Fox started their own business years ago.

Faith Healer exploits the background of the fit-up but stylization is drastic in terms of structure and form as '[s]tage directions have been kept to a minimum', leaving the director free to take all decisions about timing and movements (331). The challenge to dramatic action (Kilroy 91) embedded in the sequence of four subsequent monologues telling divergent truths is a test also for stage directions and structure. The former are not the only features to be kept to a minimum. Action itself is. The play *'tells* us what has happened and *shows* nothing' (Hughes 175). The play's approach to the setting is 'unique' (Burke, 'As if Language … ' 21) and the use of props draws attention to the fiction and the structure of drama *per se*. In fact, both the rows of chairs and the poster (331) that are revealed while Frank is absorbed reciting his litany of place names (Aberarder, Aberayron / Llangranog, Llangurig, and so forth) at the opening of the play, purposefully disclose the play as a work about itself (Kiberd 108). The poster is present in all monologues but the final one, while the three rows of chairs occupy the stage only during Frank's first monologue. In a way the unseen audience heard off-stage in *Crystal and Fox* is carried onto the stage in *Faith Healer*. Yet, the stage is empty, the chairs are there only to imply the possibility of a performance. 'By the power of the narrative the empty chairs will fill up with … invisible audiences' (Worth 82), who in turn are participants in the faith healing process, so that stage and auditorium become one (Roche 108). Thus the empty chairs enhance Frank Hardy's role as a performer. And, as Joe Dowling pointed out, *Faith Healer* is 'about actors communicating with their audiences and understanding how to develop a relationship with an audience' (qtd. in Wallace 8). This is accomplished through the technique of story-telling, which is the reading and structuring principle for *Faith Healer* and which makes the play a sort of manifesto for creative art, if not just a 'metaphor for writing' (Andrews 159).

The 'critical process of self-reflection' (Kearney 24) which is staged and performed in *Faith Healer* is enacted by the abolition of the 'fourth wall', as the faith healer talks directly to the audience. And again, which audience is it? Is it the audience 'physically' listening to him in a theatre? Or is he talking *through* us to the stylized audience on stage? Or the other way round? Audiences past? Or audiences future? The elusive quality of this timeless retelling is enhanced by Frank Hardy's introduction of himself: 'The man on the tatty banner' (332). This identifies the faith healer, who, in turn, identifies himself with the poster. In a play in which the spoken word is everything, it is the written word – both the tatty banner and the newspaper clipping in which his name is spelt wrong – that identifies Frank Hardy and his 'vocation without a ministry' (333). Again, if compared to *Crystal and Fox*, a process of stylization has taken place: the banner is the quintessential Frank Hardy, much in the same way as Fox Melarkey *is* his own show. Identity is provided by the fiction of the fit-up, 'the performer can never be released from his performance' (Kearney 31). Fox's existence, like the faith healer's, is provided and guaranteed by the existence of his show and by the presence of an audience. Fox's restlessness begins when he does not believe in his audience any more, that is when his own fiction ceases to be meaningful. As a performer, he has been released from his performance, and he spends the rest of his life trying to reconcile himself with it.

Fox's self-analysis becomes exasperated in Frank. His tormenting questions overcome Fox's practical concern and disappointment with the travelling show. Frank's considerations are metaphysical, they invest his identity as an artist and the extent of his gift. He keeps questioning himself about the nature of his power. In other words, he scrutinizes the nature of his art and performance and his role as an artist and a performer. The central obsession in *Faith Healer*, tormenting Frank, but also raising disquietude in the audience, is the issue of fiction, 'the notion of the artist as inspired con man' (Kiberd 108). 'Am I a con man?' (333) wonders Frank Hardy, aware that this is only one of the questions obsessing him, 'those nagging, tormenting, maddening questions that rotted my life' (334). The question involves Frank and his intermittent power of faith healing, a gift he cannot control or summon up at will – like a shaman, he has 'no control over the spirits' (Throne 22) – but it is extended also to drama and art at large. In *Faith Healer* Frank reinterprets Fox's weariness: 'It was always like this – shabby, shabby, bleak, derelict' (372). 'Like this' works at different levels, shedding light on the contingency of the wandering life, but also on the fiction of his performance. At the same time the nature of faith healing is questioned: is it part of the 'shabby,

bleak, derelict'? Is it a power to heal and reinvigorate or is it a
non-power? Is it only a fiction, just as the show is a fiction?

On Pretending

To some extent *Crystal and Fox* foreshadows Frank's concern
and obsession with his fiction. Even though Fox does not seem
to be disturbed by the *nature* of performance and his role as a
performer, some of his observations are suggestive of the
metatheatrical dimension embedded in a play which is based on
the fiction of drama. Towards the end of Episode 2, Fox points
out his own weariness, he is tired of 'this making-do, of
conning people that know they're being conned' (36). On the
level of plot these words recall the layout of the Fox Melarkey
show, which opens on a double fiction, the melodrama and the
fake raffle. But on the level of structure, they reveal the
consciousness of the theatrical situation: he (the actor and
stage-manager) knows he is consciously conning us, the
audience, who, on our part, are aware of the conning that is
going on. Different roles are at stake, various personae are
called onto the stage and released, illusions take form and are
dispelled again. The show must go on. Fox is a showman, an
illusionist, an entertainer, a great pretender who has grown tired
of pretending. His multiple personae lose ground while he is
sustaining them, because he does not believe in the fiction he is
performing. Fox has no faith whatsoever in the other half that
should provide strength or fuel the show, that is, the audience –
in the play and the 'real' audience. Neither of them can corroborate the illusions he keeps building on stage, so he offers
them what they want: 'a happy ending' (13).

As a showman, Fox has spent his life pretending to be what
he is not (O'Brien 64), his role as entertainer has given him a
'god-like' power of transformation which involves himself and
others; 'he is an impresario of other worlds, a truly mythic
ringmaster' (Andrews 105). He imposes roles and changes
them, manipulating identities for the sake of the show. From
this point of view Fox does not seem to possess any control
over the power as illusionist he is endowed with, rather he is
carried away by it, not unlike Frank Hardy's faith healing. He is

mesmerized by Pedro's fingers and arbitrarily decides that Pedro is to play Doctor Giroux (27). When Pedro refuses, Fox casts the role on Crystal's father (28). Yet, in his dramatic metarole of stage-manager and director, Fox is also an actor who role-plays before the policeman when he comes searching for Gabriel. That is why he is putting on another illusion for the sake of an audience. He manipulates his voice, his face, his identity, in the same way in which he manipulates other people's identities.

Frank Hardy, too, is a manipulator of identities. Grace is never his wife but his mistress. She is from Yorkshire (335) but then she is from Scarborough, Knaresborough, Kerry, London, Belfast (345) and he does not remember her family name, he keeps changing it all the time (345). By inventing new names and new identities for Grace, Frank is casting her into different roles, including the role of somebody he has cured (345). He is probably conscious of what he is doing and this is what makes it harder for Grace: 'I'm one of his fictions too' (353). Is this what Frank has made of Grace? A product of his imagination? An invented role? A persona inside his travelling show? Grace herself gives evidence of the twisted workings of Frank's mind in that he mixes fiction and reality. They overlap and get blurred in a new, liminal area: 'Even the people who came to him ... were ... real as fictions ... And if he cured a man, that man became for him a successful fiction and therefore actually real' (345).

Grace is also reflecting on herself while noticing she is only 'one of his fictions', as she is giving voice to her dramatic metarole inside the play. She is questioning her own being and existence as a character, a persona in Frank Hardy's imaginings, but also within the construct of the play. So, in a way, *Faith Healer* is not only about the art of writing and about the artist's creative power and imagination, it is also about the production's awareness of being fiction. From this point of view, Grace's cry 'I am one of his fictions' is not far from the six characters' dramatic awareness of being living constructions in Pirandello's *Six Characters in Search of an Author.*

By becoming aware of being a fiction, Grace lays bare the final illusion of drama as substitute reality. The relationship with the audience is thus stripped of the element of lying that is 'embedded in the theatrical phenomenon' (Almansi 87) and drama puts forward what for Declan Kiberd is the key element in *Faith Healer*: 'the first audience the artist must con is himself' (109). Grace recalls Frank's aggressive and provocative questions: 'Just a con, isn't it? Just an illusion, isn't it?' (350). Again, such questions as these work on a double axis, as they corroborate the faith healing process in terms of plot, but they also draw attention to the performance as con and illusion, questioning the nature of drama itself. Not by chance does the first monologue close on a metadramatic note. The faith healer informs the audience – the audiences? – that his narration will have a sequel later, and at the same time he sheds light on the fiction that characterizes his existence: 'The first Irish tour! ... And there I am, *pretending to subscribe to the charade* ...' (340-41, emphasis added).

Ambiguity arises in the deictic embedded in 'there I am' – is it 'here I am', now, or 'there I was', then? Such ambiguity is also part of the fiction, since 'the fictional past is ... simultaneously there before us' (Roche 108), which is corroborated by Frank's 'pretending to subscribe to the charade', a game of words, but also an absurd pretense.

In a play dominated by fiction at different levels, the fiction of the monologists' narration, the fiction of the performance and the fiction of drama, Teddy sheds different light on the consciousness of fiction. His voice is the most reliable, while his monologue sheds light on the trio's nomadic life (Roche 123) with references to financial problems and scanty audiences. In spite of, or maybe because of, his position as a stage-manager, he can have a detached perspective, showing 'a subtle awareness of the power of illusion' (Kiberd 117). For him, Frank is thwarted by his 'brains', which makes him mediocre (357). Teddy is questioning the whole enterprise the audience has contemplated so far: Frank's monologue is dominated by his self-analysis and by his unanswered questions. This is what makes him mediocre, so in a way also *this* performance is mediocre, because his monologue is nothing but a continuous self-reflection, a steady repetition of questions, the effect of his 'brains'. Maybe it is only a lie.

Both Frank and Fox consciously or unconsciously base their lives on the act of lying. Right from the start in *Faith Healer* doubts arise about the authenticity of the truth in each monologue. Grace calls Frank a liar, 'whose fictions are to be believed' (Roche 108). And the impulse to lie comes from an inexplicable need to both hurt and create; it is a 'compulsion he had to adjust, to recreate everything around him' (345).

Fox has a similar compulsion to recreate, and to recreate himself and Crystal as they were years ago. In fact, what he wants to restore is a perfect image of his own past with Crystal and yet such recreation is accompanied by an inexplicable need to lie. At the end of the play, when he seems to have reached what he wanted, he tells Crystal he has given their son Gabriel away to the police in order to obtain the reward. Crystal's iterated accusation of lying is re-echoed again by Fox himself, who is unable to explain why he has done it: 'It's a lie, Crystal, all a lie, … I made it all up … I tried to stop myself and I couldn't' (64). Fox's admission of lying opens the final moment in *Crystal and Fox*, a breathless, frantic accumulation of words and snatches of discourse with no consequential or logical connection or construction. The lack of punctuation, or the sparse use of it, is indicative of the disorder Fox is undergoing. The iterative use of connectors (and, but), of 'that's', and the frequency of pauses, graphically rendered with dashes, highlight Fox's lack of control on language and on reality, as he cannot control the fulfilment of his dream and his own power of recreation:

> Red-yellow-black or blue, whatever it is that tickles your fancy, now's your chance to turn a bad penny into a decent pound, I love you, my Crystal, and you are the best part of me and I don't know where I'm going or what will become of me (64).

The play closes on the paradoxical destruction of what Fox thinks he has just restored. As an actor and stage-manager he used to restore the show as soon as he had destroyed part of it;

in his private life he was obsessed with preserving and restoring a personal dream, and by doing so he has enacted a process of destruction. Going onwards for him means going backwards, his greatest achievement is to be 'back at the start' (69), 'just ... you and me and the old accordion and the old rickety wheel' (55), which echoes the song in *Philadelphia, Here I Come!*: 'Philadelphia, Here I come, right back where I started from' (30). The use of the song in *Philadelphia* is ironical: Gar has never been to the United States, so his departure can never be a return. The irony exists in *Crystal and Fox* as well. In fact, here '[I]t's all about to begin' and 'it's all over' (31); destroyer and preserver, Fox wants to keep Crystal but ends up by losing her.

Crystal is 'central' to Fox's dream (O'Brien 67), just as Grace is central to *Faith Healer*. The two characters have a lot in common, so that some of their words are taken nearly verbatim from play to play. Crystal in her dedication to Fox expresses her own anxiety with words later echoed by Grace: 'I never understood why you did those things ... And maybe I didn't want to know, ... because ... I was terrified that you were going to shake me off too' (60). Likewise, Grace's greatest suffering stems from the awareness that she has to sacrifice herself for the intermittent power of faith healing: 'And then, for him, I didn't exist ... he obliterated me' (344).

Both sets of characters undergo regression to childhood. This comes to the fore in the final episode of *Crystal and Fox*, when dizzy with drink Crystal and Fox behave like children. According to stage directions, their arrival is announced by 'so much noise' that 'one would expect to see a dozen happy children appear' (55). This childish behaviour also belongs to *Faith Healer*, as the most trustworthy of the narrators, Teddy, recollects Frank and Grace's behaviour as childish: 'What a pair! ... Like kids they were' (369).

The relationship between the plays is enhanced by such cross-references. Moreover, in the structure of *Crystal and Fox*, the presence of folklore and fairy tales, from Goldilocks to Little Red Riding Hood, is a fundamental structuring principle (see Robbins). This is taken up again in *Faith Healer* at occasional points, such as the fairy-tale image evoked by Frank:

> I had a fairy-tale image of us being summoned to some royal bedroom … and I'd raise the sleeping princess to life and we'd be wined and dined for seven days and sent on our way with bags of sovereigns (335).

Also Fox's account of his first meeting Crystal is a significant memory translated according to the formula of fairy-tale, with three golden vans and a princess. *Faith Healer* exploits the traditional form of the oral narration, the art of storytelling which is its basic principle. In a way, this is the expansion of the presence of storytelling that is vital in Friel's production and especially in *Faith Healer*, where 'the story is everything' (Worth 74), but in the specific case of *Crystal and Fox* personal anecdotes and episodes from the past are recast into the mythic code of fables and fairy-tales. Fox's memory of a swim with Crystal, and of plaiting seaweed into her hair (53-55) has a magic timelessness. The episode is said to have happened at dawn, and also Episode 6 of the play takes place at dawn at a more than overtly symbolic crossroads, 'a critical place in destiny' (Burke, 'As if Language … ' 18). This is the time in which beginning and end overlap, which draws the play closer to *Faith Healer*. In the latter play, too, the end of Frank's monologue and of his life coincide with a new beginning, as he dies at dawn: 'And as I moved across the yard towards them … for the first time I had a simple and genuine sense of home-coming. Then for the first time … the maddening questions were silent' (376).

The temporal space of dawn is enlarged in the physical space of the courtyard where Frank meets his death, where his end overlaps with various beginnings, and the crossroads, where Fox is left with more and more maddening questions. 'He ends the play by mocking himself in a long, disjointed speech' (Robbins 74) – a monologue – accompanied by the rickety wheel. The latter does not simply work as a prop, but it is a leitmotif, recalling the wheel of life, fortune or torture, but also drawing attention to Fox's obsession that 'the whole thing's fixed' (65). Thus, Fox is giving voice to what later on Frank Hardy will materialize as his 'maddening questions'.

Obsessions take different forms. Even the song Fox sings, 'A-Hunting We Will Go', which is the theme song for the Fox Melarkey Show, becomes a maddening question, as it torments Fox at the conclusion of the play. The song, however, has its own significance within Friel's play (not just Fox's show), in the same way as the inconsequential use of 'The Way You Look Tonight' underlies *Faith Healer* and the faith healing performance. One line in particular attracts attention, a line which changes significantly between beginning and end:

> we'll catch a fox
> and put him in a box (18).

In Fox's embittered monologue 'we'll catch a fox' becomes 'you'll catch no fox' (64), with a double change in pronoun and mode, an 'emendation' (Burke, 'Heard and Imagined' 44) that highlights Fox's failure. 'Ironically, it is the Fox himself who traps himself in an empty box' (Robbins 76) in an attempt to escape from whatever is 'fixed – fixed – fixed'. The faith healer, too, has trapped himself in a series of boxes: the company's van is a box, the various halls and rooms where he performs are boxes, also the format of the play is a box with its four monologues, which contain various acts of narration, which contain different stories, or snatches of stories (Deane 19). A box is also the theatre/stage where these monologues are performed. Yet, being imprisoned in monologues points out the shifting perspective in *Faith Healer*. Here things may be 'fixed', yet they elude fixity by the elusive quality of words, capable of changing or moulding reality.

A final cross reference lies in the need and desire of both Fox and Frank to step out of their world of fiction and pretence and reach something better 'than this' (48). 'This' can be read or decoded at different levels: is it their show? Their itinerant life? Their misery? Or is it the restlessness and recklessness that plague them? Only occasionally can Fox perceive that something better may happen, when 'the fog lifts' (47). This is the moment in which Fox Melarkey, the great pretender, casts off his borrowed robes and reveals his desire for transcendence (Kenneally 275). Frank Hardy can intermittently reach what Fox has only got a glimpse of, 'the kind of wholeness and harmony that Fox Melarkey seeks' (Kenneally 275). When occasionally his power is effective (333), leading to the long-expected miracle (337), the wholeness of the man he has cured has a cathartic effect on the faith healer: 'For these few hours I had become whole in myself' (333).

Conclusion

The restless wanderers, the great pretenders, both liars and artists (Kerwin xvi), are magicians and masters of words. Yet, ironically, words have deceived them and what remains is a fiction of 'truth'. At the end of *Faith Healer* the obsession with questions has dispelled: 'For the first time … the maddening questions were silent' (376). For the first time ever Frank has reconciled with his questions and his experience of 'a simple and genuine sense of homecoming' (376) provides the sense of order that the words in his story have not managed to give. In Friel's earlier play, instead, Fox remains trapped in the deliberate disorder he has provoked. There is no sense of homecoming for him, rather he is lost forever at the final crossroads, lost also in the chaos of his words, while claiming paradoxically to possess 'all the answers'. Frank's tormenting questions have a counterpart in Fox's tormenting answers. Yet, again, his answers belong to the fiction, they are part of the recital of his travelling show: 'whatever it is that tickles your fancy, the Fox knows all the answers … he's learned the secrets of the universe, strike me dead if I'm telling a lie' (64-65).

Fox's monologue is potentially endless, the recital of his invention could go on forever. Frank takes up this legacy, and the recital of his monologues has a similar quality of 'wanderlust', in space and in time, in words and in fiction. In their destiny to cheat and deceive a power of transformation is revealed, which invests themselves and the Other, crossing the barriers of all possible worlds and striving to make whole what was not whole. Frank's displaced voice is the voice of a pretender trying to confront his own imaginings, trying to control the uncontrollable flow of language that makes up the play. *Faith Healer* itself possesses the quintessential quality of faith healing as described in Grace's disturbed voice: 'this gift, this craft, this talent, this art, this magic' (349).

Works Cited

Almansi, Guido. 'Harold Pinter's Idiom of Lies'. *Contemporary English Drama.* Ed. C.W.E. Bigsby. London: Arnold, 1981. 79-92.

Andrews, Elmer. *The Art of Brian Friel.* London: Macmillan; New York: St. Martin, 1995.

Burke, Patrick. '"Both Heard and Imagined": Music as Structuring Principle in the Plays of Brian Friel'. *A Small Nation's Contribution to the World: Essays on Anglo-Irish Literature and Language.* Ed. Donald Morse, Csilla Bertha, and István Pálffy. Gerrards Cross: Smythe, 1993. 43-52.

--- '"As if Language No Longer Existed": Non-Verbal Theatricality in the Plays of Friel'. In Kerwin. 13-22.

Carberry, Sean. 'The Morality of a Fox'. *The Sunday Press* 17 Nov. 1968: 27.

Corcoran, Neil. *Seamus Heaney.* London: Faber, 1986.

--- 'The Penalties of Retrospect: Continuities in Brian Friel'. In Peacock. 14-28.

Dantanus, Ulf. *Brian Friel: A Study.* London: Faber, 1988.

Esslin, Martin. *An Anatomy of Drama.* London: Smith, 1976.

Friel, Brian. *Crystal and Fox.* London: Faber, 1970; Dublin: Gallery, 1984.

--- *Faith Healer.* London: Faber, 1980; *Selected Plays.* London: Faber, 1984.

--- *Philadelphia, Here I Come!* London: Faber, 1965. *Selected Plays.* London: Faber, 1984.

--- *The Gentle Island.* London: Davis-Pyntner, 1973; Dublin: Gallery, 1993.

Harding, Tim. 'What a Way to Go'. *The Sunday Press* 7 Sept. 1980: 20.

Heaney, Seamus. *Selected Poems.* London: Faber, 1980.

Hogan, Robert. *Since O'Casey and Other Essays on Irish Drama.* Gerrards Cross: Smythe, 1983.

Hughes, George. 'Ghosts and Ritual in Brian Friel's *Faith Healer*'. *Irish University Review* 24.2 (1994): 175-85.

Kelly, Seamus. 'New Friel Play at the Gaiety Theatre'. *The Irish Times* 13 Nov. 1968: 10.

Kearney, Richard. 'Language Play: Brian Friel and Ireland's Verbal Drama'. *Studies* 72. 1 (1983): 20-56.

Kenneally, Michael. 'The Transcendent Impulse in Contemporary Irish Drama'. *International Aspects of Irish Literature.* Ed. Toshi Furomoto, *et al.* Gerrards Cross: Smythe, 1996. 272-82.

Kerwin, William, ed. *Brian Friel. A Casebook.* London: Garland, 1997.

Kiberd, Declan. 'Brian Friel's *Faith Healer*'. *Irish Writers and Society at Large*. Ed. Masaru Sekine. Gerrards Cross: Smythe, 1985. 106-21.

Kilroy, Thomas. 'Theatrical Text and Literary Text'. In Peacock. 91-102.

Maxwell, D.E.S. *A Critical History of Modern Irish Drama 1891-1980*. Cambridge: Cambridge UP, 1984.

O'Brien, George. *Brian Friel*. Dublin: Gill & Macmillan, 1989.

Orr, John. *Tragicomedy and Contemporary Culture. Plays and Performance from Beckett to Shepard*. London: Macmillan, 1991.

O'Toole, Fintan. 'Friel's Lost Tribe'. *The Sunday Tribune* 24 March 1985: 20.

Paine, Basil. 'Friel's New Play Disappoints'. *The Irish Press* 13 Nov. 1968: 4.

Pine, Richard. *Brian Friel and Ireland's Drama*. London: Routledge, 1990.

Peacock, Alan, ed. *The Achievement of Brian Friel*. Gerrards Cross: Smythe, 1992.

Robbins, Ronald. 'Friel's Modern "Fox and the Grapes" Fable'. *Eire-Ireland* 21.4 (1986): 66-76.

Robinson, Paul N. 'Brian Friel's *Faith Healer*: An Irishman Comes Back Home'. *Literary Interrelations. Ireland, England and the World*. Vol. 3. *National Images and Stereotypes*. Ed. Wolfgang Zach and Heinz Kosok. Tübingen: Narr, 1987. 223-27.

Roche, Anthony. *Contemporary Irish Drama: From Beckett to McGuinness*. Dublin: Gill & Macmillan, 1994.

Rushe, Desmond. 'Friel's New Play. "A Thing of Shreds and Patches"'. *The Irish Independent* 13 Nov. 1968: 3.

Throne, Marilyn. 'Brian Friel's *Faith Healer*: Portrait of a Shaman'. *The Journal of Irish Literature* 16.3 (1987): 18-24.

Wallace, Arminta. 'Great Faith in Friel, Confidence in his Cast'. *The Irish Times* 27 Nov. 1990: 8.

Worth, Katherine. 'Translations of History: Story-Telling in Brian Friel's Theatre'. *British and Irish Drama Since 1960*. Ed. James Acheson. London: Macmillan; New York: St. Martin, 1993. 73-87.

4 | Music And Words In Brian Friel's *Performances*

Csilla Bertha

Music is a 'much more demanding language' than words because music is 'the language of feeling itself; a unique vocabulary of sounds created by feeling itself' (31) – proudly declares Leoš Janáček, the Czech composer-protagonist in Brian Friel's *Performances*. Questioning the power of words versus other forms of expression is a well-known recurring theme in Friel's *oeuvre*. In 'Seven Notes for a Festival Programme (1999)' he confesses that he often used music in his plays, sometimes at points where words offer neither an adequate means of expression nor a valve for emotional release. Because at that specific point emotion has staggered into inarticulacy beyond the boundaries of language. And that is what music can provide in the theatre: another way of talking, a language without words. And because it is wordless it can hit straight and unmediated into the vein of deep emotion (177).

The famous closing sentences of *Dancing at Lughnasa* (1990), for instance, assert the superiority of dance to words in its power to 'whisper private and sacred things, to be in touch with some otherness' so 'words were no longer necessary' (71). But, as Nicholas Grene helpfully observes: 'it is with the hypnotic suggestiveness of language itself that language is renounced' (142). In *Wonderful Tennessee* (1993), the verbal utterances are often silenced or counterpointed by music, and George's accordion-playing conveys his whole life story more potently than words could. Or in *Give Me Your Answer, Do!* the dried-up writer Tom is silenced by the tragedy in his family and his career is continuously juxtaposed to his wife's musical talent which circumstances do not allow her to use. In 2002, before *Performances* appeared, Richard Pine argued that musicality seems 'to be the overriding characteristic of what he [Friel] is writing at the moment' perhaps as a response to the fact that 'our modern society ... has exhausted our traditional strategies of speaking to ourselves, and ... some kind of "music" is necessary even if only to give language a rest and an opportunity to reformulate itself' ('World' 236). He speaks about 'musicality' in a broad sense, the way he had already talked about it in his book on Friel, *The Diviner*, as the exploration of 'the inner chambers of the heart and the imagination' ('World' 236), the expression of what lies 'beyond' the ordinary, visible, mundane. But in *Performances* Friel goes furthest in dramatizing directly the language-music dichotomy, giving music centre stage, letting it occupy a huge proportion of performance time.

The survival of Janáček's love letters written to a young woman at the time of (and for years before) composing his *Second String Quartet* called *Intimate Letters*, gives Friel a splendid opportunity to raise questions and then let them linger throughout the play, such as whether the *words* of love in these famous love letters can be ignored as negligible in appreciating Janáček's music. Does the music express the passion the letters speak about? Is the quartet superior not only because it is a lasting creation but also because it appears in the form of music rather than language? And, in the final analysis, in the formation of pieces of art what is the importance of the inspiring life experience behind all that – that is, Janáček's love for the young, married woman, Kamila Stösslová? Does art elevate life or simply feed on it? Does life – relationships with other people, invigorating passions, stimulating experiences – merely exist to provide the artist with material and inspiration for the creative work? Does the awareness of the life experience that prompted the conception and formation of the work of art illuminate it and help in interpreting or, at least, better understanding it or does it become entirely forgettable once the piece is created? Such and similar questions inform the play-long debate between the seventy-year dead Janáček and Anezka Ungrova, the contemporary Ph.D. student writing her dissertation on his work. While these dilemmas define the structure and mode of Friel's *Performances*, he leaves readers and audiences with the questions reverberating with strong ambiguities, always avoiding final answers as he turns and twists them with his usual sensitivity, subtlety, and ambivalence.

Performance, a key term today not only in theatre but also in everyday life, from psychoanalysis to identity theories, refers to and emphasizes the performative aspect of all human behaviour. Just as the title of *Translations*, with its plural form, called attention to the manifold meaning of the translating act, including translating between languages, cultures, individuals, past and present and/or transgressing those boundaries, so the plural in *Performances* suggests the multiplicity of forms and levels of performance, such as verbal, musical, intellectual, psychological, and theatrical. Obviously, the play itself is being performed in the theatre. Having a composer for its protagonist, the performance of music becomes a natural part of the play. As a unique theatrical act, a real string quartet plays Janáček's music on the stage, performing a whole movement there (and another off-stage), while the members of the quartet also appear as characters, speaking and acting as the composer's younger contemporaries. But throughout most of the play we can witness Janáček's 'performance' in front of the enthusiastic young scholar, Anezka, as he tries to explain away the mystery of his great, stimulating passion for Kamila in the last several years of his life. His 'performance' takes a further twist by his being dead for decades at the time of the play and yet he is fully, corporeally present on the stage, so he performs simultaneously his live self and his remembering, judging, contemplating dead self.

Friel has already travelled the twilight country between life and death in *Faith Healer* where not only does it transpire after each monologue that the previous speaker is dead but also in the last section Frank Hardy, the faith healer, that great performer, now known to be dead by the audience, talks about his own death and also establishes the co-existence of his living and dead selves by acting out on stage what he recalls he did while alive, 'that night in that pub in Ballybeg', as he crumples up and throws away the newspaper clipping with the description of his successful faith healing (371). This co-existence is carried much further in *Performances* where Janáček's being dead becomes clear to the audience very soon after the beginning, often in some comic remarks, for instance as he grudgingly mentions the publication of one of his pieces twenty years after his burial (15), yet, at the same time, he complains of asthma or boasts how healthy and 'life-enhancing' lettuce is as he eats it with relish. The setting also reflects a collapsed time: it is his house complete with his piano where he lived in the late twenties, at the end of his life and it also functions as a museum to which the contemporary Ph.D. student travels by computer-run trains. The string quartet plays his last piece, *Intimate Letters*, in this collapsed time which is *both* the biographically true occasion of the Moravian String Quartet playing in the house of the real composer briefly before his death in 1928 and also during the visit of the contemporary student. The external action is minimal, it consists in Anezka's visit, her debate with Janáček, her departure followed by the concert of a part of the string quartet. Or, in other words, with Anezka the reality principle intrudes into the quiet afterlife of the composer, stirs up life-memories which then, after the visit, keep resonating further as he listens to the performance of his own music.

In Janáček's words, music is a more perfect medium than language for expressing feelings because 'people who huckster in words merely report on feeling' while 'we' – that is, musicians, composers, singers – '*speak* feeling' (31). Friel here echoes George Steiner's ideas about the superiority of music to language, as Richard Pine has already pointed out in the *Programme Notes* to the performance (n.p.). Poets, masters of language, always acknowledged, claims Steiner 'that music is the deeper, more numinous code, that language, when truly comprehended, aspires to the condition of music' (62).

Philosophical discourse on feeling often focuses on the question whether it is related to subjectivity or not, whether 'emotion exceeds subjectivity' or not? (Deleuze, qtd. in Terada 92) In its turn, philosophy of music strives to puzzle out *if* and *how* music relates to emotion, and if emotion needs to be personal or can be impersonal and only resemble 'pieces of expressive behaviour' (Terada 98) and evoke 'an emotional reaction' because of the perception 'of a corresponding emotional quality in it' (Ridley, qtd. in Terada 96). Even those among contemporary philosophers of music who affirm the emotional expressiveness of music, qualify it by asserting, as for instance, Jerrold Levinson does, that 'music impresses us ultimately *as if* it were actually someone's expression of such-and-such emotion' and 'we cannot get the impression of expressiveness without imagining some expresser' – so this expresser is actually the embodiment of the listener's ima-gination or desire. Then he adds that 'musical expressiveness should be seen to belong unequivocally to the music … and not to the listener or performer or composer' (qtd. in Terada 94). Even this qualified acceptance of emotion in music is criticized (for instance, by Peter Kivy) for maintaining the view that 'music can be *about* the emotions it displays' and thus for the 'compulsion to see music as another example of literary or painterly values' (qtd. in Terada 96-97).

This argument appears to lie in the centre of Janáček and Anezka's exchanges in *Performances*. Janáček's *Second String Quartet* is music text that, by Rei Terada's definition 'seems to fill space or even emanate from within, unfurling feeling inside us. Music is all too transparent, a language so fine that no content can penetrate it' (92). Similarly, in 'Schiller's view … music has the capacity to create meaning without reference to a world beyond itself' (Pine, *Diviner* 258). Music's non-referentiality proves similar to that of painting, which, in Jack B. Yeats's words: 'does not need translation … A creative work happens' (qtd. in Arnold, 134). Anezka, on the other hand, insists that the music is the expression of the composer's great passion for the young woman, Kamila to whom he wrote the 700 love letters. She endeavours to read content into the musical piece, to enhance the importance of the literary within the musical medium. Janáček, however, while referring to the poor style of his own letters with contempt, also dismisses the significance of the actual experience finding it merely the embodiment of his desire for the perfect music. After his death, therefore, the woman herself and his own passion for her seem to have lost all meaningfulness in the face of the existing work.

His meditation on the relationship between the individual, subjective feeling and its effect on other people, that is, on the particularity and universality of the work and the emotions carried by it, also pertains to one of the dilemmas in the philosophy of music: 'if particular emotions involve particular beliefs, how can music create such keen emotions without, usually, seeming to refer to anything non-musical, anything not utterly formal?' (Terada 92-93). Janáček's view seems to accord with Schopenhauer's, among others, who sees music as the art that grants rare access to generality; yet listeners react to this 'invisible yet vividly aroused spirit-world' by refacing it, clothing the abstract universal in 'flesh and bone' (qtd. in Terada 98). Similarly, Levinson contends that 'Musical expressiveness should be such that, when perceived or registered by a listener, evocation of feeling or affect, or the imagination of feeling, naturally, if not inevitably, ensues' (qtd. in Terada 94). But again, Friel is most indebted to George Steiner (and he duly acknowledges his indebtedness to his observations in the printed script). Steiner maintains in 'Silence and the Poet' that '[i]t is in music that the poet hopes to find the paradox resolved of an act of creation singular to the creator, bearing the shape of his own spirit, yet definitely renewed in each listener' (62). As opposed to the impoverishment of language, the 'exhaustion of verbal resources', the brutalization and devaluation of the word in modern civilization, '[m]usic alone can fulfil the two requirements of a truly rigorous communicative or semiological system: to be unique to itself (untranslatable) yet immediately comprehensible' (65). These statements recur almost *verbatim* when the long-dead Janáček in Friel's play recalls his feeling when alive:

> I remember when I finished it [*the Quartet*] I really thought that
> – yes! – this time I had solved the great paradox: had created
> something that was singular to me, uniquely mine, bearing the
> imprint of my spirit only; and at the same time was made new
> again in every listener who was attentive and assented to its
> strange individuality and to its arrogance and indeed to its
> hesitancies (31).

But then, since he is not a philosopher but a true artist, he
dismisses it all, with self-mocking laughter as 'Vanity' (31).

Janáček's own version, his memory of the creation process,
however, is continuously juxtaposed to the evidence of his own
words written in the famous letters reflecting on the creative
process itself as well as the inspiration and the emotions leading
to creation. The letters themselves describe his earlier creative
process using the Wordsworthian concept of 'feeling
recollected in perfect calm' – as Janáček puts it – but juxtaposed
to the case of the *Intimate Letters* with 'feelings experienced
directly and vividly' (30). But if Janáček himself dismisses the
truth or at least the significance of his own words in his letters
to his love, then how much truth and value do his present
words of dismissal carry as against the evidence of his past
passion? Among the *words* opposed to *words*, which should be
trusted? Why those of the all-too-lively dead man? The play
keeps 'hesitancies' vivid, balancing between the two truths, one
of which holds that experienced passion becomes a significant
part of the created work while the other claims that nothing
matters only the work, everything else is 'ancillary'. If the
beloved young woman was actually an ordinary woman clothed
into the dream-figure of the desired imaginative perfection that
at last took form in the music – as Janáček insists – then the
words of the letters become just another form of his
imagination incorporated. Then personal emotion is, indeed,
not necessary for expressing emotion in music. However,
without that personal experience the work would never have
been created – as evidenced in the imperfect and sentimental
but honest words of the letters – so the paradox remains
unresolved but vividly hovering above the perfection of the
musical form. Just as music transcends words, so the image of

the imaginary young woman transcends the real Kamila, thus the object of Janáček's adoration was not so much a Muse as the catalyst of all those feelings and desires that are needed for creation and that make it possible for listeners to relate to the work and allow it to evoke their own feelings whether knowing about the actual life story of the composer or not.

The music-language tension is polarized between Janáček, the musician and Anezka, the scholar dealing in words. Anezka knows all the facts, recognizes all the pieces of music when put to the test. But she hardly listens to the music, and refuses to stay to hear the string quartet play. Preoccupied with her thesis and trying to prove herself right, she does not pay attention even when Janáček confesses something that may have evoked a more lasting and deeper emotion in his life: the death of his son and the resulting lullabies that he wrote for his birthday each year for forty years after his death. The figure of the critic overwhelmed by his or her own theory has been the target of Friel's mockery in earlier plays (for instance, the sociologist Dr. Dodds in *The Freedom of the City*). Yet despite all his irony, Friel here allows Anezka to bring Janáček back to look at his own experience, which he keeps trying to avoid all through the play. Janáček's seemingly easy and self-ironic dismissal of all her claims, his interpretation of his own memories turns more and more clearly into a suspicious performance of indifference including his distancing his old self by his sometimes using the third person singular 'he' to refer to himself. His performance then is questioned by the whole play.

When, in the final scene, the music plays in Janáček's (and the audience's) presence and present, he, now alone with his art, without the necessity to act, to 'perform', turns back to his memories, reads into his own letters and becomes emotionally affected by them. The play ends on a richly ambiguous note with the last movement of his *Intimate Letters* playing, Janáček listening and slowly leafing through his letters, '*pausing now and then to read a line or two. Now he leans his head back and closes his eyes*' (39) according to the stage directions before the final blackout. In the Dublin Gate Theatre performance, he uttered a heavy sigh in the closing moment, further emphasizing the full circle he has travelled back to re-live part of his one-time passion. Janáček's unghostly ghost – in accordance with the Irish tradition in which ghosts usually appear in their full corporeality (Anthony Roche 41-44) – goes through an inverted Yeatsean 'dreaming back' of life's passionate moments. Although he seems to be – pretends to be? – rather free of his one-time great earthly passion, unlike Yeats's agonized ghosts, who hope to expiate guilt or achieve release from pain in their afterlife, yet by the end, ironically enough, with the help of the only half-understanding but enthusiastic critic, the created work itself leads Janáček back and makes him re-immerse in that passion. This might create that 'equilibrium' (38) in which the two readings of his letters – as real love letters and as metaphors for his musical creation – can exist, as he suggests a few minutes earlier. The difference between the two moments is that at that point he still insists – verbally – that 'the work is the thing', everything else must be 'ancillary to the work' (38) but by the end, when only the music – his music, his 'work' – can be heard, the re-evoked joy and pain of life seem to overwhelm him. Love triumphs even in death.

Yet all this time we remain in a liminal space, between life and death, life and art. 'Liminality [always] intensifies signification' (Joseph R. Roche 107). Only the Ph.D. student belongs undoubtedly to the matter-of-fact, real world. Does that suggest that all the other characters – the musicians and Janáček himself – are conjured up out of her imagination? Called up by her intensely thinking about them? We are dangerously close again to the Yeatsean territory, the 'call[ing] to the eye [– or here rather: ear –] of the mind' another world. If so, what does that say about the work itself? This representative of posterity still, seventy years after Janáček's death, finds his life and love affair more interesting than his music? Her definite resistance to engaging with the music itself, even when it is being played in her presence might question its value. But again, if the whole scene, with the composer, musicians, and the music itself is conjured up in her imagination or 'the ear of the mind', does it not attest to its power to fill the space and to live on, whether she wants to listen to it or not?

Even though the student-scholar – who prefers studying, interpreting, theorizing to enjoying the music – departs before the musicians play the last movement on stage, the music triumphantly goes on and the audience (of the play) hears it, without interpretation, sharing it only with the composer. In a very unusual and daring way Friel allows the music to play on for the last 10-12 minutes of the play, to carry its own effect and let the audience decide whether it speaks for itself or not, whether it 'speaks feeling' or not. But, with another twist, since this scene comes after all the passionate appeal of Anezka to Janáček to admit that the music is the expression of his love for the young woman, the audience cannot help listening to the music with that knowledge. Thus, the research, the excavation of the important inspiring experience in life influences and colours the way the audience hears the music, which then, totally differs from listening to the same piece at home. Janáček's minimal stage gesture, his deep sigh clutching the folder of his love letters in the last moment indicates that personal passion distilled into the non-subjective emotion conveyed by music, evokes again the very personal passion of love within the artist himself.

Patrick Burke suggested several years ago that 'those plays of Friel in which music is a prominent presence … in general tend to be at once celebratory of life and affirmative of women' (46). If this observation holds true for *Performances*, as it appears to, then it celebrates the importance of life experience and affirms the role of the inspiring woman in creating art, despite the protagonist's protest. Music itself contradicts its creator's words. Contradicts, that is, his spoken words (within the play) while actually confirming his written words (in the love letters). But, for the audience all that becomes manifest through the playwright's work, the beautiful, elegant play itself, which is, itself, created out of *words* on paper brought to life by the *performances* in the theatre. This resolves Friel's somewhat disingenuous juxtaposition of music and words at his own, the writer's expense. If music as it appears in the polished composition of *Intimate Letters* proves superior to language as manifested in the love letters and in Anezka's comments, then the comparison itself already puts words into a disadvantageous position since neither the love letters nor, obviously, the young woman's speeches are or were meant to be artefacts. Janáček himself can mock the sentimentality, cheap effects of his own letters as much as he likes, his derision targets only his momentary expression of his feelings and not the power of language itself, as if a writer were criticizing his own style in his diary kept while writing a masterpiece of literature. What then compares with the musical composition, is the play itself with its highly polished language, strict structure, and intricate balance of music and words, past and present, the living and the dead, life and art.

Music 'seems to fill space or even emanate from within, unfurling feeling inside us. Music is all too transparent, a language so fine that no content can penetrate it' (Terada 92). But can that have been Friel's purpose: the ultimate refinement of the arts through music into silence? Even the envied potential 'last book ever written, … the most wonderful book … the book without words' of *Wonderful Tennessee* contains all the mystery, 'the inexpressible', yet it is not without content although all written down 'without the benefit of words' (41). In the last scene the artist is silent, speechlessly listening to his own music, but now without narcissism or the self-congratulatory mood that he performed in the presence of Anezka. No more words are necessary; nor are words adequate to express the feelings of the one-time existing and now re-emerging passion and loss. As if dramatizing Steiner's idea that language 'borders on three other modes of statement – [divine] light, music, and silence – that gives proof of a transcendent presence in the fabric of the world' (58), the artist's *words* on paper, his *music* and *silence* together, create a sublime moment which borders on the divine or at least superhuman *light* that, in the last analysis, the playwright's play, words incorporating music, evoked. Friel, thus, by connecting language with what lies beyond Steiner's three frontiers of language, also increases the hesitancies and 'necessary uncertainties' concerning the nature and power of words and the created work.

The critic then, trying to talk about the play, falls into the same trap as the Ph.D. student, since in talking about the play and the performance one can use only words to describe the combined effect of the words, gestures, sounds, and music on the stage, can only speak *about* the emotions conveyed and evoked but one cannot *speak them*. That is the limitation of the critic compared to the artist.

Works Cited

Arnold, Bruce. *A Concise History of Irish Art*. London: Thames and Hudson, 1977.

Burke, Patrick. "'Both Heard and Imagined'": Music as Structuring Principle in the Works of Brian Friel'. *A Small Nation's Contribution to the World. Essays on Anglo-Irish Literature and Language*. Ed. Donald E. Morse, Csilla Bertha and István Pálffy. Debrecen: Kossuth University, 1993. 43-52.

Friel, Brian. *Faith Healer. Selected Plays*. London: Faber, 1986.

--- *Dancing at Lughnasa*. London: Faber, 1998.

--- 'Seven Notes for a Festival Programme'. *Brian Friel: Essays, Diaries, Interviews, 1964-1999*. Ed. Christopher Murray. London: Faber, 1999. 173-80.

--- *Performances*. Dublin: Gallery, 2003.

Grene, Nicholas. 'Friel and Transparency'. *Irish University Review* 29.1 (Spring/Summer 1999): 136-44.

Pine, Richard. *The Diviner: The Art of Brian Friel*. Dublin: University College Dublin Press, 1999.

--- Programme Notes to *Performances*, Dublin: The Gate Theatre, n.p.

--- 'The World and Work of Brian Friel'. Interview with Mária Kurdi. *The AnaChronisT*. Budapest: ELTE, 2003. 233-52.

Roche, Anthony. 'Ghosts in Irish Drama'. *More Real than Reality: The Fantastic in Irish Literature and the Arts*. Ed. Donald E. Morse and Csilla Bertha. New York: Greenwood, 1991. 41-66.

Roche, Joseph R. 'Power's Body. The Inscription of Morality as Style'. *Interpreting the Theatrical Past: Essays in the Historiography of Performance*. Ed. Thomas Postlewait and Bruce A. McConachie. Iowa City: University of Iowa, 1989. 99-118.

Steiner, George. *Language and Silence*. London: Faber, 1967.

Terada, Rei. *Feeling in Theory: Emotion after the 'Death of the Subject'*. Cambridge, MA, and London: Harvard UP, 2001.

AMBIGUITIES OF LANGUAGE

5| Interpreting Between Privacies:
Brian Friel and the Boundaries of
Language
Ger FitzGibbon

Private Lives, Public Issues, and the Aesthetics of Theme

Towards the end of one of Brian Friel's most public plays, *Translations* (1980), Hugh, the old, drunken schoolmaster, finally bows to what seems a historical inevitability and agrees to teach Maire, one of his pupils, English. He adds a question, however: 'But will that help you to interpret between privacies?' (*Plays* 446). The question is arresting for a number of reasons. On the grand thematic scale, it is an extension of and an ironic coda to some of the play's central concerns with issues of the relation of language to culture, and the role of language/culture in framing the intellectual, political, historical possibilities of a people. In terms of the specific scene, it is also a particularly pertinent question for Maire, whose short-lived affair with Yolland, the young English army officer, had managed to overcome the absence of a common language. They had, as it were, found other means for interpreting each other's privacies. The question of 'interpreting between privacies' is, however, a particularly odd one for Hugh to raise. He, of all the characters in the play, is imperviously self-obsessed: he spends most of the play drunk on a combination of Anna-na-mBréag's poteen, pedagogic power and heavily-carried learning. So, even though (courtesy of an anachronistic acquaintance with the writings of George Steiner) he shows some sense of the larger historical picture – of the rise and fall of civilizations, of the need to change or die – he is spectacularly unaware of the attitudes and needs of his own students, of the realities of the National School job he hopes to be offered, or of his own literally and metaphorically crippling effect on his son Manus. In short, even though it is imaginable that he might be interested in the theoretical issue, there is nothing at all in the play to suggest that Hugh as a character has ever had the slightest consciousness of the interiority of other people. And even putting aside questions of character, motive, and situation, dramaturgically the question comes too late in the play and at too melodramatic a juncture to allow room for its exploration in the context of this particular work. So why does Friel introduce such a question at this juncture?

At a symposium with Kevin Barry and John Andrews in January 1983, Friel declared that prior to *Translations* he had for some time been pondering the possibility of writing a play about the loss of the Irish language and what must have been the attendant psychic trauma for individuals (Barry 122). While he was actually in the process of writing *Translations*, he recorded in his journal a worry that the play was becoming too 'public' and that it was moving away from 'the dark and private places of individual souls' (*Essays* 77). If the latter was his focus of interest, his unease was well founded.

Few Friel plays so consistently refuse to focus on the private lives of the characters, or so deliberately disperse attention among their *dramatis personae*. Further, while at first glance the characters seem to be a relatively homogenous representation of the more-or-less stable society of an early nineteenth-century Irish village, Friel goes to some lengths to reveal quite rapidly the forces of individual desire, ambition or desperation that are ready to fragment this community from within. One character wants to learn English as she is considering going to America; her fiancé, meanwhile, plans to go to the Irish-speaking Aran islands; another spends his days reciting

Greek and enjoying geriatric fantasies about Greek goddesses; one loves her teacher but can barely speak her own name, let alone communicate her love; and the one apparently fulfilled and successful member of the village blindly facilitates the social and cultural destruction of his native place. Even among the British army, there is divergence of purpose, for Lancey is intent on subduing the native chaos of the Irish countryside to cartographic and military order while his Lieutenant, Yolland, falls in love with the chaos, the poteen, and the ahistoric *terra incognita* romance of it all.

This is more methodical and significant than simple character-individuation: it is Friel's way of disrupting the simple binary oppositions of the play (Irish/English; native/colonist) and problematizing the very concept of social community even among those who share the same language. However, far from being a dramaturgical problem, this centrifugal dispersal of interest enacts the major trope of the play's narrative, which is the scattering of the hedge school community under the two pressures of internally generated need and externally generated colonial force. In doing this, it effectively images the larger scattering of Irish communities and Irish culture throughout the nineteenth century. Equally, the corresponding emphasis on action and change rather than mood and revelation is what allows the play to address questions of language, culture, and identity on a large social and historical scale. While adding greatly to the play's richness on one level, however, this dispersal of interest means that on the level of individual character-psychology (and even of character-biography) the play is almost cursory. While we may get glimpses of grief and inner turmoil, any sustained exploration of the characters' inwardness, of the private trauma of losing one's language, is precluded. Hugh's final question, then, serves to identify an absence in *Translations*, a dimension of the play's subject matter that the play has effectively skirted – the shadow of an unfulfilled authorial intention. But, in doing so, it directs attention to the prevalence elsewhere in Friel's work of this task of 'interpreting between privacies' and identifies what may be

seen as a tension between two rival centres of dramatic interest
and two corresponding modes of dramaturgy.

Friel's apparent struggle in the writing of *Translations* may
serve to reinforce the commonplace of criticism that his work
divides into two broad categories – public and private – but this
crude critical division, useful in identifying matters of broad
emphasis, needs significant modification in relation to many
works. It may appear at first glance that plays such as
Philadelphia, Here I Come! (1964), *Dancing at Lughnasa* (1990),
Aristocrats (1979) or *The Loves of Cass Maguire* (1966) deal with
predominantly domestic or 'private' matters – more or less
ordinary emotional and existential crises of individuals and
families. Others – plays such as *Making History* (1988), *The
Freedom of the City* (1973), *Volunteers* (1975) – may seem to be
unequivocally 'public' in that their primary address goes beyond
the domestic towards public events and persons of communal
or historical import, the machinery of politics and history. Yet
even where a play seems decisively centred on one kind of
matter or the other, there is often an interpenetration of public
and private matters. As early as *Philadelphia, Here I Come!* Friel
was exploring the thematic and stylistic dimensions of this
collision. The matter of the play, with its village context,
domestic setting, and family situation is grounded in the entirely
familiar material of the rural Irish domestic drama. Yet Friel
uses the small episode of Gar O'Donnell's impending emigration to America to articulate the massive social and cultural
changes facing Ireland in the early sixties. In the play, the world
of Gar's home is one in which flour is bought by the sack and
made up by hand into two-pound pokes, tincans are bought
directly from the local tinkers, fish are bought from the local
boatmen and gutted and salted by hand; it is a world haunted by
the memory of Gar's mother arriving barefoot at the edge of
the village with her shoes under her arm. So even though the
play is set in the present as it premiered in 1964, its primary
dramatic world is constructed as a place of premodern, rural
simplicity and innocence, a place almost untouched by tech-
nology, a place where childhood still clings to a twenty-five-
year-old. By contrast, the 'other world' that Gar hopes to join is

a world of jet travel, fashion shows, international hotels, orchestral concerts; it is also an adult world of freedom and loneliness, isolation and autonomy. Thus, through the very private story of the individual's departure from home and family, Friel offers a view of a much larger cultural shift in the Ireland of his time – the abandonment of the isolationist De Valera vision of 'lives of frugal comfort', and the decision to join the bleak excitements of the modern, international world.

This oscillation of focus has its parallel in Friel's use of dramatic form, for while the familiar subject matter might have a stylistic corollary in traditional rural realism, Friel defamiliarizes his material by a number of consciously contemporary theatrical devices: fluid use of stage space, disruption of chronological sequence with segments of flashback and fantasy and, most tellingly, the splitting of the central role of Gar O'Donnell between two actors, one of whom represents Gar Public – the gauche, churlish, tongue-tied country boy as seen by other characters – while the other represents his Gar Private, his inner, witty, sardonic, articulate, alter ego. This also allows the play to speak with two voices: one the voice of the traditional Irish kitchen drama, the other the voice of sixties cinema, of television, of satire. The dramaturgy thus stylistically enacts the cultural and historical schism which is the core of the play's public concern as well as the personal disjunction which is the central character's condition.

But the interpenetration of public and private is not the only issue here. The other is the role of language in answering the emotional and psychic needs of the individual. Gar's departure is made more painful by his intensifying isolation as the play progresses. Yet, even as he steels himself for departure, he longs for the affirmation of sharing with his father his one golden memory of warmth and happiness between them. When he eventually does find courage to utter to his father the memory he has been treasuring in private, the result is bathos. The father not only fails to remember, but he also contradicts the very details of the incident as narrated by Gar. No matter how apparently authoritative the Private voice may be, it cannot authenticate itself as a truthful witness. This suggests that language is hopelessly crude as a means of communication with others and that, in any event, the memories to which it attempts to give utterance are themselves fictive and unreliable. On the level of the characters, however, such recognitions merely problematize the whole business of emotional connection, they do not obviate the individual's need. Robert Welch implies that the force of the theatrical expression refutes the argument advanced by the play and that while characters of the play cannot manage the act of communication required, 'Friel's theatre *does* translate it' (138). Yet this somehow degrades the core issue of Friel's play to a mere rhetorical ploy, and Friel's almost obsessive probing of this conundrum suggests that for the writer this represents a genuine crux, a logical and aesthetic paradox where the more effectively he expresses his argument, the more he refutes its validity.

The implications are almost Beckettian. Time and again Friel's characters glimpse the complete illogicality of their position, caught between a momentary intellectual recognition of their own existential isolation and the emotional need which repeatedly demands that insight, meaning, communication and even perhaps some kind of communion with others and with ourselves is possible. *Aristocrats*, centred on an upper-middle class Catholic family, seems to show how a family mythology crumples at the touch of 'fact and reason'. Yet, as one of the family says of the visiting historian, '[t]here are certain facts, certain truths, ... that are beyond Tom's kind of scrutiny' (*Plays* 309-10). *The Freedom of the City*, a fiction about the shooting dead of three civil rights marchers, is based on actualities in substance and method. The material echoes Bloody Sunday in Derry; the structure is based on the form of a television drama-documentary; parts of the text draw upon the Widgery Tribunal. And yet thematically it addresses a very large-scale theme – the problem of a community who cannot agree upon a shared history. The play radiates journalistic immediacy and a specific and literal sense of 'public address' quite distinct from the sense employed by Richard Pine (69-186), yet its most telling moment is an utterly private revelation by one of the three of the civil rights marchers killed. In this moment – when

Lily Doherty confesses that she goes on civil rights marches because one of her children has Down's Syndrome – the painful disconnection between political expression and private pain is made manifest. *Making History* explores the gap between the fiction of official published history and the (fictional but notionally 'true') story of the individuals' lives. The stylistic virtuosity Friel displays in these plays does not, however, conceal what is finally an aesthetic issue: ultimately, how can the writer translate into theatre that which, by definition is private, inaccessible, untranslatable?

Art and Transformation

In *Philadelphia, Here I Come!* the Private Gar, watching the local priest playing draughts with his father, suddenly utters an uncharacteristically serious (if silent) plea to the cleric:

> you're warm and kind and soft and sympathetic … you could translate all this loneliness, this groping, this dreadful bloody buffoonery into Christian terms that will make life bearable for us all. And yet you don't say a word. Why Canon? Why, arid Canon? Isn't this your job? – to translate? Why don't you speak then? (*Plays* 88)

It is a plea on the part of the character, but also, perhaps, a kind of mission statement on the part of the dramatist. However dark his vision may be, however strong the repeated recognition of the ultimate privacy of individual experience, much of Friel's drama is, I believe, animated by such a sacerdotal impulse – a sense that, despite the flawed means, there is an artistic imperative to find images, emblems, gestures, narratives, which can transcend existential isolation and which can allow individual human needs and experiences to find communal articulation, recognition and release.

It was not until *Faith Healer* (1979) that Friel took a much closer, colder look at this territory. In its very form, by renouncing the most basic dramatic element of dialogue, the four monologues of *Faith Healer* – an opening and closing one by Hardy, and one each by Grace, his mistress, and Teddy, his manager – articulate the inescapability of existential isolation. We are left with four bleak narratives of a life spent traipsing

from one small town to another in an old van, ministering to
and deceiving the desperate, the hopeless, the maimed and the
wounded. We hear of the still-birth of Frank and Grace's child,
of minor betrayals, disappointments, and attritions. But Frank
Hardy's weird and intermittent gift of healing is the core of the
play, a mystery to the man who carries it, and as odd in its
operation and ambiguous in effect as creativity itself: 'A craft
without an apprenticeship, a ministry without responsibility, a
vocation without a ministry ... And occasionally it worked – oh
yes, occasionally it *did* work' (*Plays* 333).

As many of the commentators on the play have observed,
Frank Hardy is obviously a version of the dramatist as
confidence trickster, but as a trickster who occasionally and
unpredictably creates the conditions within which a miracle can
happen:

> Was it all chance? – or skill? – or illusion? – or delusion? –
> Precisely what power did I possess? ... Was I its servant? Did it
> reside in my ability to invest someone with faith in me or did I
> evoke from him a faith in himself? Could my healing be
> effected without faith? (*Plays* 333-34)

And if Frank Hardy is, to adapt Alan Bennett's phrase, 'the
writer in disguise' (7), then the interrogation to which Friel
subjects himself and the conclusions he apparently reaches are
grim in the extreme. Hardy spends a tortured, egocentric existence, ministering to a largely thankless but desperate public,
offering them disappointment after disappointment, enlivened
only by the added torture of occasional success. Far from being,
as Pine would have it, a reconciliation of the artist 'to his
privacy' (144), this seems like a spiralling death-dive into despair
– a vision of the artist as victim, scapegoat and charlatan.

Almost like a defiance of this grim vision, within a year of
the first production of *Faith Healer* came the founding of Field
Day Theatre Company, and the opening of Friel's own
Translations (1980). That play's priest-healer is Manus, who
through the force of his faith in the teaching process makes the
dumb Sarah speak. But Manus is not strong enough to heal a
whole community, and the magus of the play, Hugh, the master

of languages, is a drunken bore full of the wisdom and cynicism of the ages and egocentrically blind to the people around him. His sacred art (reflected in its purer form in Manus, his apprentice, as the capacity to liberate through speech and through literature, to give people a kind of mastery of their universe) has become curdled and sour, an instrument of petty authority, a living, and a bitter retreat. But even while the struggle for an adequate syntax was reaching its high tragic moment in *Translations* and its comic apogee in that play's parodic shadow, *The Communication Cord* (1982), Friel was already exploring alternative and perhaps more authentic modes of expression and communication.

In *Aristocrats,* Friel's most Chekovian play, music is the crucial new element that supplements and partly replaces language. As both Harry White and Patrick Burke have observed, as far back as *Philadelphia, Here I Come!* Friel had used the music of Gar's record player (Ceili band, Mendelsshon's *Violin Concerto*, etc.) to shift and to reflect the central character's moods (White 8, Burke 47). But, here as elsewhere, the music is not merely a commentary upon character; it operates directly to manipulate and focus the audience's emotional responses and, indeed, in some plays, forms a complete textual layer. Set in the disintegrating wreck of a once-proud Big House, Ballybeg Hall, *Aristocrats* is drenched with the sound of Chopin. For many scenes the off-stage piano playing of Claire, the youngest of the O'Donnell family, forms a virtual musical score, counter-pointing or reinforcing the ongoing action. At its simplest, Claire's music signals the delicate gifts, sensitivities, and lost opportunities of this pivotal character, but it also operates to evoke the *haut-bourgeois* family history and, by historical reference, to create a sense of the more distant heritage of houses and families such as this – the emotional and artistic textures of nineteenth-century Europe with all its accomplishments and civilities, its cultural *richesse*. The cultural connotations of Chopin's music are startlingly at odds with the political turbulence out of which it was born and equally the harmony and comfort the music evokes for a modern audience is in sharp theatrical contrast to the leaking shell of Ballybeg Hall out of which it emerges. As Patrick Burke has noted, the music acts as a reminder of the intransigence of the Father in suppressing artistic self-expression among his family (49), although in performance this point might hinge upon the actual quality of Claire's piano-playing as registered by the theatre audience. On a larger scale however, the music acts as a reminder of the full depth of the temporal and cultural dislocation of the O'Donnell family, the discontinuities between their social status and their economic condition, their inherited expectations and their lives. White's claim that Friel uses music as a 'subversive metalanguage' (7) may go so far that it misses the point: in the multiple-signing system that is theatre performance, the music forms a crucial additional layer. And in the case of *Aristocrats* it contributes its own commentary on one of the play's major themes – that, to paraphrase Shakespeare, time moves in diverse paces with diverse persons. The gap between Claire's rendering of Chopin and Eamonn's crooner impression as he drunkenly sings 'So Deep is the Night' perfectly images the family's social and cultural slide and, behind it, the decline of a whole class. '*Semper permanemus*' may, according to Eamonn, be the family motto, but the play and its music tell us that this family and all it represents is disintegrating, dying. Not until *Wonderful Tennessee* (1993) does Friel again so saturate a play with music, using it to generate a 'rival discourse of song' (White 13). But by then he had begun to extend his dramaturgy in other directions.

The crucial music of *Dancing at Lughnasa* is quite different in its quality, connotations and, most importantly, in its effects. There Friel uses the device of a whimsically faulty radio that turns on and off at will to fill the stage with random and magical bursts of music, a bit like Shakespeare's Ariel, who fills Prospero's island with 'sounds and sweet airs that give delight and hurt not' (*The Tempest* 3.2.134). It is such a burst of music – the lively Irish tune called 'The Mason's Apron' – which triggers the outburst of dancing that becomes the central transforming image of *Dancing at Lughnasa*. The stage directions regarding the quality of the music are significant, for Friel describes it as '*very fast*', '*a raucous sound*', '*this too loud music, this pounding beat'* (21-22). The excess and the loss of control in the music itself triggers the response of the women, who, one by one, enter into the wild dance. The terms Friel uses all point towards the dance as frenzy, as Dionysian release:

> arms, legs, hair, long bootlaces flying. ... a white-faced, frantic dervish. ... the movements seem caricatured. ... shouting – calling – singing, this parodic reel ... there is a sense of order being consciously subverted, of the women consciously and crudely caricaturing themselves, indeed of near-hysteria being induced (21-22).

This is a new direction in Friel – celebration of loss of control, of the release of energies that are pre-intellectual and atavistic and which, through art and frenzy, find a truer expression of the moment. The same image flashes through *Molly Sweeney* a few years later when we hear of the blind heroine on the eve of her operation, dancing:

> I found myself on my feet in the middle of the sitting-room and calling, 'A hornpipe, Tom! A mad, fast hornpipe!' And ... in a rage of anger and defiance I danced a wild and furious dance round and round that room; then out to the hall; then round the kitchen; ... Mad and wild and frenzied. ... No timidity, no hesitation, no falterings (31).

Momentarily the disciplined fury of the dance allows her a more total, intuitive and self-expressive life – qualities that will be entirely lost when Molly's sight is surgically restored.

Ritual, Myth, and Altered States

But it is not just that explosion into dance that marks the aesthetic shift in *Dancing at Lughnasa*; it is also utilization of myth as a frame of reference, a structure and a thematic focus. As Alan Peacock has pointed out, the world of *Translations* overtly commutes between a small Donegal village and the world of Classical myth ('Translating the Past' 121-33). Jimmy Jack spends his time in a kind of meta-erotic fever over Pallas Athene; Hugh, faced with the destruction of everything around him, recites like a mantra the story of the fall of Libya. But in *Dancing at Lughnasa* and *Wonderful Tennessee*, classical and Celtic myths form a constant point of reference within the dialogue and a covert underpinning for action and character. Under the apparently naïve, autobiographical narrative of *Lughnasa,* for example, Friel sets up a most elaborate system of structurally related folk-ritual, myths and figures. Some of this is obvious on the surface of the play – in the references to Lughnasa and the Lughnasa fires for instance.

> **Kate:** Festival of Lughnasa! what sort of –
> **Rose:** First they light a bonfire beside a spring well. Then they dance around it. Then they drive their cattle through the flames to banish the devil out of them (16).

This is overtly cross-related with Father Jack's (sentimentalized) accounts of Ugandan harvest ceremonies, where formal religious ceremonial flows unselfconsciously into community celebration, the lighting of fires, singing, drinking and dancing. Such conscious patterning signals Friel's concern with the need to merge religious rite with personal release, and suggests that the overt cultural differences (between Uganda and Donegal) disguise deeper correspondences of human need. But the strongest recurrent reference points for such mergings of self and society, psychic release and religious fervour, are the ceremonies associated with the god Dionysus. Many plays mention in one guise or another the story of the maenads, followers of Dionysus, who in a holy orgy, frenziedly kill a young man (Pentheus) and awake purified and innocent. As far back as *The Gentle Island* (1971) a young man is savagely killed for having offended the local gods, although there the killing is punitive rather than celebratory. In *Faith Healer,* a wild night in an Irish pub – a 'Dionysian night' as Frank calls it – precedes the killing of Frank Hardy himself. *Dancing at Lughnasa,* however, is the first play in which such a frenzy is imaged on stage and the first in which, while overtly constructing a semi-autobiographical narrative of recollected childhood, Friel develops a densely-textured system of mythic reference.

It may be useful to isolate some of the mythic and folkloric elements in *Dancing at Lughnasa* which find echoes in Classical or Celtic sources. The stage-directions in the famous 'dancing' scene clearly emphasize loss of control, abandon, transgression, even temporary craziness. And the relation to more formal kinds of religious ritual is suggested by the white mask of flour smeared on Maggie's face and by Christina's donning of Father Jack's surplice to do her dance. That Kate's dance is described as '*out of character*' but adumbrating '*some deep and true emotion*' (22) clearly suggests that, for Friel, this is a moment of truth, a moment of restored wholeness, rather than an aberration. The more the play is explored, the more we find echoes of gods, goddesses, fertility rites, and religious rituals compiled, apparently from a variety of sources, and thematically cross-related. From the evidence of Máire MacNeill's study of Lughnasa lore and customs, it is clear that Friel's text gathers from different areas elements of well-documented tradition: hilltop fires; large all-night gatherings of people; dancing, courting, and matchmaking; games; bilberry-picking; drinking, and picnicking. Nowhere is there evidence in Ireland of the driving of cattle through fires or of people ritually leaping over the fires – key features of the customs described in the play. It is possible that Friel may have taken these elements from James Frazer's accounts of European midsummer fires: 'In the valley of the Orne the custom was to kindle the bonfire just at the moment when the sun was about to dip below the horizon; and the peasants drove their cattle through the fires to protect them against witchcraft' … (823). Frazer also lists instances of Bealtaine fires and of people running through fires as part of the ritual (808-14), an aspect of the ritual that is echoed in the fate of the Sweeney boy who gets burned in the Lughnasa fire. Based on MacNeill's evidence, it appears the vast majority of Lughnasa festival practices had died out or been suppressed well over a hundred years ago. Interestingly, one of the few exceptions comes from Friel's own region and survived down to the early 1930s; it took the form of a gathering, berry-picking, and celebration by a small lake near a hilltop (MacNeill 146-47).

The women in the play may be denied the ritual of the Lughnasa fires or the harvest dance, but their own, private Lughnasa rite has the appropriate effect: it conjures up the

annual return of the Celtic god, Lugh, in the unlikely figure of
Gerry Evans, the improbable, Welsh, dancing salesman. Lugh,
also known as the Celtic Mercury, is described by Proinsias
MacCana in the following terms: 'the inventor of all the arts ...
a guide ... influential for money-making and commerce ...
youthful, beardless, equipped with caduceus, petasus and purse.
... his arts include that of war' (27-28). According to Dáithí Ó
hÓgáin, traditionally the god Lugh also has other features such
as agility, magic, the ability to enchant (272-77). Gerry Evans,
like Lugh, has a mastery of many arts, including song, dance,
and mastery of craft; the gramophones he sells are classical,
named after Minerva, patroness of arts and crafts; and his identifying marks are a straw hat and a walking cane (*Lughnasa* 25),
corresponding to Mercury's distinctive hat and staff. He is
linked with male fertility through his fathering of Michael, his
effect on the women of the play and semiotically through the
wearing of Father Jack's old ceremonial hat, complete with high
cock-comb of feathers. The strange, one-horned cow he claims
to have met seems to echo the magically fruitful cow of Irish
lore, the *Glas Goibhneann*, sometimes linked with Lugh (Ó
hÓgáin 240). The correspondences even extend to the business
of having two wives in different locations (Ó hÓgáin 274),
although in Gerry Evans's case the doubling of wives is more
complex, for he is linked with both Agnes and Chris Mundy,
and we later discover that he has a household and children in
Wales as well as in Ballybeg (*Lughnasa* 61). And Gerry Evans is
finally associated with warriorship, as he enlists in the international brigade to fight in the Spanish Civil War.

   The Mundy sisters themselves are not without mythological
antecedents. As MacCana points out, two of the principal sites
in the worship of Lugh 'were the burial places of female deities
who are clearly associated with the earth and its fertility' (28).
And there are other Celtic references also, some of them given
an ironic twist. The Mundy home has strange correspondences
to *Tír inna mBan*, for example, – the Land of Women – 'a land
of primeval innocence where the pleasures of love are untainted
by guilt', a land which is 'filled with enchanting music ... from

instruments which sound without being played', and which has 'abundance of exquisite food and drink' (MacCana 124).

In combing through Friel's text to find echoes of myth or documented folk custom (such as Rose and Agnes's berry picking, or Rose's picnic with Danny), it is easy to miss the bigger issues. Central to Friel's play is a yearning for the customs which allow for an unselfconscious celebration of dance, sensuality and passion – what Anna McMullan refers to as a desire for 'a fusion of the rational with the affective and the compassionate' (100). Equally, to see Friel's use of references to Celtic deities as entirely ironic or even parodic is to miss the crucial ambivalences of viewpoint the play offers. It is through those echoes, through the pervasiveness of essentially literary intertextual references, that Friel opens up and sustains the duality of the play's imaginative world where we are simultaneously aware of the adult knowingness of the narrator and the wide-eyed fantasy of the child. On another level this dualism allows the author/narrator's reminiscences of a 'real' childhood in a narrow-minded and repressive 1930s Donegal to interpenetrate with an alternative and ahistoric world of myth and folk ritual that touches and illuminates the mundane and that offers glimpses of a less rational, more violent but also fuller and more human existence.

Wonderful Tennessee continues the exploration of myth, but takes it in a different direction. As the action takes place on a pier on the Donegal coast where a group of middle-aged friends await the arrival of a boat to take them to a magical island, *Oileán Draíochta*, the setting and situation clearly mark this as a play about liminality. They never get to the island because their boatman never arrives, but the night spent on the pier seems to offer a substitute for whatever they had hoped to encounter on the island, as the characters get drunk, sing, tell stories, make suicidal gestures and have epiphanies. As the play is quite cursory in its handling of realist trappings like motivation, plausibility and plot, the focus shifts to the inner lives and relationships of the characters and the effect upon them of this strange combination of pilgrimage, drinking session and encounter group. And gradually it becomes clear that the play is an extended dramatic essay on the nature of myth, reason, religion and ritual, played out on a threshold between land and water, culture and nature, order and chaos.

Throughout the play, Friel cross references his characters' particular experiences with familiar and half-familiar other-worldly myths and encounters. As Csilla Bertha has so cogently argued ('Otherness' 133-34 and *passim*), the play as a whole seems to be structured around a version of the Eleusynian Mysteries – an ancient initiation rite to Demeter and Dionysus, involving an all-night vigil, wine, food, dance, song, and so forth. However, many other elements of Celtic and Greek myth are included. The *Oileán Draíochta* that changes shape, character, and location depending on the viewer is clearly a version of the mysterious island of Hi-Brasil, which was supposed to appear and disappear off the west coast of Ireland. Terry the bookie tells of fourteen young men and women returning from a Eucharistic Congress, going out to a mysterious island and having an orgy during which they ritually kill one of their number – clearly a transformation of the story of Pentheus and the Maenads. There is a pervasive use of religious song, ranging in style from the Irish Catholic hymn 'O Mother I could weep for mirth' to the more celebratory American Baptist mode of 'Heavenly Sunshine' and 'Oh Them Golden Slippers'. One character has a vision of a dolphin dancing on the sea 'like a faun, a satyr; with its manic, leering face' (*Tennessee* 70) – a description that disturbingly echoes the descriptions we get of Carlin, the boatman who does not arrive. As Bertha notes, Carlin himself has resonances of the classical underworld boat-man, Chaaron ('Otherness' 131), but his name also links him with a symbolic figure of derision from Bealtaine harvest rites, the carline or carlin (Frazer 810). At the end of the play the Pentheus story is symbolically repeated when the characters construct their own ritual. They make a little altar to the deity of the island, adorn it with sacrificed possessions, and symbolically dismember the leader of the group by tearing his shirtsleeves off. Bertha's reading of the play as intimately related to an Irish desire for transcendence ('Otherness' *passim*) or as a quest for 'redemption' on the part of the characters ('Six Characters' 135)

is persuasive in many respects, though perhaps a little optimistic, as if the substructural form of the play, based on
romantic comedy, were a guarantee of a positive outcome. But
many readings are possible. Taken in one way, the play can, for
example, be read on a secular, psychotherapeutic level: jaded
humanity journeys to the outer edge of its own domain (the
pier) and, through its encounter with a densely encoded version
of nature, reintegrates the lost, suppressed or irrational aspects
of itself. In this respect, it is almost a Friel transposition of *As
You Like It* with Terry as the deposed Duke Senior, leading his
court on their quest. But the play's final ritual, which mingles
ancient and modern, Celtic and Greek, Pagan and Christian
around a lifebuoy stand whose shape echoes a Celtic cross
seems to argue that the author is suggesting that such impulses
to sacrifice and worship are both authentic and universal. For
underlying this play is a longing for a reunification of religion,
myth, art and social ritual to accommodate and express the
complexities of the whole person, to celebrate Dionysian excess
as well as Apollonian control. There is even a sense that the
theatre might become the site of such a reunification.

Beyond Language

As with Samuel Beckett, the engine at the centre of Friel's work
is the refusal of Friel the artist to listen to the arguments of
Friel the intellectual sceptic. From *Philadelphia, Here I Come!*
onwards Friel is fascinated by two equally powerful and contrary positions. On the one hand is the conviction of the
ultimately unbreakable hermetic seal on individual existence, the
privacy of experience and the inadequacy of language as an
instrument in which to construct ourselves or each other. On
the other is the equally strong conviction that most human
beings need to deny or escape this existential isolation – to
establish through love, friendship, worship or art, a way out of
that hermetic privacy, a sense of real contact with another.
Thematizing that contradiction in his plays, however, only
serves to intensify its implications in terms of his dramatic
aesthetic. Friel is one of the clearest, most articulate,
playwrights of our time. If, as he insistently suggests, language is

implicitly untrustworthy because words represent the self-serving rationalizations of a tortured self-consciousness, he cannot, as an artist, avoid the consequence: that the nature of the words he writes and the distorting mediations inherent in theatre performance – actors, director, theatre conditions, audience – mean that real communication is an illusion and that the theatrical enterprise itself is futile. *Faith Healer* certainly offers this possibility for consideration. But Friel also offers himself, and us, an escape through the possibility that music, dance, myth and ritual can circumvent or subvert that crippling, questioning consciousness and offer alternative modes of self-liberation. The move is best captured in the final lines of *Dancing at Lughnasa*, delivered by a narrator who fully articulates his own unreliabilty:

> But there is one memory of that Lughnasa time that visits me most often; ... memory ... that owes nothing to fact. ... When I remember it, I think of it as dancing. Dancing with eyes half-closed because to open them would be to break the spell. Dancing as if language had surrendered to movement – as if this ritual, this wordless ceremony, was now the way to speak, to whisper private and sacred things, to be in touch with some otherness. ... Dancing as if language no longer existed because words were no longer necessary (71).

Despite that apparent renunciation, Friel's later work continues to assert that it is the business of the dramatist to generate images, characters, and moments that will allow an audience to share an experience with him and each other and that, at its occasional best, that process has the potential to be healing, mysterious, and sacerdotal. The use of pan-European myth, gesture, ritual, and fable is part of that attempt to deepen the nature of his theatrical exploration, to escape the super-ficialities of the detailed surface, and bring his characters to deeper, more visceral modes of communication, or even com-munion, with themselves and each other. Through that process he is attempting to return the theatre to its cathartic and transformative roots.

Works Cited

Barry, Kevin. '*Translations* and *A Paper Landscape*: Between Fiction and History'. *The Crane Bag* 7.2 (1983): 118-24.

Bennett, Alan. *The Writer in Disguise*. London: Faber, 1985.

Bertha, Csilla. '"Island of Otherness": Images of Irishness in Brian Friel's *Wonderful Tennessee*'. *Hungarian Journal of English and American Studies* 2.2 (1996): 129-42.

--- 'Six Characters in Search of a Faith: The Mythic and Mundane in *Wonderful Tennessee*'. *Irish University Review* 29.1 (1999): 119-35.

Burke, Patrick. '"Both Heard and Imagined": Music as Structuring Principle in the Plays of Brian Friel'. *A Small Nation's Contribution to the World*. Ed. Donald E. Morse, Csilla Bertha, and István Pálffy. Gerrards Cross: Smythe, 1993. 43-52.

Frazer, James G. *The Golden Bough: A Study in Magic and Religion*. Abr. ed. London: Macmillan, 1963.

Friel, Brian. *Brian Friel Essays, Diaries, Interviews: 1964-1999*. Ed. Christopher Murray. London: Faber, 1999.

--- *Dancing at Lughnasa*. London: Faber, 1990.

--- *Molly Sweeney*. Oldcastle: Gallery, 1994.

--- *Plays 1*. London: Faber, 1998.

--- *Wonderful Tennessee*. Oldcastle: Gallery, 1993.

MacCana, Proinsias. *Celtic Mythology*. London: Hamlyn, 1970.

McMullan, Anna. '"In Touch with Some Otherness": Gender, Authority and the Body in *Dancing at Lughnasa*'. *Irish University Review* 29.1 (1999): 90-100.

MacNeill, Máire. *The Festival of Lughnasa: A Study of the Survival of the Celtic Festival of the Beginning of the Harvest*. 2 vols. Dublin: Comhairle Bhéaloideas Éireann, 1962.

Ó hÓgáin, Dáithí. *Myth, Legend and Romance: An Encyclopaedia of the Irish Folk Tradition*. London: Prentice, 1991.

Peacock, Alan. 'Translating the Past: Friel, Greece and Rome'. *The Achievement of Brian Friel*. Ed. Alan Peacock. Gerrards Cross: Smythe, 1993. 113-33.

Pine, Richard. *Brian Friel and Ireland's Drama*. London: Routledge, 1990.

Welch, Robert. '"Isn't This Your Job? – to Translate?": Brian Friel's Language Plays'. In Peacock 134-48.

White, Harry. 'Brian Friel and the Condition of Music'. *Irish University Review* 29.1 (1999): 6-15.

6 | Palimpsest: Two Languages as One in *Translations*

Christopher Murray

In the year 1980 Brian Friel got together with the actor Stephen Rea, and, between them, they set up a new theatre company, which they decided to call Field Day. Thereby hangs an oft-told tale. In this paper I shall strictly limit the information about Field Day to Friel's own involvement in it and, in particular, to the play he wrote for its first production, *Translations* (1980). The original board of directors for Field Day (established in September 1981) numbered six in number, all from Northern Ireland, three Protestants and three Catholics. All were men, a matter that was to create problems when the *Field Day Anthology* was published later on. Apart from Friel and Rea, the original directors were: Seamus Heaney, Tom Paulin, Seamus Deane, and David Hammond.

It is important to keep in mind that Friel's play came first, with its successful production in September 1980, and after that the establishment of the Field Day board, and only after that the definitions and the pamphlets. As artist, Friel was concerned with getting a play written, rehearsed, and staged. He was not at this time or at any time interested in the larger questions, ideological and political, raised by Seamus Deane as central to the Field Day project. To say that Friel was not interested is to exaggerate: he must have approved what was happening in the 1980s, when no less than fifteen pamphlets were published. But it should be understood that there was not one single pamphlet on theatre or drama in all the fifteen, nothing on the theory of drama, or performance, or the relationships between theatre and politics, nothing to suggest that either Friel or Rea, the two theatre people on the board until Tom Kilroy joined in 1986, was central to the intellectual drive mounted by Field Day in the 1980s culminating in the *Anthology* in 1991.

Accordingly, there were two Field Days and not just one. There was the Field Day established by Friel and Rea to write, perform, and tour plays throughout Ireland north and south. And there was the Field Day which was largely Seamus Deane's invention, a cultural experiment dedicated to intervening in the Northern situation and changing it. To be sure, a separate company was set up to publish the anthology. Yet, although the board members remained the same, the fact that a separation of purposes was then acknowledged is crucial to the understanding of the whole enterprise of the Field Day Theatre Company. Because this dual set of purposes was never properly addressed and its implications dealt with, Friel as artist found himself more and more on the margins of what Field Day was doing after 1982. He wrote no plays between 1982 and 1988 when Field Day produced his *Making History*, the closest Friel ever came to writing a pamphlet. Two years later he gave *Dancing at Lughnasa* to the Abbey Theatre in a gesture that has to be seen as a judgement on Field Day. By 1990 he regarded Field Day as an 'institution' injurious to his talent (Deane 21). He wrote nothing further for Field Day from this point, and resigned from the board in 1994. Field Day now continues mainly as a publishing concern (in association with Cork University Press). The Field Day Theatre Company, while it has flickered briefly into life with Frank McGuinness's version of Chekhov's *Uncle Vanya* in 1995 and again with a co-production of Stewart Parker's *Northern Star* in 1998, virtually collapsed once Friel resigned.

Brian Friel, then, set up the Field Day Theatre Company only to see it overtaken by intellectuals who wanted to use it to promote a debate in which Friel as artist had no obvious part to play. Therefore, it is best to regard *Translations* as a play which, like W.B. Yeats's *Cathleen ni Houlihan* in 1902, surprised its author by the immediate and long-lasting effects it had on cultural nationalism. The proof of this lies in Friel's *The Communication Cord* (1982), a farce written to counteract what he saw as the excessive reverence accorded to *Translations*. More-over, we have to remember that the play staged immediately after *Translations* was Friel's version of Chekhov's *Three Sisters,* written before *Translations*. In other words, if we take those three plays together, what they tell us is that Friel was occupied with questions of language and translation at this time, and shied away from the possibility of propaganda. Years earlier, he stated his opposition to propagandist art: 'I do not believe that art is a servant of any movement' ('Plays Peasant' 306). What we must see in *Translations*, in fact, is a play that confronts history in such a way as to maximize the artist's vision of Ireland today.

It is clear from the published extracts from the diary he kept at the time of writing *Translations* that Friel was determined to keep language as his main theme, in spite of the political implications of the action. On 29 May 1979 he tried to clear the way by declaring what he did *not* want to write about:

> I don't want to write a play about Irish peasants being suppressed by English sappers [soldiers working on the survey]. I don't want to write a threnody [lament] on the death of the Irish language. I don't want to write a play about land-surveying. Indeed I don't want to write a play about naming places. And yet portions of all these are relevant. Each is part of the atmosphere in which the real play lurks ('Extracts' 58).

That atmosphere is one of unease, of imminent crisis. As the play opens we hear of two major changes about to happen in this peasant society and one positive threat, namely of potato famine. The 'sweet smell', which forebodes the failure of the main crop on which depends the survival of this community, is given much concerned comment at first and then recedes from the play until the end, when it reappears in a transformed way

to reinforce the sense of crisis following the disappearance of
Yolland:

> **Bridget:** The sweet smell! Smell it! It's the sweet smell! Jesus,
> it's the potato blight!
> **Doalty:** It's the army tents burning, Bridget.
> **Bridget:** Is it? Are you sure? Is that what it is? God, I thought
> we were destroyed altogether (*Selected Plays* 441).

For these people, nothing would be more devastating than
the failure of the potatoes. This dependency is the key to the
atmosphere Friel wants to evoke. The cultural and political
crises that develop from the opening scene, from the two areas
of change about to encroach, namely the initiation of a national
system of education in which English will replace Irish as the
sole medium of instruction, and the mapping of the countryside
with translations of place names, are both framed in this
material consideration, the fear of a famine.

This is a point which critics tend to miss. The framework of
the famine lends an acute sense of instability to this peasant
people. It is a metaphor to place beside the master metaphor in
the play of translation itself. It helps to create the atmosphere
Friel wants. So, too, does the birth and almost immediate death
of the baby we hear about in the first scene. Whereas a certain
amount of ribald comedy is created from the speculation about
who the father of this illegitimate baby is, the comedy is
overshadowed by the dark, even tragic implications of his
sudden death. Hugh is barely home from the celebrations for
the baptism when he is off again to the wake. The two rituals,
so close together, remind the audience how close death is in
this exposed and vulnerable community. Only a thin line
divides joy from sorrow here, and in this atmosphere of
brittleness the play takes place.

It may be agreed, then, that as *Translations* opens this
community is balanced on a knife-edge. A major shift, a re-
volution indeed, is about to take place whereby an old world, a
world of traditional modes of education and of communication, will yield to a new world, let us call it modernity.
The basic conflict in the play is between tradition and

modernity. Yet Friel was apprehensive that the play he was writing would be too political in theme and emphasis. 'What worries me about the play', he confided in his diary on 1 June, 'are … the political elements. Because the play has to do with language and only language' ('Extracts' 58). This is where one must begin any serious excavation into the meaning of *Translations*.

Marilynn Richtarik, in her book on Field Day, makes the significant point that 'when an Irish playwright talks about language, it has a political edge' (35). Like Stephen Dedalus in James Joyce's *Portrait*, every Irish writer has the sensation that his/her soul frets in the shadow of the language of the conqueror, England. Language can never be a neutral force or medium in Ireland. Therefore, Friel can only attempt to make the political implications of his subject less urgent than they might be if he gave them free rein. The language question, historically bound up in the suppression of Irish (i.e., Gaelic), and the consequent insecurity in standard English by a colonized people, is invariably politicized, even in postcolonial Ireland. The question here is, what are the politics that result from a self-conscious focusing on the language question?

A brief glance at one of Friel's sources which comment on the loss of Irish in the nineteenth century may assist with this question. In P.J. Dowling's *The Hedge Schools of Ireland,* extracts from which appeared in the Field Day theatre programme when *Translations* was first staged, we read that at the beginning of the nineteenth century about one and a half million people spoke *only* Irish, out of a population of under eight million, while over two million people commonly used the Irish language (57). Dowling refers also to the establishment in 1832 of the National Board of Education which 'witnessed the passing of the old Hedge Schools, slowly giving way to the schools under the National Board' (122). It has to be remembered that these hedge schools were illegal schools until the passing of the Catholic Emancipation Act in 1829. They became redundant as soon as they were legal. The old order gave way to the new, and with it Irish gave way to English as the vernacular. By the time J.M. Synge visited the Aran Islands in 1898, the people even in this remote part of Ireland were bilingual. By 1983, just after Friel's play was first staged, the number of people using the Irish language daily was only 4% of the population of 3.5 million, and only one quarter of that group, a mere 35,000 people, lived in the Gaelic-speaking areas known as the Gaeltacht (Hussey 495-96). Friel looks back from this situation and finds the roots of it in 1833. What he finds he presents as tragic.

The failure to restore Irish as a speaking language has left the country in what Gemma Hussey calls 'a cultural vacuum' (498). The issue is a significant means of measuring national consciousness. Thus the modern historian J.J. Lee has commented:

> It is hardly going too far to say that but for the loss of the language, there would be little discussion about identity in the Republic. With language, little else seems to be required. Without language, only the most unusual historical circumstances suffice to develop a sense of identity,

as happened during the Irish revival at the turn of the century. But in the later twentieth century, Lee continues:

> the importance of the lost language as a distinguishing mark becomes more rather than less evident. As circumstances normalize, only the husk of identity is left without the language (662).

Thus in focusing on the inevitability of the decline of Irish once the national school system was established and in focusing on the replacing of Gaelic place names, with all their traditional associations, by English equivalents, Friel is necessarily intervening in a debate on national identity. The way in which he makes translation the key to this issue is masterly. As Declan Kiberd has said, 'the Irish Renaissance had been essentially an exercise in translation, in carrying over aspects of Gaelic culture into English' (624). Indeed, Kiberd goes so far as to claim that the writers at the turn of the century recognized that 'to translate Ireland was but another way of bringing it into being' (624). One would have to say, however, that Friel's notion of translation is a lot more complex than the re-writing of one version in another form.

For Friel, the whole business is bound up with communication. Communication, specifically the problematizing of communication, was Friel's theme ever since his first major success, *Philadelphia, Here I Come!* (1964). That play is concerned with a young man's inability to communicate with his father. The loneliness that results from this inability is presented as intense and at the same time as rooted in cultural malaise: Friel's drama is usually diagnostic. Thus he sees the silence between father and son as partly the result of Gar's mother's death in childbirth and partly because of the failure of anybody in society, any cultural or religious figure, to intervene. In particular, Friel accuses the parish priest, who is represented as wilfully ignoring the reality of suffering in the house he visits nightly. The inner self of the young man, played by a second actor deemed invisible on stage, attacks the priest in these words:

> because you could translate all this loneliness, this groping, this dreadful, bloody buffoonery into Christian terms that will make life bearable for us all … Isn't this your job, to translate? (*Selected Plays* 88).

Here one sees the special sense in which Friel understands the term. To translate is to communicate or to make communication possible.

Friel's point, however, is that this possibility is tragically unavailable in the conditions life offers. It is fair to say that when he read George Steiner's *After Babel* (1975) Friel found there a confirmation of what he already believed. Steiner talks in his first chapter about understanding as translation, and about all communication as a form of translation or transfer of meaning. Steiner also argues that pure communication, true translation, is impossible: 'Each communicatory gesture has a private residue' (46). And, again, 'all communication "interprets" between privacies' (198). Friel twice uses a similar kind of language in his play *Translations*. The first instance is where Yolland, yearning to learn Irish and go native, but aware that he was doomed to be an outsider: 'Even if I did speak Irish I'd always be an outsider here, wouldn't I? I may learn the password but the language of the tribe will always elude me, won't it? The private core will always be … hermetic, won't it?' (*Selected Plays* 416). And the other occasion is when Hugh finally agrees to teach Maire English: 'We'll begin tomorrow. But don't expect too much. I will provide you with the available words and the available grammar. But will that help you to interpret between privacies? I have no idea. But it's all we have' (446). In other words, Friel believes that each individual exists to some extent in a world of private discourse, where language is private and incommunicable. As soon as one begins to translate, the thing or feeling one wished to communicate vanishes. In the play the glaring examples are the place names, but these also stand for the general problem of communication between people who each have their own language. As Steiner puts it: '*inside or between languages, human communication equals translation*' (47).

What is happening in Friel's play, then, is a process that I tend to call 'palimpsest'. *The Oxford English Dictionary* defines palimpsest as follows: 'a parchment or other writing-material written upon twice, the original writing having been erased or rubbed out to make place for the second; a manuscript in which a later writing is written over an effaced earlier writing'. This process is a constant factor in Irish writing. The style or the use of form is habitually to superimpose one story or discourse on to another. It follows that Irish writing is often revisionary, a form of re-writing of some earlier version, and is sometimes also revisionist, that is, deliberately and critically a re-interpretation. The result is intertextuality as translation in the sense I am employing it here. For example, Seamus Heaney in writing a poem about a pilgrimage to Lough Derg in *Station Island*, a poem dedicated to Brian Friel, rewrites the earlier texts of William Carleton and Patrick Kavanagh. The presence of Carleton and Kavanagh in the poem serves to authorize a new version of a narrative about pilgrimage in a new historical period. The appearance of Joyce within this new narrative has no textual basis: Joyce never wrote about Lough Derg. But he is translated into the narrative in order to rewrite it and give it a new, secular direction. The palimpsest is thus a form of assimilation. One does not find this in the English tradition *per se*: when William Wordsworth revisits Tintern Abbey, he does not seek to conflate the modern with the medieval landscape, much less his own writing with that of a medieval manuscript: he is sufficiently secure in his cultural identity to bypass the ruins for the landscape 'A Few Miles above Tintern Abbey'. The Abbey's history, its suppression by Henry VIII, could never impinge on Church-of-England Wordsworth as it would to an Irish (Roman Catholic) writer were the ruins in Ireland. For Wordsworth the Abbey is already invisible. It is the landscape of river and pantheistic presence that claim his attention, reflect his personal history and act as the occasion of his sustaining memories. The revisiting is just that: a return to a source that is used as a peg, an *aide mémoire*, rather than as appropriated as a text to be rewritten. Wordsworth's process is the English process, seen clearly again, for example, in Waugh's *Brideshead Revisited* or, for that matter, the whole corpus of Philip Larkin's poetry, high windows and all. In this respect, English art aspires to the photograph album, whereas Irish art aspires to appropriative refiguration.

Joyce's own works provide rich examples of this technique, from the rewriting of *Stephen Hero* as *A Portrait* to the rewriting of the *Odyssey* as *Ulysses,* not to mention the glorious palimpsest he called *Finnegans Wake*. The tenor and mode of Paul Muldoon's poetry rely almost entirely upon palimpsest; his 'play' derives from little else. The fondness among contemporary Irish writers for creating versions of classical plays, moreover – for example, Heaney's *The Cure at Troy*, a version of Sophocles' *Philoctetes*, and more recently his *The Burial at Thebes*, or the three earlier versions of *Antigone* from Brendan Kennelly, Tom Paulin, and Aidan Mathews – clearly indicates the persistence of palimpsest. The work of Tom Mac Intyre for the stage offers yet another case in point. It is a form of dynamic spoliation of existing texts, such as Patrick Kavanagh's *The Great Hunger* or Eibhlín Dubh Ní Chonaill's *Caoineadh Airt Uí Laoghaire*.

Brian Friel's versions of Chekhov's *Three Sisters* and *Uncle Vanya* are in the same category, as indeed are the many successful versions of Ibsen's plays made in the past ten years by Frank McGuinness (notably *The Wild Duck* and *A Doll's House*), plus the excellent version of Pirandello's *Six Characters in Search of an Author* that Tom Kilroy did for the Abbey Theatre in 1996. There are other examples, too many to mention. Heinz Kosok (2004) has recently written about this Irish fondness for translations and adaptations. All of this dramatic activity is not just opportunism, nor can it justifiably be called a lazy or easy option exercised by Irish playwrights, a climbing upon the back of some original author. On the contrary, it is something more profoundly indicative of the peculiar, productive nature of the Irish imagination writing in English, some kind of response to history and the problem of identity raised by that history. In contrast, the translations done by English writers – for instance, Michael Frayn or Tony Harrison – make no attempt to superimpose an English text as culturally revisionist. By the same token, it may be as dangerous to fault Friel for 'poor' translation of Chekhov as it is to accuse him of 'poor' history in *Translations* (see below). In both instances he knew what he was doing.

Moreover, as regards the play *Translations*, it is obvious that there is no original *text* as such for Friel to translate or adapt, a point well made by Kiberd (624). Instead, the play dramatizes the process of palimpsest itself. When Owen is asked to translate Captain Lancey's message in Act 1, he gives only a rough version of the message, altered to suit his audience, as Manus quickly notices. Owen was disguising what Lancey said. Decoding, Manus superimposes his version onto Owen's: 'it's a bloody military operation' (*Selected Plays* 408). The action bears out the truth of Manus's translation. Again, the treatment of the place names provides a key to the action. Instead of a direct translation what Owen supplies is a superimposition on top of the old word or group of words. For example, Burnfoot for *Bun na hAbhann,* or Roland for Owen. The latter example shows clearly how a shift in identity is involved. In the action of the play Friel shows at large how the process works. There is an entrance, not to say an invasion, in the first scene, by which a group of strangers occupy the space inhabited by the natives. Doalty's little story of how he shifted the surveyor's pole (389-90), while the soldiers were mapping, is correctly perceived by Manus as Doalty's gesture: aboriginal land is being traversed by men who are reinscribing it with new names; Doalty moves their equipment so that their means of measuring the terrain is subverted. Manus comments: 'it was a gesture … Just to indicate … a presence' (391). Gesture is also a form of language, although a silent form. But the key example and the key scene in the whole play is when Maire and Yolland exchange place names as an expression of their lovemaking. It is worthwhile looking briefly at this scene.

Most Friel critics have seen this love scene as the heart of the play. It shows, really, that no amount of philosophy or language theory can adequately account for a scene where human feeling comes across on the stage. In drama, it is important that there should be this kind of release of feeling, so that the audience is drawn in and can empathize with the characters' predicament. In Greek drama, this necessity was provided for by the chorus; in Shakespeare by the soliloquy; but in modern drama, it is usually provided by the dialogue alone. Friel goes further by replacing dialogue with lines that cannot communicate because spoken in a language other than the one used by the other lover. A bridge is found by the place names in their Irish form only. A form of unity is suggested by the use of a single language. All through the play, of course, there is only one language – apart from the bits of Greek and Latin – and that is English. But the convention Friel uses, the 'conceit' as one might say (following Dürrenmatt, a playwright Friel greatly admires), is that the peasants are speaking Gaelic and the soldiers English. Interestingly, when the *Taidhbhearch*, Ireland's national Gaelic theatre in Galway, wanted to stage the play half in Gaelic and half in English Friel refused permission, saying it had to be entirely in one language. It is only in that way that the irony of lack of unity of culture is emphasized. In the scene in question, Act 2, Scene 2, the pathos of the Romeo and Juliet love affair is underlined by this convention. The passage (426-

27) is too long to quote in full here, and must be familiar to all interested in Friel's work: though speaking in different languages, as each is reported in English we see that they are as lovers virtually using the same words (signs). It is not the words but the sound that matters to them. Also, it is to be noted that in this opening section they use names only, emphasizing that it is a matter of identity that is at stake. When Juliet leans out the balcony, likewise, in Shakespeare's play, she speaks aloud to herself, not knowing that Romeo is below, and what she says is to question why he is named Romeo and thus a Montague:

> What's Montague? It is nor hand, nor foot,
> Nor arm, nor face, nor any other part
> Belonging to a man. O, be some other name!
> What's in a name? That which we call a rose
> By any other word would smell as sweet.
> So Romeo would, were he not Romeo called (2.2.40-45).

Friel adapts Shakespeare's scenario in his own play. We bear in mind what Jimmy Jack says in Act 3 when he is seriously discussing the fantasy marriage between himself and the goddess Athene: 'the word *exogamein* means to marry outside the tribe. And you don't cross those borders casually – both sides get very angry' (446). Crossing tribal borders is also a form of translation. And that is exactly the situation Maire and George are on the brink of in this love scene. Unlike Romeo and Juliet, however, they have no common language and so must communicate by other means, by sound and by movement or body language. And so the scene progresses. Anything beyond the use of first name leaves the other character lost in incomprehension. Maire tries Latin, but this is a failure. She recites the one bit of English she knows, and this has electrifying results. No matter that it is a nonsensical sentence about maypole dancing in Norfolk, a phonetic exercise in the letter 'o'. Yolland hears the place name 'Norfolk' and he responds with such enthusiasm that Maire has to consider if her Aunt Mary might not have taught her an obscene phrase. All of this exchange is bound up with place names. And it is at this point that Yolland begins to recite the Gaelic place names he and Owen have been translating. He says the first one '*almost privately, very tentatively, as if he were searching for a sound she might respond to*' (428-29). Maire moves away at first, and then stops and listens to his litany. On the fifth name she replies with another place name. Friel says in his stage direction that each of them speaks almost to himself and herself (429). This is a private and secret language they use. As they exchange the words they move across the stage until they meet and touch hands. The contact is extremely important. It is the highpoint of the dramatic action. It translates for the audience a love that challenges division.

The political implications of Friel's play are well known and need no elaboration here. Some critics, such as Edna Longley, were outraged at what they saw as Friel's irresponsible revision of nineteenth-century Irish history as a means of reinforcing the nationalist position in the North. Indeed, Longley says that Friel 'translates contemporary Northern Catholic feeling into historical terms' (29). The phrasing is unfortunate. Nowhere in *Translations* does Friel refer to Catholics or Protestants. Yet his hostile critics insist that he takes sides. This is not so. He shows how a resistance movement can begin. He shows how retaliation breeds only further retaliation. He is not interested as a playwright in championing any side or cause but in seeking to lay out the tragic conditions which make a course of events inevitable. Indeed, it is the English soldier, and not any of the native Irish, who describes the Ordnance Survey as 'an eviction of sorts' (420).

The psychological implications of the play are equally important. Obviously, Sarah is traumatized in Act 3 so that she falls silent, probably forever. She is as affected by Manus's disappearance as Maire is by Yolland's. When Maire appears in Act 3 she is close to breakdown. Like Nora Clitheroe in O'Casey's *The Plough and the Stars* (1926), Maire is bereft when her man is needlessly taken away from her. It is interesting to see the new use made here of the mapping metaphor. In her distraction, Maire drops on her hands and knees on the floor and, with her finger, traces an outline map of Norfolk and of the district from which Yolland comes. Is this map a text? It is rather the translation of a text, since Maire is recomposing a map Yolland earlier drew on the wet sand and on which he wrote the English place names. Maire is compelled literally to go over the old ground. She recites the place names: 'Strange sounds, aren't they?' They are 'like Jimmy Jack reciting his Homer' (438). She has the map in her head now. The text has been translated into memory. Thus Friel takes 'text' to be unstable, like the wet sand and yet capable of recording experience by the process of superimposition. One thinks of Daniel Corkery, and his famous claim: 'Everywhere in the mentality of the Irish people are flux and uncertainty. Our national consciousness may be described, in a native phrase, as a quaking sod. It gives no footing. It is not English, nor Irish, nor Anglo-Irish' (14). For 'quaking sod' read 'wet sand'. Friel brings *Translations* into a focus upon both the need to re-draw landscape and the pathos of the transaction. In any case, it is wrong to see Yolland's writing on the sand as signifying only futility and sentimentality (Kiberd 619). The pathos of Maire's re-drawing of the map is central to the emotional impact of the play and hence to its meaning. Maire on her knees tracing a map based on another map on sand: this is the image of love, need, and loss we carry with us from *Translations*.

At the close of the play we see, too, the breakdown of Hugh as he stumbles over a translation with which he is entirely familiar, a passage from Virgil's *Aeneid*. 'What the hell's wrong with me? Sure I know it backwards. I'll begin again' (447). The idiom of 'replay' once again simultaneously reinforces the meaning and the pathos. The parallel of futures, of Carthage and of Ballybeg, is firmly drawn. We might stop to ask what language Hugh is translating into. Irish, one supposes. But what we hear is English, once again. Why is the audience being given this translation on which the play ends? It can only be so that the audience can hear in the use of English the language that Hugh did *not* use but which was about to replace his own. In short, the audience gets a palimpsest. The concept, George Steiner says in *Real Presences*, 'is crucial to the Freudian reading of the relations, always both true and false or true in their falsehood, between the word and the self' (110). Steiner is here talking about the language of psychoanalysis, and the way in which it redeploys a speaker's words in order to create meaning and to heal. 'Thus psychoanalytic interpretation does not define: it translates into other, momentary translations' (110). Friel seems to be primarily interested in the healing power of language, or of language as sound. In *Translations* we see the destroying power, but the audience is brought, through the love affair, into such close contact with a possible alternative to division and conflict that, as with the ending of *Romeo and Juliet*, we are left with not just a warning but with an impulse towards reconciliation.

Ten years later *Dancing at Lughnasa* (1990) was to end with an idealized version of the past, into which the audience gain access through language which denies the value of language. The closure of *Translations* is similarly contradictory or ambiguous. The ominousness of the opening scene is fully intensified, and yet, ironic though it is, Hugh's text, recycled into no language we can be sure of, prophesies the foundation of a new age and a new dispensation. Of course, it also prophesies doom, at least for the Carthaginians. With this liminality, the play fades out rather than concludes. We are left inhabiting two time scales simultaneously, sensed through two languages superimposed.

Works Cited

Corkery, Daniel. *Synge and Anglo-Irish Literature*. Cork: Mercier, 1966.
Dean, Joan Fitzgerald. *Ireland into Film: Dancing at Lughnasa*. Cork: Cork University Press, in Association with the Film Institute of Ireland, 2003.
Dowling, P.J. *The Hedge Schools of Ireland*. Cork: Mercier, 1968.
Friel, Brian. 'Plays Peasant and Unpeasant'. *Times Literary Supplement* 17 March 1972: 305-06.
--- 'Extracts from a Sporadic Diary'. *Ireland and the Arts: A Special Issue of Literary Review*. Ed. Tim Pat Coogan. London: Namara, n.d. [1985]: 56-61.
--- *Selected Plays*. London: Faber, 1984.
Hussey, Gemma. *Ireland Today*. London: Penguin, 1995.
Kiberd, Declan. *Inventing Ireland*. London: Cape, 1995.
Kosok, Heinz. 'Cracks in the Jug: Recent Translations/Adaptations of Continental Plays by Irish Dramatists'. *Drama Translation and Theatre*

Practice. Ed. Sabine Coelsch-Foisner and Holger Klein. Frankfurt-on-Main: Peter Lang, 2004: 99-120.

Lee, J.J. *Ireland 1912-1985: Politics and Society*. Cambridge: Cambridge University Press, 1989.

Longley, Edna. 'Poetry and Politics in Northern Ireland'. *Crane Bag* 9.1 (1985): 26-40.

'Palimpsest'. Def. *The Oxford English Dictionary*. 2nd ed. 1989.

Richtarik, Marilynn J. *Acting Between the Lines: The Field Day Theatre Company and Irish Cultural Politics 1980-1984*. Oxford: Clarendon, 1994.

Shakespeare, William. *William Shakespeare: The Complete Works: Compact Edition*. Ed. Stanley Wells and Gary Taylor. Oxford: Clarendon, 1988.

Steiner, George. *After Babel: Aspects of Language and Translation*. London: Oxford UP, 1975.

--- *Real Presences: Is There Anything in What We Say?* London: Faber, 1989.

7 | The Hungarian Translator's View of Brian Friel's *Translations* and The Problems in Translating it into Hungarian

Márton Mesterházi

No one reads a drama text as closely as the translator; he has to decode the allusions and quotations of the original, unravel its secrets, absorb the work as a whole with such strong love as will make all his efforts self-evident, even enjoyable. He must interpret, first for himself, the structure, the situations, the characters, the style(s) of the original, then re-invent them in his mother tongue. A good play will shine through bad acting, even bad directing; but a bad translation makes everybody else's work impossible, and stifles all potential productions in the bud. That is why we can proclaim that the translator – like the wolf in Phaedrus's fable – *superior stat*.

Inspired by this type of close reading of Brian Friel's *Translations*, I wish to deal with two major problems: the basic linguistic set-up (two languages in one), and history as the basic situation of Friel's play. Probably the most essential characteristic of the play is that the two sets of characters are supposed to speak two languages, Irish and English, mutually foreign to each other, excepting (in order of appearance) Manus, Hugh, and Owen, who are bilingual.

Brian Friel wrote his play in English. It would have been quite obvious for him to use some sort of Synge-ese – English bearing strong traces of having been translated from Irish to differentiate his Irish-speaking characters. But he most carefully avoided reconstructing a conjectural 1833 Irish usage (and I about four; we are after celebrating, and so forth.)

The only remainders of Irish usage are a few little-known dialect words (for example, footering about, to jouk, footless) emerging in the speech of the less educated characters. Similarly, though much more often, well-known dialectal phonetic forms and idioms (aul fella, be Jasus, ate=eat, yella, wee get, to leave home=see home) appear in the speech of the same characters. To render these and similar cases I used words and idioms easy to understand for the present-day Hungarian urban reader, but with a definite flavour of countryside origins.

To pursue the subject of how Brian Friel differentiates between the two sets of characters, let me have a look at the Irish speakers' idea of the English language. Maire knows, and tells with the strange accent of an unknown, foreign language 'In Norfolk we besport ourselves around the maypoll' (388). This is a 'rhyme' sentence, reappearing in the love-scene (428) – where she will remember three more words – and quoted after Yolland's disappearance (437). Jimmy knows 'Bo-som' (388). Doalty tries farcically to imitate the debate of the sappers (391).

The first important moment of the Irish characters meeting English is drowned in twofold farce. Lancey first speaks as if addressing a group of deaf children: loudly repeating and explaining the words his audience will not understand (405). The farcical effect is irresistible, both on the reader/audience, and on the Irish characters. Lancey then proceeds, reassured by Owen's promise to translate.

> **Lancey:** His Majesty's government has ordered the first ever comprehensive survey of this entire country – a general triangulation which will embrace detailed hydrographic and topographic information and which will be executed to a scale of six inches to the English mile. ...
> **Owen:** A new map is made of the whole country.
> **Lancey:** (*Looks to OWEN*) Is that all?

OWEN smiles reassuringly and indicates to proceed (406).

Friel uses here a different, but just as irresistible, age-old farcical effect based on the first childish surprise felt at hearing a foreign language in action, and *ad absurdum* exaggerating the sameness/difference shock. Which is the reverse replica of Molière's *Le bourgeois gentilhomme*:

> **Cléont:** Bel-men.
> **Coviell:** Il dit que vous alliez vite avec lui vous préparer pour la cérémonie, afin de voir ensuite votre fille et de conclure le mariage.
> **M. Jourdain:** Tant de choses en deux mots?
> **Covielle:** Oui, la langue turque est comme cela, elle dit beaucoup en peu de paroles (105).

The translator has to do full justice to the farce for two reasons. Yolland will drop into the same trap in the love-scene (*'raising his voice … articulating in a staccato style … with equal and absurd emphasis on each word'* 427); and Lancey will have a chilling translation scene with nearly the same characters in Act 3 (439-40), the contrasting effect of which must be established here, at the end of Act 1, when the Captain makes a clown of himself.

Finally, Maire will quote the key-words of her beloved: 'Winfarthing – Barton Bendish – Saxingham Nethergate – Little Walsingham' (437) and 'always' (446). As I decided to translate the local place names into Hungarian (to be explained below), it logically follows that I put special importance on translating also Yolland's native place names, and make Maire mispronounce them the same way as Yolland mispronounces their Irish equivalents.

The only English speaker who tries to form an idea of the Irish language is Yolland. He even gets involved in a situation (inconceivable for Captain Lancey, the other English speaker) where Manus, with scarcely hidden offensiveness, speaks Irish to him (411, 412). The translator must bear in mind that the situation will be repeated – off-stage, reported with bitter irony by Manus – in Act 3 when he shouts his curses in Irish to a politely apologizing Yolland (432). However, apart from those two instances, the only examples which might give Yolland, the enthusiastic Hibernophile, any idea of the language he wants so much to learn, are the line of place names to be Anglicized.

At this point I cannot delay quoting a translation of my introductory note, 'The Translator's Apology' ('A fordító mentsége'), any longer:

> In the original text the Irish place names stand in Gaelic as long as, by superior order, they do not become Anglicized – the process the play is about. (Friel also introduces a couple of English place names, of course in English.) If I leave those place names untranslated, the (Hungarian version of the) play will be about nothing. If I translate only the English place names, it is the Irish ones (the very ones outraged in their dignity) from which I estrange Hungarian readers. If I translate only the Irish/Gaelic place names, I leave pieces of English text in the play every (English) sentence of which I have translated into Hungarian. Only desperate audacity seemed to be logical here. As for the Hungarian equivalents, Balázs Orbán was most helpful. Commonly known place names (like Dublin) have been left unchanged (Friel, *Helynevek* 100).

Two notes seem necessary. Hungarian readers would look with Lancey's indolence at Irish/Gaelic names, and would never notice that the play is about them: about us. About the Hungarian place names chauvinistic régimes around Hungary furiously turned into Romanian, Slovakian, Serbocroat, and so forth after the 1920 Trianon Treaty. Balázs Orbán's *Descriptio Transsylvaniae* was first published in 1868, when the age-old logic of the myriad local names had not yet been violated by '*edictum imperatoris*', and merely thirty-five years after the time in which Friel's play is set, 1833.

Thus 'Bun na hAbhann' (410), on which Owen and Yolland demonstrate the phonetic, etymological, and aesthetic (ideological) methods of their joint work, is 'Gyöngyöstorka' (with some of the most difficult Hungarian sounds in it) for Owen, mispronounced 'Dondos-tarka' by Yolland, and 'Forró Föveny' (138) for the Name-Book.

And there is the final, tragic showdown, when the real ideological (political/strategic) purpose of the 'worthy enterprise' gets demonstrated by the contrast of the native and the Anglicized forms:

> **Lancey:** 'Sertésdomb'.
> **Owen:** Disznóvár.
> **Lancey:** 'Forró Föveny'.
> **Owen:** Gyöngyöstorka.
> **Lancey:** 'Feketekó'.
> **Owen:** Feketekő.
> **Lancey:** 'Fennsík'.
> **Owen:** Fejérláz.
> **Lancey:** 'Királyszikla'.
> **Owen:** Királyfő. (176)[1]

I cannot thank my Irish colleague, Bill McCormack, enough for the help he gave me, during a talk we had in Budapest in the late 1980s, in decoding the logic of the Irish names in the love-scene. He explained to me that however mutual their feelings, Yolland picks at random among the place names he remembers, while Maire, who knows their meaning, chooses hers to tell something gentle, nice or favourable to her love. I think that in this respect the Hungarian text is as telling as the original would be for a bilingual audience.

In the same scene, the translator must hear the 'rhymes' Maire and Yolland cannot hear:

> **Maire:** The grass must be wet. My feet are soaking.
> **Yolland:** Your feet must be wet. The grass is soaking.
> …
> **Yolland:** I would tell you how I want to be here – to live here – always – with you – always, always.
> **Maire:** 'always'? What is that word – 'always'? …
> **Maire:** I want to live with you – anywhere – anywhere at all – always – always.
> **Yolland:** 'always'? What is that word – 'always'? (426, 429, 430)

Maire will even ask Hugh about the meaning of Yolland's 'always' in the last scene of Act 3 (446).

To round off the analysis of how Friel differentiates between his two sets of characters, we must recall that both the English and the Irish language are conceptually analysed in the play. English is first described by Hugh – the only professional linguist among the characters with sufficient self-confidence and discipline for philosophy. He tells how he explained to Captain Lancey that some people did speak his language, 'outside the parish of course ... usually for ... purposes of commerce, a use to which his tongue seemed particularly suited' (399). Maire – partly quoting Daniel O'Connell, the Liberator – voices a radically opposite opinion when she asserts that they should be learning English since '[t]he old language is a barrier to modern progress' (399-400). Hugh considers such insolence as open revolt, and crushes it with his usual arrogance. Owen, the professional interpreter in the play, amply seasons his contrastive image of the two languages with irony: 'My job is to translate the quaint, archaic tongue you people persist in speaking into the King's good English' (404).

In Act 2 Hugh, still proudly optimistic, makes an unusually philosophical confession about the Irish language, as a means of collective self-deception (418-19). As Ulf Dantanus argues, the 'central argument of his belief is taken verbatim from Steiner's *After Babel*' (193). Then, after the tragedies set in, Hugh will be the man to accept English as an inevitability (444-45).

Thus, if we accept the characters' own judgement: English is reliable, efficient, professional, whereas Irish, as the quaint, archaic language of self-deception, is a barrier to progress. How should this be translated into the two Hungarians that would express the two sets of characters?

Morphology gave me the first evident idea. In English, 'only God is Thou', in Irish everybody is 'tu'. In Hungarian 'on se tutoie' if on familiar terms, and 'on se vousoie' if on formal ones. Consequently, in my translation the Irish 'se tutoient', the English 'se vousoient'. This was one of the few instances of poetic licence I was glad to take. Another was making the Hungarian of the Irish as idiomatic as possible, with a very mild taste of – no, not dialect, but definitely not city-speech; and the Hungarian of the English as strict, as matter-of-fact as possible.

If we accept the idea that a drama-translator renders characters, and that character is best defined by style, we can easily use the extremes, and define the Irish as 'Hugh-style', and the English as 'Lancey-style'. *Licentia poetica?* I am not quite sure. If we compare the two soul-searching tirades devoted to the past of Hugh (445-46) and Yolland (415-16), the quixotic English dream-eater's text is definitely Lancey-like structurally; at any rate much more so than Hugh's. Besides, I had to articulate some things more precisely than the author: I was translating the play for an audience who think of Irish history as of something very remote, and whose attention should not be diverted (*diverto, divertere*) by lack or laxity of information about the speaker's language-group identity.

Owen calls the Irish language quaint and archaic. However, following Friel's unmistakable instructions concerning the text, I avoided any form of archaization, while keeping away from anachronisms and city-language neologisms even more carefully.

If the problem of two languages in one provides the basic set-up of the play, history has, perhaps, an even deeper role in it: history is its basic situation. At the beginning of Act 1, Manus's innocent question about the Donnelly twins changes the so far jocular atmosphere: unexpected tension sets in, then Bridget blurts out a half-sentence about two of the soldiers' horses, but stops short (393). By common consent, the Donnellys are a subject not to be spoken about. When some minutes later Hugh asks about them, Bridget tells a white lie – they must be digging turf – with routine ease, though after a brief pause (398).

At the beginning of Act 2 we learn that the Donnellys are very good fishermen and Lancey would want them for questioning. So they might be in some sort of conflict with the British military authorities.

At the beginning of Act 3 when Owen begs for information about his friend, Doalty tells him that the Donnellys were about when Yolland was kidnapped and probably killed. So they, quite clearly, seem to be the local armed resistance.

After Lancey's ultimatum we know they are:

> **Doalty:** I've damned little to defend but he [Lancey]'ll not put me out without a fight. And there'll be others who think the same as me ... If we knew how to defend ourselves.

Owen: Against a trained army.
Doalty: The Donnelly twins know how. (441-42)

They 'know how': the same primitive, ineffectual way their fathers and grandfathers had learned in 1798.

Another motif pointing, unlike that of the Donnelly-twins, forward in history is 'the sweet smell' – the first ominous sign of decay in the potato crops – discussed in detail at the beginning of Act 1 and brushed off as a false alarm in Act 3, after Lancey's ultimatum. It figures like some kind of historical frame, and both times in very near textual vicinity to the Donnellys. It is as though Brian Friel's *Translations* were in deliberate dialogue with Tom Murphy's *Famine* (another play I had the honour to translate), set in 1846-47. Murphy's equivalents of the Donnelly twins are the O'Leary brothers, Mickeleen, the hunchbacked ideologist, and Malachy, the action-man. In Scene 2, when the possibility of the starved villagers raiding one of the corn-carts (which are taking away Irish corn into well-off England) seriously emerges, Mickeleen is quite outspoken about the source of his ideas: 'The men of '98 shed their blood ... Were they murderers? ... And the priests – the real priests – who led and fought and died – were they murderers?' (28-29). But the local leaders, indeed the whole community are so fully aware of what a blind alley 1798 was, they nearly kick him to death.

As an alternative to dying of hunger, in Scene 3 the uncouth Malachy proposes the Donnelly twins' method: 'Soldiers! – Anyone! – I – know – we – can't – ["kill"] – them – all! Some of them. One now, and maybe two after a while as we get better. But make such a job of that one he'd count for ten' (39). After a short debate the community outlaws him. He will kill two policemen for their guns (Scene 6), then shoot the Justice of the Peace (Scene 9), the only person in power who did real work in order to help the community.

The thinking of Friel and Murphy is parallel (though Murphy's is more categorical): between the blind alley of 1798 and the trap of the Famine, armed resistance will crop up, but only to add to the misery. It is never the oppressors, the

Lanceys, or the Shines, the Simmingtons (in Murphy's play) who get killed.

What use does the translator have to make of all this in his work? Misquoting Hamlet, 'awareness is all' is the more important part of my answer. As to the rest: the translator should by all means keep up the special tension of the dialogues about the Donnelly twins and the sweet smell, the tension created in the speakers by subjects which are not meant to be spoken about, and yet are.

History is the basic situation of *Translations*. The statement can be pushed further: history is the style of the characters in the play. This is especially valid for the two authoritative, no-longer-young father-figures: Hugh Mor O'Donnell and Captain Lancey. 'Old Hugh, O'Caseyan Paycock though he in part is, seems to be the guide to what Friel is saying' – suggests Christopher Murray (211). O'Caseyan Paycock: the epithet is precise. But while we have no idea where 'Captain' Boyle lost his moral sanity, we have full information of where Hugh lost his:

> The road to Sligo. A spring morning, 1798. Going into battle ... Two young gallants with pikes across their shoulders and the *Aeneid* in their pockets ... We marched as far as – ... Glenties! All of twenty-three miles ... And it was there, in Phelan's pub ... we got homesick for Athens, just like Ulysses. The *desiderium nostrorum* – the need for our own. Our *pietas*, James, was for older, quieter things. And that was the longest twenty-three miles back I ever made (445-46).

Humiliation made the length of those twenty-three miles. Humiliation worsened by catastrophic collective defeat. (Victory means a world of difference, we know.) Not to be there among the dead pikemen shot into raw meat by professional artillery at Vinegar Hill, when you had pledged your honour to the cause. Such deep, and, to a good extent, self-inflicted humiliation can only be cured in the typical Irish way: drinking oneself senseless, so that one falls across the 'infant son in his cradle' (412), and drives the 'recently married goddess' (412) into premature death. Hugh, after innumerable bouts of drunken senselessness, realized he was too strong for premature death, and accommodated to the poison of humiliation by drinking himself morally insane.

This is manifested in his style: a complete set of mannerisms, so characteristic of him as though he were badly imitating (or parodying) himself. It is no mere chance that Hugh gets parodied twice in Act 1. First in a crude way, by Doalty (390), then in a loving way by Owen:

> **Owen:** ... the younger man that I travelled with from Dublin, his name is Lieutenant Yolland ... attached to the toponymic department – Father? – *responde – responde!*
> **Hugh:** He gives names to places.
> **Owen:** Indeed – although he is in fact an orthographer – Doalty? – too slow – Manus?
> **Manus:** The correct spelling of those names.
> **Owen:** Indeed – indeed! (403)

The translator must make the absolute best of Hugh's intellectual superiority, the ease with which he treats other people as servants; the speed of his ripostes; the erratic flow of his speech; in one word, his brilliance. The translator must do his best to be brilliant – but in full awareness of Hugh's last two great tirades: the one about the spring of 1798, and the out-of-joint quotation from the *Aeneid* (N.B. 'the *Aeneid* in their pockets' 445). There the translator must give the reader (the director, the actor, the audience) a sense of tragic dignity.

Friel is so gracious as to identify the sources of his quotations. Jimmy quotes some lines from Homer's *Odyssey* (384-87), and some of Virgil's *Georgica* (392) at the beginning of Act 1. Not much later Hugh quotes one line from Sophocles to mock Doalty. In Act 3 even his one line from Ovid (442) will have much more sincerity; and his substantial recital from the *Aeneid* (446-47) gains special significance as the closing statement of the play.

I admit having been unable to find the exact Sophoclean line; so I used one from *Oedipus at Colonus*, which I know quite well: 'As long as youth flourishes, it has stupidity sitting on its arm' (390, Babits Mihály's Hungarian translation, my English). But the problem is more intricate than that. We have wonderful – and, as our tradition prescribes, true to form – Hungarian translations of both Homer and Virgil. But the translator cannot quote Gábor Devecseri or István Lakatos, however temptingly beautiful their texts are, because neither Jimmy Jack nor Hugh are professional translators of great talent or ambition, not mentioning the radical difference between the translating traditions of the two languages/literatures. However, I had to look up the exact equivalent Hungarian texts, in order to use, in a sort of oblique quotation, the most characteristic words of Devecseri and Lakatos, to give a taste of the poetic quality of the texts, to 'elevate' them above the rest of the play.

The other character whose style is rooted in history is Captain Lancey. And the solution to his riddle (as to Hugh's) can be found in a soul-searching tirade, though not his own. It is Yolland, coalescing him with his father (415), who sounds the keynote, provides the key ideas about him:

> The perfect colonial servant: not only must the job be done – it must be done with excellence. Father has that drive, too; that dedication; that indefatigable energy ... He inherited a new world ... There were no longer any frontiers to man's potential. Possibilities were endless and exciting (415-16).

Drive, dedication, energy; there are no frontiers to the human potential. The English variant of '*le siècle des lumières*', with Reason as common goddess. Even when Lancey makes a clown of himself, he is a clown of reason and efficiency, showing a shy but deeply felt belief in the Common Good he serves (406-07). The same character will reappear in Act 3 as a figure of Nemesis: primitive, superstitious natives have responded with violence to the message of Reason, so law and order have to be restored: with drive, dedication, and energy, because 'not only must the job be done – it must be done with excellence' (415).

Friel describes Lancey as small and crisp: so his style must be, too. Thus, beyond the general rule for the Hungarian equivalent of English to be strict and matter-of-fact, I intended Lancey's text to be very precise, professionally reasonable, and efficient; that is, to be, textually, the diametrical opposite of Hugh's. Lancey's enlightened humanism will be irrefutably subverted by England's behaviour during the Famine years; and will find consolation in the Irish reform movement, to be led later by Parnell and Gladstone. Of course, that is already after Lancey's lifetime, and beyond the scope of the play. However, I presume one of the Captain's great-grandsons may very easily be called Tom Broadbent.

As a result of serious study and relentless heart-searching, Friel has come to see the deeper logic of post-1833 Irish history. He places his Irish characters between two crippling humiliations: between 'Ninety-eight and the Famine, and makes them face the task of fighting out a new identity after the loss of their mother-tongue. 'We must learn those new names ... We must learn where we live. We must learn to make them our own. We must make them our new home' (444).

This is miles, light-years, off 'The Patriotic Schoolmaster's History of Ireland' (419). To mitigate the contradiction, can we declare that Friel is looking back at a disturbing past from a modern state of national identity the Irish have victoriously achieved by now? Some of the hostile reactions following the hugely successful performances of the play suggest that not only the Irish past but the Irish present also has disturbing elements. Yet, contradictory as it is, the achievement of the Irish people has great and undeniable dignity. Whoever does not understand the bitter truth-seeking passion and the simultaneous historical optimism of Brian Friel, will never be able to translate *Translations*.

Note

[1] A re-translation of the Hungarian might be useful:
   Lancey: 'Swinefort'.
   Owen: Pig Fort. (for Lis na Muc)
   Lancey: 'Burnfoot'.
   Owen: Mouth of the Gyöngyös River (for Bun na hAbhann)
   Lancey: 'Blackstunn'. (form showing incorrect pronunciation)
   Owen: Black Stone. (for Druim Dubh)
   Lancey: 'Plateau'.
   Owen: White Plains. (archaic dialect word; for Machaire Ban)
   Lancey: 'King's Cliff'.
   Owen: King's Head. (archaic form; for Cnoc na Ri)

Works Cited

Dantanus, Ulf. *Brian Friel: A Study.* London: Faber, 1988.

Friel, Brian. *Translations. Selected Plays.* London: Faber, 1988. 377-455.

--- *Helynevek. Philadelphia, itt vagyok! Három dráma.* Budapest: Európa, 1990. 99-186.

Molière. *Le bourgeois gentilhomme.* Paris: Le livre de poche, 1985.

Murphy, Thomas. *Famine.* Dublin: Gallery, 1984.

Murray, Christopher. *Twentieth-Century Irish Drama: Mirror up to Nation.* Manchester: Manchester UP, 1997.

Szophoklész. *Oedipus Kolonosban. Szophoklész drámái.* Trans. Babits Mihály. Budapest: Helikon, 1959. 329-412.

PSYCHOLOGICAL AND SPIRITUAL TORMENTS

8 | Unveiling the Vice: A Reading of *Faith Healer*

Giovanna Tallone

Faith Healer looks back at, among other traditions, the legacy of medieval drama, however loosely the term may be used so as to include Tudor interludes. This recognition provides an additional reading in terms of organization, structure and narrative strategy, so that features of miracle and morality plays may be identified in the play. *Faith Healer* thus exploits strategies and gives new life to an earlier form of drama, and, at the same time, rewrites a tradition that is apparently alien to the play. Not by chance does *Faith Healer* open with a list of 'dying Welsh villages'.

> Aberarder, Aberayron,
> Llangranog, Llangurig,
> Abergorlech, Abergynolwyn (*Selected Plays* 331-32).

The place names of '[a]ll those dying Welsh villages' (332), recited in darkness by the play's protagonist evoked from a blurred past, both tell a story and accompany the telling of that story. They mark the reconstruction of a personal history that has developed along the route from village to village. They represent a storehouse for the protagonist's personal myth as he uses his list of place names to convey his restlessness and to silence it, to assert his identity, and to forget who he is. In its different forms and variations, the recital of place names becomes a catalyst and a continuum, a sort of *fil rouge* in the subtext of this play which remains – perhaps – the most experimental and impressive of those in the Friel canon.

The sound of 'Aberarder, Aberayron ...' has a soothing and hypnotic effect; these are the signs of a mysterious code, the words of an unknown language. But for Frank and Grace they are a living part of their recitation, speaking of shared yet divergent experiences, revealing the mythical proportion of their personal past, pure sounds in which the speakers indulge. 'The very word-form itself even unassociated with notions is capable of giving pleasure', offering speakers and listeners alike the 'phonetic pleasure' that J.R.R. Tolkien found in unknown or invented languages (207, 218). This is what Frank calls 'the mesmerism, the sedation, of the incantation' (332) which provides a sort of ecstasy (Kiberd, *Inventing Ireland* 617), a trance-like condition (Throne 22) rooted in the repetitive quality of family daily prayer and devotion (Robbins 78). The technique of listing place names is further exploited in Friel's *Translations*, where pure sounds are capable of bridging the gap of language barriers. For Maire and Yolland, Gaelic place names acquire a semantic value beyond signifier and signified: they become a new language.

But Friel has always indulged in the 'phonetic pleasure' of place names. The 'emphasis on place' (Murray 6) and the significance of place and place names is evident already in his stories. In 'The Wee Lake Beyond', for instance, the first-person narrator calls back to mind the lakes of his childhood: 'Lough Fada, the long lake; Lough Na Noillean, the lake with the islands; Lough Gorm, the blue lake; Lough Rower, the fat lake' (*Gold in the Sea* 70). A private *amor loci* mythologizes the protagonist's personal history, the past comes back to life by recollecting places and reciting place names. In 'The Saucer of Larks' the Sergeant identifies the beauty of the valley of the larks with its name: '"Glen-na-fuiseog", said the Sergeant, pronouncing the Gaelic name properly' (*Diviner* 141). In 'Among the Ruins' Joe's children repeat the name 'Corradinna' 'sampling the word', flavouring its sound (*Diviner* 127). The 'threnodical litanies of locales in *Faith Healer* and *Translations*'

(O'Brien 25) are anticipated in 'The Flower of Kiltymore' by the private quality of continuous removal from village to village which marks the life of the Sergeant's wife: 'from Kiltymore to Culdreivne, from Culdreivne to Ballybeg, from Ballybeg to Beannafreaghan, from Beannafreaghan back to Kiltymore' (*Gold in the Sea* 134).

In these cases an echo of the mythic tradition of *dindshenchas* recurs, the lore of prominent places, which was part of what the *fili* was trained to narrate (Knott and Murphy 102). Its purpose to 'explain the names of famous places, rivers, lakes or hills' (Dillon xvii) translates places into stories: 'each place has a history which is continuously retold' (Welch 150). The lure of place names is magnified by the stories behind them, and a recital of lists of place names thus results in a multiple recounting of multiple stories.

In Friel's plays, lists of various sorts appear, always revealing of states of mind. In *Philadelphia, Here I Come!* Aunt Lizzie recites the litany of the Gallagher girls – 'Una and Agnes and Rose and Mother and me'; 'Poor Aggie – dead. Maire – dead. Rose, Una Lizzie – dead – all gone – all dead and gone' (60, 64) – as a sort of anticipation of the catalogue of her possessions ('this ground-floor apartment, and a car that's air-conditioned, and colour TV' [65]). Her list magnifies the country of emigration that has become her own, and by doing so Aunt Lizzie writes the place(s) of Gar's future. She indulges in this verbal accumulation in part to lure Gar to America, but also for the instinctive and childlike pleasure of the listing itself, which implies boasting possession, gaining control, and keeping order in a familiar world.

In *Faith Healer*, the strategy of listing place names is ambivalent and works on different levels both in terms of rhetorical strategy and structure. Each character recites his/her monologue in isolation, so that the formal compactness of the monologue contrasts with and highlights the protagonists' psychic fragmentation and inability to communicate. It provides both imaginative freedom and confinement – a retreating into privacy by eliminating the Other. Each monologist indulges in his/her own version or distortion of things, each speech is 'a

worrying of hidden or half-hidden obsessions' which are
brought to 'conscious life' (Kilroy 100). Frank's obsessions take
the form of the 'maddening questions' (334) about his faith
healing power, which are counterbalanced by Grace's obsession
of being only one of Frank's 'fictions' (353) and by Teddy's
obsessive recounting of other people's stories. The monologue
is well-suited to express Friel's development and deepening of
psychological insight, at the same time providing a theatrical
device, turning inwards into utter privacy, and outwards to the
audience of public listeners.[1]

Faith Healer opens with a singsong, 'Aberarder, Aberayron',
which is broken by Frank Hardy's explanation of its mesmeric
power, soon to be resumed again:

> Kinlochbervie, Inverbervie,
> Inverdruie, Invergordon,
> Badachroo, Kinlochewe (332).

So at the *opening* of the play the narration appears unable to
get started, as it cannot leave its claustrophobic container. The
routine of performance itself is nothing but a list of actions –
'We'd arrive in the van usually in the early evening. Pin up the
poster. Arrange the chairs and benches . . .' (335) – an inventory
overcome by another list of place names:

> Penllech, Pencader,
> Dunvegan, Dunblane (335-36).

This further list does not interrupt Frank's narration: listing
and recounting are interwoven and inseparable. For Frank, the
recital of place names is a sort of drug, like his addiction to
whiskey. Both have the purpose of silencing the questions that
keep tormenting him. The questions themselves are proposed
in the manner of a list, the strategy of someone who is trying to
keep control, but who is rather controlled and trapped by the
very list he is building:

> *Am I endowed with a unique and awesome gift?* – ... *Am I a con man?*
> ... Was it all chance? – or skill? – ... what power did I possess?
> ... Could my healing be effected without faith? But faith in
> what? – in me? – in the possibility? – faith in faith? (333-34)

The structure of the list of place names is thus repeated and is functional to the organization of the play. With the growing of psychic tension, listing becomes a form of self-defence, a self-induced drug as appears clearly in Grace's monologue, which opens repeating the place names almost verbatim, highlighting her dependence on Frank, making his mythology hers.[2] Her first sentence following the list is broken and un-completed – 'That most persistent of all the memories, … that most persistent and most agonizing' (341) – thus revealing her fragmented consciousness. In her recitation the name of Kinlochbervie becomes central, the place where she gave birth to a stillborn child. The repetition of this name (353) con-tinuously retells Grace's story in a sort of personal *dindsheanchas* and is an obsessive death knell (Roche 112).

The strategy of listing in *Faith Healer,* as a technical and structural device, belongs to the postmodern construction of the play, whose 'knowing intertextuality' is part of Friel's experimentation (Kiberd, *Inventing Ireland* 618). *Faith Healer* has an 'intergeneric' form, half-way between novel and drama (Kiberd, '*Faith Healer*' 106), between stream of consciousness and straightforward narration. The play's monologic structure is indebted to Faulkner's *The Sound and the Fury* and close to Akira Kurosawa's film *Rashomon,* where different stories of the same incident are told by dead characters. The play is akin also to Brechtian epic theatre in its focus on process rather than action as, in a reversal of Coleridge's *Rhyme of the Ancient Mariner,* it recalls the eternally repeated story of the Ancient Mariner. *Faith Healer,* a rewriting of ancient myth and Old Irish legend, casts an old story into a new frame and recontextualizes its history. In fact, Declan Kiberd reads in *Faith Healer* a rewriting of the Old-Irish legend of *Longes mac Uisneach,* the story of Deirdre ('*Faith Healer*' 106). It is worth noticing that in the version of the legend contained in the Glenmasan MS, *Oidhe Chloinne Uisneach,* Deirdre's farewell to Scotland indulges in the names of Caill Cuan, Glenn Láid, Glenn Masán, Glenn Etive, Glenn Urcháin, Glenn Dá-Rúad, making a personal myth out of them (Stokes and Windisch 158), following the tradition of keening and providing the same soothing and hypnotic effect that will be later part of the faith healer's monologue.

Faith Healer is 'revenant drama' (Grene 136), dead characters tell stories of different deaths, Frank's father and mother, Grace's mother, the pigeons of Miss Mulatto that had died during a cold winter (356), the stillborn baby at the heart of the Kinlochbervie episode, Grace's death as recounted by Teddy, all these anticipating the faith healer's death. This final episode, too, has multiple recountings, by Grace, by Teddy, and by Frank himself. With dead characters on stage *Faith Healer* turns out to be a variation of the Dance of Death (Wickham, *Medieval Theatre* 110; Chambers 153; Margeson 33). This impression is enhanced by the evocation of the unseen presences of the desperate multitude (336) turning to the faith healer to be confirmed they cannot be cured (337). In this pantomime of dead wanderers, the speakers' verbal activity is the technical counterpart of the homiletic tradition. The visual impact of the Dance of Death in medieval iconography is verbalized by preachers and sermons. In medieval tradition 'the subject of drama and sermon were often the same'; a sermon is nothing but 'a dramatic monologue with the preacher as actor' (Cawley et al. 86). The most famous of morality plays, *Everyman*, is nothing but an 'effectively dramatized sermon' (Cawley et al. 223), exploiting the strategy of parable, allegory, typology, and cautionary tale (Wickham, *Medieval Theatre* 109, 110), thus assembling different stories. *Faith Healer* exploits a similar strategy, while attention is drawn to the faith healing art itself with a language which bears religious overtones, identifying the realms of artistry and vocation: 'A craft without an apprenticeship, a *ministry* without a responsibility, a *vocation* without a *ministry*' (333; emphasis added). The sacral or ritual recurs a few lines later, when Frank describes the nights of his success as 'nights of exultation, of consummation' (333). The human world is juxtaposed to the ritual of 'consummation' in its idea of perfection, but it also recalls Christ's words on the cross: 'Consummatum est'. As a priest, minister, or shaman, Frank is an *alter Christus*, whose death can be read as a sacrifice.

Frank, too, is word made flesh (Roche 113). His monologue(s) can be read or listened to as a sermon. And as the *Artes Praedicandi*, or preaching manuals, emphasize repetition as a technique for capturing the audience's attention (Neuss 43), so *Faith Healer* is based on repetition, of the same story, of the same episodes, of the same or similar words, of different details, of divergent truths. Repetition also characterizes the structural organization of Old Irish sagas, since in *Táin Bó Cuailnge*, as well as in all the early heroic tales, 'the repetition of themes, or rather of variants on a basic theme' are 'demonstrable formulas' representing a 'stylistic device' to 'provide some special emphasis' (O'Rahilly 67, 74). The repetition of episodes in the great medieval cycles aims at the restatement of truths (Bevington, *Marlowe* 4), while repetition in *Faith Healer* restates the elusiveness of truth.

In medieval drama the traditional allegorical character of the Vice, who is a master of words, typically employs both direct address to the audience and repetition. This character in all its variations can be identified as a prototype of Frank Hardy. Like the devil from which he departs, the Vice makes use of grotesque and erratic language. Courtly Abusyon in Skelton's *Magnyfycence* (1533) enters singing 'Huffa, huffa taunderum, taunderum tayne, huffa, huffa!' (Happé 224). 'Mish, mash! Driff, draff', says Mischief early in *Mankind* (1465-70), anticipating the disorder he is going to bring about (Wickham, *Moral Interludes* 8). The Vice Sedicyon in John Bale's *King Johan* (1538) calls England's complaints to Johan 'bablyng matters': 'they are dyble-dable … byble-bable' (Happé 323). With such alliterating and rhyming words the Vice minimizes what his interlocutor says, considering it to be worthless, thus exercising his power through the medium of nonsense language (Cushman 109). And, in the 14th-century *The Last Judgement*, the first demon interrupts the devil Tutivillus's list of sinners saying: 'With words will thou fill us' (Bevington, *Medieval Drama* 646), shedding light on the hypnotic and secret power of words. The Vice's 'easy familiarity with the audience' (Salgādo 33) recurs from play to play and in his development from medieval to Elizabethan drama he becomes the epitome of evil (Spivack, *Allegory of Evil* passim).

His importance increases as a tempter and deceiver, but also as intriguer and stage manager, so that plays become 'a demonstration of his skill' (Margeson 35). As a central theatrical figure, the Vice compresses the earlier vices and deadly sins in a process of simplification. His dangerous deception and disruptive power are revealed in a series of asides in which he involves the audience (Margeson 38; Happé 15). He uses soliloquies to inform the audience of what he is about to do. The Vice is a seducer (Spivack, 'Vice' 140; Tydeman 31). Unable to control his language, he cannot 'keep his council telling us how evil he is' (Davison 81). Falstaff later, like the Vice to whom he is indebted, *seduces* 'the audience to his point of view' (Davison 64).

Frank Hardy bears a similarity with the Vice character as Grace and Teddy often say he is 'twisted' (345, 349) or 'convoluted' (346). As a performer, Frank is also a liar (345), a creator of fictions. Obsessed only by his intermittent art, he uses people as he uses words. For instance, he changes Grace's surname all the time – Dodsmith, Elliot, O'Connell, McPherson, McClure (345). And like the Vice, Frank also uses language as a tool for seduction. When he recites his list of place names, he does so for 'the mesmerism, the sedation of the incantation', where 'sedation' can be easily read as 'seduction'. This sedation/seduction is twofold, turning to himself to silence his obsessive questions (334), seducing himself out of his torment by hypnotism, but also seducing his listeners who indulge in the 'phonetic pleasure' of his list.

Frank's opening speech in *Faith Healer*, the stylization of a journey, re-proposes or reproduces one of the oldest mythological motifs and tale types in the Irish tradition, the *immram*, or voyage. Its focus of interest often lies 'in the account of the visit to the other world' (Dillon 124), the quintessential undiscovered mysterious place. By repeating the names of the villages he has visited Frank is accompanying the audience and himself along the steps of his mysterious faith healing art. Similarly, the Vice's traditional opening speech often gives an 'account of an imaginary or nonsense journey' (Sanders et al. 203). In Francis Merbury's interlude *The Marriage Between Wit and Wisdom* (1571-78), Idleness recounts his unlikely adventures, mythologizing the places he has been to:

> I have been at St Quintin's where I was twice kill'd;
> I have been at Musselborough at the Scottish field;
> I have been in the land of green gingers and many a-where
> (Wickham, *Moral Interludes* 184).

Frank Hardy's obsessive repetitions thus bear an echo of the Vice's verbal activity. The 'playful attitude towards language' in Skelton's political interlude *Magnyfycence* (1522) takes the form of 'long lists of names' and repetitions (Sanders et al. 173). As Idleness in *The Marriage Between Wit and Wisdom* lists his qualities in a long monologue (Wickham, *Moral Interludes* 170-71), so Magnyfycence boasts of his qualities as a prince quoting a long sequence of kings, princes, and tyrants from history and mythology (Happé 270-71, lines 1466-1515). Likewise, the recitation of male lineage is a characteristic feature of History plays (Howard 130) while the 'delight in listing of places and people and food' belongs to folk drama (Axton 12). This popular catalogue motif finds a variation in the list of evil actions in the moral interlude *Nice Wanton* (1560) – 'Swear, lie, steal, scold, or fight; / Cards, dice, kiss, clip, and so forth' – (Wickham, *Moral Interludes* 159) and in *King Johan*, where Sedicyon exhibits his collection of relics, 'giving a complete inventory of all sorts of repulsive and impossible objects' to sustain Protestant polemical propaganda (Cushman 87; Happé 369-70, lines 1215-1230).

The Vice's role often arouses laughter and his comic traits, too, have the power of seducing the audience, because he keeps the spectator involved in the play through an 'effervescent bubbling over of words' in the form of lists of place names and 'long catalogues of words' he loves to 'rattle off' (Nicoll 54). The Vice narrates his experiences as a traveller in a number of plays, such as *The World and the Child*, *Hickscorner*, *Like Will to Like*, and *All for Money* (Cushman 136). He is the one who seems to have greater power on the audience, as he uses the list of place names as an incantatory formula, which is conducive to the 'phonetic pleasure' of 'a pure sound', 'a complete sound' (345), as is the name Kinlochbervie.

In *The Last Judgement* from the Corpus Christi Cycle, Christ enumerates the corporal works of mercy (Bevington, *Medieval Drama* 637), while the devils have their register of sinful deeds (640) and Tutivillus his own list of fools and sinners (645, 650). In this catalogue Tutivillus also identifies himself with no restraints on language:

> My name is Tutivillus.
> My horne is blawen;
> Fragmina verborum, Tutivillus colligit horum,
> Belzabub algorum, Belial Belium doliorum (647).

His 'Latin gibberish', to the effect of: 'Tutivillus strings together the scraps of their words, Beelzebub of the cold regions, Belial of sorrows' (647), is an epitome of creativity and of the power Tutivillus has over language. The devil mockingly distorts the language of the Church, but also indulges in the pleasure he can get from such invention. In this way he is a destroyer and a creator of a new and mysterious, if not ritual, language.

Tutivillus, or Titivillus, is also a key character in the morality play *Mankind*. His task there is to lead Mankind astray, so that he is a prey of Sloth. The good and bad characters use the same language when addressing the audience: Mercy opens the play with a direct address to the audience ('ye sovereigns'), and Mischief uses his same words 'I beseech you' (Wickham, *Moral Interludes* 7, 8). Like Tutivillus, Mischief revolves in a verbal labyrinth in the guise of latinized words – 'Corn serveth breadibus, chaff, horsibus, straw firibusque' (8) – whose effect lies in the incantatory sound of alliteration and assonance. A list of parts of the body anticipates a long list of names and places uttered by the Vice New Guise, who mentions 'master Huntington of Sawston', 'William Thurlay of Hauxton', 'Pycharde of Trumpington' (21). Mischief's henchmen, the Vices New Guise, Now-a-day and Nought, who recite the singsong, appeal to the familiarity of the names to the audience in the area of Cambridge and Norfolk (Bevington, *Medieval*

Drama 921; Kahrl 118; Hattaway 20) and follow a consolidated tradition repeating the cliché of Vices reciting lists of place names.[3]

Likewise, in *The Castle of Perseverance* (1400-1475), the earliest and the most comprehensive morality play to survive, Mundus boasts his fame in a long alliterative recital of place names whose rhythm is given by accumulation. He is sitting on the same scaffold as Covetousness, so that his list resorts to figural allegory:

> Assarye, Acaye, and Almayne,
> Cavadoyse, Capadoyse, and Cananee,
> Babyloyne, Brabon, Burgoyne and Bretayne,
> Grece, Galys, and to the Grychysch See;
> I meve also Mesadoyne in mykyl mayne, Frauns, Flaundrys, and
> Freslonde, and also Normande,
> Pyncecras, Parys, and long Pygmayne,
> And every toun in Trage, evyn to the Drey Tre,
> Rodys and riche Rome.
> All those londys at myn a-wyse
> Arn castyn to my werdly wyse.
> My tresore, Syr Covetyse,
> Hath sesyd hem holy to me. (Happé 89-90)

'This alliterative list is a conventional boast' (Happé 621) and part of a personal myth, and it is worth noticing that the place names appear in roughly alphabetical order on the part of a character, who aims at disorder. Frank Hardy, too, exploits alliteration and assonance in his list of Welsh and Scottish villages, but no order seems to be present, which enhances the elusiveness of order and truth and the 'phonetic pleasure' *per se*. His breathless recital both aims at and eludes a public declaration of identity, as the reciter is made by the places he has visited. Frank's fragmented lists emphasize his vain effort to say who he is, while the Vice's uncontainable boastings repeatedly assert his identity by making reference to extensive journeys.

In John Heywood's interlude *The Play of the Weather* (1525-33), the Vice character, Merry-Report keeps in line with the tradition of the Vice as reciter of alliterative lists of place names, boasting the places he has visited and thus publicly declaring his kinship to the devil, who could not 'have gone halfe thus mych':

> I have ben from hevyn as farre as heve is hens.
> At Lorryn, at London, and in Lombardy,
> At Baldock, at Barfolde, and in Barbary,
> At Canterbury, at Coventré, at Colchester,
> At Wansworth and Welbeck, at Westchster,
> At Fullam, at Faleborne, and at Fenlow,
> At Tawton, at Tiptré, and at Totnan,
> At Glouce(s)ter, at Gilford, and at Gotham,
> At Hartforde, at Harwicke, at Harrow on the hill,
> At Sudbery, S(o)uthampton, at Shoters Hill,
> At Walsingham, at Wittam, and at Werwicke,
> At Boston, at Bristow, and at Berwicke,
> At Gravelyn, at Gravesend, and at Glastynbery,
> Ynge Gingiang Jayberd, the parishe of Butsbery –
> The devill himselfe, without more leasure,
> Could not have gone halfe thus mych, I am sure!
> (Bevington, *Medieval Drama* 998-99)

In the interlude *Hickscorner* the Vice bearing that name announces his arrival on stage as a ship's master – 'Alee the helm, alee! Veer! Shoot off! Veer sail! Vera!' (Lancashire 183). He recounts his experiences as a traveller to real and imagined lands, at times giving details about their location:

> Sir, I have been in many a country,
> As in France, Ireland, and in Spain,
> Portingale, Seville, also in Almain,
> Friesland, Flanders and in Bourgogne,
> Calabre, Pouille and Arragogne,
> Brittany, Biscay and also in Gascogne,
> Naples, Greece and in mids of Scotland,
> At Cape Saint Vincent and in the new found island.
> I have been in Gene and in Cowe,
> Also in the land of rumbelow,
> Three miles out of hell,
> At Rhodes, Constantine and in Babyland,
> In Cornwall and in Northumberland,
> Where men seethe rushes in gruel.
> Yea, sir, in Chaldee, Tartare and Inde,

And in the land of women, that few men doth find,
In all these countries have I be (Lancashire 184-87).

Hickscorner's list of place names is followed by the catalogue of ships he knows as a ship's master, in which names of ships are juxtaposed to the names of the harbours the ships come from:

First was the Regent with the Michael of Briskilsea,
The George with the Gabriel and the Anne of Foy,
The Star of Saltash with the Jesus of Plymouth,
Also the Hermitage with the Barbara of Dartmouth,
The Nicholas and the Mary Bellouse of Bristow
With the Ellen of London and James also (Lancashire 187-88).

These long conventional stretches fall into the same category as Frank Hardy's 'incantation'. The incantatory effect of the sound of place names is, however, overwhelming and may be the source for the faith healer's litany alongside the mythical native tradition of *dindshenchas* and *immram*.

Moreover, in *Faith Healer* the lists are not just occasional or incidental. The 'twists and turns of the four monologues, and their progress through the winding back roads of Wales and Scotland' (Roche 104) lead back home to Ireland and represent a paradigm of the play. Place names are the route of the play which winds in the same way, so as the voices recounting the story wind, twist, and turn in accordance with the wandering of their minds. Lists of place names are the equivalent to musical themes (Hughes 179), and an incantatory formula has the 'thematic spell of a *Leitmotif*' (White 12). The ritual incantation is thus at the centre of the play, as the tragic counterpart of comic listings on the part of the medieval Vice. *Faith Healer* is a sort of twentieth-century *Psychomachia*, or inner warfare, where Frank is not a bone of contention between the categories of good and evil, but a victim of his own torments and questionings, like the Vice, a destroyer going towards self-destruction, a creator in the use of what Grace cannot understand and tries to grasp resorting once again to the strategy of a list: 'this gift, this craft, this talent, this art, this magic' (349).

In *Translations*, while searching for a suitable English rendition for the crossroads known in Irish as Tobair Vree, Owen tells the story that lies behind that place name, the story of old Brian who was drowned in a well (420). Brian's story survives in a place name, the 'mythological geography' (MacCana 17) keeping alive his personal history. The faith healer's mythical geography is similarly kept alive by the 'mesmerism' and the 'incantation' that sustain the recounting of his wanderings, a personal history made of the accumulation of words. Nothing else exists.

Notes

[1] Lists of place names appear four times in Frank's first monologue and eight in Grace's, they disappear in Teddy's and come back again twice in a more contained and fragmented way in Frank's final monologue. They accompany the whole play as a subtext, representing set-pieces within the set-pieces. They highlight the journey of the travelling trio, framing and containing the development of action and narration. They are a précis of narrative, containing and codifying the story, anticipating the recitation of a story which is nothing but a list, at some stages lost in the disorder it tries in vain to overcome. Being self-contained, the list *is* in a way action itself: deed and word coincide.

[2] Her monologue is magnified by the obsessive repetition of conjunctions and pauses, semantic voids, and her discourse is an overflowing of the 'and and' pattern: 'And, as they say, I've got a lot to be thankful for ... And I like living in London. And the bedsitter's small but it's warm and comfortable ... And at night I listen to the radio or I read ... And on Thursday afternoons I go to the doctor to get my pills renewed' (341-42). This breathless *tour de force* is not episodic, as it is a variation of the pattern of listing. The frantic accumulation of 'and and' reminds the reader or listener of children's language habits, and it is revelatory both of the strenuous effort to control reality and of the limited capacity, or impossibility, to do so. The conjunction 'and' ceases to be a link as Grace stumbles on it as she stumbles in her repetition of 'or – or – ', leaving the sentence unfinished.

[3] The cliché is used also in John Bale's interlude *The Temptation of Our Lord* (1540), in which Satan shows Christ 'all the world's delight' using the technique of listing as a form of verbal seduction (Wickham, *Moral Interludes* 138).

Works Cited

Andrews, Elmer. *The Art of Brian Friel*. London: Macmillan, 1995.

Axton, Richard. 'Folk Play in Tudor Interlude'. *English Drama: Forms and Development*. Ed. Marie Axton and Raymond Williams. Cambridge: Cambridge UP, 1977. 1-23.

Bevington, David. *From 'Mankind' to Marlowe*. Cambridge: Harvard UP, 1962.

--- *Medieval Drama*. Boston: Houghton, 1975.

Cawley, A.C., Marion Jones, Peter F. McDonald, and David Mills. *Medieval Drama*. Vol. 1 of *The Revels History of Drama in English*. London: Methuen, 1983.

Chambers, E.K. *The Medieval Stage*. Vol. 2. Oxford: Oxford UP, 1903.

Cushmann, L.W. *The Devil and the Vice in the English Dramatic Literature before Shakespeare*. 1900. London: Cass, 1970.

Davison, Peter. *Popular Appeal in English Drama to 1850*. London: Macmillan, 1982.

Dillon, Myles. *Early Irish Literature*. Chicago: University of Chicago Press, 1948.

Friel, Brian. *The Diviner: The Best Stories of Brian Friel*. Introd. by Seamus Deane. Dublin: O'Brien, 1979.

--- *Brian Friel. Essays, Diaries, Interviews: 1964-1999*. Ed. Christopher Murray. London: Faber, 1999.

--- *The Gold in the Sea*. London: Gollancz, 1966.

--- *Selected Plays of Brian Friel. (Philadelphia, Here I Come!, The Freedom of the City, Living Quarters, Aristocrats, Faith Healer, Translations.)* London: Faber, 1984.

Grene, Nicholas. 'Friel and Transparency'. *Irish University Review* 29.1 (1999): 136-44.

Happé, Peter, ed. *Four Morality Plays*. Harmondsworth: Penguin, 1979.

Hattaway, Michael. *Elizabethan Popular Theatre: Plays in Performance*. London: Routledge, 1982.

Howard, Jean E. *The Stage and Social Struggle in Early Modern England*. London: Routledge, 1994.

Hughes, George. 'Ghosts and Ritual in Brian Friel's *Faith Healer*'. *Irish University Review* 24.2 (1994): 175-85.

Kahrl, Stanley J. *Traditions of Medieval English Drama*. London: Hutchinson, 1974.

Kelly, Colm. 'Homecomings and Diversions: Cultural Nationalism and the Recent Drama of Brian Friel'. *Studies* 76 (1987): 452-62.

Kerwin, William, ed. *Brian Friel. A Casebook*. New York: Garlan, 1997.

Kiberd, Declan. 'Brian Friel's *Faith Healer*'. *Irish Writers and Society at Large*. Ed. Masaru Sekine. Gerrards Cross: Smythe, 1985. 106-21.

--- *Inventing Ireland*. London: Cape, 1995.

Kilroy, Thomas. 'Theatrical Text and Literary Text'. *The Achievement of Brian Friel*. Ed. Alan Peacock. Gerrards Cross: Smythe, 1993. 91-102.

Knott, Eleanor, and Gerard Murphy. *Early Irish Literature*. London: Routledge, 1966.

Lancashire, Ian, ed. *Two Tudor Interludes*. 'The Interlude of Youth' and 'Hickscorner'. Manchester: Manchester UP, 1980.

MacCana, Proinsias. *Celtic Mythology*. London: Hamlyn, 1970.

Mahony, Christina. *Contemporary Irish Literature. Transforming Tradition*. London: Macmillan, 1998.

Margeson, J. M. R. *The Origins of English Tragedy*. Oxford: Clarendon, 1967.

Neuss, Paula. 'Active and Idle Language: Dramatic Images in *Mankind*'. *Medieval Drama*. Stratford-upon-Avon Studies 16. Ed. Neville Denny. London: Arnold, 1973. 41-67.

Nicoll, Allardyce. *British Drama*. London: Harrap, 1925.

Niel, Ruth. 'Non-Realistic Techniques in the Plays of Brian Friel: The Debt to International Drama'. In Zach and Kosok. 349-59.

O'Brien, George. *Brian Friel*. Dublin: Gill, 1989.

O'Rahilly, Cecile. 'Repetition; A Narrative Device in TBC'. *Ériu* 30 (1979): 66-74.

Pine, Richard. *Brian Friel and Ireland's Drama*. London: Routledge, 1990.

--- *The Diviner: The Art of Brian Friel*. Dublin: University College Dublin, 1999.

Robbins, Joan E. 'Conjuring the Life of the Spirit in the Plays of Brian Friel'. *Canadian Journal of Irish Studies* 18.2 (1992): 75-87.

Robinson, P. N. 'Brian Friel's *Faith Healer*: An Irishman Comes Back Home'. In Zach and Kosok. 223-27.

Roche, Anthony. *Contemporary Irish Drama*. Dublin: Gill, 1994.

Salgādo, Gāmini. *English Drama: A Critical Introduction*. London: Arnold, 1980.

Sanders, Norman, Richard Southern, T. W. Craick, and Lois Potter. *The Revels History of Drama in English*. Vol. 2: 1500–1576. London: Methuen, 1980.

Spivack, Bernard. *Shakespeare and the Allegory of Evil*. New York: Columbia UP, 1958.

--- 'The Vice as a Stage Metaphor'. *Medieval English Drama*. Ed. Peter Happé. London: Macmillan, 1984. 140-44.

Stokes, W., and E. Windisch. *Irische Texte*. Zweite Serie, 2. Heft. Leipzig: Hirzel, 1887.

Throne, Marilynn. 'Brian Friel's *Faith Healer*: Portrait of a Shaman'. *Journal of Irish Literature* 16.3 (1987): 18-24.

Tolkien, J.R.R. 'A Secret Vice'. *The Monsters and the Critics*. Ed. Christopher Tolkien. London: Allen, 1983. 198-223.

Tydeman, William. 'An Introduction to Medieval English Theatre'. *The Cambridge Companion to Medieval English Theatre*. Ed. Richard Beadle. Cambridge: Cambridge UP, 1994. 1-36.

Welch, Robert, ed. *The Oxford Companion to Irish Literature*. Oxford: Clarendon, 1996.

Wickham, Glynne. *The Medieval Theatre*. London: Weidenfeld, 1974.

--- ed. *English Moral Interludes*. London: Dent, 1976.

White, Harry. 'Brian Friel and the Condition of Music'. *Irish University Review* 29.1 (1999): 6-15.

Witoszek, Walentina, and Patrick F. Sheeran. 'Irish Culture: The Desire for Transcendence'. *Cultural Contexts and Literary Idioms in Contemporary Irish Literature*. Ed. Michael Kenneally. Gerrards Cross: Smythe, 1988. 73-78.

Zach, Wolfgang, and Heinz Kosok, eds. *Literary Interrelations: Ireland, England and the World*. Vol. 2. Tübingen: Narr, 1987.

9 | Telling Tales: Narratives of Politics and Sexuality in *The Gentle Island*

Michael Parker

> In a society like ours, the procedures of exclusion are well known. The most obvious and familiar is the prohibition. We know quite well that we do not have the right to say everything, that we cannot speak of just anything in any circumstances whatever. In the taboo on the object of speech, and the ritual of the circumstances of speech, and the privileged or exclusive right of the speaking subject, we have the play of three types of prohibition which intersect, reinforce or compensate for each other, forming a complex grid which changes constantly. I will merely note that at the present time the regions where the grid is tightest … are those of sexuality and politics; as if discourse, far from being that transparent or neutral element in which sexuality is disarmed and politics pacified, is in fact one of the places where sexuality and politics exercise in a privileged way some of their most formidable powers.
>
> Michel Foucault, *Untying the Text*

The nets and networks of meaning within *The Gentle Island*, Brian Friel's eighth stage play, take shape primarily from the intersections of politics and sexuality, which function as both signifieds and signifiers, interactive subjects and metaphors. Within its play of narratives are inscribed crucial issues of Irish culture, questions about language and authority, about sexuality and gender, about how different generations construct conflicting narratives in response to disorientations and discontinuities – issues that changes in the South and the collapse of the North had brought into even sharper focus. It is, perhaps, useful to recall the contexts of its composition and first performance in late November 1971, which was a period which witnessed a major deterioration in the social and political situation in Northern Ireland, a process that would accelerate in the wake of the introduction of Internment without trial.

From 1 January to 8 August 1971 34 people had been killed in the North; eleven British soldiers, four RUC men, and nineteen civilians. From 9 August (the date on which Internment came into effect) to the end of the year the figure was 139 dead; 32 British soldiers, seven RUC men, five UDR men and 95 civilians. Internment had turned a campaign of pin-pricks into an all out war (Farrell 287).

Yet rather than reflecting the steadily worsening British-Irish, and Nationalist-Unionist relationships in his work, at first sight Friel's play seems to be deliberately turning its gaze away, inward and westward. The central concern of *The Gentle Island* appears to be familial and sexual politics within a tiny, 'claustrophobic' (Friel, 'Self-Portrait' 20), exclusively Catholic community on Inishkeen off the coast of Donegal.[1] Its action is taken up with the tensions between a father, a daughter-in-law, and his two sons, exacerbated by the departure of the rest of the islanders, and the arrival of two outsiders, whose presence ignites the sexual, political tinder. In contrast to the minority population in the North in the early 1970s, 'remarkably united' (Farrell 330) by what they perceived as the twin threats of Loyalist and British violence,[2] the community Friel evokes is captured at the moment of its dissolution. Due largely to economic factors, their democratic vote to abandon the island represents a rejection of the myth of the rural Gaelic 'good life' successive Irish governments had fostered. According to the stage directions in the text, *The Gentle Island* is set in the present, yet the mass emigration with which it begins might have occurred at any date within the previous two centuries.[3]

To a superficial eye, the narratives, the situation and the location depicted in *The Gentle Island*, and, indeed in most of Friel's writing, might appear to be parochial, marginal, limiting, a wilful denial of those political realities facing the North. In fact, as I will demonstrate, Friel's plays are deeply engaged with issues, including political ones, affecting the whole of Ireland and far beyond in the late 1960s and early 1970s, a period which saw rapid cultural, economic and technological changes world-wide. Friel's artistic enterprise, like Patrick Kavanagh's and Seamus Heaney's, locates itself in the parish, not as a secure, unchanging centre, but as a valid and validating locus for exploring the prevailing, interconnected concerns of the time.

Friel's dramatic fictions certainly are political to the extent that they reflect how external public forces and pressures affect and afflict individuals, families and communities, but they do not come equipped with a set of ideological prescriptions which will heal the national wound. Like Seamus Heaney's *Wintering Out* (1972), *The Gentle Island* brings together many of the factors that have contributed to the Troubles, but does not seek to impose an analysis, or proffer a remedy, for 'dramatists have no solutions. Furthermore, it is not their function to give answers' (Friel, 'Theatre of Hope' 21).[4] In his various occasional writings, such as the *Extracts from a Sporadic Diary*, Friel has expressed similar anxieties to Heaney's over allowing political concerns to overshadow aesthetic and artistic ones. Yet, the pressure of public events at various moments during the past twenty-five years has often compelled him to address those very concerns, overtly in some plays, such as *The Freedom of the City* and *Translations*, and more obliquely in others, such as *The Gentle Island* and *Faith Healer*. Fintan O'Toole is surely right in drawing attention to 'the often anguished dignity of his work [that] comes from its demonstration of the fact that in a society where people are willing to kill for certainties and out of commitment, confusion, as Hugh puts it in *Translations*, "is not an ignoble condition"' ('Keeper of the Faith' 6).

Given political and cultural attitudes North and South of the border, not to mention the 'commercial theatrical set-up' in Ireland, Britain and America, the only way that the playwright felt he might be allowed in his plays to approach the critical, changing issues 'of his time' was by means of 'indirection', 'necessary caution', 'obligatory deviousness' ('Theatre of Hope' 19) – a canniness, like Shakespeare's, which deceives some audiences, readers and commentators, and perhaps sometimes even the writer himself, into underestimating the political import of his writing.

The Gentle Island, like *Faith Healer* (1979) and *Molly Sweeney* (1994), is very much a play of and about narratives, about who controls the narratives and about the responses they generate. Threaded into and between the relatively few key actions on stage – the islanders' exodus at the opening, the proposition scene, the dance at the end of Act 1, the card game at the start of Act 2, the indictment and the shooting scenes – are the drama's literally most telling points when characters disclose equally dubious versions of themselves and events to each other, and to themselves, deploying 'fiction as a strategy of psychological survival' (Kearney 130). Repeatedly characters use phrases which make reference to something called 'the truth' – 'that's the truth' (Shane, 32), 'the truth is' (Joe, 51), 'tell him the truth' (Sarah, 55), 'Is it the truth or is it a lie?' (Sarah, 69), 'Is it the truth?' (Manus, 70) – but the play seems to imply that there is no such thing; and there are only 'imaginings' (33) which they are prepared to pain, maim, and kill for.

That time is out of joint, that past, present and future are blurred and undetermined, are immediately established in the unsettling opening scenes, and by the set itself. Although outwardly Manus Sweeney's cottage, comprising of a kitchen flanked by a bedroom on each side, and 'curragh, fishing nets, lobster pots, farming equipment' (11) against the gable wall – seems to belong to an earlier period of continuities, the siting of the central patriarchal character, '*sitting in an airplane seat, his back to the audience, staring resolutely into the fire*' (11), suggests a figure suspended between two worlds and times; while the airplane seat implies a connection with this century of rapid movement and widening spaces – as well as an ironic intertextual nod to *Buile Suibhne* and the legend of King Sweeney[5] – his fixed inward-looking gaze on the hearth signifies an attempt to suppress the present, a denial of external realities.

Significantly the play opens with an act of narration, a sense of division. In contrast to his father's apparently unmoved, resolutely silent response to the disintegration of the island community, the audience witnesses son Joe's excitement and amusement at the sight of two young locals trying 'pulling and tearing at' the massive bulk of the aged Nora Dan on board one of the boats (12). By using Joe as the medium through which Nora Dan's resistance is viewed, Friel quickly sets in play the contrastive attitudes of younger and older generations towards exile, and the violence changes and perceived betrayals generate. Manus's refusal to budge appears to have fixed his sons' futures, restricting Joe to a passive role as a commentator on others' actions. From an early snatch of conversation between Joe and Tom, one of his contemporaries leaving for a 'better life', the audience learn that Joe's brother, Philly, missed the islanders' farewell fling because he was working at the salmon, which might indicate an obsessiveness about his work, and/or that, like his father, he finds it difficult to accommodate change. When set alongside the crude, boisterous Bosco's comment, 'It's a buck like me Sarah should have got. Jaysus, I'd never rise out of bed except to eat' (12), the suggestion that all might not be well in the Sarah-Philly marriage directs the audience/reader perhaps to re-interpret their first sighting of Sarah – conventionally, 'femininely', '*sewing at the kitchen table*' (11), yet glancing out of the window like some confined nineteenth-century heroine at an outer world of alternative possibilities.

Conflict across the generations and between the genders is endorsed with the arrival of the next two figures on stage, Con and his daughter, Anna – the second in a procession of four pairs of characters who make just one brief entry. Whereas Bosco relishes the sexual freedoms that he imagines exile will bring – 'Get the knickers off, all you Glasgow women! The Inishkeen stallions is coming!' (12) – the drunken Con, in a moment of lucidity, recognizes that all that he will gain in exchange for the ancestral home is '[o]ne bloody room in bloody Kilburn' (14). His parting question, 'Do you think was the Flight of the Earls anything like this?' (14) and parting song should perhaps be read as sardonic comments not only on the unheroic Irish present, but also on the unreliability of mythic representations of the Irish past. From Anna's curt responses to Joe it is evident that an unsatisfying relationship existed between them, a situation, one learns subsequently, that parallels his brother and sister-in-law's emotionally and physically barren marriage. Sensing that he has 'missed the boat' with her, as well as with his friends, a growing desperation enters into Joe's promises and pleas for some kind of link beyond exile, clearly marked by his repetitions and clinging to the future tense. By contrast her last words to him already place her and her presence on the island in the past:

> **Joe:**   Anna, I'll write to you, Anna.
> **Anna:**   You hadn't much to say to me when I was here.
> (*She goes off down left*) (13-14).

This latest communication failure, which has the effect of intensifying Joe's acute sense of isolation and linguistic inadequacy, since he has admitted to being illiterate or, at best, semiliterate,[6] is followed by a shocking, ferocious outburst, which again calls into question the island's epithet. Following on from the 'biting and spitting and butting' (12) accompanying Nora Dan's departure, Mary's (Sarah's mother's) request to 'put a shot' (15) in her dog, and the account of the farewell party at which two cats were tied together and scalded, Joe's misdirected rage anticipates subsequent acts of sadistic cruelty: 'Did you see Con . . .? Full as a bloody skin, the bastard. Jaysus, he hasn't sobered for nine days, that fella. Wants his head kicked in. That's what he wants. His bloody head kicked in' (14).

Much of the rest of Act 1, Scene 1, and indeed much of the rest of the text, is taken up by different, contradictory 'readings' of the island, which, like Ireland, is imagined as a place of plenty, as a prison, as a paradise and spiritual haven, as a site of violence where emotional growth is stunted and sexuality repressed. The very name of the island is problematic and proves deeply ironic; embedded, embodied within its two elements is, one might suggest, a history of linguistic, cultural and political

violence. Inishkeen⁷ is an anglicization of the Gaelic *Inis*
('island', a *feminine* noun) and *caoin* ('beautiful', 'pleasant',
'gentle'), though this latter element once anglicized has
associations with sharpness, bitterness, loss, and grief.⁸

The character who decodes the island's name for the
visitors from the mainland – and, of course, for the audience/-
readers – is pivotal in the rest of the play's translations. As un-
knowable and unreadable as, for example, Anne Devlin's
Finnula in 'Naming the Names' (*The Way-Paver*), Sarah
functions as a disturbing text, a richly ambiguous presence
within the *The Gentle Island*'s metanarratives and charac-
terization.⁹

For the childless, now parentless and, in her eyes, virtually
husbandless Sarah, Inishkeen is a 'nothing' (28), a place of
constraint and constraining expectations, the mocking antithesis
of the beautiful island of her memory, the Isle of Man.¹⁰ That
equally significantly named island has acquired a mythic status
in her selective recollections, which have edited out the
drudgery of her time at the *Arcadia* Hotel (emphasis added),
working 'from seven in the morning till ten at night' (28-29),
and foregrounded the 'forbidden' experiences, its comradely
danger, its social and sexual excitement: 'And every night when
the housekeeper went to bed, we slipped down the fire-escape
and went to a dance … In the eight weeks I was in Douglas I
was at fifty-one dances. I wore out three pair of shoes. I never
had a time like it' (29).

When she first encounters Shane, even though his only
words in front of her have been asides to Peter, Sarah immediately sets about 'reading' him, connecting him with that lost
other world of effervacious, desirable young men when she says
of Man, 'You would like it … He would have crack' (29). The
animation Sarah shows in these early exchanges with the
outsiders, and her eagerness to initiate narration and share
'memories', are in marked contrast to the dialogue that occurred
between her and her husband a few pages earlier. These are
characterized initially by a series of peremptory, mechanical
questions concerning Philly's welfare and his catch, and
contains a pointed reference to his father as the one person he

is able to satisfy. However, when the marital conversation moves on to the islanders' departure, her mother's parting present, a cradle (23), and her own father's pathetic actions, Sarah's sentences lengthen frenetically, until finally her narrative drives her back to what she perceives as the major sources of her past, present, and future unhappiness, her desperate sense of isolation and, above all, her 'failure' as a woman in the eyes of her mother, Philly's father, their culture – all of whom long for her confinement, 'and she says they'll be back next summer for two full months or sooner she says any time at all she's needed she says' (23). Close to tears, but uncomforted by Philly, who *'watches her closely but makes no move towards her'* (24), apparently unmoved by her distress, she regains control and changes tack, speaking *'almost formally, choosing her words with care'* (24). Having got nowhere with the coded reminder of his failure to fulfil his conjugal duties, she tries safer ground by repeatedly appealing to his sense of comradeship as a member of the same generation and by stressing the potential dangers of her loneliness: 'I want to go with them; not with my father and mother, but with all of them and you, all of us together. I'll go out of my head with loneliness, I know I will ... We belong with the others. We should be with them ... They're too old to change. But we're not' (24).

Her acute frustration with Philly's conservatism, materialism, and imperviousness to her every word/desire is evident in the last of her exchanges with him before the arrival of Shane and Peter, and perhaps helps to 'explain' her later actions:

> **Sarah:** Maybe if you spent less time on it [fishing] we might be better off.
> **Philly:** Farming? Here?
> **Sarah:** You and me.
> (*Pause*)
> **Philly:** I'm tired.
> **Sarah:** You're always tired when you're at home.
> **Philly:** I was up all night, woman. When you and the rest of them were away drinking and dancing I was working.
> **Sarah:** So you were (25).

Sarah's contemptuous attitude towards Inishkeen, like her subsequent sexual advances towards Shane, is, therefore, very much bound up with her hostility towards Manus and what she views as the pernicious authority he exerts over her husband. She pictures her own narrative of neglect as a consequence of, and indeed repetition of that meted out by Manus on his wife, Rosie Dubh, his Dark Rosaleen[11] – an abuse leading to madness. Philly's sexual indifference and impotence are, according to her interpretation of psychological 'truth', the direct product of Manus's promiscuity and its aftermath, marital negligence, moral dereliction: 'Joe doesn't know the truth. But Philly does. And he'll never forgive you for it. And if he can't father a family, you're the cause of it' (57). Whether one accepts the authenticity of her later devastating 'disclosure' in Act 2,[12] – or believe, as Joe would like to, that she 'could have made a mistake' (63), or regard her accounts as the fabrications of a vicious/unhappy woman, her actions and words prior to the two indictment scenes suggest that she has had enough of being authored by others and that she is determined to impose her own narrative on events.

Even before the strangers' arrival, it is apparent from Manus's speeches that his faith in the island along with his sway over his sons, have been seriously undermined by their neighbours' departure. His first words display an anxiety about the home ground and its ability to sustain life (18-19), but with the return of Philly, the beloved son (*filius*) in whom he is well pleased, these fears at first seem dispelled. His eldest's account of one splendid night's fishing sees the island transmuted into a place of confirmation and benison, as rich as the waters of Galilee, 'They were that thick in the water you could have walked on them' (20). For Manus, as for 'Bull' McCabe in John B. Keane's *The Field* or Michael Moran in John McGahern's *Amongst Women* and scores of past generations of Irish men, the land is held in a sacred trust. The hallowed bond between a father, son, and the ancestral soil of far more significance than marriage, women, or the lives of strangers.

For his two sons, however, the island – like the Irish state? – no longer functions as a secure ground, stable centre or transcendental signified, exerting an unquestioning faith and loyalty. Like the divided Gar in *Philadelphia, Here I Come!*, who is also struggling to achieve a measure of individuation, Joe and Philly fluctuate between a scepticism about and deep attachment to 'home'. (An emblem of Joe's weakness and splintered state is the broken spade he carries.) Despite envy of those who have left – 'Whatever wind there is is with them' (17) – contempt for a life spent tending 'bloody cattle' and 'scrabbling a mouthful of spuds from the sand' (18), and angry scorn for Manus whom he names the 'King of nothing' (18), Joe abides until his father's spell is finally broken at the play's end. After his one and only overt confrontation with paternal authority, when ironically he accuses Manus of cowardice – 'You – you – you haven't even the guts to bid them goodbye' (18) – he almost bursts into tears when he is given leave to leave, according to Sarah's reading.[13] Part of him badly wants to trust in his father's words, and though one minute in an ensuing exchange on stage with Philly, he dismisses Manus as 'the aul bastard' (21), the next he is faithfully recycling for his brother's benefit their daddy's comic and maudlin tales, his views on the exiles' future, and the terms of his will.

A gap in the text of both brothers' lives remains the absence of their mother, an absence which clearly strengthened their father's psychological grip on them. (In this respect their situation is analogous to Shane's.) In their only scene alone together, Philly shows some curiosity about what the 'Mouth' (21) had to say about her, only to be disappointed by another of Manus's blatant fabrications, this time on the somewhat touchy theme of marital togetherness:

> **Philly:** What did he say about mother?
> **Joe:** She had long fair hair. I never knew that, Philly, did you?
> … And his job was to plait it every night before she went to
> bed. And you should have seen his face when he was telling me.
> **Philly:** With one hand?
> **Joe:** One hand what?
> **Philly:** How did he plait it with one hand? (21)

Although it is Philly who presents himself as the more detached of the two, claiming to view the island merely as a convenient economic resource, it is Joe who eventually makes his escape. Under threat from Sarah in their first conversation, Philly strikes a utilitarian note – 'Stick it out until the end of the summer. I'll have made the most of £200 then. Then we'll pack up and off and bugger the lot … Any hard cash that comes into this house comes from the sea … And as long as I make money from it I'll fish it' (24) – yet one suspects that these assertions and the promise of future release they contain may be simply a device resorted to when he seeks to deflect attention, hers and his, from the emotional and sexual pressures she exerts, and the absence that lies at his core.

With the introduction onto the island stage of the outsiders, Shane and Peter, the highly 'schematic' nature of the play becomes increasingly apparent.[14] While at the outset the islanders seize upon the pair for the relief and diversion they might bring, their effect is to accelerate the processes of disintegration and change; Shane's 'presence', and Sarah's overt and Philly's ambiguous sexual reactions to it, will further destabilize an already fraught domestic 'political' scene.

Ironically, though their departure from Inishkeen sees the bonds of mutual dependency horribly strengthened, in our first encounter with Peter and Shane there is a strong suggestion that a parting is coming. They are dressed similarly '*in summer slacks and open shirts*' (25) and wrongly identified as 'Yanks' by Sarah, yet the marked differences in their ages, personalities, perspectives and languages are quickly established.[15] Whereas the '*plump, balding, middle-aged*' Peter puffs onto the stage, Shane, '*twenty years younger*' (25), enters calmly peeling an orange, a symbolic fruit of youth. Initially, and repeatedly as he becomes further enmeshed in his own myth-making, Peter reads the island awry, envisioning it in terms that anticipate Lieutenant Yolland's idealization of Ballybeg in *Translations*, as 'heavenly', 'heaven' (25), 'lovely', 'beautiful' (28), a place of 'sheer delight' (40), where there is 'calm', 'stability', 'self-possession. Everything has its own good pace', 'everything's so … constant … part of a permanence' (54). Significantly, and perhaps ironically considering his job as the music teacher, Peter cherishes most of all Inishkeen's exterior, visual qualities, its illusory 'clarity', and its absence of sound, picturing it as a summer and winter retreat where his relationship with Shane can achieve reaffirmation, away from suspicious and condemnatory voices.[16] Shane's reactions to the island, however, prove to be astute. Though at first his frenetic clowning seems a strategy to undercut his partner's narrative – Shane is resisting the Romance genre, by situating himself in Western territory – his dubbing of Inishkeen as 'Apache' (25), alien territory, as 'Sinister', 'Too quiet' (26), also serves to underscore the audience's awareness of its violent undertext. His playful glossing of its name as 'scalping island' (26) turns out to be both accurate and prophetic.[17] Many of the subsequent analyses and intertextual references he makes similarly show his gift for reading the signs, though like any other reader he can seriously misinterpret and undervalue some texts. By means of the allusions Shane makes to Nazi Germany and to the Pied Piper legend, for example, Friel may be suggesting that post-independence Ireland – and, equally, the patriarchal, Protestant-run northern state – had in fact translated itself into a 'country for old men' (Yeats 217), which sought through its institutions to exercise an almost totalitarian control over the young, depriving them of choice and speech, or driving them into exile: 'They reach the mountain. A door opens. They all march through. Disappear. Door shuts. Then silence. Not a sound. Just like here' (27).

Through Shane, the playwright decodes Manus's construction of the island text, recognizing how its defining values, 'confining prejudices' and 'saleable images' (Heaney, 'Synge-Song' 55) are rooted in an earlier phase of Irish cultural development, the 30s, 40s, 50s and early 60s. These decades, Friel's formative years, saw the heyday of De Valera's Ireland, at the centre of whose vision was 'the small independent farmer, who had his land, who had his house, who had his family', 'a family society with every family having sufficient for its needs and not dependent on anybody else' (Joseph Lee in O'Toole, 'Dancing'). Essentially Manus subscribes to Dev's dream of a future island/Ireland:

self-supporting and self-reliant; a land whose countryside would be bright with cosy homesteads, whose fields and villages would be joyous with the sounds of industry, with the romping of sturdy children and the laughter of happy maidens; whose firesides would be forms for the wisdom of serene old age (Eamon de Valera, 1933 qtd. in O'Toole, 'Dancing').

a cosy, rosy *Tir-na-Óg*, from which no-one would dream of emigrating. Shane's analysis has much in common with Seán O'Faoláin's critique of 'Silent Ireland' in *The Bell*:

> The old patriarchal, rural Ireland is slowly beginning to disintegrate. And it is disintegrating just at the moment when the classes who, as I have said, normally provide the intellect … can do nothing than wail for the past … dig their heads in the sand and try by repression to hold back the tide … If there once was an old association of the Peasant with Liberty it is all over. The romantic illusion, fostered by the Celtic Twilight, that the West of Ireland … is for some reason more Irish than Guinness' Brewery or Dwyer's Sunbeam-Wolsey factory, has no longer any basis whatsoever (qtd. in Brown 200).[18]

Though scathing in his denunciation of the Synge-song, rugged, close-to-nature, *Man of Aran*[19] stuff served up to them, and merciless in his parodying of Manus's crude and dated stage Oirish *persona*

> (*He slips his left arm out of his sleeve and tucks it into his belt.*) Be Jaysus, Shane boy, you're a quare comedian. You should be on the stage. Like me. Look at the act I have – the simple, upright, hardworking island peasant holding on manfully to the *real* values in life, sustained by a thousand-year-old culture, preserving for my people a really worthwhile inheritance (40)

at the same time Shane recognizes the incipient threat posed by him should his tenuous faith in the 'Gaelic way' be disturbed. Unlike Peter, he detects an ideological subtext to Manus's hospitality, and perhaps how, like himself, he is a man rapt in a role. When Peter asserts that their host 'genuinely wants us back', Shane replies 'Of course he does. Because we give support to his illusion that the place isn't a cemetery. But it is. And he knows it. The place and his way of life and everything he believes in and all he touches – dead, finished, spent. And when he finally faces that, he's liable to become dangerous' (41).[20]

His trenchant attack is consistent with his initial uneasy response to the island, but needs to be seen also within its dramatic contexts. It follows hard on the heels of Sarah's sexual invitation, 'Will you lie with me?' (39), and Peter's proposition that they return at Christmas, the one disrupting the relaxed, settled rhythm he appears to have settled into, the other a plea for a continuation of their chafing relationship. As the exchange between the two Dubliners develops, Shane's anger switches from their island host to its real object, Peter and himself, the sham and shame of their acts. Earlier in the same scene (Act 1, Scene 2), in his fateful confidences with Sarah, Shane had confessed to his frustration at what appeared to be turning into a life sentence, screwed by a 'spook called Obligation, *sired by* Duty out of Liability' (37, emphasis added). The autobiographical, and, therefore, suspect sketch he presents to Sarah places him as one of ten orphans sent to Peter's school, but one in whom Peter had taken a special 'interest' (36). Although at first sight his grammar seems 'innocent' and many of his verb choices purely descriptive – 'bought me', 'kept me', 'released me', 'got me', 'sent me' (36) – in fact, like that word 'interest', they express Shane's sense of himself as victim, as a subject being turned object.[21] Whether Peter really supplied him with fur-lined boots and leather helmets, or whether they are metaphors coined for the occasion, they form part of a pattern Shane is constructing to legitimize his escape from what he now views as Peter's obsessive, possessive, over-protective, over-directive, more-than-paternal care. The psychological strategy he had developed to mask his anxieties about himself, his 'uncertain' origins (42),[22] and, almost certainly, his sexual orientation, which manifests itself in a constant need to 'perform', to lay claim to other voices – and which prompted him to submit himself to Peter's custody – has now lost its value and validity. (He has reached a point where he is tired of putting on an antic disposition, playing Hamlet to Peter's leaden Polonius.) When Peter tries reassuring him, 'They all like you', his answer is significant, 'Which of me?' (41). This self-reflexive question heralds a brief, but crucial moment in the dialogue, in which Shane's speech ceases to be a 'tissue of quotations', to use Roland Barthes' phrase; it also marks a hinge-point in the plot. The combined effect of Sarah's advances and Peter's pleading drives him away from the house into alternative male company (Philly's), creating a 'separation' as momentous in its way as that effected by Iago between Othello and Cassio, Othello and Desdemona.[23] Resentment at his past dependency, at having played out the role of dutiful follower, mingles with a growing distaste for Peter, his age, his body, his language, his façade, his moral dubiousness.

Encoded within Peter's praise of Manus's consistent kindness (41) is a commendation of his own, under which lies, Shane now feels, a crass manipulativeness, crude materialism. His resistance surfaces in a series of acerbic, economic metaphors, references to Peter possessing 'the gauche subtlety of an insurance man', 'our lease', 'the ledgers', 'obligations … fully satisfied' (41-42). These finally tell on Peter, forcing him to adopt a similar *lexis*, and to admit this sullied aspect of their relationship, 'an understanding' contracted between unequal partners, a matter of capital, emotional and financial. Despite his denial that his interest is a material one, his diction clearly fixes Shane as a pensionable asset, 'I've got to a stage when I need *a – a – modest permanence*', 'I've never asked you for *a commitment*, have I? Just a *reasonable expectation*', 'You *owe* it to me, Shane', 'Love, Shane, love, love – all I have is *invested* in you – everything – for the best years of my life. There must be some *return*. It's not extravagant to expect *something*' (42, emphasis added). Outed unwillingly, his need exposed, Peter veers from temper to repentance, first making a humiliating allusion to Shane's illegitimacy, then abjectly apologizing for it: 'Shane, I'm sorry – my God I'm sorry – I'm sorry, Shane – I didn't mean a word of it – I'm tired – I'm jittery – I'm jealous of Sarah, of Philly, of everyone – forgive me, Shane, please forgive me' (42-43). That Peter might be conceivably jealous of Sarah can be explained from the fact that she has spent so much more of the day with Shane while he has been mending the radio and the gramophone. His jealousy of Philly at this stage, however, is harder to fathom, unless he means he is jealous of his youth, or of his future ownership of the island.[24]

Ironically, in the bizarre, violent scene that ensues, Philly's interest in Shane clearly awakened, and by its close Peter is given cause to feel displaced. The hurt Shane feels is stressed in his reverting to the manic, attention-seeking behaviour we witnessed earlier. According to Friel's stage directions, '*SHANE dashes into the kitchen. Searches feverishly … for a record … He speaks at an almost hysterical speed and pitch*' (42). His speeches contain three pointed, class-conscious references to 'Sir Peter' (43-44). Mockingly he throws back at Peter his own superlatives, 'it reminds me of a *memorable* holiday I once had on a *heavenly* island one *divine* summer' (emphasis added), and takes another swipe at the phoney Gaelicism of the Sweeneys.[25] He also makes what could be taken as a significant sexual reference to 'the barren island' (43), which may suggest an awareness that Sarah had not only sex, but conception in mind.

The scene which witnesses the restoration of music, dancing, and clapping to the island, brought about by Shane the engineer's skill, culminates in deeper discord.[26] Essentially Shane's song-and-dance is a sexual display, and read as such by Sarah and Philly. Peter rightly interprets it as a piece of wounded defiance. The very qualities that Sarah found appealing in Shane – his charm, wit, energy, dexterity, his apparent 'openness', vulnerability, parentlessness, unattachedness, which excited her desire and sympathy, quickened her acute sense of absence, and encouraged her to recognize affinities between her plight and his – now in the wake of his rejection of her render him repellent.[27] Previously she had spoken in praise of music and dancing on the Isle of Man, and laughed at Shane's black slave *persona*. Now his choice of a plantation/minstrel song, 'Oh, Susanna', with its reference to an abandoned, tearful, black woman, whose fate and name almost rhyme with her own, and his attempted cavorting with her, she reads as a further humiliation, a mocking response to her offer of herself.

Friel deploys symbolic action to convey the accelerating deterioration of relationships on the island – from frustration and paralysis through to violence. Shane's dance and fall, like the articulate blows that fell him, speak and enact a move away from language and dialogue. Initially, especially for an audience, it is difficult to comprehend the causes of Philly's manic, sadistic glee. Almost certainly it is bound up with the often un-verbalized contest between Sarah and himself. It could be that he feels his wife's dignity has been affronted by Shane's pre-sumptuous gesture, that he is simply defending his 'possession', but equally it is possible that his actions originate in a more complex, contradictory set of motives and emotions. His repeated punches may be simultaneously an expression of an unconscious hostility/subconscious sexual attraction towards Shane, a kind of initiation rite, a warning to Sarah, a further illustration of the endemic brutality on 'scalping island' (26). Significantly, once assured that 'aul Sean' (46), as Joe has rechristened him,[28] is 'unhurt' (46), and that he can accept punishment *like a man*, he invites him for a 'run' (46) on his boat to 'show you the caves' (46), dismissing Peter's prior claim and his excessive response to what after all was merely boyish horseplay.[29] His hostile, derisive attitude towards Peter may be partly because he looks upon him as another pitiable, yet empowered father-figure, but also because he is so obviously a 'townie', and thus lacking the genuine *male*, physical attributes. From Joe's comments it emerges that earlier in the day Philly had been amusing himself sadistically at Peter's expense, while he was attempting to keep up with him at the turf. ('You're a bugger, too', exclaims Joe [47].)

The act ends, as it began, with more uncertainties over identity. When yelping breaks out, initially it is unclear whether the source is Shane or Sarah's maimed dog, an ominous blur-ring.[30] By imitating the dog, Shane colludes with the cruelty, *machismo* and deceptions on the island; by failing to enlist his better judgement, to act on his intuitions, 'Single yelp shatters fragile peace. Acute unease on paradise island. War thought imminent. All men over seventeen report for military service' (50), he connives unwittingly in his own diminution to the status of casualty.

The opening of Act 2 initially dwells on the two patriarchs' attempts to reconstruct their pasts for external consumption,

appearing to offer each other their 'innocent outspread hands'
(Friel, 'Self-Portrait' 22).[31] For a while the threat of physical
violence is suspended, in favour of the ritualized combat of the
card game, which in its turn gives way to a genial swapping of
narratives, until Sarah takes a hand. The contest pitches the
older against the younger generation, and, anticipating the play's
outcome shows the senior partners, Manus and Peter, finding it
difficult to submit to defeat gracefully; if they lose, it must be
because their opponents are playing with marked cards. (It is
Manus who gives this reason for their defeat. Peter, always
quick to ingratiate himself, is swift in endorsing his host's
words. Ironically in the larger contest of the play, it seems that
it is the old who have marked the cards of the young.) During
the game of *solo* – another apt choice on Friel's part – Sarah has
to be advised as to which card to play, the Jack.[32] Any illusion of
domestic integration around the hearth is undermined by
Manus's churlishness, Joe's boyish triumphalism, and, more
importantly, Sarah's distractedness and Peter's anxiety over the
absent pair. Further evidence of Philly's reluctance to return
home (and indifference to his wife and her needs) comes from
Joe's unreassuring comments to Peter that '[h]e'll probably
leave Sean off at the far slip and head out again by himself.
He'll hardly come up here' (53), and prompt a second,
melancholic allusion to the Monks' tale, that narrative of
thwarted sexual longing, which reaffirms the petrifying
authority of the old over the young.

> **Peter:** I imagine, if you could see them, they're trying to escape
> now.
> **Manus:** Who?
> **Peter:** The monks and the girl.
> **Manus:** Them. Hah! They're wasting their time. They'll make
> nothing of it (54).

Peter's recalling of the legend from the first day of his stay,
like his subsequent eulogy to the island, indicate how far he has
been drawn into its fictions. Unsatisfied, if not unsatisfiable, the
two older men voice their envy of each other's imagined
security, and then slip into heavily edited confidences, whose

primary purpose is to elicit sympathy rather than elucidate the past. However, whereas Peter is able to maintain control of his narration, and draw back under Sarah's close questioning of gaps in his text,[33] Manus is more exposed. Quietly observing the increasing warmth her father-in-law shows to Peter, symbolized in his gift of the clock and the gift of his narrative, Sarah intervenes to debunk his account of how he lost his arm in the copper mines of Montana. Denied the consummation and closure (pregnancy) she had wished for, she determines to shape his ending; her aim in seizing the role of principal narrator of *his* story is to dig beneath his self-belief, to deflate Peter's vision of him, to confront him with absence, with what should be spoken. Although prepared to tolerate his projection of himself as Inishkeen's answer to Tiger King,[34] she cannot stomach his presenting of *him*self as a martyr. In Sarah's eyes and in her account, it is always, as in Hardy's *Tess*, the woman who pays; for her, the principal victim in the Sweeney history and household was 'a gentle young girl called Rosie Dubh' (56). In place of the anticipated cowboy adventure Manus would have served up, Sarah provides a change of genre.

What begins lyrically, with many of the linguistic features of a fairy tale ends a grotesque, grim parody of one. The innocent young heroine is first glimpsed trapped between two wicked uncles, 'that *never* spoke and *never* washed and *never* lit a fire' (56, emphasis added), caught in iterated negation. Like the nun in the Monk's tale, she is an object contested by two men; like so many Irish women she is divided, 'starved and repressed' (Longley 173) by domestic and religious patriarchies. Instead of a hero appearing to rescue Rosie from the two ugly (animal-like, non-articulating) brothers, a different kind of beast arrives on the scene, a 'buck', 'a smart buck', 'smelling about the back of the hill' (56), a beast on heat. Sarah's choice of signifiers collectively stresses a predatory sexuality, which, she implies, disgusts her, and emphasizes Manus's attractive outward appearance, his intelligence, his knowledge of a wider world, America, where smart bucks can make a smart buck. The irony, of course, is that the characteristics she singles out apply equally to Shane *as she conceived him earlier*. Unlike Shane, however,

Manus used his ability 'with the tongue' to get 'Rosie Dubh pregnant' (56).[35]

While in Sarah's version of what happened next, Manus simply abandoned his victim, in his version he indeed went to London, but returned twelve months later with 'the wedding ring in my pocket' to marry her (57). Rather than suffering the loss of his arm when a mine-face collapsed, as he first claimed (56), both subsequent accounts have him mutilated by Rosie's uncles and their herring knives. For Sarah, in her self-appointed role as Justicer and Truth-Teller, it is a justifiable punishment for taking advantage of a girl's honour, for an abuse of hospitality. For Manus, the brothers' attack on him was unmerited and cowardly, and 'truth', like fiction, a complex question of angles and audiences: 'There's ways and ways of telling every story. Every story has seven faces. And there's things shouldn't be said before a stranger' (57).

Unfortunately in *The Gentle Island* the seventh face is missing; the dead Rosie Dubh, along with the dead in *The Freedom of the City*, and so many of the dead of the Troubles, suffer violence a second time when their narratives are misappropriated to service 'the needs and the demands and the expectations' of the living (Friel, *Making History* 16), to yield more dead. What is not in dispute in Friel's play, or in recent Northern history for that matter, is the outcome – loss. Manus does not challenge Sarah's bare description of his wife's disappearance, 'a month after her second son was born she went out for a walk along the cliffs on the east side and was never seen since' (57). As Hugh points out in *Translations*, however, 'it is not the literal past, the "facts" of history that shape us, but images of the past embodied in language' (Friel, *Selected Plays* 445). In Sarah's 'imaging' and imagining of the past, the evidence for Manus's responsibility for the suicide of his wife is incontrovertible. What is more, for her his criminal neglect *provides the explanation for* her husband's sexual in-difference, the fruitlessness of her own marriage. These 'facts' are clearly at the forefront of her mind as she leaves for the slip to see Philly and Shane.

In the fragmented, 'authorized' history of his marriage Manus recounts to Peter after Sarah's departure, he attempts to absolve himself from some measure of the guilt. In one sentence he mentions the whores in the camp in Montana, then backs away from that topic which might confirm Sarah's picture of him as a womanizer. Part of the attraction of Rosie Dubh, one surmises, was not so much sexual, as a matter of power and class; he enjoyed her awe of him, her submissiveness, her innocence. Poignantly, pathetically, he delights in the memory of her calling him *Mister* Manus. The fact that he makes no reference as to having contacted her or her uncles to announce his 'honourable intentions' prior to his return to Inishkeen throws some doubt on his claims, but at least he does recognize a connection between his reappearance and her death when he avers, 'It might have been better to leave her be' (57). In his interpretation of the text, his missing arm, rather than functioning as an apt metonym for his absence or reminder of his betrayal, is proffered as a *cause* for the failure of their relationship and her later suicide. 'It made her uneasy with me' (58), Manus confides. (However, it must have been only an occasional uneasiness, since she conceived a second child.) Manus tries to impose a satisfactory closure on this painful scene of disclosures by asserting the one thing he is, or rather would like to be sure of, that Philly 'holds nothing against me' (58). He designates his account as 'the whole story' (58), but if every story indeed has seven faces, how can there be a 'whole story'?

That Manus has been profoundly destabilized by Sarah's assault becomes clear when he desperately urges Joe to marry because of his intensifying anxiety over the succession. The tenuousness of the island's economy, its uncertain fertility is confirmed in a tiny snatch of highly gendered dialogue in which Joe complains 'you'd get more milk from a billy-goat than that aul heifer' (58). His companions' departure has clearly loosened the 'grip of irregular fields' on Joe, and, like Patrick Kavanagh's *persona* Maguire, he is no longer convinced of the wisdom of making the 'field his bride' (Kavanagh 35). However, despite all his scepticism about the quality and viability of life on the island, he again succumbs quickly to the force of his father's will, which would marry him to it forever. If accepted, *his father's* proposal to Anna, might have secured Joe on Inishkeen and maintained the Sweeney line. However, hardly has the glue had time to dry on the envelope, before Sarah re-enters bearing a text that trumps theirs, to return to the card metaphors from earlier.

Whether from righteous anger or cynical calculation, Sarah proves herself again an adept at story-telling and narrative craft. Instead of informing Manus immediately what she has allegedly seen in the boathouse, she maximizes his discomfiture, prolongs the suspense by inviting him to witness something that begins as 'your son' (61), but then gets translated and lost in a mocking succession of metaphors — 'bull', 'sire', 'prince', 'hero', 'apple', 'barren', 'womb', 'crop', 'seed', 'waste', 'sterile', 'king' (61) — and rhetorical questions. Even when she finally abandons these devices, and approaches in a series of sub-ordinate clauses the critical 'fact' in what she has 'witnessed', she shows a reluctance at naming the appalling deed.

No longer silently working at her sewing and furtively looking up towards the window, as she was at its outset, in *The Gentle Island*'s penultimate scene Sarah stands assertively in its frame, empowered with and by the authority of narration. That fundamental changes and reversals in the politics of the family have occurred is further indicated by the placing of the two other characters. An ironic repetition from the play's opening sets '*MANUS* ... *in the airplane seat, facing upstage*' (62), but even this physical metaphor, like all metaphors, offers only an illusion of similarity. Manus is once more at a loss, but the loss is of a different order and initially seems to have blasted his faith and his hope. Whereas Act 1, Scene 1 had seen the play springing into 'action' with Joe's rushed and impassioned entry, the later scene situates him inside the house, '*his head in his hands*', '*sitting at the kitchen table*' (62) which had previously been Sarah's place.

Again, Friel employs the present tense, heightens dramatic tension, though this time it is in anticipation of an arrival. Sarah's narrative stresses the provocative ease with which Shane progresses towards his *peripeteia* and the family home he has (supposedly) violated. Such is her assuredness that neither the father nor the son rises to verify its accuracy. From her description, Shane appears simultaneously as the man she wanted him to be – 'He's coming. He's alone. He has his jacket across his shoulder and his shoes in his left hand … He's stooping down. He's picking up something. A stone. He's skimming it across the water' (62)[36] – and the man she wants them to believe him to be, smugly indifferent to their hurt. Her confidence in her ability as a 'reader' of others can be seen when she assumes that she is privy to his thoughts, 'He's saying to himself, "My God, it's heavenly"' (62), yet, as the audience are aware, such an exclamation is much more typical of Peter.[37] Joe's appeal to Manus is unable to compete with the rhetoric of revenge.[38] Skilfully manipulating her father-in-law by appealing to his belief in the interconnectedness of narratives and narrative continuities, through her question '[w]hat about the herring knives, Manus?' (62), she relates the present 'crime' against him to his past experience of summary justice at the hands of Rosie's brothers, when he was both guilty and victim. (Manus, of course, is no stranger to traditional Catholic thinking on sexual transgressions, which classified them as 'mortal sins', and, as such, deserving of the severest 'divine' punishment.)

Though again reluctant to name the obscenity and its 'engineer' (63), Sarah alludes to it overtly and covertly in her references 'the buck', lost 'in the hollow' (62-63). Her 'technique' as a teller resembles Iago's to a certain extent, in that having provided 'ocular proof' confirming the worst fears of her hearer, she then appears to question her own testimony, admitting 'I could have made a mistake, Manus', 'How could I be sure in the dark? What do you think, Manus? Is there doubt in your mind?' (63). She promises a restoration of manliness, potency, authority, if only he will 'act'. For Manus the gun offers an escape from numbness, a way back into being. Appalled that for a second time ancestral pieties have been spat upon,[39] he is in no mood to listen to his son's increasingly desperate attempts at damage limitation, and the argument that the strangers will soon be gone. Yet again dismissed by his father, Joe rushes off in search of a substitute, a responsible adult figure, Peter. Perhaps, as Sarah implies, he is also looking for a chance to 'escape' (64), witnessing the seemingly inevitable outcome of the narrative. His departure is dramatically necessary since it leaves the unsuspecting Shane isolated on stage with his adversaries; at the same time, it presents Sarah with a further opportunity to goad Manus, by playing on his name and contrasting Joe's boyish cowardice with his own potential 'redemption' through violence. By taking up the gun, taking on the role of justicer, his own past crimes against Rosie and his shame can be annealed, 'For a while there *he* didn't know how *he* was going to escape, did he? But *he*'s only a *boy*. This time *you*'ll be a *man*, *Man*us. This time' (64, emphasis added).

Immediately on his return from the expedition with Philly, Shane reveals his new-found receptiveness to Gaelic language and culture, yet this very familiarity proves his undoing; to his accusers it seems another blatant act of expropriation. His speeches prior to his indictment are heavily larded by Friel with unconscious ironies, usually in the form of allusions to the alleged 'crime' and future 'punishment' – 'far away hills look green', 'Purest Donegal', 'untouched by human hand', 'your worthy husband', 'the Stags', 'jolly gruesome', 'where the tanker broke up', 'the broken ford' (64). Necessarily in view of the impending dramatic climax, the character is recklessly unaware of the extent to which he is further antagonizing his stage audience with his verbal ostentatiousness, his flip 'translations' of Philly and his sayings. What had been represented in the previous scene as 'more entertainment for the young people than the instruments he set going again' (55), the Dubliner's playfulness with language, is now read by Manus, in the light of Sarah's narrative, as evidence of moral degeneracy. Even Shane's 'admission', uncovered through Sarah's interrogation, that up until 'half an hour ago' he and Philly had been swimming 'in the moonlight' (65) is made to appear deviant behaviour; would normal people go swimming '[I]n the dark?' (65).

Although twice picking up on Manus's uncharacteristic quietness – like his host, Shane prefers talking to listening – he singularly fails to recognize the warning signals implicit within that silence, the subsequent narrative that breaks it, or Sarah's directorial manner. Several times she intervenes in Manus's narrative in an effort to maintain control over the situation, 'Listen' (65), 'Quicker, Manus', 'That's what happened. What do you make of that story, engineer?', 'Savages! Listen!' (66) Six times Shane interrupts Manus's parable with interjections, which seem confirmation to his accusers of his wanton contempt for them and their values. Although in his first aside he rightly identifies a potential analogy between the itinerant 'niggerman' (65) and himself, in his second he wrongly anticipates, following the mention of 'holy pictures' (65) and the bent, rheumatic old couple, that the tale will be about faith healing, miraculous cures. By the time of his third interjection, 'All niggers is thieves, man' (66), one suspects that he has concluded that essentially this is a racist narrative, a story about the inherent cupidity and deceit of strangers, which indeed it is. However, as the audience are aware, it is also a parable about possessions and the vulnerability of the old; the five gold sovereigns function not only as a metonym for financial security, but also subtextually as an objective correlative for Philly, the son who will provide for him.[40] Even before Manus has reached the nub of the story, the closure he has been driving towards, Shane feels he has heard enough, as his sardonic comment, 'I'm breathless' (66), indicates.[41] Manus's aims as a narrator are to illustrate the dire penalties awaiting those who transgress the laws of ownership and decency on Inishkeen, to induce a confession, and to serve as a prelude and prompt to executive action. To Shane, however, the narration is an obscenity, another example of the sadistic cruelty of 'scalping island' (26). What appals him is not only the unquestioning assumption of the black man's guilt, but also Manus's obvious approval of 'lynch law', and the savagery meted out on both the accused and an entirely innocent animal:

Manus: Bound as he was, they harnessed him to an old donkey. Then they pumped linseed oil down into the donkey's ears. And for a full day, sir, until it dropped dead, the mad donkey dragged that niggerman across the length and breadth of this island ... But I'm thinking ... that it was a fair punishment for a thief (66).

Shane's outrage, whether stemming from an urban, liberal education, or the product of his own experience as a figure on the margins (due to his illegitimacy/homosexuality?), takes the form of a bitter, insulting riposte, 'So what's the moral? Don't attempt to peddle religion to savages?' (66), further infuriating Sarah and dragging Manus towards the deed he had wished to avoid and the deed he cannot bring himself to name. Maddened by Manus's repeated retreat into the evasions of metaphor – 'you did *a worse thing*', '*five gold sovereigns* was a small enough thing, *sir*', 'you *robbed* me, *sir*', 'you *stole* my son' (66-67, emphasis added) – his continuing deference, above all, his failure to enforce his authority by means of the gun, Sarah finally seizing the initiative, albeit with repetitions and evasions of her own. At last realizing the deadly seriousness of the situation, Shane's defence is not to explain what had happened between Philly and himself, but exclusively centres upon persuading Manus of the unreliability of the witness, 'For God's sake you don't heed her, do you?', '*She* wanted to sleep with me', 'I wouldn't have her. That's what's eating her', 'Look at her for Christ's sake! She's insane!' (67) When, however, he attempts leaving to fetch Philly to corroborate his account that nothing 'dirty' occurred between them,[42] Sarah swiftly blocks that narrative-route, 'You've had enough with Philly, engineer' (67).

In the melodramatic scene that follows, five times she calls on Manus to shoot, but though he raises the gun he does not fire. Taking advantage of this moment of indeterminacy, Shane dashes out into the street, shouting out to Peter for his salvation, only to be brought down by a shot from Sarah, who almost immediately freezes, then '*begins to lament*' (68). Although at the end of Act 2, Scene 1, Sarah had demanded that Manus kill both Shane and Philly, throughout Scene 2 her will has been wholly focussed on the destruction of the engineer, who she succeeds in leaving broken like the black man in Manus's story, maimed like the dog, that other object of her need. When the stage directions talk of how '*Very softly*' Sarah '*begins to lament*' and to make '*an almost animal noise*' (68), the moment seems an echo of the ending of *The Playboy and the Western World*, with its '*wild lamentations*' (Synge 77). Both Sarah and Synge's Pegeen Mike create icons of the men they briefly love, yet later fell the objects of their fictions.

The Gentle Island's concluding scene returns to the narrative that has haunted Irish social life throughout Friel's lifetime and long before, the seemingly unremitting process of emigration. In contrast to the mass exodus of the opening, the play closes with a single figure passing into exile, and a newly cold hearth. It begins intruding into the mind of an increasingly solitary, confused old man, a far cry from the resolute, enthroned patriarch of Act 1. Appropriately, given his sons' resistance to or inability to produce heirs, Manus is presented symbolically located '*huddled over a dead fire*' (69). According to the stage directions, he has '*aged a lot*', lost '*the assurance from his bearing*' (69) after the shooting, and drifts uncertainly between past and present. One minute he is twenty years back in time addressing the dead Rosie and bemoaning the burden of a baby, the next – somewhat unconvincingly in my opinion – he is fully alert, summoning Sarah as he pumps an exhausted Joe for information about the strangers. Showing neither pity nor remorse at the news of Shane's condition, 'Even if he lives he'll never walk again. His spine's shattered' (70), Manus is more concerned about the legal repercussions of the incident.[43] Once assured that there will be none, he determines, like Sarah, to delete the whole episode from his memory, hence his request to her to suppress from her husband the previous night's events, his own lies to his son about the real circumstances of their departure, and his resistance to the thought of Philly salvaging the Dubliners' paraffin fire and the canvas. Having lost the younger, Manus strives to maintain control over the elder son by placing a taboo on the most recent of narratives.

Another clear indication that a definite power shift has occurred within the Sweeney family lies in Joe's changed attitudes, in particular towards his father and the island which has become a tainted place. The animated boy narrator of the first scene, eager to engage his father's attention, now '*walks briskly past*' (69) Manus on his final entry, and responds curtly, sombrely to his questioning. The combined effect of having his pleas ignored in the previous scene and of witnessing at first-hand the shattering, perhaps fatal consequences for a young body of his father's and sister-in-law's folly, has hardened him. No doubt he is sickened also by Manus's attempts to deflect guilt from himself ('It was a sorry day Red Doherty brought them in among us', 'They cankered us! They blackened the bud that was beginning to grow again!' [70]) and from Philly ('Philly had nothing to do with' [71]). None of the tactics Manus employs to persuade Joe to stay seems to weaken his resolve to abandon Inishkeen – imperatives ('Put that away, boy' [71]); cajoling ('Wait a month. Wait a week. Wait till you're settled' [71]); physical restraint ('*He grabs JOE's arm. JOE stands rigid. The grip is relaxed*' [71]); emotional blackmail ('It doesn't matter to you that your father's handicapped' [71]) – though under the pressure of the latter he does offer his father the chance to escape, too. Still clinging for dear life to his 'phoney dream' of his sons' success,[44] Manus is possessed by the past, unwilling to rid himself of the fictions he has made to mask his actual failures. Desperately he tries to will Joe's departure and his defeat into a future victory, by constructing a London-marriage-children-grandchildren scenario, but his younger son can no longer be bought off with bribes or promises.[45] By way of answer, Joe takes only the money he needs to get to Glasgow, rips up and burns the proposal to Anna Con, and finally throws down the key to her abandoned house. Like Gar in *Philadelphia, Here I Come!*, he has by now had enough of '[a]ll this bloody yap about father and son and all this sentimental rubbish about "homeland" and "birthplace" – yap! Bloody yap! Impermanence – anonymity – that's what I'm looking for' (Friel, *Selected Plays* 79).

In the encounter with Sarah that follows, Manus fares little better. She also declines to offer Manus any consolation, either by commiserating with him over the loss of Joe – rather she endorses the wisdom of the decision to emigrate – or by retracting her account of Philly's activities in the boathouse. Her reply to his tentative suggestion that she might have mistaken what she had 'seen' is also to walk away; she has no intention of restoring his idealized image of his son to him, of envisioning a re-vision. To do so would be to admit her moral responsibility for the crippling of Shane, and she is no more keen on that prospect than those who have pulled triggers and set off bombs in the North for the past twenty-five years. From her final exchanges with Manus and Philly one might imagine that nothing had changed substantially within her. The night before she had exposed her husband's alleged sexual deviance to his father and brother, called for his immediate death, and shot a man. The morning after she expresses her quiet content with her memories of Man, and shows wifely obedience preparing food for Philly, kneeling at his feet and helping him off with his thigh-boots, asking how the salmon were. Seemingly all her anger is spent, and she slips back as so many Irishwomen have over the years into the resignation they have been encouraged to live by. Her final words, 'We'll get used to it' (77), refer not only to the quiet of the house without Joe, but also to the life sentence she has received – a future of endlessly deferred gratification.[46]

George O'Brien opens his remarks on *The Gentle Island* in his valuable study of Friel's work by setting a distance between it and the political satire of *The Mundy Scheme*. The later play, he asserts, 'contains nothing of cultural commentary. Its central figure is a woman. And it has a remote rural setting' (71). On the contrary, as I have sought to prove in this essay, *The Gentle Island* in fact is a play with a very substantial cultural and political charge. The fact that its 'central figure is a woman' is also of great cultural and political significance; Sarah's 'presence', along with Roisin Dubh's 'absence', are means through which Friel can raise issues about power and gender in

Ireland, and expose the repressive status quo on both sides of the border.

Although *The Gentle Island* clearly can be read in terms of its treatment of interpersonal relationships, as D.E.S. Maxwell read it in 1973, 'as a parable of human groping after communion and permanence, and the elisions of contact that frustrate it' (99-100),[47] its concern with the psychic and spiritual paralysis of its characterizations should not lead to ignore the deep political and cultural watermarks it so evidently bears, or the context in which it was composed. *The Gentle Island* belongs to a period when, like his dramatic art, Friel was heading in 'a completely new direction' (qtd. in Hickey and Smith 222), and when Ireland faced the greatest turmoil since the War of Independence. During the years immediately prior to its composition, the late 1960s, Friel had shifted ground literally by leaving one state, Northern Ireland, for another, the Republic, when he moved from Derry, where he had lived since 1939, to Muff in County Donegal, a partly practical, partly symbolic re-location, like Seamus Heaney's move to Glanmore, towards country and the margins and away from an explosive urban centre. Some two years previously – in 1966 or 1967 – he had also severed a longstanding family connection with the Nationalist Party, which he felt had lost initiative and impetus (Hickey and Smith 221). Both *The Mundy Scheme* and *The Gentle Island* bespeak a gathering and profound disillusion with both states of Ireland, North and South, and a determination on the part of the forty-year old author to review the ideological baggage he had inherited.[48] As a child and as a young Northern Catholic, no doubt, he had been encouraged to regard the Twenty-Six Counties as a kind of dream locus, a home for heroes, a place of coherence, an equivalent perhaps to Sarah's vision of the Isle of Man. His 'sense of frustration' with the corrupt, 'tight', seemingly 'immovable Unionist regime' (Hickey and Smith 221) did not blind him to the stifling 'moral authoritarianism' (Longley 14) and venality within Southern public life. Coming three years after the fiftieth anniversary of the Easter Rising, *The Mundy Scheme*, with its sub title, 'May We Write Your Epitaph Now, Mr Emmet?' – like the reference to

the Flight of the Earls in *The Gentle Island* – draws attention to
the gulf between the idealized, heroic fictions of Ireland past
and the present political scene, with its narratives of sordid self-
interest and duplicity. Not surprisingly given the events of the
following three years, 1969-72, motifs of betrayal surface
prominently in his next two plays.

While continuing and developing Friel's existing preoccupations with language and authority, with the price of exile
and the cost of staying on, *The Gentle Island* marks an interesting
departure from his previous work in the attention it pays to
'thwarted sexuality' (Maxwell in Peacock 55) as a force within
'interpersonal and family dynamics' (O'Brien 76), but this, too,
functions at least in part as political metaphor. It is, perhaps,
not entirely fanciful to characterize the play's younger
generation, particularly Sarah and Shane, as 'the rebellious
oppressed', to use Elmer Andrews' phrase (Peacock 34), and
their aspirations for radical change in the quality of their
personal lives as bearing some affinity with those of the young
people who thronged to the Civil Rights movement, like those
he depicts in *The Freedom of the City*.

Having emphasized at every opportunity throughout this
essay the possible political and historical subtexts operating
within this important, underestimated, transitional play, it is
perhaps appropriate to end with something of a counter-view.
In a recent essay, entitled 'Marking Time' (Peacock 202-14),
Fintan O'Toole offers an appropriate and persuasive corrective,
however, to those who *over*-politicize Friel's work, as he
suggests Seamus Deane has tended to do:

> Because his work deals in the stuff of history, it is tempting to
> understand him as a fundamentally political writer. In his
> introduction to Friel's *Selected Plays*, his friend and Field Day
> collaborator feels it necessary to point out that Friel's work is
> not 'wholly political in its motivations and obsessions', (which
> implies, of course that it is largely so) … History and politics …
> may well floor Friel's house, but they do not contain the drama
> that happens in that house.[49]

Although one respects the obvious legitimacy of re-considering an author's earlier texts in the light of subsequent work, since 'when a new work of art is created … something happens simultaneously to all the works of art which preceded it' (Eliot 80), there can be a danger in trying to impose a single coherent narrative on an author's work, in constructing a retrospective fiction, just as there can be drawbacks in interpreting *solely* by reference to its contexts, social, political, cultural, or intellectual. My contention remains, however, that *The Gentle Island*'s position in Friel's work should be seen as analogous to that of *Wintering Out* in Seamus Heaney's, permeated as they are by the intensely politicized 'climate and condition' of their time (Friel, 'Theatre of Hope' 18). Both texts reflect their authors' increasingly urgent search for forms, parables, images, symbols, a language 'adequate to our pre-dicament' (Heaney, *Preoccupations* 56), as things fell apart, and earlier hopes of the possibility of a 'liberating breakdown of order' (O'Toole in Peacock 207) were dashed.

Notes

[1] Brian Friel's time in America in 1963, watching Tyrone Guthrie producing Shakespeare, he describes as 'my first parole from inbred claustrophobic Ireland'.

[2] I am thinking in particular of such events as the riots in Derry and Belfast in August 1969, the Falls Road curfew of July 1970, the introduction of internment in August 1971, and Bloody Sunday in January 1972.

[3] The subject of emigration and its cultural, social and economic consequences, is obviously a highly charged one for an Irish audience. For an account of how island life in post-independence Ireland was idealized, see Terence Brown (93-96).

[4] In a letter to the author, Friel wrote in May 1987 that he had made a 'stern decision not to do interviews because I discovered that … I was beginning to myself formulating complete answers'.

[5] *Buile Suibhne*, a medieval poem deals with the story of a King of Ulster, Sweeney, cursed by a cleric for a profane act, turned into a bird and forced into exile. The story was revitalized with comic effect by Flann O'Brien's *At Swim Two Birds* (1939). In the summer of 1972, Friel's close friend, the poet Seamus Heaney, began a modern-day translation of the poem which eventually appeared in 1984, under the

title *Sweeney Astray*. The name clearly has resonances for Friel since he has employed it again in *Molly Sweeney* (1994).

6 This is one of many instances of Friel using disability as a metaphor. Within this play Manus is missing his left arm, and Shane's spine is shattered; in *Translations* he gives Manus a limp and Sarah speech problems, and at the (absent) centre in *Aristocrats* is the father, a stroke-victim. For the use of this common motif in postcolonial texts, see Parker and Starkey and for a further discussion of its use in Friel's plays see Ruth Niel's essay in this volume.

7 I am grateful to Professor Emrys Evans of the University of Manchester for his 'translation' back into Gaelic of the name, Inishkeen, which is referred to in *The Annals of the Four Masters* as *Iniscaein*. Interestingly, there is an Inishkeen in Co. Louth, which possesses 'the scant remains of the early monastery founded by St Daig mac Cairill' (see Killanin and Duignan 241), and is where the poet Patrick Kavanagh – a writer much admired by Friel and Heaney – was born and buried. It is interesting to note that Seamus Heaney's place-name poems, 'Anahorish', 'Broagh', 'Toome' and 'A New Song' from *Wintering Out*, which play with Gaelic etymology belong to the same period as *The Gentle Island*.

8 The Hiberno-English word 'keen', the sound mourners make at a wake, comes from the Gaelic word *caoineadh*. The islanders' decision to leave may be linked to the process of anglicization, to the hard economic facts that they must abandon their birthplace to 'enjoy' what is termed a 'decent living' in London or Glasgow.

9 On a simple level, she serves as an agent or 'presence' who causes dramatic shocks, readjustments and transformations in the other characters. If, however, the play is interpreted as representing political, cultural and sexual dysfunction, Sarah could be 'read' as an embodiment of those elements – within the state of Northern Ireland /within the nationalist community of the North/within 'Catholic Ireland'/within any society/within the human psyche – that, if repressed, excluded, silenced, are likely at some stage to blaze into violence. A feminist reading of the character might well emphasize her status as victim, abused and confused by male hegemony, subjected by Family, Church and State. A more traditional, perhaps less reflective reading and audience, however, might choose to view her as one of many victim figures in the play, a product of frustration, humiliation, and jealous anger. *The Gentle Island's* narratives are littered with casualties, and Peter and Shane will become part of a line stretching back past the 'niggerman' (65-67), back to the monks (32-33).

10 Again, one suspects the choice of the name, Man, is not entirely

accidental; it is a place she associates with physical, sensual pleasure.

[11] Given his strong sense of the intertextual, the literary dialogue going on within and between his own plays and those of the Irish dramatic tradition, it seems likely that Friel intends the absent Rose as a contrast to those idealized, distorted representations of Mother Ireland and Dark Rosaleen in nationalist mythology. Brian Moore similarly deconstructs these male-constructed, nationalist archetypes in his novel, *The Mangan Inheritance.*

[12] Her first disclosure to Peter of Manus's 'deceit' is partly to break up what seems to be the cosy alliance developing between the Sweeneys and the visitors, and occurs immediately after Manus has presented Peter with one of his 'acquired' treasures, and while Philly has stolen away with Shane. Her second, more devastating disclosure comes when she reports sighting Philly and Shane making love in the boat-house. Whether this is true or entirely her fabrication, the main targets for her rage or revenge appear to be Shane *and* Manus, rather than her husband. Certainly she regards both men as thieves of her happiness, and projects Philly's failings onto them.

[13] Sarah's 'reading' of Joe's features may be inaccurate. She may be again attempting to make mischief between father and son. Certainly she takes every opportunity that presents itself to challenge Manus's authority.

[14] Within the text the outsiders perform a multiple function in terms of theme, characterization and dramatic structure; generational conflict and issues of patriarchy are replicated and developed in their relationship; opportunities for retailing fresh readings of the island and re-telling self-justifying narratives are created; contrasts and collisions are set up between an urban, professional, technologically-skilled, geographically-mobile, anglophone Ireland and its rural, peasant, manually skilled, 'static', marginally Gaelic Other.

[15] Even their names and occupations hint at separation. Peter Quinn, the 'freelance" music teacher/piano tuner, like Shakespeare's Peter Quince, is a would-be director, a somewhat fumbling manipulator of men. 'Peter' also has associations with clerical authority, and given Friel's understandable reticence about his 'very disturbing experience' as a student at Maynooth, may have some private significance. The name of his travelling companion, Shane Harrison, the engineer, sounds distinctly Anglo-American, suggesting perhaps that he belongs to the post-De Valera, multinational Ireland of the 1960s.

[16] Although Friel typically does not make it explicit, most commentators seem to agree that Peter and Shane are homosexuals. Evidently they have lived together in economic partnership for some time (55). From the same conversation with Manus, we learn from Peter that

they once taught in the same school until 'the principal and I had a row' (54). When Sarah interjects, 'About the engineer?', rightly divining the cause, Peter does not contradict her. From this one deduces that some aspect of his relationship with Shane caused the conflict, which resulted in his subsequent inability to gain a permanent teaching post. It is certainly significant that the true cause of the shooting is kept from the doctor (70), presumably to 'protect' Shane from a painful court case and possible prosecution. In *Ireland – A Social and Cultural History: 1922-1985,* Terence Brown cites the attempt by David Norris in the early 1980s to challenge the two Acts in the Irish Republic's constitution which made homosexual acts and behaviour illegal (349-50).

[17] Long exposure to the island, and to the 'madness' of 'King' Sweeney, takes the heads off Sarah and Philly, and Rosie Dubh, before them.

[18] Friel's first published short story appeared in *The Bell* in July 1952.

[19] Fintan O'Toole and Angela Bourke expose the contrivances employed in the making of *Man of Aran* (1934), Robert Flaherty's classic film, which was received rapturously in Europe, America and Ireland, for its authentic representation of peasant life. Its 'timeless truths', O'Toole comments, turned out to be 'lies'. For its key scene, the shark hunt, American experts had to be flown in to teach the islanders a method for catching the fish that they had not used for the last hundred years. The film, Angela Bourke points out, was deliberately shot on the rocky, unsheltered part of the island, thus giving a misleading picture of life there ('Dancing at the Crossroads').

[20] Shane's idea of the island as a cemetery echoes the central premise of Friel's earlier satirical play, *The Mundy Scheme* (1969), in which there is a proposal to turn the west of Ireland into a giant, international burial ground.

[21] His reading of himself in these terms corresponds with Sarah's reading of herself, and perhaps helps to explain the fateful attraction.

[22] When asked about his parents, he has previously informed Sarah and the audience, 'I never knew either of them' (35).

[23] Like *Othello, The Gentle Island* is a tale of betrayals, or rather perceived betrayals, a popular Irish theme. Both words play variations on the verb 'to lie' (see *Othello,* III, iii, 410, 'I lay with Cassio lately', or IV, i, 33-38, 'Lie with her? Lie on her?'), and Sarah's account of what she saw in the boathouse could be seen as an ambiguous counterpart to the 'ocular proof' Iago offers. Certainly it induces a disorientation in Manus which may lead '[e]ven unto madness' (*Othello,* II, i, 311). Later in *The Gentle Lsland,* Joe warns Sarah, 'Put none of your *poison* into my father's head' an image which Iago frequently employs, but also recalls Claudius' crime. As I have indicated in the main text,

there are many other Shakespearean echoes within the play, reverberations perhaps of Friel's intense experience in Minneapolis watching Tyrone Guthrie's productions of Shakespeare.

24 Earlier, on his return from the turf-cutting, he had spoken admiringly of Philly's physical prowess and expertise, his silent, uncomplicated charm, 'sheer delight to watch him' (40). The subtext of these comments, if we assume that Peter and Shane are homosexuals, might be that he finds Philly sexually attractive. Peter no doubt finds Philly less verbally threatening.

25 Instead of an authentic, 'ancient Gaelic folk-song' (43), the first record he turns up is an American one, 'Oh, Susanna', attributed to Stephen Foster (1826-64), who acquired many of his songs from the black plantations. At the opening of Act 1, Scene 2, Shane had briefly adopted a black slave *persona* –'Ole Joshua he sure fix you' music box real good now' (34) – which re-emerges when later Manus draws analogies between Shane's 'crime' and that of the thieving niggerman (65-67). Northern Irish Catholics in the late 1960s commonly made comparisons between their plight as an underclass and that of the American blacks, most notably in the founding of their own Civil Rights Movement in 1967. (See Seamus Heaney's comments in his interview with James Randall 18-20.)

26 The three machines fixed by Shane – the radio, gramophone, the outboard motor – symbolize the already existing 'intrusion' of the external, industrial world on the mythic 'self-sufficient' Inishkeen of Manus's and Philly's imagination.

27 Her bitter hostility towards Shane may also be 'explained' as a manifestation of that very 'human' tendency to abuse beings deemed even lower in the scale of social acceptability; 'I may be only a woman, but at least I'm not a queer'.

28 Tired of the role-playing involved in living with Peter, Shane finds himself recast by the islanders. His manual dexterity and technological skills have made him acceptable, hence his new life as 'Sean'. The act of re-naming in Friel's plays often has violent consequences, as can be seen in *Translations*.

29 Peter's switching off of the record and later smashing of it is obviously an attempt to halt the beating Shane is receiving, but also suggests that he has learnt something from his afternoon experience with Philly. It challenges Philly's dominance, and can be seen as another example of the older generation endeavouring to restore their hegemony and control. Part of him perhaps finds Philly's violence exciting, but only when it is directed at him. Is there not something masochistic in Shane's and Peter's acceptance of punishment?

30 Friel cleverly uses the dog to delineate character further. Increasingly it

becomes apparent from Philly's responses to the news that Sarah has been feeding it (anger and incredulity) and that Joe thinks of turning it into a pet (withering contempt), that underneath Philly's solid, solitary, self-sufficiency lies a similar cruel insensitivity to his father's. Philly, like Manus, shows no qualms about taking a pitchfork to the dog. By contrast, one observes the affectionate way Joe views both the dog and Shane, regarding them as possible replacement companions to those he had lost through emigration. Although Sarah has begun by befriending both, acting as a mother to one, longing to be made a mother by the other, her rejection by Shane has dehumanized him in her eyes, reduced him to something less than an animal. It is a way of thinking that recalls the Nazi attitude to Jews and Slavs, but equally how sectarianism in Northern Ireland constructs the 'enemy'. See Padraic Fiacc's poem, 'Elegy for a Fenian Get' (112-13).

31 Friel voices here an almost Shane-like distaste for the 'exhibitionism', 'ostentation', 'parade', 'swagger of the first person singular', his suspicion of his own rationalized, sanitized, heavily edited auto-biographical snatches.

32 Definitions of 'Jack' in *The Shorter Oxford English Dictionary* (3rd edition) include 'one who does odd jobs' (L4), 'the knave of trumps in all-fours' (L5), and a Shakespearean usage meaning 'a mad-cap ruffian' (L6). In mining, a 'jack' is 'a wooden wedge used to assist in cleaving strata' (II.6b). The phrase to 'play the jack' means 'to play the knave', which would fit what Sarah does if one assumes that she is guilty of slandering Shane. The unresolved question at the end of the play is the identity of the 'Jack' – Sarah, Shane or Philly?

33 Once again Sarah's questions are unanswered, see her appeal to Shane earlier (39).

34 The heroic farmer-fisherman of *Man of Aran*.

35 A further irony, of course, is that her 'tongue' and gun will cripple Shane for life.

36 She depicts him as if he were a figure who had just stepped out of a romantic film or advertisement.

37 It may be that in her own mind Sarah sees little cause now to differentiate between Peter the Elder and Shane the Younger Pervert. His 'rejection' of her has rendered him an object of disgust.

38 One might draw a comparison between Joe's pleas and those of constitutional Nationalists to their hurt community after such events as Internment and Bloody Sunday to think rationally and act justly.

39 'People have lived here for hundreds of years, thousands of years', 'There were people here before Christ was born' (63). These two lines may seem non-sequiturs, but in fact reflect Manus's shocked

acceptance of the plausibility of Sarah's evidence and his own evident sense of betrayal.

[40] Like Peter remonstrating with Shane (41-42), Manus easily resorts to economic metaphors to describe his relationship with his son. As Sarah recognizes, Manus is more concerned with the damage to his property – 'He robbed you, Manus' – than with her loss.

[41] The not-uncommon gulf between authorial/narratorial intention and narrative reception is manifest here.

[42] He might be attempting either to prove that the sexual encounter described by Sarah is a complete fabrication, or, if one accepts the reading of Shane and Philly as homosexuals, that it was an act between two consenting adults.

[43] A curious gap in the text is introduced at this point as to why neither Shane nor Peter inform the doctor or the police as to the real cause of his injuries. Sarah, like Manus, shows a similar indifference to the state she has left Shane in.

[44] In his role of failed patriarch, Manus could be seen as analogous to Arthur Miller's Willy Loman, from *Death of a Salesman*. The phrase 'phoney dream' is from Miller's play.

[45] Earlier in the play (22), we learn that Manus had bequeathed these self-same, choicest parts of his property to Philly.

[46] The profound sense of resignation Sarah articulates at the end of the play may be seen as characteristic of the Northern Irish Catholic psyche in the post-partition era. Politically it manifested itself in the abstentionist policies of the Nationalist Party, which were attacked by John Hume in his *Irish Times* articles of 1964. (See Michael Parker, *Seamus Heaney* 14; Seamus Heaney's poem 'From the Canton of Expectation', *The Haw Lantern* 46-47; Padraic Fiacc's poem 'Credo Credo', *Ruined Pages* 141).

[47] Earlier in this pioneering study of Friel's drama, written before the text of *The Gentle Island* had been finally published, Maxwell makes the important point – one which Frank Ormsby would reiterate some twenty years later in his introduction to *A Rage for Order: Poetry of the Northern Ireland Troubles* – that often 'the Northern situation' operates as 'a kind of subterranean presence in works that ostensibly have nothing to do with it'. He goes on to cite Seamus Heaney's comment about 'The Last Mummer', a poem whose composition is probably contemporaneous with that of *The Gentle Island* – 'I didn't mean this to be a poem about Northern Ireland, but in some way I think it is' (29).

[48] Together these plays set up a pattern that I see as a recurring tendency in Friel's work from the 1970s onwards. The composition of an overtly political play (*The Mundy Scheme, The Freedom of the City,*

Volunteers, Translations) is generally followed up with a much more oblique one *(The Gentle Island, Living Quarters, Aristocrats,* and *Faith Healer).*

[49] O'Toole's well-written essay focuses largely, as its title suggests, on more recent developments in Friel's career which postdate Seamus Deane's introduction to the *Selected Plays* (1984).

Works Cited

Brown, Terence. *Ireland: A Social and Cultural History: 1922-1985*. London: Fontana, 1986.

Devlin, Anne. *The Way-Paver*. London: Faber, 1986.

Farrell, Michael. *The Orange State*. London: Pluto, 1976.

Fiacc, Padraic. *Ruined Pages*. Belfast: Blackstaff, 1994.

Eliot, T.S. 'Traditional and the Individual Talent'. (1919) *Twentieth Century Poetry: Critical Essays and Documents*. Ed. Graham Martin and P.N. Furbank. Milton Keynes: The Open UP, 1975.

Foucault, Michel. *Untying the Text*. Ed. Robert Young. London: Routledge, 1971.

Friel, Brian. *Aristocrats*. London: Faber, 1980.

--- *The Gentle Island*. Oldcastle: Gallery, 1993.

--- *Making History*. London: Faber, 1989.

--- *The Mundy Scheme*. New York: Farrar, 1970.

--- *Philadelphia, Here I Come!* (1965). *Selected Plays*. London: Faber, 1984. 21-99.

--- *Selected Plays*. London: Faber, 1984.

--- 'The Theatre of Hope and Despair'. *Everyman* 1 (1968): 17-22.

---*Translations*. 1981. *Selected Plays*. London: Faber, 1984. 377-451.

--- 'Self-Portrait'. *Aquarius* 5 (1972): 17-22.

Heaney, Seamus. *Wintering Out*. London: Faber, 1972.

--- *Preoccupations: Selected Prose 1968-1978*. London: Faber, 1980.

--- *Sweeney Astray*. London: Faber, 1984.

--- 'After the Synge-Song – Seamus Heaney on the Writings of Patrick Kavanagh'. *The Listener*. 13 Jan. 1972: 55-56.

--- Interview with James Randall. *Ploughshares* 5.3 (1979): 7-22.

Hickey, Des, and Gus Smith. *A Paler Shade of Green*. London: Frewin, 1972.

Kavanagh, Patrick. *Collected Poems*. Dublin: Brian and O'Keeffe, 1972.

Kearney, Richard. *Transitions*. Dublin: Wolfhound, 1988.

Killanin, Lord, and Michael Duignan. *The Shell Guide to Ireland*. Basingstoke: Macmillan, 1989.

Longley, Edna. *The Living Stream: Literature and Revisionism in Ireland*. Newcastle-upon-Tyne: Bloodaxe, 1994.

Martin, Graham, and P.N. Furbank. *Twentieth Century Poetry: Critical Essays and Documents*. Milton Keynes: The Open UP, 1975.

Maxwell, D.E.S. *Brian Friel*. Lewisburg: Bucknell UP, 1973.

Moore, Brian. *The Mangan Inheritance*. London: Cape, 1979.

O'Brien George. *Brian Friel*. Dublin: Gill-Macmillan, 1989.

O'Faolain, Sean. 'Silent Ireland'. *The Bell* 6 (1943): 460-64.

O'Toole, Fintan. 'Keeper of the Faith'. *The Guardian* 16 Jan. 1992: 6.

--- 'Dancing at the Crossroads: A Portrait of Modern Ireland'. *The Late Show*. BBC2. 6 Mar. 1995.

--- 'Marking Time: From Making History to Dancing at Lughnasa'. In Peacock. 202-14.

Ormsby, Frank. *A Rage for Order: Poetry of the Northern Ireland Troubles*. Belfast: Blackstaff, 1992.

Parker, Michael, ed. *The Hurt World: Short Stories of the Troubles*. Belfast: Blackstaff, 1995.

--- *Seamus Heaney: The Making of the Poet*. Basingstoke: Macmillan, 1993.

Parker, Michael, and Roger Starkey, eds. *Postcolonial Literatures*. Basingstoke: Macmillan. 1995.

Peacock, Alan, ed. *The Achievement of Brian Friel*. Gerrards Cross: Colin Smythe, 1994.

Synge, J.M. *The Playboy of the Western World*. London: Unwin, 1968.

Yeats, W.B. *The Collected Poems of W. B. Yeats*. London: Macmillan, 1933.

RITUAL AND CEREMONY

10 | Questing for Ritual and Ceremony in a Godforsaken World: *Dancing at Lughnasa* and *Wonderful Tennessee*

Richard Allen Cave

Anna McMullan begins an essay on *Dancing at Lughnasa* with the pertinent observation: 'In the late nineteen nineties, the body is in vogue: Irish theatre from the Abbey to the fringe is drawing on the energies of physical performance' (90). She proceeds to explore the extent to which Friel anticipates this 'vogue' with that play of 1990, as if he stated the theme at the opening of the decade on which subsequent theatre would play multiple variations. Her main focus, however, is on the issue of women's authority over their own bodies and their capacity for unique expression through those bodies as gendered. While I would agree that *Dancing at Lughnasa* sets a particular trend, I would also argue that it pursues a delicate line of enquiry into the nature and function of ritual in contemporary life, which links it retrospectively with *Faith Healer* (1979) and with the later play, *Wonderful Tennessee* (1993). It would be useful here to ponder briefly on the title of a talk that Seamus Deane gave about the same time in the Peacock Theatre, Dublin, as part of the *Writers on Stage* series: 'Irish Theatre: A Secular Space?' (163). Given the Abbey's long tradition of stage realism (and Deane is much concerned with the work of Ireland's *national* theatre), the idea of the stage as a 'secular space' would seem fittingly apt. But there is a cunning dubiety implicit in that final use of the question mark. None of the founders of the theatre movement (not even the Ibsen-obsessed Edward Martyn) saw theatre as exclusively secular and Yeats in theory and practice was deeply opposed to such a limiting view of drama's potential. Friel has relentlessly pushed at the borders of conventional stage realism, searching for dramatic structures that will embrace not only the secular but psychological and spiritual intensities, which traditionally do not find expression within that mode of re-presentation. His most remarkable breakthrough in this regard was *Faith Healer*.

Faith Healer

Despite an unwarrantably poor reception at the time of its first performance in New York, the play has come to be seen as a seminal inspiration for much drama conceived since by younger dramatists such as Frank McGuinness, Sebastian Barry, Dermot Bolger, and Conor McPherson. Yet as a play that dramatizes the mind's processes of recall or 'dreaming back' and as a play that creates a stage for ghosts to explore their tortured spiritual and emotional condition, *Faith Healer* continues a tradition of Irish drama that recedes through Beckett and Johnston to Yeats's *The Dreaming of the Bones*, *The Words Upon the Window-Pane*, and *Purgatory*.[1] In the period after the initial production of *Faith Healer*, when Friel joined forces with Stephen Rea in founding Field Day Theatre Company, he began with *Translations* (1980) to devise plays to a precise political agenda. The plays of the 1980s culminating in *Making History* (1989) have an epic scale and ambition in interrogating colonialism and the cultural and spiritual consequences of suffering invasion or defeat in warring against an aggressor. There is little scope here for exploring the private metaphysical quests of individuals, which had brought such innovations in dramatic form and structuring to *Faith Healer*, making for both profundity and intensity in performance. But the plays of the 1990s return to the territory of spiritual anguish with renewed confidence, showing us more clearly by their example how to 'read' and appraise that earlier play with which they have much in

common. While even earlier plays by Friel had examined
questions of faith and found ways of introducing elements of
ritual within a prevailing realism, *Faith Healer* was the first to
juxtapose against such thematic and structural interests a new
preoccupation with the language of the body as an equivocal,
challenging and potent source of symbolic expression.[2] Where
Faith Healer differs from the later two plays under discussion is
the mode in which physicality is realized dramatically.[3] The
body is continually described in *Faith Healer* in ways that
provoke (indeed at times haunt) the imagination of the
audience; in *Dancing at Lughnasa* and *Wonderful Tennessee* the
bodies in motion of the performers are intricate signifiers,
having at times as in Yeats's dance plays the status of metaphor:
allusive, complex, intimating meanings which lie beyond the
analytical powers of language to convey. They are plays which
require performance as the basis of study, not merely the text.
James Hillman, the Jungian analyst, has observed: 'The names
of European potentates and heroic scientists colonized all sorts
of natural phenomena: planets, plants, processes. Liberation
movements cast off the oppression of words that represented
the old order' (275). After a decade of playwriting for Field
Day, which interrogated colonial systems by which language
was subject to oppression, manipulation, fracturings and de-
stabilizings of root-meanings, it would seem appropriate for
Friel to look elsewhere for more 'innocent' means of theatrical
expression. His growing fascination with the 'speaking' body in
this political context is again wholly apt, for as Martha Graham,
that most self-possessed and enquiring of dancers, was fond of
informing her pupils: 'Movement never lies. It is a barometer
telling the state of the soul's weather to all who can read it' (4).

During Frank's opening monologue in *Faith Healer*, he
describes the kind of dilapidated church or school hall in which
he generally was required to perform, observing how these
places often had remnants of a long-ago harvest thanksgiving
service or a bit of left-over Christmas decoration. He promptly
dismisses these ageing festive tokens as 'relics of abandoned
rituals' and defines his audiences as 'beyond that kind of
celebration' (*Selected Plays* 332). The somewhat archaic form,

'relicts', suggests a time now long past, while the placing of the epithet 'abandoned' in relation to the rituals rather than the decaying objects creates a potent ambiguity. Harvest festivals and Christmas are communal celebrations; but here such social gatherings are deliberately distanced to some remote past; Frank and his audiences are 'beyond' all that. 'Beyond' might imply a superiority, a being *above* the need to celebrate, or of being at one with a community; but it can also mean 'outside' in the sense of 'beyond the reach of' festive sharing. In that one word is intimated all the strange pride coupled with solipsistic despair, which we later learn characterizes the people who come in pursuit of Frank's healing gifts. Frank is their last resort: the ghost of a hope which lies within utter hopelessness which, being frustrated or denied, as they expect it will be, will confirm for these people a sense of their complete abjection:

> they defied me to endow them with hopelessness. But I couldn't do even that for them. And they knew I couldn't. A peculiar situation . . .? No, ... eerie. But occasionally ... the miracle would happen. And then ... – panic! Their ripping apart! The explosion of their careful calculations! The sudden flooding of dreadful, hopeless hope! I often thought it would have been a kindness ... not to go near them (336-37).

Frank's art of faith healing is a strange gift, given his wavering rate of success in effecting cures. In a world that has abandoned the outward manifestations of faith (those dusty 'relicts') what can the term and the experience of faith healing *mean*? Is Frank being required to restore faith along with hope and physical reparation to the benighted? If neither he nor his audience have faith, then what is the nature of the power invested in him from time to time to effect a cure? Can miracles, achievings of the impossible, occur outside of faith? Questions undermine Frank's trust and confidence in what he does, and then his power wanes; and yet, paradoxically, he always knows when he will succeed and when fail. Cruelly the power invariably leaves him when he might wish to help those closest to him (wife, parents, mother-in-law, manager). Deepening anguish provokes ever more searching metaphysical probing until at the last Frank chooses death by a kind of

martyrdom for the sake of his 'gift', in order to still the doubts
for ever; at that moment he no longer felt any 'atrophying
terror', since 'the maddening questions were silent'; finally, he
was 'renouncing chance' (376). Traditionally martyrdom
revivifies the belief of those of little faith, the doubters and
agnostics: the deeds of martyrs are told over, recalled in story,
legend and iconography in Church for precisely this end.
Frank's death may be an assertion of belief in himself, of faith
in his special vocation, but it reduces his wife, Grace, to despair
and suicide and his manager, Teddy, to emotional collapse. For
them the questions continue, insistent and unanswerable. Four
times the story of a death is told through monologues (twice by
Frank, once by Grace and then Teddy); that death which Frank
tries to define as sacrifice, Grace and Teddy judge as murder.
How an audience interprets the event depends on the degree to
which spiritual awareness and faith shape their individual
perceptions or whether such metaphysical propositions are
'relicts' merely.

Perhaps because so much of the fabric of *Faith Healer* is
made up of stories, often of moments etched vividly in a
character's memory, greater attention is given than in earlier
plays by Friel to descriptions of body language: appearance,
posture, movement. These are all evoked with remarkable
visual clarity, suggesting either that the speaker is confident of
her or his interpretation of what was seen and noted as
distinctive or that the speaker was bemused or teased by an
inherent ambiguity and indeed continues to think through the
episode in search of some conclusive explanation of its
significance. What has been witnessed has the status of an
epiphany that both demands and eludes definition. A
representative example would be Teddy's recollection of
assisting at the birth of Grace's still-born child:

> all that blood … her bare feet pushing, kicking … then … that
> little wet thing with the black face and … black body, … no
> size at all … a boy … afterwards she was … fantastic … She
> held it in her arms, just sitting there on the roadside … her back
> leaning against the … wall … her legs stretched out … sitting
> … looking down at it … (363-64)

Grace sustains that posture for over half-an-hour, before she calmly announces that it is time to bury the child. This has visual immediacy for the audience because it has all the clarity of an icon for Teddy: the episode is both nativity and pieta at once, a birth and a burial. What time for mothering the child is given to Grace is no more than a brief tender honouring of its corpse. And Teddy watches, participates, emotionally supports, plays the role of attendant father because Frank has inexplicably raced away (Frank longs for a child, but *knows* instinctively that the baby will be still-born); in his so honouring Grace, Teddy expresses a love for her which he cannot ever voice aloud and of which she seems wholly oblivious. It is in the precision and detail of the recall that much of the emotional content is contained: the subtext of feeling implied by the style here enriches the representation of Teddy's character. He never once admits to his love for Grace, for all the confessional quality that the monologue invites as a dramatic form. The audience are presented with an image and must explore the range of meanings for themselves. Movement has this same power on stage to be at once immediate in its physicality but allusive and enigmatic as to its meaning.

In his plays of the 1990s Friel begins to explore this potential in body language, finding ways of creating contexts within which ever-increasingly subtle deployments of move-ment may be read by an attentive audience. Interestingly those plays return to addressing the question of whether ritual has a necessary function in modern, materially-conscious society after the collapse of organized forms of religion. Traditional rituals are expressed through movement in a stylized mode. Frequently in *Dancing at Lughnasa* (1990) and *Wonderful Tennessee* (1993) the characters turn to movement in the hope that it will express themselves more fully by encompassing some spiritual di-mension which otherwise their lives lack.

Dancing at Lughnasa

Early in *Dancing at Lughnasa* four of the five Mundy sisters contemplate going to the forthcoming harvest dance; it would be the first time they had attended in some years. Quickly the

eldest sister, Kate, aborts their musing on possibilities by
asserting what she clearly sees is the commonsense view: 'Look
at yourselves, will you! Just look at yourselves! Dancing at our
time of day? That's for young people with no duties and no
responsibilities and nothing in their heads but pleasure ... Do
you want the whole countryside to be laughing at us? – women
of our years? mature women, *dancing*?' (13). Later in the play,
their brother Jack, returned from his years as a missionary priest
in a leper colony in Africa, recalls times of communal
celebration there amongst the Ryangans: 'And then we dance –
and dance – and dance – children, men, women, most of them
lepers, many of them with misshapen limbs, with missing limbs,
dancing, believe it or not, for days on end! It is the most
wonderful sight you have ever seen!' (48). Dancing for Jack in
contemplating the Africans is defined as a free expression of
inner joy in the spirit; there is no suggestion of criticism,
condemnation, superiority in his account, no hint of caricature
that would intimate a tendency to laugh at these people as
grotesque. Significantly Jack's perspective is all-inclusive: his is
not a judging, distancing, *gazing* eye but the view of a participant
('And then *we* dance') in which everyone is embraced by the
experiential epithet, 'wonderful'. Dancing is *seen* to be uplifting
because it is *felt and known in the body* to be so. Kate is continually
preoccupied with the 'norm' in rural Ballybeg, where the norm
in the eyes of a schoolteacher who is ever conscious of the need
to be an exemplary role model in the community is Catholic
and strict to a puritanical extreme. The body in her view should
be above the need to express itself; movement that risks
upsetting one's dignity hovers precariously for Kate in the
vicinity of the sinful. And so her viewpoint is tainted with the
judgemental to a degree that verges on the cruelty of caricature
and derision: 'mature women, *dancing*'. (One comes to feel
greater sympathy for Kate the more one appreciates the extent
to which her insistence on orthodoxy at all costs is driven by
her own fears of letting go.) These two subjective opinions help
in performance to direct the audience's visual reading of bodies
in movement and, crucially, their reading of bodies (young and
middle-aged, women and men) *dancing*.

A further perspective on the issue is offered us by the narrator-figure, Michael. His boyhood presence pervades every scene just as his adult self now watches the recreation of what is *his* remembered past. That older, more compassionate and understanding self voices the child's sharply dismissive attitudes to this family of single women and *places* them objectively as an expression of that aggrieved but wilfully accepted loneliness, which is often experienced by children deprived of a father-figure and of siblings. The child clearly shares his aunt Kate's conservative view that adults should preserve their proper dignity (though on the basis that not to do so dreadfully embarrasses the young). Michael observes the sisters 'suddenly catching hands and dancing a spontaneous step-dance and laughing – screaming! – like excited schoolgirls' when they hear the beat of an Irish jig over their old wireless set; the remarkable transformation in them startles him (the boy sees them as 'deranged') and causes him to blame it all on 'Marconi's voodoo' (2). 'Voodoo' finds an answering chime in Kate's favourite adjective 'pagan', which comes promptly to her tongue whenever she is describing activity she considers in-decorous. Two views of dancing as sacred and profane: yet both epithets are attempts in language to define a process of bodily transformation, a taking-out of one's mundane selfhood, which one view dismisses as demeaning, becoming less than human, and the other as achieving true unity of being when the body is at one with the spirit and rapture ensues.

Dancing becomes a unifying symbol throughout the play, initiating and developing the complex thematic explorations that lie beneath the surface of Michael's autobiographical narrative. Dance is enacted: the sisters' wild step-dance; Gerry's waltzing with Chris and later his whirling of Agnes into a quick-step; Rose and Maggie's music-hall-style 'shuffles' in their big boots, which lie somewhere between the clog and the sand dance; Jack's stranger, more rhythmic 'shuffle' with bent body and accompanied by his drumming together of two sticks in a measured tattoo, when – oblivious to the world around him – he returns in memory to Ryanga so powerfully that its cultural expression takes complete possession of him and, despite the watching presences of his sisters, he 'goes native'; and the stately ritual for the exchange of gifts which Jack meticulously stage manages with no sense of absurdity when he swaps hats with Gerry. And dance as formal ritual is described in detail: Rose's excited account of the age-old Lughnasa celebrations in 'the Back Hills' where, in an annual re-enactment of Celtic rites, fires are built and leapt over, which is paralleled by Jack's equally lengthy tale of the festivals in Uganda honouring the Great Goddess, Obi, involving sacrifice, incantation and communal celebrations. Significantly, though both festivals are times of thanksgiving for plenty and harvest at a turning point of the year, the former is a secret occasion and largely the preserve of the young while the latter is open and available to all. This material is all contained within a plot that explores through traditional realistic means the hardship of daily living within a punitive small-town society, whose quiet ways of earning a secure enough income to survive (providing one is willing to conform to agreed patterns of behaviour) are being threatened by encroaching materialism and industrialization: it is 1936 and cottage industries such as sock and glove knitting are being replaced by factory labour. The dialogue is focused on the pressures and anxieties of social change and the private tragedies these bring in their wake, while movement evokes experiences which are either ageless (being traditional rituals) or seemingly outside the dictates of chronological time (the dancing).

This is difficult territory to explore without succumbing to the sentimentality of either nostalgia (old ways are best ways) or romanticism (the attraction of the exotic, the pagan; or the cult of the noble savage, whether African or Celt), while the concern for the contrast between the sacred and the profane might lead to too easy a resorting to binary oppositions. The strength of the play lies in Friel's refusal to take such simplistic ways with his material. Jack's immersion in his memories of Ryangan ritual withdraws him into a solipsistic world where he has little social engagement with his sisters' household; he has to relearn his own language, and generally behaves like a great child in need of direction and constant mothering. The

Lughnasa fire ceremonies pose considerable dangers to the participants: we learn of one young man who has been severely burned and will be scarred for life. The lure of both rituals is seen to be disabling rather than ennobling. Gerry, the dapper partner with the winsome manner and the neat footwork, is in time discovered to be a two-timing cad who consciously exploits his skills, offering women momentary escape from the burdensome routines of their lives. He may whirl them off their feet; but the consequences are that Chris has an illegitimate child to bring up without his support, while his toying with Agnes provokes jealousies in Chris and leaves Agnes herself to nurse a passion she dares not admit to. For all its physical grace, technical expertise and seemingly transcendental quality, which leaves each of the women 'breathless' in turn, dancing with Gerry is emotionally hazardous; and in his easygoing irresponsibility Gerry himself comes to more than merit Kate's fiercest condemnation as 'pagan'. Friel sustains a profound and disturbing tension throughout the play between the social context of the Mundy household as realized by conventional dramatic means (dialogue, *mise-en-scène*) and the sudden in-trusions into that representational mode of extended passages of dance. The occasion whereby each episode of dancing is introduced into the fabric of the play is wholly credible in terms of stage realism, yet in each case the episode immediately takes on symbolic and metaphorical resonances which are complex in their ambiguity, because they seem to relate (like the actual dancing) to a wholly different dimension of reality. That there is considerable difficulty in reconciling these two 'worlds' is precisely Friel's theme, as is evident from a close scrutiny of the first episode in which dance occurs, indeed when it decidedly erupts onto the stage.

The sisters are quietly going about their household tasks in the family kitchen when Chris turns on the wireless; the sound of traditional Irish dance music establishes itself as a background to their working but begins insidiously to get louder. One by one they leave their chores and join Maggie, the first to abandon her cooking in response to the lilt of the music; she has streaked her face with flour in her first gestures of releasing herself to the seductive power of the rhythm. Three of the others join her in a frantic reel, while Kate remonstrates in an attempt to restore some vestige of order; but Kate too suddenly becomes possessed by the impulsive movements of her limbs and feet and careers wildly round the garden and back into the kitchen in a display of intricate footwork of a dazzling technical brilliance. Though the four, their arms joining them tightly at neck and waist, sing and shriek with merriment that in time edges towards hysteria, Kate preserves a studied silence, lost in a kind of deep communion with herself that her complete absorption in the dance demands. The experience is exhilarating (for audience and performers as well as the characters) but it has too a manic quality that brings it all close to a caricature of the contained orderliness of traditional Irish dance. The *need* those women have to dance takes control as the dominant impression in performance: a need that is sensed as 'frantic' in the grotesque ways it sets them flying and wheeling, yelling ecstatically with heads thrown back. This is little short of frenzy. More is involved here than merely joy in dancing. When the wireless suddenly goes silent, they come to an embarrassed stillness, try to avoid each other's looks or grin nervously, and the atmosphere between them becomes tense with degrees of shame and defiance (21-22).

We are of course to suppose this episode is being presented to us as through the memory of the adult Michael, his perspective influenced by the remembered awe and fear of his childhood self as he watched his mother and his aunts become 'shrieking strangers' (2). But this only in part explains the degree of exaggeration present in the experience. When Maggie first responds to the music, she transforms her features to a white mask with flour, she 'emits a wild, raucous "Yaaah!"' (21), and then everything about her (arms, legs, hair, bootlaces) seems to be 'flying'. The image created onstage is a potent one. Friel chooses to evoke the effect he is after by referring in his stage directions to a 'dervish', presumably to determine in the actress's performance a quality of abandoned whirling. But that mask and cry as forcefully call to mind the traditional image of the Maenad or Bacchante of classical lore, a woman totally given over to bodily impulse and the sensuality of movement in celebration of the power of the god, Dionysus. (It is worth recalling that in Euripides' tragedy, *Bacchae*, the women of Pentheus' kingdom, including his own mother and his aunt, succumb to the lure of the troupe of Maenads surrounding the god in reaction against the strict, puritanical, masculinist values that Pentheus seeks to impose on his subjects.) For a true dervish, the whirling is not 'frantic' but an experience of union with the divine through the medium of the dance; the image created by the fast-turning figure is actually one of total (but transcendent) physical control, where indeed – to quote Yeats – it is impossible to 'know the dancer from the dance' (245). Movement for the dervish is a rite of prayer. Religious expression in the lives of the sisters by contrast is confined to a scrupulous attention to duties and a willed abnegation of all delight in the body's expressiveness. The dancing is in that respect wholly transforming of their habitual, work-weary postures and as such inevitably a welcome release. Reference to the Celtic-derived rites of Lughnasa intimate another such means of release, where celebration is focused on body awareness, the thrill and satisfaction of demonstrating physical prowess and accomplishment during the challenging and rigorous games involved in the fire ceremony. These complex and in some ways conflicting significations are presented to the viewer; and, because dance is not contained within the logical structures of language, they remain potent and challenging since they are not reducible to precise definition. Shift one's mode of perception somewhat and one might argue that, from the standpoint of a punitive orthodoxy (such as the Catholicism practised in the world of the play), bodily expressiveness is subversive precisely because it embraces ambiguity, given its capacity to contain both release and mania, expertise and impulse, sensuousness and sensuality, frenzy and transfiguring ecstasy. Shift that perspective again, and one might argue that it is the very presence of a suspicious and judgmental Catholicism in the society of Ballybeg, which is actually responsible for rendering ambiguous the experience of both dancing and a refined body awareness, by judging impulsive needs as *sinful,* '*pagan*'. The stark moral binaries of that ethical system ensure that the experience of dancing inevitably partakes of escapism, while awareness that dancing is subversive of the prevailing orthodoxies in behaviour must needs bring to such a pursuit a degree of tension or outright fear, which invests the practice with the quality of mania. Dancing, tragically, in the world of Ballybeg as depicted here by Friel can never be *innocent*; and 'pagan' can never be freed of its pejorative connotations.

It is Kate, the eldest sister, who is perhaps the strongest signifier in the scene. When the others begin to cavort together, she (seated) is wholly antagonistic. As the embodiment of what is proper, she refuses to demean herself with such antics until some force within her takes her over completely, brings her smartly to her feet and sets her demonstrating that she is a remarkably skilled practitioner. Friel requires that the director take care to ensure that an audience registers how in dancing Kate enters a completely 'private' world in her rapt concentration. Isolating her from the group in this way (and her dance takes her away from the others and into the garden) allows the audience to focus attention firmly on her within the larger stage picture. In his stage directions at this point Friel tries to suggest a particular effect that the actress should endeavour to communicate through her performance: the audience are to read in her figure '*a pattern of action that is out of character and at the same time ominous of some deep and true emotion*' (22). Friel never uses words loosely and the whole rhythm of the phrasing stresses as significant the word, 'ominous'. It would seem to hold the key to the entire episode. The O.E.D. defines the word as meaning variously 'portentous'; 'fortunate' together with its antithesis, 'inauspicious', extending even to the 'disastrous'; and 'of doubtful or menacing aspect'. Again: a tension between opposites. 'Portentous' is apt since Kate's dance is the outward sign of a profound, because normally suppressed, emotional state. Because it is fiercely repressed, the emotion in the force with which it demands expression is indeed 'menacing'. It is 'fortunate' that this driven impulse finds release in the spontaneity of dance; but equally it is 'disastrous' (in the sense of tragic) in that such expertise as Kate demonstrates is generally withheld and so unrecognized socially for the aesthetic accomplishment that it represents.

But this still does not exhaust the potential of both word and experience. 'Ominous' in deriving from 'omen' refers too to the practice of scrupulously reading signs and symbols, icons and metaphors. In that figure of Kate as mature woman dancing is briefly imaged the pattern of a very different lifestyle which would respect her wealth of emotion, her creativity and zest, her capacity for joy and inner richness of being, her gifts of exquisite co-ordination and physical rhythm, her *beauty*. When silence overtakes the wireless, she is again reduced to the tetchily efficient organizer, whose creativity finds outlet in the controlled mothering of her wayward siblings. Kate fights against her moments of 'otherness', because her return to her mundane self is the harsher for the contrast. In Jack she recognizes one who has given up the struggle, has assumed 'otherness' in imitation of his Ryangan charges and is in consequence 'lost' in terms of conventional Catholic ethics; yet at the last, judging from within her own experience and out of the well of that 'deep and true emotion', she finds the compassion and the integrity to describe her brother as pursuing 'his own distinctive spiritual search' (60). What *Dancing at Lughnasa* represents critically is a society where faith is restricted to the practice of simplistic ethical codes and so has lost all concern with spiritual fulfilment; and most crucially has in the process come to deny that there is any connection between sensual and spiritual awareness. Dance in the play has richly symbolic and metaphysical connotations; that the dancing is not readily containable within the conventions of realism is in itself a deep-rooted criticism of the prevailing mode of theatrical representation on the grounds that it has no means of expressing metaphysical dimensions of experience. The distinctive 'otherness' of dance, emphasized here by its compelled separateness within the dramatic structure, is a source in the play of both anger and a sense of profound, tragic loss.[4]

Wonderful Tennessee

The conscious stylistic disjunctions within *Dancing at Lughnasa* invite audiences to be flexible in the ways they read performance: dancing requires a wholly different mode of interpretation from codes of stage realism and the theme of the play, the penetrating spiritual enquiry, lies in the gap created by the disjunctions. *Wonderful Tennessee* engages with contemporary spiritual consciousness (as distinct from the 1930s world of the earlier play) through even subtler processes of disjunction, in which again bodily movement makes a profound contribution to the shaping of meaning by largely subverting the prevailing stylistic mode.[5] We begin with a protracted experience of silence and the image onstage of an abandoned jetty reaching into the sea; the scene is filled with early morning sunshine and the random sounds of birdsong only emphasize the prevailing quiet. Into this seeming haven of rest erupts a party of holidaymakers, three married couples intent on raucously celebrating the birthday of Terry, who has organized the event; the plan is to be ferried from this spot to a distant island beyond, where they will spend the ensuing night. Ferryman and boat are never to appear and these middle-class, middle-aged roisterers are left waiting with time on their hands. In their efforts to cope with disappointment and the enforced change of plan, we begin to observe the relationships more closely: the six have a long history of shared experience; the husband of one pair (Terry) and the wife of another (Trish) are siblings; the other two wives (Berna and Angela) are sisters; George (Trish's husband) is dying of cancer; Angela impulsively married Frank when clearly Terry would have been a preferable mate; Terry's continuing infatuation with Angela has reduced his marriage to a round of carefully performed duties; Berna, his wife, suffers periods of mental disturbance. Little of this is openly stated; the frictions and tensions, the anxieties and yearnings, the repressed anger and subdued fatalism are rather *sensed*. Friel has long admired Chekhov and Turgenev and the play in part subscribes to the conventions of their mode of naturalism, where meaning lies behind what is actually uttered and is to be inferred through details of tone, placings of actors in relation to each other within the stage space, gesture. It is an admirable choice of style as the dominant mode, since it immediately invites us to read the performance in a particular kind of way: to perceive that what is spoken is frequently a veiled surface behind which profounder, more urgent and private dramas are being played out by the characters.

But a group of characters forcibly whiling away the time inevitably calls to mind Beckett's *Waiting for Godot* (Friel continually pays his respects to his Irish theatrical heritage) and the prevailing party atmosphere allows Friel repeatedly yet plausibly to fracture the naturalistic mode with games and bursts of song, though in a more sustained manner than Didi and Gogo's sudden, frantic 'canters' to relieve their boredom. George is an accomplished accordion player whose fingers pick up any request for a tune and, even when the others are silent, his music contributes to the mood. Cancer in the throat makes it difficult for him to speak, and his playing is his way of supporting the conversation. What is noticeable after a while is the frequency with which the tenor of his music intimates an emotional tone within a particular episode that is very different from what the other characters' talk at the moment seems to be aimed at defining. He starts popular or music-hall songs but often changes the pace and harmonies in ways that invest such tunes with the stateliness of hymns; and while this is explicable in terms of his own mind set, the mood he establishes seems peculiarly sensitive to what one might term the Chekhovian subtext of the given moment, as is evident from the ease with which the other characters succumb to the music's influence. It is as if through responding promptly to the music they can give expression to aspects of themselves to which they cannot openly give voice. Music along with gesture, tone and the spatial relations between the actors is encouraging spectators to explore the emotional currents, which lie behind what words immediately convey. Music in time is found to offer other possibilities to the characters: chiefly a means of escaping the divisive, if petty, strains provoked by simply being together socially for a length of time. When one of them spontaneously,

or taking a cue from George, launches into a song, it is not long
before one or more of the others joins in till sometimes the
choral effort results in a riotous 'performance' in the style of
music hall or instils momentarily a shared seriousness and
intense commitment. The music at such times offers a brief
respite from division and creates in them a sense of community.
What is noticeable in this respect is that the songs like the
hymns are not immediately contemporary but derive either
from the time of the characters' youth or from earlier times still
when the melody brings recall of childhood and family
('Mother's song!'; 'Remember Father singing that every
Christmas?'). What unites the characters in singing is a controlled nostalgia. Within a naturalistic framework situated in the
immediate present, Friel is finding ways through subtextual
devices to intimate the fabric of cultural history that has shaped
his characters' emotional lives: songs, sacred and secular, define
their background and upbringing from which they are now
entirely dissociated and at a cost.

To interpret what that cost entails, it is necessary to engage
with another dimension to the play, which Friel introduces with
studied casualness from the moment of the characters' arrival in
the scene. George, Angela, Frank and Trish appear dancing a
'clownish, parodic conga dance, heads rolling, arms flying – a
hint of the *maenadic*' (17). To establish the point more strongly,
Friel a short while later has Angela imagine George, who has
just obligingly accompanied her through a rendition of 'I Don't
Know Why I'm Happy', as an honoured musician of classical
times: 'You should be wearing a toga and playing a lyre and
gorging yourself with black grapes' and, placing a trail of dry
seaweed on his head like a wreath, she salutes him in his new
guise – 'There! Dionysus!' (21-22). Angela, trapped in a loveless
marriage to Frank and pestered with Terry's attentions, is for
much of the play poised on the edge of hysteria; she several
times tells the others stories of Dionysus but in the telling
seems to withdraw completely into herself; the most extended
tale is of the god, caught and trapped by pirates, but finding
escape through transforming himself and the ship on which
they all travel, which drives his captors to jump overboard

whereupon they were themselves transformed into dolphins (Angela is a classics teacher, and the tale is the subject of one of the Homeric Hymns). We are entering Jungian territory here, where the mythical story reflects an anguish in the narrator suffered in the deeps of the mind.

All the characters tell extended stories during the central scene set in the early hours of the morning following their arrival at the jetty; each tale carries symbolic overtones revealing the psyche of the teller. (Friel is carrying his interest in the potential of monologue within drama into new creative territory here, as each character is unwittingly isolated in a vulnerable moment of truth while performing for the gathering.) Trish recalls at length her wedding to George and his late arrival for the ceremony, which Terry and Frank treat with some ribaldry while George drowns her out with bursts of 'There Was I Waiting at the Church', the painful music hall ditty about a woman being 'left in the lurch'. The episode does much to explain Trish's overly protective solicitude for her husband. Berna tells the story of how the Holy House of Loreto flew there miraculously from Nazareth in 1294, because in her view the event totally defies reason and all the values focused on a right use of logic that she has been trained to respect as a lawyer. George's contribution takes the form of a virtuosic display of technical accomplishment: a breathtakingly 'presto' and impassioned rendering of the third movement of Beethoven's 'Moonlight' sonata which he suddenly breaks off in mid-phrase. After bowing to the others with cold formality, he returns the accordion to its case. The playing, Friel indicates, should express 'internal fury'; it is a cruel, self-inflicted parody of his imminent fate. Frank, seemingly the most cynical and reductive of the men, later tells in awe how on a walk along the beach at dawn he saw the island which is their hoped-for destination emerging from a veil of mist and then watched a dolphin careering above the waves. Embarrassed, he searches for words to define his feelings – 'thrilling', 'wonderful', 'somehow very disturbing' (70) – as if startled by the discovery in himself of the very capacity to *feel*. Terry tells the final tale; it is about the recent history of that island, Oilean Draiochta, where he hoped they would celebrate his birthday; he risks dispelling the group's sense of wonder and mystery about the place by revealing how it was the site of a murder.[6]

The death came as the climax of a time of revelry and is rumoured to have taken the form of a sacrificial rite; reference to the dismembering of the victim and the sense that the perpetrators were in a heightened state of elation verging on trance links the story with Dionysus in his darker aspects and his revenge, as recorded in many myths, on those who deny his power. The young people involved in the incident were, according to Terry, newly returned from the celebrated Dublin Eucharistic Congress in 1932 and in a state of considerable euphoria; and behind this information lie intimations of the links between Christianity and earlier religions focused on sacrifice and atonement. The Christian and the Dionysiac are deftly brought into a precise relationship. The story is a re-markable outpouring from Terry, the genial socializer, whose only care till now seems to have been for everyone else's happiness. But we learn that it is his generosity that has kept Frank and Trish's marriages financially secure; the extent of his magnanimity is evident in the lavish picnic and supply of drink that he endlessly proffers to the group throughout the play; he has been sacrifice and scapegoat for them, as is parodically revealed in a game when they literally 'have the shirt off his back' to a chanted chorus: 'The shirt! – the shirt! – the shirt! … We want it – we want it! … Need it – need it!' (80-81). Again the story intimates a tragic perception of the self, which the play's naturalistic surface sustains in a more banal style. But this tale of Oilean Draiochta is not the only story Terry tells of the island. On their arrival at the jetty he encourages the group to view the island on the horizon and informs them of a ruined monastery there and of Celtic saints associated with the place. To his sister's surprise, he recalls having visited it before as a child with his father, when they came with others on a pilgrimage: he tells of a vigil, of going barefoot and encircling a group of stone mounds where in sequence each visitor lifted a stone from the base of the pile only to replace it on the summit, of a holy well surrounded with votive offerings suggestive of successful cures, of his agnostic father filling a bottle with water at the well and sealing it with a twist of dry grasses. The visit in the present would seem an attempt to relive that occasion and recover the emotions of the former time; but the failure of the ferryman to appear frustrates Terry's intent.

It has been necessary to rehearse so many details of the play the better to appreciate the remarkable originality of the dramaturgy in the final scene. By morning the postures and movement of the characters show that they are wholly exhausted for want of sleep; randomly they begin to pack up their belongings ready for the return journey. While the dialogue continues to flow about her, Angela starts to play an invented game, throwing stones from a set distance to get as close as possible to, but without touching, an empty bottle which she has set up as marker. Just as casually the other women join her in turn, becoming quite focused on the game even while pretending to scorn it: 'What sort of a makey-up game is that?' (67). The lingo, 'makey-up', is significant: they have found a corporate identity through childish invention and with no hint of self-consciousness. By the time the game concludes there is a mound of stones at the foot of a stand on which hangs a remnant of a lifebelt; the stand 'listing and rotting', according to Friel's prescriptions for the set, is 'cruciform in shape' (8). On it various pieces of clothing have been hung throughout the action, which in the tidying are now recovered. Berna on impulse re-ties her silk scarf round one of its arms; and, one by one noticing what is happening, the others hang there some object of personal worth. All the time the conversation continues on the level of trivial matter, making no reference whatever to what the group are severally *doing*. No one questions when Angela suggests they leave an uneaten honey cake by the mound; and shortly afterwards Frank absentmindedly empties some drops of liqueur beside it. (Honey and wine are traditional classical offerings to the gods; but to balance this awareness, we know that, on a more practical and mundane level, Frank needs an empty bottle to fill with rainwater from a puddle on the jetty to mix with his whisky on the return journey.) Their minibus arrives but, having continually voiced a longing to go, they now seem held by the place. Quietly humming a melody in unison, they one by one, barefoot, approach the mound of stones, encircle it twice, each time raising a pebble from the base and replacing it on the summit, touch the votive gift each has left and leave the stage, their postures confidently erect and inwardly seemingly at peace. There is no admission verbally that they have individually accomplished a pilgrimage, but each has exactly enacted the patterned ritual that Terry recalled from his childhood visit to the island.

Evoking this episode in words does a disservice to the artistry of what an audience are clearly to *experience*. The cast are required to speak the dialogue naturalistically, while their bodies move to the wholly different rhythm of ritual: while a banal surface is maintained in the performance, a profound instinctual drive takes possession of the characters on a different level of being, where they acknowledge they have shared a communal spiritual journey throughout that night on the jetty. The ritual they shape together has no specific religious or Catholic connotations; the 'point' lies in the fact simply of its shaping as a shared endeavour. Their talk, their songs, their chatter, their hymns, their feasting and their confessional monologues have veered precariously between the profane and the sacred. They have revealed their private desperations and found some measure of healing. Continually out of the comic spectacle of adults indulging boozily in childish games, moments of revelation have arisen: Terry, the erstwhile provider, is now known to be the archetypal victim; and Angela (appropriately named), the most urbane and svelte of the women, has through a bored form of hopscotch found the means to transform her angry defiance into a kind of belief. We have watched a mystery enacted (formerly, the slain god did ensure survival), and yet the dramatic artistry, the simultaneous playing of Chekhovian naturalism with stylized ritual, saves the experience from a descent into the overly pious or the crassly portentous: the episode remains in consequence an approach to ritual for an agnostic world, an admission of loss and a gesture of hope, an expression of fear at the cultural cost of that loss (and of danger through the story of the murder with its undertones intimating the penalty of suppression) and an assertion that instinct is a valid approach to the mystical. When the idea of pilgrimage is first talked of in the play, the initial interpretation offered is confined to the material ('people went there to be cured'); quietly Berna, the trained lawyer, offers a different explanation: 'To remember again – to be reminded. ... To be in touch again – to attest' (31). 'Attest' is a legal term meaning 'to bear witness to', 'to affirm the truth of', 'to be evidence of' or 'to vouch for'. By the end of *Wonderful Tennessee* it is the *body* that has found its own means of affirmation, quite apart from the play of the mind as registered in the voice. The physical affirms the need for recognition of the spiritual.

What is remarkable about the play is Friel's refusal, given his theme, of the format of parable or allegory. Classical reference (the waiting for the churlish boatman, Dionysus in his life-enhancing and his destructive manifestations, the Orphic and the Eleusinian mysteries) and Christian practice (the hymns, a baptism when Berna jumps into the sea without warning, wedding celebrations, the Eucharist) exist as palimpsests within the flow of the dialogue, hints merely, gestures which may or may not be registered by an audience; but they help increasingly to focus attention for the alert spectator on the actors' bodies as signifiers pointing to a different and independent mode of communication from speech. The play ends as boldly as it began with a protracted silence descending on the scene before the lights fade: all that has changed in the image before us is the careful heap of stones and the objects hanging from the lifebelt stand and yet they are the modest tokens of a search and a discovery. Impressively in both *Dancing at Lughnasa* and *Wonderful Tennessee*, Friel has found a dramatic means of deploying movement and the sheer physicality of his actors to give audiences access to a special subtext in the plays which, in exploring the relation of the spiritual to the social life of an individual, confronts the inexpressible but in a manner that allows it to be respectfully *apprehended*, even if not exhaustively understood. The suggestive nuances of the moving body become metaphors for the numinous.

Notes

[1] Christopher Murray has examined in particular Friel's debts to Yeats (69-90).

[2] Several critics have investigated the deployment of ritual in *Faith Healer*, most notably George Hughes in 'Ghosts and Ritual in Brian Friel's *Faith Healer*'; but his focus is on the structural innovations of the play and their resemblance to aspects of Japanese Noh drama. Ritual is for Hughes most forcefully present in Friel's play in its incantatory mode, where the medium is language rather than the body in movement, stylized or abandoned.

[3] Though a number of critics have examined Friel's new-found interest in the body, their discussions have tended to be thematic rather than analytical of the processes whereby the body becomes a medium of distinctive expression in the process of performance. For example, McMullan's focus in the work cited is on the relation of gender to authority rather than on the functions of dance in the performance text of *Dancing at Lughnasa*; and, though Elmer Andrews claims that 'Yolland and Maire's kiss in *Translations* and Tim and Claire's embrace at the end of *The Communication Cord* (1983) speak volumes, in-augurating a new language of the body beyond the falsifying rituals of the word' in his study of *Wonderful Tennessee*, he does not examine how this new language is given theatrical realization in the ensuing essay. (See '"The Necessity for Paganism": Brian Friel's *Wonderful Tennessee*' [Kamm 513].)

[4] See my essay 'The City Versus the Village' where I have discussed the issue of anger as manifest in the initial production of *Dancing at Lughnasa* at the Abbey Theatre, Dublin, and how this quality was slowly dissipated as the play's popularity required the production to go through several re-castings of the roles.

[5] Csilla Bertha covers rather similar territory to this essay, but she is throughout preoccupied with the finished effects of the drama as they may be applied to specific themes rather than with how those effects are steadily created in performance, which is the focus here.

[6] For a detailed discussion of the function of violence and sacrifice in *Wonderful Tennessee*, see José Lanters.

Works Cited

Bertha, Csilla. 'Six Characters in Search of a Faith: The Mythic and the Mundane in *Wonderful Tennessee*'. *Irish University Review* 29.1 (1999): 119-35.

Cave, Richard Allen. 'The City Versus The Village'. *Literary Inter-Relations: Ireland, Egypt and the Far East*. Ed. Mary Massoud. Gerrards Cross: Smythe, 1996. 281-96.

Deane, Seamus. 'Irish Theatre: A Secular Space?' *Irish University Review* 28.1 (1998): 163-74.

Friel, Brian. *Selected Plays*. London: Faber, 1984.

--- *Dancing at Lughnasa*. London: Faber, 1990.

--- *Wonderful Tennessee*. Oldcastle: Gallery, 1993.

Graham, Martha. *Blood Memory: An Autobiography*. New York: Doubleday, 1991.

Hillman, James. *The Soul's Code*. London: Bantam, 1997.

Hughes, George. 'Ghosts and Ritual in Brian Friel's *Faith Healer*'. *Irish University Review* 24.2 (1994): 175-85.

Kamm, Jürgen, ed. *Twentieth-Century Theatre and Drama in English: Festschrift for Heinz Kosok on the Occasion of his 65th Birthday*. Trier: Wissenschaftlicher, 1999.

Lanters, José. 'Violence and Sacrifice in Brian Friel's *The Gentle Island* and *Wonderful Tennessee*'. *Irish University Review* 26.1 (1996): 163-76.

McMullan, Anna. '"In touch with some otherness": Gender, Authority and the Body in *Dancing at Lughnasa*'. *Irish University Review* 29.1 (1999): 90-100.

Murray, Christopher. 'Friel's Emblems of Adversity and the Yeatsian Example'. In Peacock. 69-90.

Peacock, Alan, ed. *The Achievement of Brian Friel*. Gerrards Cross: Smythe, 1993.

Yeats, W.B. *Collected Poems*. 1939 London: Macmillan, 1950.

DISABILITY AND EMPOWERMENT

11 | Disability as Motif and Meaning in Friel's Drama
Ruth Niel

A Disabled Universe?

Whether at the centre of the action or, more frequently, in peripheral roles, the disabled are a constant presence in Friel's drama. So pervasive is this presence that one is led to ask not only about their function in individual plays in terms of character, theme and symbolic force, but, over and above this, about the significance of disability itself for the writer and his work. The data are impressive. There is hardly a play of Friel's in which at least one character is not physically handicapped or mentally disabled or disturbed. We meet people who are lame, deaf, colour-blind, blind or dumb, many *dramatis personae* have suffered nervous breakdowns, some spend or have spent part of their lives in mental homes or have had a stroke, others are mentally confused or retarded. In response to this, the present essay will initially outline the types of disabilities the reader or spectator is confronted with in Friel's *oeuvre,* and investigate the functions they serve in their particular context. Their number and variety suggest that there is no single answer to the question what the disabilities stand for. Nevertheless, per-meating the plays like a *leitmotif,* they seem to indicate a whole that is more than merely the sum of its parts. In this they are like other motifs in Friel's work, which may not be particularly obtrusive within the individual plays, where other issues are larger and more immediate, but which take on a wider implication in the context of the drama as a whole.[1] In Friel's plays these motifs indicate a world, a mental universe actively informing the limited scope of the drama. The essay's underlying question is concerned with this universe and the place taken in it by disability.

The Individual in Society

Friel's plays – or particular aspects of his work – have often been interpreted as emphasizing either private or public concerns. His plays dealing with the question of language, such as *Translations* or *The Communication Cord*, have thus been seen primarily as comments on society, whereas *Molly Sweeney* or *Dancing at Lughnasa* were thought to emphasize individual psychological problems.[2] It is clear, however, that while such distinctions can be useful interpretative tools, one should not forget that they are only tools. Friel's plays usually combine the public and the private levels. This is also true of his use of disabilities. Thus nervous breakdowns often indicate a private, psychological event, a disability standing for a character's inability to cope with his or her life. But families in Friel's plays often function like microcosms. The lack of communication that reveals the problems of an individual or a family can, therefore, at the same time, be symptomatic of society as a whole.

Manus, the father in *The Gentle Island* can serve as an example of the duality of the private and public function of disabilities in Friel's work.[3] Manus lost an arm as a young man, and there are conflicting versions of how this happened. Manus's own version – that it was the result of a mining accident in Montana (55) – serves to create and to support the myth of the strong man who left his island to work but finally came back 'home' where he belongs. His embittered daughter-in-law, Sarah, however, tells the visitors Shane and Peter that on his return to Inishkeen, Manus still had both his arms, and that he was attacked and wounded by the two uncles of Rosie, the woman whom Manus had left with a baby son without marrying her. After the fight Manus, according to Sarah, had to stay on the island because there was no work for one-armed labourers. He married Rosie, but, shortly after the second son's birth, she committed suicide.

Thus, the facts themselves are shrouded in the needs of those who relate them. Manus obviously needs his own story because he cannot face up to his behaviour towards Rosie. When faced with Sarah's version, he admits its basic truth and claims that he only returned to marry Rosie; but the relationship failed because after the fight she was uneasy with a disabled man. This again, however, might be invented. Manus's sons are split in their attitudes towards their father's behaviour: Joe, the younger son, believes him; Philly is convinced that Manus betrayed their mother. There are indications that Manus is at least partly honest, as he tries to persuade Joe to marry his girl and tells him not to risk losing her; but there is no proof. He might simply be feeling guilty in hindsight for his own behaviour. This scenario is typical of the whole play: the main characters never really know whether anything anybody else says is true; they cannot communicate, they cannot trust each other, and there are different versions of every tale.

This opaqueness casts its shadow on the attack on Shane. Again, this is caused by a supposed betrayal, and, again, Sarah is the one who reveals it when she says she saw Shane in a homosexual encounter with her husband. Although this story is never verified either, Manus and Sarah believe Shane has to be punished, and she wounds him with a gun. These 'private' events have a public side to them, however; for it is the need to find work abroad that leads to separation and broken relationships in the first place. Nor can outsiders be accepted or returned emigrants reintegrated – the world of the islanders remains isolated, hermetic. This world is so sterile that there can be no new life: all the islanders, apart from Manus's family, leave Inishkeen at the opening of the play, and Sarah, the only woman left, has no children. The only new arrivals from outside are two men, probably homosexuals (although, again, this is never verified), who cannot solve anything. Shane is a scapegoat (see Lanters, 'Violence' 164) and the violence against him is a logical consequence of a form of life that has lost all meaning and perspective. Manus's severed arm becomes a symbol of this impoverished, violent situation, of the cruelty of the world these people inhabit and of a society that is breaking apart.

Other figures represent a similar duality. Thus Manus in *Translations* is lame, because his father Hugh fell over his cradle (412). Owen, Hugh's younger son, believes this is why Manus has always felt responsible for his father. What looks like a paradox at first glance – that the lame son feels responsible for the father and not the other way round – makes sense in the complex world of *Translations*, where the father, for all his learning and understanding, is an alcoholic who neglects his duties and leaves his son to do all the work.[4] The relationship between father and son is more ambiguous than it seems, and the same can be said of the play as a whole. *Translations* is not a simple, nostalgic play about Ireland's loss of identity as a result of British colonialism. The Irish *dramatis personae* are depicted too subtly and have too many negative traits to allow for such a straightforward reading.

The opening scene already indicates this: we see three characters on stage – Manus, Sarah and Jimmy Jack. Manus is lame, Sarah is dumb, Jimmy Jack lives in a mental world of his own. 'For Jimmy the world of the gods and the ancient myths is as real and as immediate as everyday life in the townland of Baile Beag', the stage direction comments (384). But, as Hugh indicates towards the end of the play, this has another side to it: Jimmy Jack has ceased to distinguish between the literal past and the images of the past embodied in language. This, for Friel, is central: Friel himself has rejected the notion that the rural Ireland represented by Baile Beag was meant to be identified with Eden. The idyll, he observes, is an illusion, and his remark highlights the wider dimensions of the dramatic issue: 'you have on stage the representatives of a certain community – one is dumb, one is lame and one is an alcoholic, a physical maiming which is a public representation of their spiritual deprivation' (qtd. in O'Toole, 'Hesitant Move' 5).

The figure of Sarah shows this aspect of the play particularly clearly. As the curtain rises, Manus is teaching Sarah to speak. The stage directions read: 'Sarah's speech defect is so bad that all her life she has been considered locally to be dumb and she has accepted this' (383). Manus holds her hands, he is gentle with her, and, in this situation of trust, Sarah is able to utter her first sentence: 'My name is Sarah' (384). Manus sees this as the beginning of a new life for her: 'Now we've really started! ... Soon you'll be telling me all the secrets that have been in that head of yours all these years' (385). The ironic twist in this relationship is that the only secret which Sarah will ever tell Manus – she calls him when she sees Maire and Yolland kissing – will lead to the destruction of his hope for love and to the catastrophe at the end of the play.

Sarah, only once, manages to use her new-found ability to communicate through language. When Owen asks her who she is, she can state her name and the place she comes from – she can state her identity.[5] But her ability to speak leaves her when the situation changes. When Lancey, announcing the evictions at the end of the play, shouts the question at her: 'Who are you? Name!' (440), she frantically tries to answer but cannot. And she knows she cannot. She ceases even to try. Seamus Heaney makes explicit the wider significance of this action, reading Sarah at a necessary public level of interpretation: 'It is as if some symbolic figure of Ireland from an eighteenth-century vision poem, the one who once confidently called herself Cathleen ni Houlihan, has been struck dumb by the shock of modernity' (1199). A world is coming to an end, is losing its coherence and meaning, and speechlessness is the result.

Children and Fathers

Emotional crippling and the inability to communicate recur particularly frequently in relationships between adult children and their fathers. In Friel's plays most relationships between fathers and their children, especially their sons, are fraught with problems and tensions. Marilyn Throne argues that 'It is clear ... that Friel is emphasizing not the parents' role, but rather the father's role [and] ... that in all of the plays the children are

presented as actually or psychologically crippled by their
fathers' (163) – mothers often being absent, dead or without
influence.[6] In general, father figures have no real authority any
more, but most fathers still act out of a need for dominance
over their offspring.

The most striking example of a father who has lost his
authority is Judge O'Donnell in *Aristocrats*. He used to be a
powerful man: owner of Ballybeg Hall, residence of the influential Catholic O'Donnell family, and district judge.[7] But he
has suffered a stroke; he is now reduced to a state of confusion
and physical disability and is totally dependent on his children,
who have even installed a baby-alarm to help supervise him.
The five children are, all in their own way, crippled by their
father. Judith, the eldest, had to give up her illegitimate child in
order to look after him. Alice is married to a local man, but she
lives with him in London and is an alcoholic. Anna is a nun,
working as a missionary in Africa. She is present through a tape
sent to her family; when the others listen to it, it becomes clear
that she still speaks and thinks like a child, frozen in a world
that has long since vanished. Claire, the youngest daughter, is a
talented pianist but, like their mother, who committed suicide,
she suffers from depressions: her father did not allow her to
pursue an artistic career.[8] Out of all of them, however, it is the
son Casimir who has been most damaged by his father. The
stage directions describe him as 'erratic' but not 'disturbed': 'He
is a perfectly normal man with distinctive and perhaps slightly
exaggerated mannerisms' (255). When he was nine years old,
Casimir was forced to realize that he was in some way different
from others, that others found him peculiar; and it was his
father who made him cruelly aware of this:

> I remember the day he said to me: 'Had you been born down
> there' – we were in the library and he pointed down to Ballybeg
> – 'Had you been born down there, you'd have become the
> village idiot. Fortunately for you, you were born here and we
> can absorb you' ... So at nine years of age I knew certain
> things: that certain kinds of people laughed at me; that the easy
> relationships that other men enjoy would always elude me; that

– that – that I would never succeed in life, whatever – you know – whatever 'succeed' means (310).

Casimir has found his own way of at least partly coming to terms with this fact: he lives in a world of memories and stories from the past. He constantly talks about their childhood, telling anecdotes from the O'Donnells' past – though most of them do not coincide with historical fact and refer only to the family's connections with artists and intellectuals, never to the power of the O'Donnells as representatives of a particular political past and of the institutions of the law. Casimir has escaped from his father's example: he did not finish law school; he married a German woman, lives in Germany, and has three sons who cannot speak English: he will never be able to say such cruel things to them as his father said to him, for he speaks hardly any German. By his own admission he does not seem to have much authority (278), but maybe he will find a way of communicating with them without words, at least without destructive words. Through privation he may have discovered something unique and worthwhile:

> once I acknowledged that the larger areas were not accessible to me, I discovered … smaller, much smaller areas that were … I find that I can live with these smaller, perhaps very confined territories without exposure to too much hurt. Indeed I find that I can experience some happiness and perhaps give a measure of happiness, too (310-11).

Ironically, the family, gathered for Claire's wedding (again, to a much older man), have to attend their father's funeral instead. An old world is coming to an end, Ballybeg Hall will be given up and the O'Donnell children finally get the chance to live their own lives.

Marilyn Throne and Edna Longley have both interpreted the public level of the father figures in Friel. Longley calls Judge O'Donnell 'symbolically maimed by a stroke' (93).[9] Marilyn Throne points out that several fathers – including Grace's father in *Faith Healer* – have professions which make them re-presentatives of authority in public life – judge, teacher, doctor, army commandant:

> However, whatever titles and real or titular power Friel's fathers
> have, they also have a shared impotence. ... [The] combination
> in the fathers of a power of authority, which is sometimes
> crippling to their children, and an impotence in solving the
> problems of life in general and Ireland in particular creates
> conflicts with and within those children (162-63).

Friel, Throne continues, 'is exposing the failure of the Irish
culture to communicate its heritage to its offspring' (171). The
fathers themselves might still believe in this heritage, but can
only pass on negative, destructive authority, devoid of meaning.
Paradoxically, the crippled children love their fathers, but few
of them can find any escape. Through his representation of the
patriarchal judges in *Aristocrats* and *Faith Healer*, Friel shows the
crippling effects of systems without respect for the individual –
both at a political and a personal level.

Gar's father, S.B. O'Donnell in *Philadelphia, Here I Come!*, is
another character who lacks individual authority. Unable to
communicate with his son, he still dictates Gar's life, and their
unequal and repressed relationship is one of the main reasons
why Gar will emigrate – if his father showed any signs of
changing the way they lived together, he would probably stay.
Father and son have no way of communicating, they are both
speechless, and the love which exists between them can only be
expressed through the medium of a third person: in Gar's case
his 'other' self, Private Gar.

Maureen Hawkins interprets Gar's split personality as an
example of literal as well as literary schizophrenia (*passim*).
Basing her conclusions on the theories of R.D. Laing and on
Nancy Scheper-Hughes's study of *Saints, Scholars, and Schizo-
phrenics*, she sees Friel's plays as representations of a schizophrenic society and some of his characters as symbolic
embodiments of this state. Her examples are Gar in *Philadelphia*,
the three protagonists in *The Freedom of the City* (taken together
as one), and Hugh, Jimmy Jack and Owen in *Translations*.
Schizophrenia, according to Laing, is generated by the inability
of the individual to validate and integrate experience – either on
his own or through significant other people (usually the family).

In the context of drama, this becomes rather a blunt weapon. It may apply to the examples Hawkins mentions, but it is equally true of most other characters in Friel's plays. Gar's split character enables the spectator to hear and see hidden aspects of his personality, which we would otherwise never know, for Public Gar is as speechless as his father. Whether this duality – and the duality one can observe in other characters – really implies symptoms of schizophrenia may, however, be doubted. One could equally argue that Gar is yet another 'normal' person, and that his split character represents a psychological state, which many people share. Nevertheless, one can agree with Hawkins that there is a symbolism of schizophrenia at work in this play: Friel has indeed spoken of himself as living 'in a schizophrenic community' ('Self-Portrait' 19), and several other critics have indicated the schizophrenic elements in the society he portrays (see O'Toole, 'Silicon' *passim* or Longley *passim*). Irish society, and in particular Northern Irish society, is divided; it does not constitute a unified whole, which could offer its people harmony and meaning.

Longley makes the interesting further point that some of the critical writing on Friel's *oeuvre* also uses terminology from psychology. In his introduction to the *Selected Plays* Seamus Deane uses terms like depression, apathy, desolation, crisis and dislocation. Longley comments: 'This language partly derives from psychology: the terminology of depressive psychosis. Friel in *Translations* applies a kind of therapy to this psychosis by offering Northern Catholics an alternative history ...' (98). Seamus Heaney had also used the term therapy in his review of *Translations*: 'Friel's work, not just here but in his fourteen preceding plays, constitutes a powerful therapy, a set of imaginative exercises that give her [Cathleen ni Houlihan] the chance to know and say herself properly again' (1980). While it undoubtedly has this local symbolic force, mental disability in its various manifestations has a further dimension of (public) significance in Friel's plays, for it is a major element in his conception of the human being – and this in turn reflects on the conflicting cultural philosophies of present-day Ireland.

The Disabled Soul

In many Friel plays we encounter (or hear about) characters who suffer nervous breakdowns or depression; such as Ben and Helen in *Living Quarters*, Grace and Grace's mother in *Faith Healer*, Claire and her mother in *Aristocrats*, Berna in *Wonderful Tennessee*, Maggie's mother in *Lovers*, and Molly's mother in *Molly Sweeney*, to name only some of them. Most of these are women, who in Friel's plays find it even more difficult to live with the complexities and pain of existence than men – they, faced with similar problems, try to find other solutions. For a lot of women characters, the inability to cope with the 'realities of life' and history leads to depression or to a retreat into a private world that is no longer considered 'normal' by society. Cass, Trilbe and Ingram in *The Loves of Cass McGuire* are notable examples. When Cass is forced to live in Eden House, an old people's home she calls the workhouse, she gradually gives up her attempt to make meaning of the harsh circumstances of her life and weaves her own truth instead, a beautiful truth in which love and understanding enrich existence. Friel does not present this as a failure but as a meaningful form of escape. Very few characters in his plays are able to find such a positive solution, however: Grace Hardy kills herself, as did the (absent) mother in *Aristocrats*, and Ben and Helen in *Living Quarters* slide further into depression and alcoholism. Mental instability in Friel's work thus becomes a recurrent pointer to its source in the instability of the family and its social and political environment.

Some figures seek a more positive, active solution within the outside world. Berna in *Wonderful Tennessee* has spent time in a nursing home because of a nervous breakdown and alcohol problems. She is one of six people in the play who go on an outing: the three couples want to visit a small island but never get further than the pier on the mainland. In the course of the highly symbolic action, tensions, problems and conflicts become apparent, but also love, desire and hope.[10] The island used to be a place of pilgrimage but was also the site of a cruel, perhaps ritual murder. Its name Oileán Draíochta means 'Island of Otherness' or 'Island of Mystery' (28), and it stands among other things for the unattainable, the elusive. The situation presented in the play, removed from everyday life and experience, a borderland setting with vagueness and fluidity as major elements, corresponds directly to Berna's personality and circumstances. She says of herself: 'There are times when I feel I'm … "about to be happy" … Maybe that's how most people manage to carry on – 'about to be happy'; the real thing almost within grasp, just a step away. Maybe that's the norm. But then there are periods – occasions – when just being alive is … unbearable!' (43-44). Csilla Bertha comments:

> Berna … seems to be the most sensitive to the meaning of time and place … She, the one who finds it most difficult to adjust to everyday life and to the forced cheerfulness of the others, understands most fully and is able to express the meaning of the island … ('Island of Otherness' 132).

Berna wants to defy reason and believes in memory as a healing force. Thus, when they are discussing why people used to go on pilgrimages to the island, and someone asks: 'But years ago people went to be cured?', she replies: 'To remember again – to be reminded. … To be in touch again – to attest' (31).

The theme of memory and healing evoked in this sequence of verbs echoes two other plays in which the same elements are crucial: *Translations*, in which Hugh comes to the conclusion: 'To remember everything is a form of madness' (445), and *Faith Healer*, which offers yet another variation of the theme remembering – madness – healing. The three characters in this play are haunted by their memories of the past. Terry seeks salvation by concentrating on positive memories (although in this he fails); Grace finds no escape and commits suicide; Frank needs to silence the torment of inner questioning. Frank, the healer with an erratic gift, knowingly seeks the ultimate nexus of failure and death as the embodiment of man's existential need and its incurability. He goes out into the backyard to meet the disabled man he is supposed to cure, and as he does so his feelings focus and intensify. He knows that 'nothing was going to happen', but despite – or because of – knowing this

> I became possessed of a strange and trembling intimation: that
> the whole corporeal world ... had shed [its] physical reality ...,
> and that in all existence there was only myself and the wedding
> guests. And that intimation in turn gave way to a stronger sense:
> that even we had ceased to be physical and existed only in spirit,
> only in the need we had for each other ... And as I moved
> across the yard towards them and offered myself to them, then
> for the first time there was no atrophying terror (375-76).

The questioning had ceased. What makes it cease, however, is
no passive succumbing to fate – it is an active step.[11]

The play's final speech and action provide a complex commentary on faith and healing. The act of faith has a twofold
significance: on the one hand it effects a momentary healing,
not of its subject but of the healer. Frank has become whole
(333). His ability to heal gives him hope. Hope, however, must
learn to live with its opposite, the bleakness of despair, which is
man's final hope. Frank's abandonment to his situation touches
here to the heart of Friel's drama. The awareness on which it
rests has far-reaching cultural and political as well as philosophical implications, for its conception of man is of a being
that is incurably broken, and this strides across the theological
premises of the sectarian divide – inasmuch as that divide can
be said to have such premises. It is to reinforce their faith in the
ineluctable finality of despair that the cripples assemble. They
had come 'not in hope but for the elimination of hope', for the
'confirmation that they were incurable' (336-37). Reality becomes bearable when it is understood and accepted, even if this
means the loss of hope and optimism.

Order and Disorder

Friel's use of characters who are mentally retarded or confused
often highlights a particular aspect of problems related to reality
and fiction and to the validity of distinguishing between the
two. What is real, what is imagined, what is sane, what is insane
– these are questions that run through the whole of his *oeuvre*.
Two minor figures that raise the issue are Declan in *The Freedom
of the City* and Jimmy Jack in *Translations*. Two others are
particularly interesting: Rose and Jack in *Dancing At Lughnasa*.

Rose is described as 'simple' in the opening stage directions. Her sisters feel protective towards her. Right from the beginning of the play it is obvious that she 'moves to a different rhythm from that of the world. Indeed her grasp of the empirical world is uncertain, as her faltering notions of geography indicate. Yet, Rose has intuitive knowledge in other areas of experience', as Peacock and Devine comment (120). She is in love with a married man – a relationship her sisters watch with suspicion but which she refuses to give up. He takes her to the symbolic 'back hills', which were and obviously still are at the time of Lughnasa the site of pagan rituals. More acutely than her 'normal' sisters, she senses the importance of these rituals, of a world that reaches beyond the ordinary and visible. Thus she strongly opposes Kate, the most traditionally Christian of the sisters, when they talk of Lughnasa and rituals (16).[12] With her direct, innocent approach Rose shows how questionable a value-system is which believes in only one set of rules and in a norm that alone is 'healthy'.

The figure of Father Jack adds a further dimension to the same theme. Jack has recently returned from Africa, where he spent most of his life as a missionary. His mental confusion becomes apparent when he enters the scene: he does not recognize the room or his sisters immediately. He cannot remember the correct words for objects – the place and the language are obviously no longer his own. Nor can he distinguish clearly between Christian and pagan beliefs; but he does not seem to recognize this as unusual. Jack has partly 'gone native' in Africa, giving up those aspects of Christianity which ordain rules and restrict people. Ancestral spirits, rituals, sacrifice, ceremonies seem closer to his thought than the Catholic faith. His confusion is a blending of different worlds and realities. What is presented, as an acceptable system of personal beliefs cannot, however, be accepted by the society he has been forced to return to. He is suspended as a priest and his sister Kate consequently loses her job as a teacher, a job the whole Mundy family depends on financially.

The sanity and insanity of the human condition is also the issue where Friel sets the lives of his characters more or less permanently in a mental home. All of the figures in question are women. One of them is Bridget, the daughter of the writer Tom Connolly in *Give Me Your Answer, Do!* We learn nothing about the reasons why Bridget lives in a home; we only witness her outward state. She is in her early twenties, her room in the basement contains only an iron bed with an uncovered mattress. She never speaks, although a nurse reports that she sometimes screams and goes wild. Her father visits her regularly – her mother never does – and tells her wonderful stories, all of them invented, full of ideas, comic and entertaining. As a writer he has no ideas at all any more. He tells Bridget of his hopes, weaving a beautiful image of the future for them and tenderly calling her 'my silent love, my strange little offspring' (15, 84). Tom accepts his daughter as she is, but there are hints in the play that he cannot come to terms with the fact that she has changed so utterly.

Give Me Your Answer, Do! is, among other things, a play about art and the creative process. Two of its figures are writers; another, Tom's wife Daisy, is a talented pianist without a career, and her father is a failed musician. The play abounds in quotations from literary and musical sources that have in common that they are symbols or metaphors both of the impossibility of seeing the world as a coherent, meaningful place and of the complexity of the creative process. José Lanters perceptively uses chaos theory and the concept of the 'theatre of chaos' to shed light on this apparent conundrum. She comments: 'Uncertainty is the key word in *Give Me Your Answer, Do!* In this play, too, entropy is all-pervasive … Sickness, madness, isolation, depression, kleptomania and alcoholism dominate the conversation: the forces of disintegration are about to prevail. Language, too, is disintegrating …' (Lanters, 'Uncertainty' 166-67). Chaos and uncertainty, however, as Lanters observes, far from being purely negative, are vital elements in the creative process; Daisy indeed speaks of 'Necessary Uncertainty' (80).

Bridget's state, veering in multiple dimensions between order and disorder, is emblematic of this situation. She also presents a foil against which the other six characters are seen and evaluated. Tom, for example, can only be creative when he speaks to his daughter in the mental asylum. When she fell ill (a few years prior to the time of the play), he wrote two un-published pornographic novels, completely untypical of the rest of his work, and has not written anything since. 'Tom', Lanters says, 'tried to express the obscenity of his daughter's condition in words . . .' ('Uncertainty' 169). Likewise Daisy's inability to meet her daughter hints at the brittleness of her own mental stability.

The play offers no concrete solutions, but, as Lanters argues, nothing is static either. Bridget's dramatic function is to embody this instability: 'The mystery of Friel's play is that the actual (madness) and the symbolic (healing, poetry) are both true at the same time: this autistic girl in whose condition there is never any change is simultaneously a source of despair to her parents and the potential source of artistic renewal' ('Uncertainty' 173). Hope resides here in the possibility of a new beginning, of the creative process starting all over again. Friel's achievement is to locate the motif of disability as an intellectually powerful symbol of the conjunction of order and disorder that activates that process.

Molly Sweeney is another woman confined in a mental institution. She has been blind nearly all her life and she too bears her family history with her. When Molly is admitted to the same mental home as her mother, the audience realizes that the characters of both her parents have to be re-evaluated. At first glance she and her mother differ completely from each other, as Molly often talks lovingly of her father (another judge), whereas references to her mother are rare and reveal facts rather than emotions. Only towards the end of the play is she able to reveal that her father was too mean to pay for a blind-school and that her mother could not accept his decision. In her fantasies she believes she meets her mother (who actually died long ago) in the hospital, and says of her: 'I think I know her better than I ever knew her and begin to love her all over again' (66). Being now in the place where her mother was, she can understand things that were formerly outside her own world. Like Cass, Trilbe and Ingram, she makes the hospital her new home (67). Richard Pine comments in his study of Friel: 'Mental hospitals, like prisons, set boundaries to both freedom and control, but, within those boundaries, allow the condition of ecstasy – that is, standing outside one's normal, social self – and permit the celebration of failure' (141).

Molly Sweeney is the most complex of all Friel's disabled characters. Her 'story' is told by the *dramatis personae* in three interweaving monologues. As in *Faith Healer*, the structure chosen underlines the importance of memory as the only valid source of truth. At the same time it presents the isolation of the individual speakers. Although their stories do not contradict each other as they did in the earlier play, the three characters never find a way of communicating in a meaningful way. That they actually interpret important events in similar terms or have similar desires makes this lack of communication all the more moving.

Molly's father introduced her as a child to her own world of sensation, particularly smell and touch. She had a job, was married and loved swimming, a sensual activity which she experienced as liberating through the harmony it brought with the physical world around her. Molly's balanced and by no means unhappy life changes radically when her husband Frank persuades her and the run-down ophthalmologist Mr. Rice to operate in order to restore her vision. Frank has been absorbed in various bizarre schemes in the past, and now he is fascinated by theories of vision and blindness. 'In entering Molly's non-visual realm of sensuality and joy', Carol-Anne Upton argues, 'we are offered a new insight into the harmonious world she has already created, if not acknowledged' (348). And this last word, 'acknowledged', hints at the problems to come, for Molly is unaware of the real value of her existence. Neither she nor Frank can imagine how her perception – and thus her world – will be altered by vision. 'What has she to lose?' Frank asks (*Molly Sweeney* 17). Only Mr. Rice has doubts. The night before the operation Molly suddenly feels uneasy, she does not know why she has agreed to it and turns Frank's question round:

> And have I anything to gain? Anything? Anything?
> And then I knew, suddenly I knew why I was so desolate. It
> was the dread of exile, of being sent away. It was the desolation
> of homesickness (31).

That is the paradox that now overtakes her; for the
operation is successful, and Molly's sight is restored. At first she
enjoys this new world which she slowly has to make her own.
She has to learn anew what she is seeing, and, after a while, she
begins to understand that she is losing the world she knows, the
specific world of her blindness. In a very touching episode
Molly realizes that her favourite flowers, to which her father
used to compare her, are visually unattractive. She is unable to
cope with her disappointment with the world of sight, and she
slides into a state which is called 'blind-sight'[13]: organically she
should be able to see, but her psychological state 'blinds' her
physically – the very opposite of her previous condition. As in
Faith Healer, we witness the miracle of a cure but, again, it is a
cure without healing. And as so frequently in Friel, this is
connected with the passage from hope to despair. Heinz Kosok
remarks that when a further dimension is added to her life and
her personality (that is, sight), Molly is thrown into an identity
crisis, which she can only escape from by returning to the world
of blindness. This, in the eyes of society, marks her as unable to
survive in the 'normal' world – the logical consequence is her
removal to a mental hospital (Kosok 27-28). The exile she was
afraid of has become reality, but Molly manages to create a new
reality for herself in this hostile environment. She ceases to
distinguish between 'ordinary' reality and fantasy. Like Cass
before her, she gathers her friends in her mind, and finally, in
the world so created, is able to accept the fact that her father
lied to her when he said that she could not attend blind-school
because her mother needed her company. She had always
known this, but had been unable to acknowledge it. In her final
speech she says:

> Anyhow my borderline country is where I live now. I'm at
> home there. Well … at ease there. It certainly doesn't worry me
> anymore that what I think I see may be fantasy or indeed what I

take to be imagined may very well be real ... – external reality.
Real – imagined – fact – fiction – fantasy – reality – there it
seems to be. And it seems to be alright. And why should I
question any of it any more? (67)

Molly has silenced her personal 'maddening questions'. But
disability is more than a metaphor here, for Molly's blindness
not only symbolizes the deficiency of the human condition, it
opens her own eyes to it. This takes the argument a step further
than *Faith Healer*, confirming at a more explicit level of consciousness the relinquishment of conventional hope that
informed the earlier play.[14]

Conclusion

The reality of Brian Friel's plays is always psychological. He
masterfully depicts the inner state of a character in a few scenes,
a few economical hints and comments about his or her past or
family history. Functioning in the same way as do the other
motifs mentioned at the beginning of this essay, the disabilities
that have become a constant feature in Friel's *oeuvre* contribute
at this level to the creation of a unique dramatic universe and
indicate its complexity. Nothing here is smooth, easy, 'healthy',
or 'normal': there are always scars, faults, disturbances and
deviations from the norm. One can argue that the disabilities in
minor characters have an additional function: they point to yet
another complex situation beyond the one at the centre of the
particular play. Friel does not have to go any further; the main
characters may set the tone, pose the central conflict, but the
hints about similar events in the past, about disabilities, nervous
breakdowns and impairments in other figures, are enough to
open the audience's awareness to the fact that everyone in the
play, however 'minor', lives in a world which is as complex,
difficult, haunting, thwarted and maimed as that of the central
characters. If the minor figures were shifted into the centre of
the play (for example, Maggie's or Molly's mothers in *Lovers,*
and *Molly Sweeney* or Bridget in *Give Me Your Answer, Do!*), their
version of the universe would be as moving and convincing as
the chosen focus.

But the focus of Friel's drama is not just psychological, not just individual. His plays present a view of life that is both striking in itself and has considerable implications for an understanding of man's place in the universe. Disability here is not merely a symbol of the human condition in an age that has lost its faith; on the contrary, the loss of conventional faith is a cornerstone of Friel's thought. Disability is part of the system, part of life; above all it cannot be redeemed. Friel's drama constantly moves against any striving for wholeness, any attempt to promote a simplistic, unified system of meaning. The faith he affirms is in one's ability to recognize and accept one's own infirmity without hope of reprieve. The desire – religious or otherwise – to find a holistic solution for the complexities of human existence is bound to fail, for it will inevitably lead to absolutism, with catastrophic results for the individual, unless he or she finds a way of accepting the brokenness of their world. That Friel should set this brokenness at the heart of the human condition has nothing to do with pessimism, but rather with a developed humanism that rejects all doctrinaire attempts to discipline the intractable awkwardness of experience. The life that shines through his plays is more convincing for not being an absolute: it is a broken, crippled thing and is affirmed as such.

Notes

[1] The townland of Ballybeg is an example of the way these motifs function; it stands for a small place in Ireland, but at the same time takes on a universal dimension: it is both concrete and abstract. For the function of Ballybeg see Richard Pine, *Brian Friel and Ireland's Drama*, *passim*. Other such motifs are Friel's use of music in his plays or the ritual of naming; see, for example Burke, "'Both Heard and Imagined'" and Deane, 'The Name of the Game'.

[2] For discussions of the public and the private levels in Friel's plays compare, for example, the relevant articles in Peacock, *The Achievement of Brian Friel*, Richard Kearney, 'Language Play', or Elmer Andrews, *The Art of Brian Friel: Neither Reality Nor Dreams*.

[3] For interpretations of this play see José Lanters, Michael Parker, and Csilla Bertha.

[4] Critics have often seen Hugh in a positive light simply because he is the figure who articulates the play's crucial insights into language. For a

summary of the early reception of the play see Lionel Pilkington's perceptive essay which also offers insights into the play's irony, particularly in connection with Hugh.

[5] It is interesting to note that the question of Owen's identity culminates in his utterance of the analogous statement 'My name is Owen' (421), when he finally acknowledges the fact that names and language do have a meaning and are vital for maintaining a sense of identity. His sentence can also be seen as a new beginning in his life.

[6] One exception as a mother figure is Lily in *The Freedom of the City*, a warm-hearted, strong personality, who goes on civil rights marches out of some vague feeling that it might protect her son Declan, who suffers from Down's syndrome. Marching for her, however, is also an act of defiance against her husband and his refusal to love and accept his handicapped son. *Living Quarters* is another play where children suffer nervous breakdowns, and the son also stammers badly when he is upset because of the unresolved tensions which lie at the core of the family history.

[7] The decline in authority can be seen in the decline of power in the line of the male O'Donnells: the great-grandfather was Lord Chief Justice, the grandfather Circuit Court Judge, the father District Judge (295).

[8] Their mother was an actress whom the judge married very soon after meeting her, when her troupe was travelling through Donegal. This indicates a long-buried side to the father's character and links him to other fathers in Friel's work, for example, S.B. O'Donnell in *Philadelphia* and Commandant Frank Butler in *Living Quarters*. They all married young, beautiful women who needed freedom – something they could not have in the claustrophobic world they were immersed in; and this, in turn, links to the function of disability as a sign of irremediable brokenness in Friel's work. Friel's socio-historical critique modulates seamlessly, here as elsewhere, into a reflection on man's existential condition. The close weft of subordinate and major theme and the referential mesh created across his work in elaborating these themes is a typical feature of Friel's writing.

[9] Longley reads this symbolism in a narrowly political sense when she says of the fathers in *Aristocrats* and *Translations*: 'In both these plays the sense of the fathers having let down their children makes a political comment on the history of Northern Catholics since 1921' (93-94). One does not have to follow this interpretation in order to see that Friel's very choice of an Irish Catholic family of judges raises the wider political issue of the integration of Irish Catholics into the British imperial system – and a long time prior to 1921.

[10] For a perceptive interpretation of the many levels of meaning see the

two essays by Bertha.

11 See Kiberd for an interpretation of Frank as Christ-figure and artist.

12 For a detailed discussion of the symbolic meaning of the Lughnasa rituals see Peacock and Devine.

13 The play is full of references to scientific theories about blindness, both historical and modern. Friel says in the programme notes for the first British production, which opened on 27 October 1994, that he feels 'indebted to Oliver Sacks' case history "To see and not to see", and the long strange tradition of such case histories'.

14 In his first published play, *The Enemy Within*, Friel had already used the metaphor in a similar way without developing it. In this play, which focuses on St. Columba's inability to choose between his responsibilities to his family and the demands of his faith, Columba's closest friend in the monastery is nearly blind. Despite this, Caornan has insights which Columba lacks. Already in this early play the physical ability to see does not necessarily imply a better understanding of the world.

Works Cited

Andrews, Elmer. *The Art of Brian Friel: Neither Reality Nor Dreams*. London: Macmillan, 1995.

Bertha, Csilla. "'Island of Otherness": Images of Irishness in Brian Friel's *Wonderful Tennessee*'. *Hungarian Journal of English and American Studies* 2.2 (1996): 131-42.

--- 'Iona – Inishkeen – Oileán Draoíchta: Island-Existence in Brian Friel's Plays'. *Worlds Visible and Invisible. Essays on Irish Literature*. Ed. Csilla Bertha and Donald E. Morse. Debrecen: Lajos Kossuth University, 1994. 87-102.

Burke, Patrick. "'Both Heard and Imagined": Music as Structuring Principle in the Plays of Brian Friel'. *A Small Nation's Contribution to the World. Essays on Anglo-Irish Literature and Language*. Ed. Donald E. Morse, Csilla Bertha, and István Pálffy. Gerrards Cross: Smythe; Debrecen: Kossuth University Press, 1993. 43-52.

Deane, Seamus. 'The Name of the Game'. In Peacock 103-12.

Friel, Brian. *Aristocrats. Selected Plays*. London: Faber, 1984.

--- *The Communication Cord*. London: Faber, 1983.

--- *Dancing At Lughnasa*. London: Faber, 1990.

--- *The Enemy Within*. Dublin: Gallery, 1979.

--- *Faith Healer. Selected Plays*. London: Faber, 1984.

--- *The Gentle Island*. London: Davis-Poynter, 1973.

--- *Give Me Your Answer, Do!* Oldcastle: Gallery, 1997.

--- *Living Quarters. Selected Plays*. London: Faber, 1984.

--- *Lovers*. Dublin: Gallery, 1984.

--- *The Loves of Cass McGuire. Dublin:* Gallery, 1984.

--- *Molly Sweeney.* Oldcastle: Gallery, 1994.

--- *Philadelphia, Here I Come! Selected Plays.* London: Faber, 1984.

--- *Translations. Selected Plays.* London: Faber, 1984.

--- *Wonderful Tennessee.* Oldcastle: Gallery, 1994.

--- 'Self-Portrait'. *Aquarius* (Everyman) 5 (1972): 17-22.

Hawkins, Maureen E. 'Schizophrenia and the Politics of Experience in Three Plays by Brian Friel'. *Modern Drama* 39.3 (1996): 465-74.

Heaney, Seamus. '. . . English and Irish'. *Times Literary Supplement* 20 Oct. 1980: 1199.

Kearney, Richard. 'Language Play: Brian Friel and Ireland's Verbal Theatre'. *Studies* 72 (1983): 20-56.

Kiberd, Declan. 'Brian Friel's *Faith Healer*'. *Irish Writers and Society at Large.* Ed. Masaru Sekine. Gerrards Cross: Smythe; Totowa, NJ: Barnes and Noble, 1985. 106-21.

Kosok, Heinz. 'Das Dramenwerk Brian Friels'. *Brian Friel. Molly Sweeney, Leben ein Tanz, Zwischen allen Sprachen, Antworte Mir!* Ed. Birgit Pargner. München: Per H. Lauke, 1998. 11-41.

Lanters, José. 'Brian Friel's Uncertainty Principle'. *Irish University Review* 29.1 (1999): 162-75.

--- 'Violence and Sacrifice in Brian Friel's *The Gentle Island* and *Wonderful Tennessee*'. *Irish University Review* 26.1 (1996): 163-76.

Longley, Edna. '"When did you last see your father?": Perceptions of the Past in Northern Irish Writing 1965-1985'. *Cultural Contexts and Literary Idioms in Contemporary Irish Literature.* Ed. Michael Kenneally. Gerrards Cross: Smythe, 1988. 88-112.

O'Toole, Fintan. 'A Hesitant Move into Unknown Territory'. *Irish Times* 24 Sept. 1988: 5.

--- 'Island of Saints and Silicon: Literature and Social Change in Contemporary Ireland'. *Cultural Contexts and Literary Idioms in Contemporary Irish Literature.* Ed. Michael Kenneally. Gerrards Cross: Smythe, 1988. 11-35.

Parker, Michael. 'Telling Tales: Narratives of Politics and Sexuality in Brian Friel's *The Gentle Island*'. *Hungarian Journal of English and American Studies* 2.2 (1996): 59-86.

Peacock, Alan, and Kathleen Devine. '"In Touch With Some Otherness": The Double Vision of Brian Friel's *Dancing at Lughnasa*'. *Etudes Irlandaises* 17.1 (1992): 113-27.

Peacock, Alan, ed. *The Achievement of Brian Friel.* Gerrards Cross: Smythe, 1993.

Pilkington, Lionel. 'Language and Politics in Brian Friel's *Translations*'. *Irish University Review* 20.2 (1990): 282-98.

Pine, Richard. *Brian Friel and Ireland's Drama.* London: Routledge, 1990.

Throne, Marilyn. 'The Disintegration of Authority: A Study of the Fathers in Five Plays of Brian Friel'. *Colby Literary Quarterly* 24.3 (1988): 162-72.

Upton, Carol-Anne. 'Visions of the Sightless in Brian Friel's *Molly Sweeney* and Synge's *The Well of the Saints*'. *Modern Drama* 40.3 (1997): 347-57.

12 | Brian Friel's *Molly Sweeney* and its Sources: A Postmodern Case History

Christopher Murray

Introduction

When Friel's *Molly Sweeney* premiered at the Gate Theatre, Dublin, in August 1994 it seemed possible that it was indebted to J.M. Synge's *The Well of the Saints* (1905). It so happened that at this time Synge's play was revived at the Abbey, from whence, despite unenthusiastic reviews at home, it travelled abroad to the Edinburgh Festival and won much applause. So, Synge's play was part of Irish theatrical discourse in that season.

On a superficial level the resemblance between the two plays is undeniable. In both, blindness is cured, a brief period of sightedness is enjoyed, and blindness returns. For the critic, a common temptation is to build interpretation of a new play in terms of the old, where that older play seems genetic through specific themes. Thus, to choose examples only from the field of drama, Eugene O'Neill's *The Iceman Cometh* tends to be viewed as a descendant of Henrik Ibsen's *The Wild Duck,* or David Mamet's *Glengarry Glen Ross* as a descendant of Arthur Miller's *Death of a Salesman.* This critical approach has its roots in the comparativist mode rendered authoritative in Anglo-American studies by René Wellek and his Yale school of the 1960s, well before the second Yale school of deconstructionists threatened to make the first obsolete. It is hardly any longer critically acceptable, however, simply to practise comparative criticism in that older form. Although to line up *Molly Sweeney* alongside *The Well of the Saints* might, indeed, yield some interesting results they are not the kind of results which greatly exercise or even interest those involved in the business of criticism today. Basically, this is because the comparativist procedure, which is allied to the formalist, either precludes the historical or subordinates it. And nowadays to ignore history is to be reactionary. I endorse this position. It seems to me the negation of what criticism stands for as mediator between artistic production and public consumption to pursue a modernist line in a postmodernist age. Synge was an early modernist; Friel is a postmodernist writer. To contrast them would serve only to measure the distance Friel has travelled in his use of language, setting, and above all of dramatic form.

As good luck would have it, Friel acknowledged (in a programme note) another and more significant source for *Molly Sweeney* as soon as the play opened in New York in January 1996: 'I'm particularly indebted to Oliver Sacks's case history "To See and Not See", and the long, strange tradition of such case histories' (*Playbill* 27). Sacks's case history had first been published in the *New Yorker* on 10 May 1993 just when Friel was working on *Molly Sweeney,* which he first called 'the blind play'. The fact that he himself underwent surgery in December 1993 for a cataract in his right eye (Friel, *Essays* 159) no doubt reinforced Friel's personal interest in the topic and helped him explore its symbolic facets. The first entries in this section of Friel's diary, dated 28 and 29 August 1992, refer to the diagnosis of his own eye problem and his slightly alarmed reflection that it might be 'just the aging process' (153). Thus the personal, experiential, source of the play must not be underestimated. But undoubtedly the main and determining source for *Molly Sweeney* lay in Sacks's essay.

My purpose now is twofold. First, I want to indicate how Friel so adapts his source in Sacks that it becomes distinctively Frielian in tone, emphasis, and form. Secondly, I want to address the question of dramatic authorship and its relation to knowledge. Uniting both aims is the conviction that Friel is an extraordinarily Protean writer, whose preoccupation with self-conscious 'translation' of one text, one moment in history, one discourse into another characterizes him as postmodernist. But in making intertextuality the key to his dramatic style and palimpsest his compositional mode, Friel challenges the critic to re-define originality. *Molly Sweeney,* being a play about perception but not a modernist text like *The Well of the Saints,* is a peculiarly appropriate text for the raising of these issues.

Friel and Translation

It is necessary here to enter into particulars so as to chart Friel's *modus operandi.* Although my own method is, accordingly, expository I am anxious to lay out in some detail Friel's simultaneous reliance upon and 'translation' of Sacks's narrative. I am using the word in the sense employed by W.B. Worthen in a comprehensive article:

> Like performance, translation is engaged in a complex project of identification, an elaborate encoding of personal and cultural identity and history through the negotiation of alterity. To claim 'translation' as a theatrical politics is to keep that alterity visible, to prevent translation from gathering the other uncritically into the authorizing narrative of the self, to see translation performing the difference between languages, cultures, agents, histories, mythologies (36).

Friel's composition process, as those familiar with his published diary notes are aware (Friel, *Essays*), involves a slow and interrupted negotiation of various very frail possibilities, usually bound up with a cluster of sources or (more properly) a number of diverse texts. It is always a struggle to get on track, to find the momentum to generate a satisfactory form. What turns out to be the major source, as here, Sacks's story, is part of a process of unrelated browsing. In this instance, Freud, Jung, Turgenev, and Wallace Stevens all appear more prominently in the diary notes for *Molly Sweeney* than does Sacks (mentioned only once). Wallace Stevens does not get into the play as performed but he is a source nonetheless. Friel quotes 'Thirteen Ways of Looking at a Blackbird' in his diary (*Essays* 155), specifically the lines distinguishing the blackbird's whistling from its aftermath or 'innuendoes'. Directly beneath these lines Friel wrote, 'The sight-blind play?' He then moved on to consider Stevens's 'Sunday Morning' and lingered on the lines in stanza four where the speaker (a woman) also calibrates the difference between the before-and-after effect of birdsong, replacing 'sweet questionings' with a sense of desolation, of a lost paradise. Friel's own cryptic comment follows: 'Blackbirds – wakened birds – innuendoes – testing reality – sight restored?' (157). It is like trying to follow Coleridge's association of ideas in reported conversations in order to decipher his poetry. Friel's imagination, too, is romantic: though resolutely subjective, it thrives on borrowed images as it creates by recreation. Here the before-and-after motif, so poetically condensed in Stevens, was the seedling of a play about hope and its removal.

On the following day (13 August 1993) he adds: 'Today I think the play is about seeking – and fabricating – paradise. (The result of reading W.S.'s poetry?)'. The word 'fabricating' is key here. Whereas Friel has always, like Beckett, been interested in the paradise which is lost (Beckett 74), he is habitually and even at times nostalgically looking back in his plays to a golden age of innocence and cultural unity, which he knowingly and therefore ironically reinvents. The shape of *Molly Sweeney*, with its blind heroine's initial reminiscences of a golden time spent in the company of her father, followed by her forced initiation into a rebirth through cure of her blindness, followed in a third stage by a total separation both from her short-lived state of wholeness and her initial stability within her blindness, remains true to Friel's own tragic vision. His narrative is 'fabricated' to correspond to this vision.

The details of Sacks's case history provide the plot of *Molly Sweeney*. Sacks tells of a fifty year-old man named Virgil, 'who had been virtually blind since early childhood'. His fiancée Amy took him to an ophthalmologist, who formed the view that a simple operation for removal of cataracts might restore sight. 'There was nothing to lose – and there might be much to gain. Amy and Virgil would be getting married soon – wouldn't it be fantastic if he could see?' (102). Taking this scenario as a kind of prologue Friel adapts it to his own purposes. He both retains details and adapts them. Both protagonists have the same profession. Sacks's Virgil 'trained as a massage therapist and soon found employment at a YMCA' (105); Friel's Molly Sweeney is a 'massage therapist in a local health club' (17). After the operation, neither can function as before and each loses the job of massage therapist. In Sacks's story Amy is a swimming instructress; in Friel's play Molly feels most at ease in a swimming pool: 'I really did believe I got more pleasure, more delight, from swimming than sighted people can ever get. Just offering yourself to the experience ... that existed only by touch and feel; ... and the sense of such assurance, such liberation, such concordance with it' (24). Poetically, however, Friel uses this imagery of a particular element to reinforce his theme of wrongful interference with learned behaviour. Unlike Sacks's Virgil, Molly has a brittle personality. The whole point in Sacks's story is the mystery, the fact that there was no good or foreseeable reason why Virgil should have gone into psychological decline after the operation. In Friel's version everything is as prepared as in a Greek tragedy.

In the action of the play, however, Friel follows Sacks's case history closely. Sacks comments as follows with regard to the post-operative dilemma facing the type of patient Virgil was. 'In the newly sighted, learning to see demands a radical change in neurological functioning and, with it, a radical change in psychological functioning, in self, in identity. The change may be experienced in literally life-and-death terms' that left the patient between two worlds (134). Virgil collapsed with pneumonia some months after the operation, after which he experienced what Sacks calls 'blindsight', a state in which Virgil 'manifestly responded to objects, could locate them, was seeing, and yet denied any consciousness of seeing' (139). It was after this point that Virgil lost his job and deteriorated into total blindness, caused by his unforeseen illness. Amy took this change very badly; Virgil philosophically. Sacks himself, while surprised at the outcome, could see Virgil as ultimate victor:

> At the beginning, there was certainly amazement, wonder, and sometimes joy. There was also, of course, great courage. It was an adventure, an excursion into a new world, the like of which is given to few. But then came the problems, the conflicts, of

seeing but not seeing, not being able to make a visual world, and at the same time of being forced to give up his own. He found himself between two worlds, at home in neither – a torment from which no escape seemed possible. But then, paradoxically, a release was given, in the form of a second and now final blindness – a blindness he received as a gift. Now, at last, Virgil is allowed to not see, allowed to escape from the glaring, confusing world of sight and space, and to return to his own true being, the intimate, concentrated world of the other senses that had been his home for almost fifty years (143-44).

Mutatis mutandis, this summary also epitomizes Act 2 of Friel's play, which is concerned with learning to see, learning the language which will allow Molly to be at home in a new world. But already striking differences of approach are visible between Friel and Sacks. Friel's central character, from the time he first began seriously to work on a play about blindness, was a woman, although unnamed. Thus on 7 August 1993 Friel records in his diary: 'The play seems to be gathering round three people. Is the blind person a man or a woman? My *instinct* at this stage is a woman' (156). The first, indeed the only, reference to Sacks in the diary is dated some two weeks later (24 August) when he includes Sacks among 'a lot of blind material from my agent' which he has been reading 'closely' (157). Although at the end of November Friel was still uncertain about his protagonist, tentatively called Martha, his decision to stay with a woman proved central to the quality of the play he was to write. Molly's gender makes her, in Friel's construction of the character, passive and malleable. The idea for the operation is not hers but that of her recent husband Frank. In the case history the partner is herself afflicted with an eye condition and in applying pressure on Virgil acts with some prior knowledge and interest. Thus Friel reverses the characterization. In Sacks's story we learn that 'Virgil was passive here as in so much else', accepting his blind state as unalterable, but Amy disagreed and insisted that 'there was nothing to lose ... [a]nd so Amy pushed for the surgery' (107). In the play it is Frank who takes the view that there is nothing to lose. But that this optimistic view is insensitive is borne out by Mr. Rice's own doubts before the operation, expressed in the lines which dramatically close Act 1, 'I was fearful, I suddenly knew that that courageous woman had everything, everything to lose' (39).

Further, it is clear from the outset that Molly was both tutored and in a sense abused by her father, a strong patriarchal figure who is accused of causing his wife's mental breakdown, a pattern to be found in some of Friel's earlier plays also, for example, *Living Quarters* (1977), *Faith Healer* (1979), and *Aristocrats* (1979). In the course of *Molly Sweeney* it is revealed that her father, a judge (always an ominous figure in Friel's work), deprived Molly of the possibility of self-advancement and refused to send her to a school for the blind in order to get at the mother; this, at any rate, is what the mother says in the mental hospital (58). Molly's own delicate balance finds its proper expression in the unlikely activities of swimming and dancing, where she finds her identity in defiance of the body and its limitations through disability.

In Molly's case, the changes in characterization point to a regendering of Sacks's material. Her subjectivity is not something to be taken for granted. The fact that Molly narrates her own part of the story should not blind us, in turn, to her subjugation. Her discourse is constructed from the males in her world, as appears when one considers the three male figures (including Molly's father, an invisible presence) in the play.

An aggressive autodidact, Frank is a complex figure, and by no means related to Sacks's Amy. Although comic in his passionate obsessions he is revealed as quite dangerous in his constant inconstancy, his habitude to intermittent projects of which Molly's case is but one among many to be fanatically taken up and as quickly laid aside. Moreover, in Sacks's story the ophthalmologist is merely a functionary, a benign and well-meaning physician. But Friel's Mr. Rice is not just an eye specialist. He is a divorcé disabled by his wife's desertion, a man with a drink problem, a doctor running to seed and desperately on the lookout for the medical case which might reconstruct a shattered career. The contrast Friel embellishes between Mr. Rice and Frank is vital to a drama which is a variation on the eternal triangle, a story of one woman and two men: according to Yeats, 'that is the quarrel / That knows no mending' (*Deirdre* 378). It is an exaggeration to suggest that this contrast is romantic, for there is no contest for Molly's heart, but the rivalry which Frank constructs and on which his ego feeds has nevertheless a sexual component. Frank makes Molly victim to his own frustrated desire to possess and displace Mr. Rice in some way, a way that centres on knowledge, as I shall indicate below. But at the same time Mr. Rice is a version of Molly's dead father: he has the same whiskey-breath, the same rhetorical usages of concluding a catechism with Molly with expressions of 'splendid' and 'clever lady' (see 14, 42). Indeed, Molly identifies Mr. Rice with her father early on in the play (25), and this identification gives a powerful subtext to the passage at the end when Molly, now in the same mental home in which her mother spent so much time, pretends to be asleep when Rice comes to say farewell:

> 'I'm sorry, Molly Sweeney. I'm so sorry.' And off he went. I suppose it was mean of me to pretend I was asleep. But the smell of whiskey was suffocating. … And sometimes Father drops in on his way from court. And we do imaginary tours of the walled garden (66-67).

The juxtaposition in Molly's discourse shows how one figure is a version of the other. Thus coded, Rice's destructiveness is inevitable. On the other hand, Molly tells us that what attracted her to Frank was 'that he was everything my father wasn't' (35). In short, Friel transforms a case history into a complex and tragic interweaving of off-stage and onstage characters.

In Act 2 the failure of the operation affects not just Molly but Mr. Rice and Frank in different but dramatically significant ways. Mr. Rice is given his own little sequel. Here Friel strays back to *Faith Healer* and to the failure of Francis Hardy. The straying leaves tracks in diction and syntax; for example, when Grace in *Faith Healer* refers to Frank's habitual use of the word 'performance' to describe the exercise of his gift (343). Reflecting in Act 2 on Molly's operation Mr. Rice falls into the tones of his Frielian predecessor:

> When I look back over my working life I suppose I must have done thousands of operations. Sorry – performed … And of those thousands I wonder how many I'll remember. I'll remember Dubai. An Arab gentleman whose left eye had been almost pecked out by one of his peregrines and who sent his private jet to New York for Hans Girder and myself. The eye was saved, really because Girder was a magician … And I'll remember a city called Frankfort in Kentucky … And I'll remember Ballybeg (46-47).

He'll remember Ballybeg, he assures us, not because the operation was other than routine but because it meant for him personally the lifting of a 'terrible darkness' in his life (47). It was thus a fateful episode, as 'the darkness miraculously lifted, and I performed – I watched myself doing it – I performed so assuredly and with such skill, so elegantly, so efficiently, so economically … [that] all the gifts were mine again, abundantly mine, joyously mine', and he felt in some measure 'restored' (47-48). Then a few months later, while Molly's future is dimming with her lost sight, Rice himself crosses a threshold into settled unhappiness. He receives word from New York of the death in an air crash of his ex-wife's second husband and his own erstwhile colleague. It is plain that at the funeral Rice had hopes his wife might turn to him again. But she did not. When he returns to Ballybeg he resigns from the hospital and moves out, to no obvious or secure destiny. But before he leaves he visits Molly in hospital, and in her somnolent state sees an image both of his failure and of 'the insane fantasy' which had led him to attempt personal rehabilitation (64). He knows that he has used her. But with Frielian irony he sees, too, that he gave her, however temporarily, a truer vision than is enjoyed by those with normal sight. One is now firmly into territory well beyond the medical case history. By 'truer' Friel does not mean accurate in the usual sense, since as his predecessor Bernard Shaw employed when describing his own ocular condition:

> I got a clue to my real condition [as artist] from a friend of mine, a physician who had devoted himself specially to ophthalmic surgery. He tested my eyesight one evening, and informed

me that it was quite normal. I naturally took this to mean that it was like everybody else's; but he rejected this construction as paradoxical, and hastened to explain to me that I was an exceptional and highly fortunate person optically, normal sight conferring the power of seeing things accurately, and being enjoyed by only about ten per cent of the population, the remaining ninety per cent being abnormal ... My mind's eye, like my body's, was 'normal': it saw things differently from other people's eyes, and saw them better (3. x).

Friel inverts the drift of this diagnosis from positive to negative, making Molly Sweeney a version of the artist as doomed, blind visionary. For Shaw, seeing things aright was the first step towards changing the process by which they became what they were; for Friel, seeing things is rather closer to Seamus Heaney's poetic notion of insight, in the volume *Seeing Things* (1991), whereby the world of the dead impinges on the world of the living to bring witness of both wonder and inalterability (Heaney 10-18, 62).

Frank, in a different way from Molly and to a different degree, has his own epiphany following the failure of the operation. He cannot avoid trying to convert the situation into financial gain: such is his character. He sells the story to a tabloid newspaper, thus sacrificing Molly's respect. As he is about to take off for Ethiopia he sees, like Gar O'Donnell in *Philadelphia, Here I Come!* (1964), that there is no actual necessity for him to go, that, indeed, his going into exile is more a sign of his own neurosis than a tactical and practical decision. Addressing himself Frank asks the questions only he can answer, 'who in his right mind wants to go there for Christ's sake? Not you. You certainly don't. Then why don't you stay where you are for Christ's sake? What are you looking for?' (62).

The characters in *Molly Sweeney* are thus three aspects of the artist as divine and thus tragic seer in a form of hypostatic union (for Friel is nothing if not theological). If we have been sensitive to the music of the play we will have picked up the one theme which all three characters have in common. They each use the same phrase for it, 'a phantom desire, a fantasy'

(18, 34, 41, 64). They each end up failing to realize it. Each ends in a kind of exile of the soul, and Molly alone is happy in hers. Before the operation, towards the end of Act 1, she identifies her trepidation with 'the dread of exile, of being sent away. It was the desolation of homesickness' (31). At the end of Act 2, broken psychologically as well as permanently blind, Molly declares herself 'at home' in her 'borderline country' (67). This tragic condition has nothing in common with Oliver Sacks's case history. Friel's action moves towards a definition of spiritual exile, a territory familiar not only from *Philadelphia, Here I Come!*, but also from *The Loves of Cass Maguire* (1967) and other plays.

It is to Cass Maguire above all that Molly Sweeney's fate sends us back. There, the dispossessed returned exile finds her home at last in a home which is no home but a twilight zone, a Frielian Bower of Bliss ironically named Eden House, the tragic destination of all of Friel's heroes and heroines alike. Thus Molly ends up deranged, whereby madness, Michel Foucault tells us, 'has become man's possibility of abolishing both man and the world – and even those images that challenge the world and deform man. It is far beyond dreams, beyond the nightmare of bestiality, the last recourse: the end and the beginning of everything' (*Madness* 281).

Appropriation and Deconstruction

In his essay 'What is an Author?' Foucault points out that the concept of ownership has 'always been subsequent to what one might call penal appropriation. Texts, books, and discourses really began to have authors ... to the extent that authors became subject to punishment, that is, to the extent that dis-courses could be transgressive' (202). As Foucault sees it, once copyright came into the picture the possibility of 'transgression' in the act of writing became more 'imperative', given his notion of the author as a participant in the struggle for power.

The relationship of the text of *Molly Sweeney* to Sacks's essay 'To See and Not See' raises the issue of authorial rights. Academics, in particular; are very aware of copyright and in re-cent years have been made more and more conscious of the necessity to obtain permission to use, that is to publish, even so much as a sentence from a text in print. A recent case in point is the published work of the late Martin Luther King, Jr., in which it was found that King had repeatedly reproduced the words of other scholars without due acknowledgement:

> Verification of authorship is assumed to be a major step toward the determination of whether a document represents the thoughts of the presumed author. But the process of transforming thoughts into words on paper is complex in ways that historians often avoid confronting. It is, first of all, not simply a one-way process for most writers (Carson 312).

But the same type of restriction, constriction, and prescription seems not to apply to authors of fiction, including playwrights.

Friel, as was mentioned previously, acknowledged his source, in a very professional way, in the playbill for the production by the Roundabout Theatre Company in New York. Yet it is worth emphasizing that the Irish edition of *Molly Sweeney* lacks the acknowledgement which the American edition carries. In that regard it might be said that the text itself exists between two worlds. The main question at issue, however, is what is implied by this artistic process of borrowing or quotation. In the drama, as opposed to the sort of allusion commonplace in the poetry of Eliot or Pound, this is a late twentieth-century phenomenon.

Friel, like Tom Stoppard, is the kind of writer who likes to make use of expertise in the service of some argument, usually philosophical or sociological. He likes to create a middleman, a mediator who can import into the play in a fairly raw state the knowledge or data necessary for the audience's fuller understanding. This choric figure is sometimes ironized, sometimes not. The sociologist Dodds in *The Freedom of the City* (1973) borrows his argument on the culture of poverty from Oscar Lewis's study *La Vida* (Pine 102). But whereas Dodds's intermittent addresses straight to the audience contain information which provides a plausible socio-economic analysis from which one may see the conflict between the three victims in the play and the state apparatus, Dodds is clearly both a bore and a representative of self-satisfied, middle-class academia and so all of his commentary is made to appear somewhat ridiculous. In fact, Dodds's knowledge is so ironized that it becomes more an obstacle than an aid to audience understanding. He is, in short, an alienation device in a play that embodies several Brechtian devices (see Birker 155-58). Friel does not name or acknowledge his source, but makes use as needed of his source material.

The quotations from George Steiner's *After Babel* which appear in the text of Friel's *Translations* (1980) are now well known, although I think I can immodestly boast of having been first in print with the news in 1981 (Murray, 'Review' 238-39; see also Kearney 20-25, McGrath 31-49, and Smith 392-409). I raise the matter in my essay on *Translations* earlier in this volume.The point to note here, however, is that no irony is involved: Steiner's words are blandly taken over by Hugh and Yolland. Friel makes no attempt to acknowledge the quotations in the text of his play, or even in the programme notes to the first production by Field Day in 1980, although he does so elsewhere. His practice, then, is to take over such statements from other authors as he finds useful or necessary for his dramatic purposes. If he needs a certain kind of language he borrows it. Footnotes do not belong in a stage script. It seems to be part of the way Friel writes to incorporate other texts silently. He does this markedly in *Molly Sweeney*. It is a procedure quite different from Stoppard's in, say, *Travesties* (1974), where postmodernist parody and/or pastiche are foregrounded. As Linda Hutcheon has pointed out, parody, 'often called ironic quotation, pastiche, appropriation, or intertextuality', is central to postmodernism (93). But in contrast to the pattern Hutcheon discerns in parody, which is discernible in Stoppard's plays *passim,* whereby irony operates as political critique, Friel avoids formalist critique in his plays.

I have already indicated (in the preceding section) how Friel makes use of Oliver Sacks's essay, but it needs now to be said that the discourse borrowed is a form of specialized knowledge. Once again Friel has his expert within the play to mediate this knowledge, but this time he plays a double trick. If Mr. Rice draws on Oliver Sacks in a straightforward way, the comic Frank Sweeney does so in ways that are confessedly second-hand and reductive. As amateur, as inveterate dabbler in ideas indiscriminately absorbed and paraded with absurd enthusiasm, Frank is a parody of the expert: he is the sociologist Dodds reduced to a caricature. Because we know that Frank is not and does not claim to be an authority on anything, the knowledge he provides is invariably suspect. It is presented within a discourse so shot through with anecdotes of personal, haphazard involvement in diverse lifestyles and experiments. Thus knowledge is destabilized. We hear of visual engrams, gnosis, blindsight, withdrawal, and even of a 'renaissance of personality' (22, 54, 57, 55). These terms are all in Sacks's essay (121, 108, 139, 129, and 137). Sometimes Sacks is quoting someone else, some authority in the field, sometimes not; sometimes Frank is quoting Mr. Rice and sometimes not. When he is not he seems to be quoting or paraphrasing Sacks, as when he introduces a passage with the phrase, 'I read a brilliant article once by a professor in an American magazine and he called this imprint an engram' (20). That particular passage leads into an account of perception by the Irish philosopher Molyneaux, modified by Locke and Berkeley, which is borrowed from Sacks (104). As Frank mediates this theory it is both interesting and comically pedantic. It has a third life in Molly's monologues, where it becomes so heavily ironized as part of her amused tolerance of Frank that 'tactical engrams' is finally undermined when it pops up as a malapropism (49). In her final monologue, Molly reports Frank as author – of a twenty-seven page letter from Ethiopia. As she summarizes its contents Molly deconstructs Frank as a credible witness; she does this by paraphrasing his discourse without comment. By this stage of the play Frank's absurdity is transparent, but it is interesting that for Molly it is now internalized. Thus Frank's invocation of yet another author can be silently dismissed. 'There is a man called Aristotle that he thinks highly of. I should read him, he says. And he sent a money order for two pounds and he'll write again soon' (66). The absurd inadequacy of the sum of money sent to support a deserted wife undermines the value of the reference to Aristotle.

And this, in short, is what happens in the play to the whole input of expert knowledge borrowed from Oliver Sacks. It is all revealed as so much dead wood. It may be true, historically and scientifically; it may have objective, intrinsic value, but it is all irrelevant to Molly's situation. She ends up broken, deserted, and drifting towards death. It is instructive that in the play the psychotherapist who provides post-operative counselling to Molly is named Jean Wallace, an actual scholar cited by Sacks (103). In the play Wallace and her husband are writing a book on Molly's case, but they do or are able to do nothing for her. She is no more than fodder for their academic careers. Wallace is credited by Frank with the term 'renaissance of personality' when he says: 'It was the clever Jean Wallace who spotted the distress signals first. She said to me: "We should be seeing a renaissance of personality at this point. Because if that doesn't take place – and it's not – then you can expect a withdrawal"' (55). But according to Sacks (137) the phrase is derived from Alberto Salvo's *Sight Restoration after Long-Term Blindness*. Is Friel making the point that experts simply steal from each other? Just as they steal other men's wives, as happens to Mr. Rice?

If I am right, Friel's point relates to the ambivalence of knowledge and authority. On the one hand, knowledge is essential; science is progressive and, theoretically at any rate, benignly utilitarian. On the other hand, knowledge is perfectly useless at a certain, fundamental, level because language itself is powerless to intervene where the human spirit is engaged in relating to environment and experience. Frank Sweeney is the butt of this attack on knowledge, but Mr. Rice's own history reinforces it at a serious level. If 'physician, heal thyself' be the eternal challenge to the discourse of medical science Rice's miserable personal failure shows how irrelevant yet deconstructive his expertise is. His knowledge propels him into exploitation, where destruction of personality is a calculated risk. That Rice and Frank are not just busybodies who mess up Molly's life is borne out by the expressive story of the badgers, the only really pregnant piece of narrative Frank has to offer in

the play. In a landscape undergoing change the badgers are en-
dangered. It is a landscape beloved of Mr. Rice also, a lake
environment where he fishes and finds peace. In the best
interests of the badgers Frank and his friend try to move them
to another habitat. These 'half-blind' creatures get into 'a mad
panic' (60) once released from the net used to move them and
plunge wildly, insanely back to their old lairs or setts which the
well-meaning deliverers have destroyed in the process of saving
the badgers. This, in a nutshell, is what befalls Molly. Indeed,
when Rice visits her for the last time he refers to the 'net' in
which her wild hair is now encased (64). The parallel is all too
clear. Even a little learning is a dangerous thing, how dangerous
we usually prefer not to consider. Mr. Rice himself cited the
odds against the chances of success in his ambitious operation:
only 'twenty people in a thousand years' have been cured of
Molly's complaint (25), a statistic, by the way, borrowed from
Sacks (103). The gamble, based on a 'phantom desire' common
to all three characters, was hubristic, and its result what Sacks,
using for the only time in this essay a theatrical term, called a
'catastrophe' (137).

In 'What is an Author?' Foucault makes a distinction
between a discourse founded by a scientist like Galileo and a
discourse established by a Freud or a Marx. The act that founds
a science 'is on an equal footing with its future transformations;
this act becomes in some respects part of the set of
modifications that it makes possible' (207). But Freud and Marx
were 'founders of discursivity' rather than founders of sciences
and so they 'have created a possibility for something other than
their discourse, yet something belonging to what they founded'
(206). Galileo's findings were reshaped by his successors and in
that sense he 'authors' the later transformations of his discourse. 'Re-examination of Galileo's text may well change our
knowledge of the history of mechanics, but it will never be able
to change mechanics itself. On the other hand, re-examining
Freud's texts, modifies psychoanalysis itself just as a re-
examination of Marx's would modify Marxism' (208). But
Foucault makes no provision for the appropriation by the artist
of either kind of discourse by, say, Brecht or O'Neill. The play-

wright literally plays with knowledge (what Aristotle in the *Poetics* calls *dianoia*) and transforms it into quite another discourse, dramatic poetry. A writer like Friel (and, in a different way, Stoppard) is author in the sense of *augere,* increasing rather than originating.

In addition, it may be said that Friel's formal achievement places the whole question of borrowing in another light. One thinks immediately, of course, of *Faith Healer* and is inclined to declare that Friel's greatest act of appropriation is against himself. In *Molly Sweeney* he is, in a sense, recycling the methodology of *Faith Healer.* He had this fear himself: he noted in his diary on 7 January 1994: 'The new play – form, theme, characters – is so like FAITH HEALER. A second candlestick on the mantelpiece; a second china dog' (162). But this is too apprehensive a view. Leaving aside the resemblance between the use of monologues in both *Molly Sweeney* and *Faith Healer* it should be noted that the issue in *Molly Sweeney* is not who is telling the truth or what is the nature of fact in its relation to creativity or love. The issue is the invention of an audience. To be sure, this is an issue Friel had been working on since *Living Quarters.* He assembles characters who inhabit no other common space than the stage. They cannot, with any conviction, be imagined to be present together within the same time frame: they never acknowledge each other's presence, and they never interact. This is a convention Friel has been developing for years, and it is a fictional rather than a dramatic convention. In *Molly Sweeney* it is extended to the point where we believe that Molly is narrating her own tragedy, even though we clearly understand by the end of the play not only what a totally unreliable narrator she must be (which is where *Faith Healer* leaves off) but also that she is not actually speaking to us or to anyone. We are simply eavesdropping on her inner thoughts as we eavesdrop on the thoughts of that other notable Molly in Irish letters, Molly Bloom. (We are now a long way from the controlled female narrator in Wallace Stevens's 'Sunday Morning' with whom Friel began his compositional dabbling.) When we step back and consider the play as a whole we must see – the pun is unavoidable – that the play as such does not

exist. These three characters come from different quarters of
the earth to speak to us in the past tense about Molly: why?
Because *we* are there rather than they: they certify our presence,
our desire for illusion, completeness, resolution. Friel goes
beyond Pirandello to assert that it is the audience rather than
the playwright who makes the final increment/increase (if we
exclude the critic) in the authorial process. (See Murray,
'Pirandello'.)

However, the ethics involved in Friel's appropriation of the
discourse of Sacks's essay remains challenging. There are
doubtless those who would feel more at ease had Friel recycled
Synge's *The Well of the Saints* after all. But Foucault persuades us
that such is an unwarranted reservation. 'The author', says
Foucault, 'is the principle of thrift in the proliferation of meaning. As a result, we must entirely reverse the traditional idea of
the author'. He explains further:

> If we are accustomed to presenting the author as a genius, as a
> perpetual surging of invention, it is because, in reality, we make
> him function in exactly the opposite fashion. One can say that
> the author is an ideological product, since we represent him as
> the opposite of his historically real function. ... The author is
> therefore the ideological figure by which one marks the manner
> in which we fear the proliferation of meaning ('What Is an
> Author?' 209).

Brendan Behan, as was his wont, put the point both more
directly and more simply in *Richard's Cork Leg*, itself a mish-
mash of appropriations and self-parody: 'Talent borrows,
genius robs' (312). The criminality of the artist is openly
heroicized. On the other hand, it will be of interest to note
what Oliver Sacks thinks of the matter:

> To speak of 'the ethics of the case' seems meaningless to me
> here. I think *Molly Sweeney* a masterpiece. I was and am delighted
> that an artist of Brian Friel's calibre was able to draw some
> inspiration from my case history, that it was a source (one of
> many) which gave nourishment to his own unique, creative, and
> personal rendering of the theme.

It seems to me of the nature of art, and all creativity, that it
should be interactive and, in a sense, dialogic and collaborative
– that a's work will nourish b, and b's work c, and c's work,
perhaps, a, completing the circle of giving-receiving-returning
(Sacks, Letter).

Conclusion

My conclusion must be that for Friel knowledge is both
enabling and a chimera. It is enabling, as source material is for
the playwright, because of the historical illusions about its
power. But in the sceptical philosophy which has always
energized Friel's drama to know is ultimately irrelevant. Indeed,
as *Faith Healer* so obviously shows, knowledge in Friel is
uncertain and relativistic. In his recent work, there is an
increasing disclaimer of the value of language itself as a medium
of understanding reality. That irony is compounded in *Wonderful
Tennessee* (1993) by the insistence that silence is a more viable
mode than language of communicating meaningfully (52-53), a
step further than Michael's declaration at the end of *Dancing at
Lughnasa* (1990): 'Dancing as if language no longer existed
because words were no longer necessary' (71, emphasis added). This
paradox is given a further twist in *Molly Sweeney* by the
proposition insisted on through hard experience by the
ophthalmologist Rice, 'seeing isn't understanding' (33). That
proposition is allowed to sound throughout the play multi-
valently. What then of the audience? Is what it sees what it
understands? Why use such a visual medium as theatre to put
that question? Again, Friel's ironic point of view must be part
of the answer. *Molly Sweeney* must be the least visual play to have
graced the world stage in a long time. Friel himself calls it 'a trio
for three voices' (*Essays* 157). At the same tune, it is noteworthy
that for the first time Friel has directed his own work in the
theatre, like Beckett in his later years, as if the better to control
meaning and interpretation, or, in short, to increase his authorship of the play.

Here, then, is one more irony surrounding a text more
heavily ironized than any other of Friel's to date. For it is

mainly through irony that Friel steadfastly redirects discourse toward the tragic finality of death, hovering always in his work at the extreme edge dividing the world of the stage from that of the audience. The lack of closure in *Molly Sweeney*, in contrast not only to the finality of Sacks's 'To See and Not See' but also to Friel's own *Faith Healer*, strongly asserts his current postmodernist interests (see Hutcheon 99). He has left Synge's modernism far behind, and is now more than ever the alchemical artist transforming public discourse into private and back again into public, performed speech, where it may establish a new form of freedom.

Works Cited

Beckett, Samuel. *Proust*. London: John Calder, 1965.

Brendan Behan. *The Complete Plays*. London: Eyre Methuen, 1978.

Birker, Klaus. 'The Relationship between the Stage and the Audience in Brian Friel's *The Freedom of the City*'. *The Irish Writer and the City*. Ed. Maurice Harmon. Gerrards Cross: Colin Smythe; Totowa: Barnes and Noble, 1984. 153-58.

Carson, Clayborne. 'Editing Martin Luther King, Jr.: Political and Scholarly Issues'. *Palimpsest: Editorial Theory in the Humanities,* Ed. George Bornstein and Ralph G. Williams. Ann Arbor: University of Michigan Press, 1993.

Friel, Brian. *Dancing at Lughnasa*. London and Boston: Faber, 1990.

--- *Essays, Diaries, Interviews: 1964-1999*. Ed. Christopher Murray. London and New York: Faber, 1999.

--- *Molly Sweeney*. Loughcrew, Oldcastle: Gallery, 1994.

--- *Molly Sweeney*. New York: Penguin/Plume, 1995.

--- *Playbill*, 96.3 (March 1996).

--- *Selected Plays*. London and Boston: Faber, 1984.

--- *Wonderful Tennessee*. Loughcrew, Oldcastle: Gallery, 1993.

Foucault, Michel. *Madness and Civilization: A History of Insanity in the Age of Reason*. Trans. Richard Howard. London: Routledge, 1991.

--- 'What Is an Author?' *Modern Criticism and Theory: A Reader*. Ed. David Lodge. London and New York: Longman, 1988. 196-210.

Heaney, Seamus. *Seeing Things*. London and Boston: Faber, 1991.

Hutcheon, Linda. *The Politics of Postmodernism*. London and New York: Routledge, 1989.

Kearney, Richard. 'Language Play: Brian Friel and Ireland's Verbal Theatre'. *Studies* 72 (1983): 20-25.

McGrath, F.C. 'Irish Babel: Brian Friel's *Translations* and George Steiner's *After Babel*. *Comparative Drama* 23.1 (1989): 31-49.

Murray, Christopher. 'Pirandello and Brian Friel: Some Affinities'. *Le Due Trilogie Pirandelliane*. Ed. John C. Barnes and Stefano Milioto. Palermo: G.B. Paiumbo, 1992. 207-15.

--- Review of *Translations*. *Irish University Review*, 11.2 (1981): 238-39.

Pine, Richard. *Brian Friel and Ireland's Drama*. London and New York: Routledge, 1990.

Sacks, Oliver. 'To See and Not See'. *The New Yorker*, 49.12 (10 May 1993): 59-73. Reprinted in *An Anthropologist on Mars: Seven Paradoxical Tales*. New York: Knopf; Toronto: Random House; London: Picador, 1995. 102-44. Citations are from the latter.

--- Letter to Christopher Murray, 29 December 1996.

Shaw, Bernard. *Complete Plays with Prefaces*. 6 vols. New York: Dodd, Mead, 1963.

Smith, Robert S. 'The Hermeneutic Motion in Brian Friel's *Translations*'. *Modern Drama* 32 (1991): 392-409.

Worthen, W.B. 'Homeless Words: Field Day and the Politics of Translation'. *Modern Drama*, 39 (1995): 22-41.

Yeats, W.B. *Deirdre. The Variorum Edition of the Plays of W. B. Yeats*. Ed. Russell K. Alspach. London: Macmillan, 1966.

POLITICS IN AND OF THE THEATRE

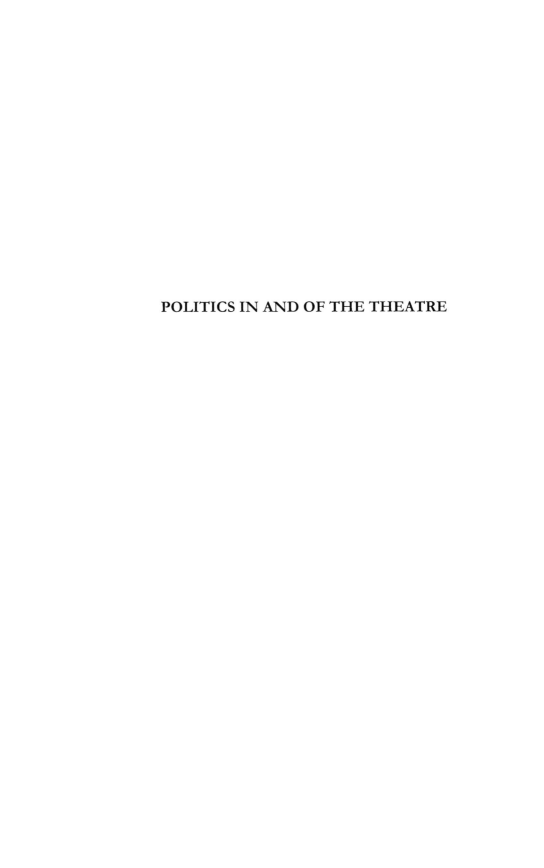

13 | About Some Healthy Intersections: Brian Friel and Field Day

Paulo Eduardo Carvalho

> Literature is the Irish ideology. This state of affairs places on the writer a particular responsibility to the reflexive relations, which necessarily link his/her art to social reality.
> – W.J. McCormack

> The problem is not how one might protect the cultural against the contamination of the political, but rather how one can mobilize both cultural and political discourse in circumstances where both appear to be exhausted and yet persist.
> – Eamon Hughes

Field Day Theatre Company, which also worked as a publishing house, is a collective initiative with a clear political purpose of intervention, with which the playwright Brian Friel collaborated from the very beginning up to his resignation from the Board of Directors in January 1994. All four monographs dedicated to Brian Friel's achievement as an artist (see Ulf Dantanus, George O'Brien, Richard Pine, and Elmer Andrews) acknowledge and integrate, even if in very different critical ways, the history, or at least part of it, of his involvement with that company. An experience of eight or fourteen years, depending on how you decide to count them,[1] in the career of so nationally and internationally prominent a playwright as Friel remains as an event which invites further consideration, especially, because throughout these years, it seems to have upset many critical voices. I'll start with three very different examples.

Some critics were soon eager to diagnose or to foresee the negative consequences that would come out of that seeming renunciation of the individual artist's aura of detachment. In 1983, reviewing Field Day's third theatrical production, Paul Hadfield and Lynda Henderson, writing for *Theatre Ireland*, were ready to state how the playwright's involvement with that Derry project was seriously affecting his dramatic production (the example here was Friel's *The Communication Cord*, the first play he wrote having that company in mind): 'There are ways in which Field Day has not been good for Brian Friel – it has largely removed him from the productive abrasion of challenge and resistance. It would be a pity if he preferred it that way' (64). Using strictly what they presented as objective dramatic and theatrical arguments, *The Communication Cord* was regarded as the negative effect of Friel's new 'burden of responsibility and inevitable level of involvement', even if their main criticism was geared to the activity of the company itself, 'an enterprise which has promised more than it has been able to deliver' (64).

In 1990 when *Dancing at Lughnasa* premiered at the Abbey, Fintan O'Toole, one of the most influential theatre critics in the Republic, hailed the event as a kind of return of the prodigal son:

> the play is appropriately housed at the Abbey rather than with Friel's own Derry-based company, Field Day. For, to put it crudely, *Dancing at Lughnasa* is a *Southern play* rather than *a Northern one*. … The escape from language in the play is also the escape from *the concerns with colonialism*, with *cultural domination*, with *the Northern questions* which have dominated Friel's work since *Translations* ('Beyond' 5, emphasis added).

Fintan O'Toole seems to be celebrating here what he interprets as Friel putting aside history. The *Irish Times'* critic would later clarify, if any clarification was still necessary, his own artistic and ideological position in a strenuous effort to dehistoricize all Friel's plays, namely *Dancing at Lughnasa* and his last contribution to Field Day, *Making History*. Because 'history changes nothing', Friel appears as O'Toole's *Irish Chekhov*, his plays being 'about the excavation of unchanging places, people and dilemmas' ('Marking Time' 202), a typical critical stance that confuses dramatic strategies with social and political concerns, a question to which I will return. Again, what is more interesting in O'Toole's interpretation is not so much his critical reading, but the way his discourse reveals what really upsets his own ideal of the great artist that he considers Brian Friel to be:

> To misread Friel's plays as history plays, or even as plays about history, is to see Friel as a writer of commitment, an *écrivain engagé,* as some of those that praise his work have done. Because his work deals in the stuff of history, and sometimes in that of politics, it is tempting to understand him as a fundamentally politic writer … The committed writer is a writer who has faith in politics, in history, and above all in the power of language, not merely to communicate things, but also to change them. Friel is a writer in despair at, or just in flight from, all of these things. *Making History* and *Dancing at Lughnasa,* far from being plays which set out to analyse society or history, are plays which deny the power of rational analysis at all (204-05).

My third and last example comes from *Acting Between the Lines,* published in 1994. In the conclusion, its author, Marilynn J. Richtarik, shows herself unable to avoid speculating on Friel's abandonment of Field Day. After expressing her suspicions that 'he felt constrained by the ideological framework Field Day had developed by 1989', she goes on to assert that 'sadly, Field Day notions of what mattered in Irish identity had ceased to accommodate one of the company's founding members' (268). She makes clear the frame of mind that conditioned this 'empirical study [of] those aspects of the Field Day project that make it unique': 'Theatre and polemics work by different means to different ends. Whereas plays suggest, pamphlets assert' (240).

This reference to the otherwise extremely well-documented work of Richtarik on the Field Day Theatre Company and Irish cultural politics is important because her approach is again extremely revealing of what I would risk calling a recurrent fear of intersections, of whatever kind one would say.[2] One of Richtarik's strongest criticisms of Field Day's evolution is the way polemics and 'pamphleteering' have insinuated themselves into the company's plays, namely Tom Paulin's *The Riot Act*, Thomas Kilroy's *Double Cross*, Terry Eagleton's *Saint Oscar*, and Friel's *Making History* (a play that she feels no obligation to come to terms with due to her very selective chronological frame: 1980-84). She does not bother to identify the way, so frequently suggested by Seamus Deane, that Friel's drama of the seventies up to *Translations* insinuated itself into the company's critical discourse, and her insistence on this separation seems to echo Edna Longley's already famous sentence that 'poetry and politics ... should be separated' (26), already in itself a rewriting of an even more famous sentence: Conor Cruise O'Brien's 1975 statement that the intersection of art and politics is an unhealthy one.

O'Brien's fear was of the damaging effect that art could have on politics; Longley was more concerned with 'aesthetic immunity', and she went to great efforts to prove the negative consequences politics could have on poetry. In the three examples mentioned above, regarding Friel, the intersections these critics fear vary a little: Hadfield and Henderson seem to be especially suspicious of the artist's abdication of his individuality and detachment, as a sure sign of a foreseeable decrease in the quality of his dramatic output. O'Toole rejoices in what he (mis)reads as Friel's demonstration that he is slowing down his too long insistence that colonialism and cultural domination are matters that the contemporary Republic needs to reconsider. The intersections he dislikes concern both the confusion between Northern and Southern Ireland and the idea that art should have anything to do with history. Finally, Richtarik sees sufficient evidence to fear the intersection of two, in her opinion, distinctly separate discourses: the artistic (the dramatic and theatrical, in this case) and the critical (which she equates with the polemical and rational).

What seems to inform all these approaches to the art and the craft of the artist is exactly what Thomas Kilroy identifies as 'the framework of thinking' inherited from the Irish colonial experience: 'the "anglophone society" still sees literature as coming from an individual mind, the act of writing is still associated with a transcendence of the common things of existence' (178). Irish twentieth-century literary history, and above all the history of that very young discipline called Irish drama, which Friel regards as starting only with J.M. Synge and W.B. Yeats, has developed as part of the dynamics of the social process. Friel's statement that the history of Irish drama should be the history of riots ('Plays Peasant' 305) is a revealing demonstration of his renewed belief in the particular place for drama in Irish cultural and political life.

Friel's assumption of a 'common place in the world', to use Kilroy's expression (186) is contemporary to the inclusion of an historical dimension in his work dating from *The Freedom of the City* (1973) and then confirmed by *Volunteers* (1975). Even if the artistic validity of that experience has been repeatedly questioned by the playwright himself (Friel, 'The Man' 22), that play marks an important change in the artist's beliefs in the nature and function of art. In the year of Bloody Sunday (and of the Widgery Report that soon followed), in a very important essay published in the pages of the *Times Literary Supplement*, 'Plays Peasant and Unpeasant', Friel was already well aware that:

> It requires no gift of prophecy to foresee that the revolt in Northern Ireland is going to spread to the Republic; and if you believe that art is an instrument of the revolutionary process, then you can look forward to a spate of committed plays: I do not believe that art is a servant of any movement. But during the period of unrest, I can foresee that the two allegiances that have bound the Irish imagination – loyalty to the most authoritarian church in the world and devotion to a romantic ideal we call Katheleen – will be radically altered. Faith and Fatherland; new definitions will be forged, and then new loyalties, and then new social groupings. It will be a bloody process. And when it has subsided, the Irish imagination will have to set about shaping and interpreting the new structure in art forms (305).

Ten years after the publication of this essay, when that bloody process was still far from having subsided and the

situation could not be better described than as 'politically
moribund', Friel would confess: '. . . I've written two or three
demonstrably political plays. And I keep saying to myself I'm
never going to write another political play because it's too
transient, and because I'm confused at it myself, but I know
damn well and I'm sure I'll have another shot at it again
sometime' ('The Man' 22). Even if always committed to a
double and oscillating balance between the private and public
dimensions that articulate his aesthetics, Friel managed in the
seventies to overcome that dominating idea of the artist as a
'true and pure thing', as a 'decontaminated' being, disengaged
from politics or society (Deane, 'The Arts' 62).

Friel would come up with *The Freedom of the City* within a
year of insisting on the impossibility of writing about the
Troubles ('The Future' 14; Untitled essay). He is the same
playwright that at the beginning of the seventies confessed that
he had never seen himself 'writing for any particular theatre
group or any particular actor or director' (Untitled 223-24) who
in the eighties would be directing and writing for Field Day.
More than accidents or contradictions these two very different
types of evolution seem to prove him right when in 1972 he
foresaw that 'what the future of Irish drama will be must
depend on the slow process of development of the Irish mind,
and it will shape and be shaped by political events' (Untitled
223). At the beginning of the seventies, somewhere between
The Gentle Island and *The Freedom of the City*, Friel confessed his
disenchantment with the theatre (Untitled 224). After three or
four years the playwright would be going through what was
perhaps his most productive period, the one that gave rise to
Aristocrats, Faith Healer, Translations, and his translation of
Chekhov, *Three Sisters*.

Global readings of Brian Friel's *oeuvre* have always, and
correctly so, it is fair to add, tended to evince the evolution of
his concerns, and if we look at the four monographs that I
mentioned before, there is a fairly general agreement on how to
divide his career or at least on the identification of its major
cornerstones or turning points (*Philadelphia, Here I Come!*, from
1964, and *Translations*, 1980, being the most consensual ones).

Even if Richard Pine's tripartite division of 'Plays of Love', 'Plays of Freedom', and 'Plays of Language' still remains as extremely operative, Elmer Andrews' stimulating, but debatable, decision to divide all Friel's plays in four successive decades somehow exposes not so much the fictional nature of these procedures as the peculiar nature of the playwright's options.

I suggest that besides the acknowledged evolution of the playwright's concerns and dramatic strategies, it is somehow possible to identify a pattern, more than thematic obsessions, in a career of almost forty years. Friel's career as a playwright shows signs of a permanent, and very fruitful, if I may say, tension between two different systems of artistic beliefs, two apparently conflicting dramatic paradigms, one which translates itself into plays like *The Freedom of the City* and another which appears perhaps best represented by *Aristocrats*. I think that Deane was somehow suggesting this when he wrote that 'Friel's writing runs in parallel worlds' ('Brian Friel' 112). The way I see it, Friel has always oscillated between those two poles in a close dialectical relation to his developments as a dramatist and to Irish society.

To understand this is important if we want to come to a proper understanding of his involvement in and his later leaving of Field Day. On the one hand we have the playwright that from a very early stage seems to have selected Chekhov as a kind of reference, more than as a model. Chekhov's dramatic strategies are the ones that Friel regards as best adapted to serve the concerns of the modern dramatist: 'man in society, in conflict with community, government, academy, church, family and essentially in conflict with himself' ('Theatre of Hope' 20). The only problem here is that, in English-speaking critical dis-course, when we say 'Chekhovian' that is frequently understood as referring to pausing, melancholic and nostalgic sets peopled by characters unable to do much more than speak about trivialities; not only is there usually, as Vera Gottlieb observed, 'a wanton disregard of the social and historical context' in which the plays were written (164), but also a prejudiced understanding of the Russian dramatist's social and political

concerns, which leads to a minimization of the play's intellectual and even ideological content. Due perhaps to the many
historical similarities that other Irish writers soon found
between Chekhov's Russia and nineteenth-century Ireland it
was surely easier for Friel to see how his dramatic strategies
could be put to use in a renewed practice, something he has
been doing from *Philadelphia, Here I Come!* at least up to *Dancing
at Lughnasa.*

But as *Philadelphia* also immediately proved, Friel's plays are
not an emulation of a master. From the very beginning, he
started combining, updating would be a very good term, the
extreme sophistication of the naturalist aesthetic with other
procedures which we would now call alienating or distancing,
not so much as a direct legacy from Brecht, but, following
along similar lines, through the application of some narrative
techniques to the stage. Friel's plays abound with breaks in the
chronological order of events, with commentators or sometimes even stage-directors, with characters that address the
audience directly, and so forth (see Niel). So, from the very
beginning, Friel broke the illusionistic convention of naturalism,
thus turning his drama into a self-reflexive and self-questioning
form. This awareness of the constructed nature of his dramatic
fictions would later evolve into an awareness of society and
history's constructed nature.

Faith Healer is a remarkable example both of these
distancing procedures and of the self-reflexive nature of his
drama. The dramatic action, understood in a more traditional
sense, is no longer between characters, but instead the relation
comes to be established between the four monologues. *Faith
Healer* will perhaps remain as Friel's most disturbing and at the
same time most revealing experiment. Because it came at the
end of a very traumatic decade – for Ireland and for the
playwright – a decade in which he produced two of the plays
which I regard as the most extreme paradigms of this tension I
identified: *The Freedom of the City* and *Aristocrats* (this last being
perhaps his most strenuous effort to prove to himself that he
was able to write a play whose characters had 'implicit in their
language, attitudes, style' all the 'politics' he needed [Friel,

'Extracts' 40-41]). After a decade filled with such extreme artistic options it is all the more compelling to find in *Faith Healer* an elaborate metaphor for the art, the craft of writing; the mysterious and unpredictable successes or failures of Frank Hardy are the complex image of the 'confusion' that all those involved in writing have about it, as the playwright himself later admitted (see 'The Man'). Just as happens between the faith healer and his audience, the relation between a writer and his readers only sometimes is transforming. In 1964, the year of *Philadelphia, Here I Come!,* Friel was already well aware of the hazardous and limited nature of his craft: 'Some people think that if they write a play and get it put on they'll change the world. But while you may move a lot of people for the moment, there will only be a very few who will think about it afterwards, maybe lie awake in bed for half-an-hour thinking over what you said' ('Delighting' 9).

The play that came next after *Faith Healer* was *Translations*, which stands as an achievement in Friel's aesthetics mainly because, as Elmer Andrews correctly saw it, the playwright succeeded 'in dissolving the distinction between political theatre which concerns itself with big "public" themes and psychological drama which sounds the depths of the individual mind' (168). *Translations* combines a highly sophisticated web of viewpoints on the nature of language and the workings of history with an arresting love story lived by deeply portrayed characters of the kind no audience will ever forget. In what is one of his most formally conservative plays, the linguistic convention on which the whole play is based (together with Hugh's choric comments) functions as a permanent reminder of the artistic (that is, constructed) nature of what the audience is watching and hearing. This is extreme distanciation combined with what might superficially be considered old-fashioned naturalism (and it is true that the play also clearly evokes the typical Abbey peasant play of the 1930s onwards). So in itself, that play was an appropriate 'translation' of his most sought-for goals as an artist. (And that he succeeded in doing this is confirmed by the delayed critical reaction to the play's historical and political dimensions, exactly the opposite of what had happened in 1973 with *The Freedom of the City*.) One of the things that perhaps explains Friel's public and academic success is his arriving at solutions for his conflicting double belief in the need of the audience's emotional engagement with what is going on up on the stage and in the possibility of making that experience last for more than two hours, the possibility of making people question some of the ideas, the pre-ordained patterns, they had for sure before sitting in the stalls. Friel's frequently praised experimentalism is perhaps more the result of the difficulties raised by the effort of holding this tension than the consequence of a deliberate will to try new forms. Mel Gussow's witty remark that Friel's work belongs to the kind 'theatregoers enjoy and academics love to sink their thesis into' (56) is somehow the acknowledgement of the very productive results of that same tension.

When critics come to the consideration of the much debated idea of the 'fifth province' launched by the directors of *The Crane Bag* and adopted by Field Day, they frequently tend to forget how difficult it would have been to go ahead with it and to keep on supporting it without the artistic developments in Irish culture which took place in the seventies. No doubt *The Crane Bag* broadened the debate over the relations between art and politics, but that was possible only because Irish artistic output made that discussion absolutely necessary. Just as Seamus Heaney would say, speaking about *Translations,* 'the excitement which this play caused was palpable and its gratifications had to do with a feeling that the dramatic form has allowed inchoate recognitions, both cultural and historical, to be clarified and comprehended' ('Field Day' 9). Friel had good reasons to believe in art as something we go to 'for perceptions of new adjustments and new arrangements' ('Extracts' 43). Art not as a commodity that made you feel nobler or worthier, but instead something that could make 'some tiny, thumbscrew adjustment on our psyche' ('Friel Spirit' 10). All this seems far from the barren scepticism O'Toole identifies in Friel's plays, which in turn should be understood as acts of 'linguistic vigilance' (Friel, 'Talking' 61): the permanent checking of the 'linguistic contours' (Friel, *Translations* 419) against the language of 'fact' (*Translations* 445). More than ever before, Friel's growing understanding of the drama text as something that means socially, politically, and discursively, reinforced his belief in its capacity to influence the thoughts and actions of other people.

Friel seems to have accepted some of the consequences of his involvement with Field Day, such as the fact of becoming a much more public figure than he has ever admitted himself to be before. In a playwright that has never shown much tendency to reflect upon his craft in more rational or critical terms, the interviews he granted to Ciaran Carty, Fintan O'Toole, and Elly Gillespie between 1980 and 1982 remain as invaluable, even if sometimes misguiding, pieces. In one of those interviews, implicitly adopting the concept of the Fifth Province first launched by the directors of *The Crane Bag* back in the seventies, Friel would go so far as to admit that the Field Day project 'should lead to a cultural state, not a political state. And I think out of that cultural state, a possibility of a political state follows' ('The Man' 23).

But these kinds of statements should not be merely interpreted, as some have done, that both Field Day's or Friel's understanding of the relationship between art and politics was a simple re-enactment or updating of the spirit of the Irish Renaissance with Yeats as its most visible protagonist. Eamonn Hughes, in one of the most penetrating and less biased essays on the 'Plays and Polemics of the Field Day Theatre Company', identifies as one of the factors in the genesis of that company 'the impact upon intellectual debate in the English-speaking world of what has come to be loosely known as structuralism and post-structuralism' (69), something that the genuine British empiricism of Edna Longley had early denounced in a more sarcastic way. Accepting this identification as true, we would also be accepting Field Day's effort to look at Irish reality (Northern and Southern, for that matter) from a renewed perspective. Their self-proclaimed effort to demythologize can perhaps be no better illustrated than in Deane's statement that 'almost everything which was believed to be nature or natural is in fact historical; more precisely, is an historical fiction' ('In Search' n. pag.).

The way Friel's drama insinuated itself into the critical and polemical discourse of the company can be found not only in the increasing historical dimension of his plays after *The Freedom of the City*, but specially in his almost unparalleled concentration on language, on linguistic codes and discourse as a dramatic strategy to expose Irish society. *Translations* is already a demonstration that 'reality' is not 'given', but instead 'constructed', and so also possible to reconstruct. Besides, *Translations* can be regarded as Field Day's founding text also because it functioned as a stimulating exercise on the way the borders between different discourses could be crossed. In this least *original* of Friel's plays, the playwright uses and translates into a dramatic wholeness an astonishing variety of sources which, through this process, end up being re-read: Irish historical documents and historical interpretations (ranging from Dowling's *The Hedge Schools of Ireland* to J.H. Andrew's *A Paper Landscape*), George Steiner's *After Babel* (extensively and boldly quoted throughout the play), classical texts like *The Odyssey* and *The Aeneid*, Shakespeare's English history plays, namely some scenes from *Henry IV*, the Irish peasant play itself, just to name some of the intertexts that are part of the play's fabric.

The vast criticism dedicated to *Translations* has not yet been able to come to terms with the seminal influence that the play has exerted upon the critical discourse not only of the other directors of the company but of some other sectors of Irish critical discourse. Charles R. Lyons, in a very positive review of Field Day's last and most debated initiative, the *Field Day Anthology of Irish Writing*, which he regards as 'a post-Foucauldian enterprise', stresses precisely this aspect when he states that *Translations* 'functions as a metonymic stimulus for the ways in which the three volumes confront the issues of language. The issues that inform the play obviously played a role in the genesis of the *Field Day Anthology of Irish Writing*, and *Translations* serves as a point of reference in several essays' (29). Deane, who repeatedly insisted on the way Field Day came to life as an extension of Friel's theatre (see 'In Search'), uses one of the most powerful and influential metaphors of the play to say exactly this: 'It was itself originating for Field Day, the more appropriate so because it quite literally mapped out a territory by writing about the remapping of a territory' ('Brian Friel' 106).

To re-write, to remap, to translate, all these have become current metaphors in Irish critical discourse. To translate became a necessary action, especially because translation is a double activity: it is first an act of hermeneutics and secondly an act of rewriting. *Translations* emerges as the culmination of Friel's increasing conviction that the reality we live in is discursively determined. The Italian writer Italo Calvino, discussing in 1976 the good and bad political uses of literature, stressed the capacity literature has to impose models of language, of visions, of imagination (82). Friel's art became simultaneously stimulating and dangerous because it started daring 'to create the possibility of another reality' (Kearney, 'Beyond Art' 75).

Friel's seemingly unbalanced or disparate dramatic output during the eighties and up to 1992 again confirms that very productive tension between the private and public paradigms I have already identified. Out of the eight plays he premiered in that twelve to thirteen-year period four were produced by Field Day, but the fact that the other four were produced elsewhere (*Fathers and Sons* at the National Theatre, *Dancing at Lughnasa* at the Abbey, *The London Vertigo* at the Andrew's Lane Theatre, Dublin, and *A Month in the County* at the Gate) does not allow us to establish a clear separation of their contribution to the playwright's political and artistic beliefs. On the one hand, something very curious happened in that period coming as a kind of aftermath to *Aristocrats*, especially if we consider the translations, adaptations, and rewritings of the Russian plays (the two Turguenev-based plays already mentioned and *Three Sisters*) and of the eighteenth-century Charles Macklin play, *The True Born Irishman or The Irish Fine Lady*. These four experiences can be both understood as efforts to map the playwright's special dramatic territory and as experiences to go on making politics by other means. The post-colonialist central concerns with language, history, place, and education which Friel had so successfully balanced in the composition of *Translations* still survive and are reworked in those other later plays. As the playwright would admit, commenting upon his translation of Chekhov into Irish-English: 'It's back to the political problem – it's our proximity to England, it's how we have been pigmented in our theatre with the English language, the use of the English language, the understanding of words, the whole cultural burden that every word in the English language carries is slightly different to our burden' ('The Man' 21).

Friel's 'estranging' translation of Chekhov then plays a cultural and political function that Tom Paulin's first Field Day pamphlet, 'A New Look at the Language Question', would make clear. That Friel was doing this in a 'theatre of moods ... where the action resides in internal motion and secret turmoil' (Friel, 'Turgenev' 10) is significant evidence that he was once more trying to explore those 'tiny, thumbscrew adjustment[s] on our psyche' ('Friel Spirit' 10) that he believed theatre was capable of operating.

The London Vertigo is not so much a further act of archaeology on his own (and Ireland's) dramatic universe, but more a kind of farcical variation and historical continuation of his concerns developed in *Translations*. Language and history remain as central in this very different type of inter-linguistic translation. The 'cutting off tongues' is still metaphorically, even if comically, presented as a 'dangerous experiment' (for the origin of Macklin's own expression see McVeagh 219).

A different type of comedy was the farce he wrote in 1982 for Field Day, *The Communication Cord,* perhaps less as an antidote to the pieties *Translations* was afforded, but instead more as a kind of dramatic paratext to that other play. The contemporary Ireland represented in *The Communication Cord* is no less overwhelmed by barriers to communication than the Ballybeg of 1833, which the playwright shows us as the result of obstinate and instrumentalizing processes of idealizing history. As Richard Kearney would later suggest, this play offers a 'playful deconstruction of words in the hope that new modes of communication may be possible' ('Language Plays' 144), thus anticipating the project of revising the 'mystique of Irishness ...

of the prevailing idea of what it is that constitutes the Irish reality' that Deane would propose in Field Day's fourth pamphlet ('Heroic Styles' 57-58).

Making History is again, on the one hand a development of a particular concern expressed in *Translations,* but perhaps not fully responded to by that play in dramatic terms: Hugh's statement that 'it is not the literal past, the "facts" of history that shape us, but images of the past embodied in language' (*Translations* 445). On the other hand, *Making History* goes further back in Irish history: to the decline of Gaelic rural society, portrayed in *Translations,* the playwright now adds the complex moment of the decline of Gaelic aristocracy. The play's main characters, Hugh O'Neill and Peter Lombard are both 'producers of history', even if in very different terms. If O'Neill emerges as 'astute' a man as the schoolmaster in *Translations,* he is likewise defeated by the social events, but this time Friel's protagonist emerges as the historically precocious personification of the complex Irish cultural identity. He is twice a translated character: first, because the complex set of cultural heritages he combines in himself condemns him to a state of permanent translation and second, because he is literally translated 'into a star' (O'Faolain vi). This daring play of ideas is not only an explicit and self-reflexive demonstration of the workings of the 'imperatives of fiction' (Friel, Andrews, and Barry 123) and thus a metadramatic exercise similar to the one we frequently find in Shakespeare's history plays, but also a renewed demonstration of how Irish drama came 'to be a factor in the re-reading and rewriting of history, a way of reshaping the consciousness of the audience in posterity, if not in the stalls' (Heaney 9). Besides offering an interpretation of the modern Irish historical condition, Friel is also attempting a challenging metahistorical reflection revealing in dramatic terms how 'history is never literal; it is a figurative reading of events by means of human thought and language' (Kearney, *The Irish Mind* 32). The conflict in *Making History* is not the traditional dramatic conflict, but is instead superseded by the confrontation of two rival hermeneutics. The fact that we again find in another Friel play the use of such different contributions as that of Paul Ricoeur's hermeneutics, particularly his work in *Histoire et Verité,* and Hayden White's *Metahistory: The Historical Imagination in Nineteenth Century* is another clear sign that the playwright has no fear of intersections, but instead a refreshing capacity to absorb and combine different discourses. *Making History* presents itself as another effort to renew the 'linguistic contours' of a civilization so that it keeps on matching the 'landscape of fact' (*Translations* 419).

Friel's involvement with Field Day came at a time when the playwright was already combining imaginative creativity with an acute sense of social commitment, always striving to find the best possible ways of making himself heard. Playing upon the title of his last contribution to Field Day, it was as if having started to unmake history back in the seventies the playwright saw the time had come to help make history. The strength of Deane's programmatic insistence that 'everything including our politics and our literature, has to be re-written – i.e., re-read' ('Heroic' 58) could not have been the same without the experience of *Translations* some years before. The whole Field Day experience is based on the possibility and the need Irish people have of reinterpreting their experience. Its most valuable contribution to the Irish cultural and political debate has been the demonstration that the crossing of borders should start being done by the cultural discourse, rejecting the idea that there are special arenas for specific purposes. In *Making History,* Mary Bagenal advises her sister not to 'plant the fennel near the dill or the two will cross-fertlize'; Mabel (Bagenal) O'Neill answers with a question: 'Is that bad?' (21-22). Cross-fertilization is a very adequate image to characterize not only Friel's drama of the eighties but also the Field Day experience.

Notes

[1] Friel's involvement with Field Day started in 1980 with the production of *Translations* and was formally concluded in January 1994 when he resigned from the Board of Directors. His more active involvement can be counted differently if we consider *Making History,* premiered in Derry in 1988, his last public contribution to that project.

[2] The juxtaposition in this essay of Paul Hadfield and Lynda Henderson's and Fintan O'Toole's *articles* and Marilynn Richtarik's *book* is perhaps

misleading if not unfair. It can be argued that the first two contributions are part of the history and the polemics (or the polemical history) induced by the Field Day project, while Richtarik's study, concentrated on the company's first five years (1980-1984), is the first major effort to chronicle Field Day's contribution to Irish cultural politics. The fact is that in Richtarik's book, superbly documented and an indispensable tool for anyone interested in the Irish contemporary scene, the neutral perspective of the cultural historian is only too often betrayed by a given set of prejudices, some of which, as I try to demonstrate, Field Day has helped to question. In this sense, and since Field Day is still an on-going reality, Richtarik's book becomes an unavoidable part of the polemics.

Works Cited

Andrews, Elmer. *The Art of Brian Friel.* London: Macmillan, 1995.

Calvino, Italo. *La Machine Littérature: Essais.* Paris: Editions du Seuil, 1984.

Dantanus, Ulf. *Brian Friel.* London: Faber, 1984.

Deane, Seamus. 'The Artist and the Troubles'. *Ireland and the Arts.* Special Number of *The Literary Review.* Ed. Tim Pat Coogan. London: Namara, 1983. 42-50.

--- 'The Arts and Ideology. A Discussion between Jennifer Fitzgerald, Joan Fowles, and Frank McGuinness.' *The Crane Bag* 9.2 (1985): 60-69.

--- 'Brian Friel: The Name of the Game'. In Peacock. 103-12.

--- 'Heroic Styles: The Tradition of an Idea'. *Ireland's Field Day.* London: Hutchinson, 1985. 45-60.

--- 'In Search of a Story'. Programme Note for the Field Day Production of *The Communication Cord.* Derry: Field Day Theatre Company, 1982. n.p.

Friel, Brian. 'Brian Friel: Delighting in Mischief, Wary of Praise'. Statements collected by Douglas Kennedy. *Irish Times* 4 July 1987: 9.

--- 'Extracts from a Sporadic Diary'. *The Writers: A Sense of Ireland.* Ed. Andrew Carpenter and Peter Fallon. Dublin: O'Brien, 1980. 39-43.

--- 'Friel Spirit in the Senate'. Statements collected by Anne Harris. *Sunday Independent* 1 May 1987: 10.

--- 'The Future of Irish Drama'. A Discussion between Fergus Linehan, Hugh Leonard, and John B. Keane. *Irish Times* 12 Feb. 1970: 14.

--- 'Ivan Turgenev (1818-1883)'. *A Month in the Country. After Turgenev.* Dublin: Gallery, 1992. 9-11.

--- *Making History.* London: Faber, 1989.

--- 'The Man From God Knows Where'. Interview with Fintan O'Toole. *In Dublin* 28 Oct. 1982: 20-23.

--- 'Plays Peasant and Unpeasant'. *Times Literary Supplement* 17 Mar. 1972: 305.

--- 'Self-Portrait'. *Aquarius* 5 (1972): 17-22.

--- 'Talking to Ourselves'. Interview with Paddy Agnew. *Magill* Dec. 1980: 59-61.

--- 'The Theatre of Hope and Despair'. *Everyman* (1968): 17-22.

--- *Translations. Selected Plays.* London: Faber, 1990.

--- Untitled essay. *A Paler Shade of Green.* Ed. Des Hickey and Gus Smith. London: Frewin, 1972. 221-25.

--- Friel, Brien, John Andrews, and Kevin Barry. '*Translations* and *A Paper Landscape:* Between Fiction and History'. *The Crane Bag* 7.2 (1983): 118-24.

Gottlieb, Vera. 'Chekhov in Limbo: British Productions of the Plays of Chekhov'. *The Play Out of Context: Transferring Plays from Culture to Culture.* Ed. Hanna Scolnikova and Peter Holland. Cambridge: Cambridge UP, 1989. 163-72.

Gussow, Mel. 'From Ballybeg to Broadway'. *New York Times Magazine* 29 Sept. 1991: 30, 55-59.

Hadfield, Paul, and Lynda Henderson. 'Field Day – The Magical Mystery'. *Theatre Ireland* Jan. 1988: 63-66.

Heaney, Seamus. 'A Field Day for the Irish'. *The Times* 5 Dec. 1988: 9.

Hughes, Eamon. '"To Define Your Dissent": The Plays and Polemics of the Field Day Theatre Company'. *Theatre Research International* 15.1 (1989): 67-77.

Kearney, Richard. 'Beyond Art and Politics'. *The Crane Bag* 1.1 (1977): 13-21.

--- *The Irish Mind: Exploring Intellectual Traditions.* Dublin: Wolfhound, 1984.

--- 'The Language Plays of Brian Friel'. *Transitions: Narratives in Modern Irish Culture.* Dublin: Wolfhound, 1988. 125-60.

Kilroy, Thomas. 'The Irish Writer: Self and Society, 1950-80'. *Literature and the Changing Ireland.* Ed. Peter Connolly. Gerrards Cross: Smythe, 1982. 175-87.

Longley, Edna. 'Poetry and Politics in Northern Ireland'. *The Crane Bag* 9.1 (1985): 26-40.

Lyons, Charles R. '"A Struggle for Definition" – *The Field Day Anthology of Irish Writing*'. *Irish Studies Review* 1 (1992): 27-30.

McCormack, W.J. *The Battle of the Books: Two Decades of Irish Cultural Debate.* Gigginstone: Lilliput, 1986.

McVeagh, John. 'A Kind of *Comhar:* Charles Macklin and Brian Friel'. In Peacock. 215-28.

Niel, Ruth. 'Non-realistic Techniques in the Plays of Brian Friel: The Debt to International Drama'. *Literary Interrelations: Ireland, England and the World*. Vol. 2. *Comparison and Impact*. Ed. Wolfgang Zach and Heinz Kosok. Tubingen: Gunter Narr, 1987. 349-59.

O'Brien, Conor Cruise. 'An Unhealthy Intersection'. *New Review* 2.16 (1975): 3-8; *Irish Times* 21 Aug. 1975: 10.

O'Brien, George. *Brian Friel*. Dublin: Gill-Macmillan, 1989.

O'Faoláin, Seán. *The Great O'Neill: A Biography of Hugh O'Neill, Earl of Tyrone, 1550-1616*. Dublin: Mercier, 1992.

O'Toole, Fintan. 'Beyond Language'. *Irish Times* 28 Apr. 1990: 5.

--- 'Marking Time: From *Making History* to *Dancing at Lughnasa*'. In Peacock. 202-14.

Peacock, Alan, ed. *The Achievement of Brian Friel*. Gerrards Cross: Colin Smythe, 1993.

Pine, Richard. *Brian Friel and Ireland's Drama*. London: Routledge, 1990.

Richtarik, Marilyn J. *Acting Between the Lines: The Field Day Theatre Company and Irish Cultural Politics 1980-1984*. Oxford: Clarendon, 1994.

14 | Forms of Redress: Structure and Characterization in *The Freedom of the City*

Michael Parker

Causes and Means for Redress

Though the specific events which occasioned Brian Friel's *The Freedom of the City* were the killings on Bloody Sunday of thirteen unarmed civilians on 30 January 1972 and the publication less than three months later of the Widgery Report which exonerated those responsible and thus compounded the gross offence, the play is best understood by placing it within a much broader narrative. It should be read not just in the context of contemporaneous political violence, which by the time of the play's premiere in February 1973 had already cost over 730 lives, but as a response to the failures of nationalist and unionist politics, Irish and British governments to fulfil their responsibilities to the peoples of Northern Ireland since the state's inception. Fifty years of institutionalized 'discrimination in housing, political representation and employment' (Foster 583) and intermittent periods of coercion had generated a profound sense of alienation within the minority community, which felt abandoned and betrayed both by their co-religionists in the South and by the British authorities. By the mid-1960s, however, an articulate, educated younger generation of northern Catholics was beginning to emerge which was not prepared to endorse the Nationalist Party's abstentionist policies, and was determined to challenge the inequities and abuses of power in the *status quo* (see, for example, Boyce 364-67).

As Friel's characterizations in *The Freedom of the City* and *Translations* make clear, nationalists in Derry – like nationalists and unionists throughout the North – did not constitute a single, homogeneous mass. Represented within their ranks was a spectrum of political opinion, ranging from constitutional nationalists such as John Hume, who co-operated with Church authorities in the Derry Housing Association,[1] to activists from the left, such as Eamonn McCann. A leading member of the Derry Housing Action Committee, McCann organized a series of demonstrations in Derry's Guildhall in the spring of 1968 in order to provoke retaliation from unionist authorities and to radicalize the nationalist community.[2]

That Brian Friel would have been extremely well-informed about such developments in the political scene and socio-economic conditions in Derry during this period cannot be doubted. The playwright's father, Patrick, served for three terms on the City Corporation as one of the eight councillors for the South Ward of the City, an area which included the Bogside, Creggan, and Brandywell (Dantanus 34). These were notorious unemployment blackspots in a city where the rate in 1966 was seven times higher than the average for the United Kingdom. Despite the fact that nationalists were in a majority in the city, local government remained in unionist hands as a result of electoral gerrymandering which had been in operation since 1924. Given this, it is hardly surprising to learn that 'seventy per cent of the Corporation's administrative, clerical, and technical employees were non-Catholics' and that Pro-testants 'held nine of the ten best paid jobs' (Buckland 116-17).

Brian Friel is known to have been an active supporter of the Civil Rights campaign and to have witnessed the events of Bloody Sunday at first hand (Pine 106). In an interview, dating from 1973, he tells of how he took part in a demonstration about housing in Derry, 'not because I was involved, but because I was an interested spectator at that point' (Maxwell,

Brian Friel 27). Like other enthusiasts for the Civil Rights cause, he would witness how the 'heady and boisterous' early years of protest in 1967 and 1968 were followed by 'an ashy aftermath' (Heaney, Letter), and in this light *The Freedom of the City* might be seen as in part a lament for lost hope.

Like Seamus Heaney's *North* (1975), Friel's play exemplifies how 'politics seizes violently upon the imagination' (Maxwell, qtd. in Connolly 168). In an interview given nine years after its first performance, he was of the opinion that *The Freedom of the City* was at best only a partial success:

> I think one of the problems with that play was that the experience of Bloody Sunday wasn't adequately distilled in me. I wrote it out of some kind of heat and some kind of immediate passion that I would want to have quieted a bit before I did it. It was really … a very emotive time. It was really a shattering experience that the British Army, this disciplined instrument, would go in as they did that time and shoot thirteen people. To be there on that occasion and – I didn't actually see people get shot – but I mean, to have to throw yourself on the ground because people are firing at you is a very terrifying experience. Then the whole cover-up afterwards was shattering too (Friel, Interview 22).

The essay that follows will in part offer an extended counter-view to Friel's assessment, and argue that much of the play's power is in fact derived from the 'immediate passion' that went into its making. It will also take issue with the verdicts of many of the British reviewers of the time who dismissed the play as propaganda, largely on the basis of its highly partial representation of the British,[3] and the man from *The New York Times* who regarded its treatment of 'recent disturbances' as 'lurid' and 'far-fetched' (Barnes 32).[4] To see *The Freedom of the City* solely as a product of a historical moment, is to ignore its concern with broader issues of authority – political, judicial, spiritual, moral and domestic – and to miss its articulation of a wider, deeper need for 'redress', for 'reparation of, compensation for a wrong sustained or the loss resulting' (*OED* 1773), and the formal, technical and verbal accomplishment with which that need is expressed.

Much of the analysis will focus closely on the structure and characterization in the play, the forms Friel has used in order to seek 'redress' and affirm art's function as 'an upright, resistant and self-bracing entity' (Heaney, *Redress* 15). A particularly fruitful source for a critique of Friel's drama, as one critic has already recognized (Andrews 45-46, 60-61, 70-71, 123, 196), is the work of the Russian theorist, Mikhail Bakhtin. Throughout *The Freedom of the City*, 'parodic stylization' (Bakhtin, qtd. in Rice and Waugh 202) is utilized specifically in order to undermine the authority figures who seek to 'manage' discourse and 'frame' the narrative, but more generally to generate continual shifts in language and perspective. *The Freedom of the City*, like Friel's other works, constantly engages the audience/reader through its 'dialogic', the plurality of its voices, which are ideologically 'disparate', yet 'mutually revealing' (Andrews 72).

An equally important feature of the play's characterization and action is its use of 'carnival' in depicting and individualizing the principal characters. Bakhtin's term is a richly suggestive one, and at a primary level refers to the transgressive quality of many literary texts, and the ways in which they subvert the official order, its ideology and practices, frequently by means of 'the permanent corrective of laughter' (Bakhtin, qtd. in Lodge 136). 'Carnivalization' deals in ambivalence and contradiction, and makes play in liminal states such as the macabre and grotesque. The most obvious instrument and agent of this element in the play is the character of Skinner, who – like his creator – regularly deploys masquerade to unmask the lofty. And yet, for all his linguistic and dramatic energy, Skinner, like his unwitting companions, will become 'a casualty of language' (Friel, *Volunteers* 28) – his own and others – and fall victim to greater force.

Structure, Sequence and Frame Narration

Writing in *Time and Narrative*, Paul Ricoeur avers that 'a discontinuous structure suits a time of dangers ... a jagged chronology, interrupted by jumps, anticipations and flashbacks ... is better suited to a view of time that has no possible over-view, no overall internal cohesiveness' (qtd. in Onega and

Landa 134). Though formally divided into two acts, *The Freedom of the City* is a play of approximately thirty-four 'scenes'. In the course of its action, which constantly shuttles backwards and forwards in time, over twenty-two different voices are heard in a range of registers and diversity of speech forms.[5] Interspersed between ten substantial sections of dialogue between the three central characters, Michael, Lily, and Skinner, a Judge delivers four monologues and cross-questions witnesses on four occasions, a priest gives two sermons, an RTE commentator two live reports, a balladeer two songs, and a sociologist, Professor Dodds, a lecture in five parts.

During Act 1 a pattern is established whereby for every one long episode in which Michael, Lily, and Skinner appear, there are generally three others involving other commentators, while in Act 2 scenes tend to alternate between the besieged and the empowered. Although the play's closure gives the last word to the media and the Judge, the time-sequencing throughout the play subverts their (and all other) authority, since the audience's direct experience of the 'live' private exchanges between Michael, Lily, and Skinner exposes the false witness of those who subsequently hold court.

The combined effect of this overtly 'loaded' structure and the irony-generating, narrative anachronies running through it is to bond the audience's sympathies with the dead – misread and outnumbered as they are from the outset. Anticipating the daring illusions in *Faith Healer*, where three out of the four Parts are delivered by 'ghosts', and *Translations*, where the audience listening to English become 'convinced' they are hearing Gaelic, *The Freedom of the City* begins establishing the fate of the protagonists – *Three bodies lie grotesquely across the front of the stage* (107) – and then proceeds to resurrect them. After having re-animated them in a series of flashbacks within Act 1 (Scenes 7, 11, 15, 19, 22), Friel disrupts the linear narrative operating for scenes inside the Guildhall at the beginning of Act 2 by a remarkable use of *prolepsis*. In a scene further confirming the 'privileged' status of the audience, Michael, Lily, and Skinner are heard lucidly articulating their thoughts at the moment of death

(149-50, scene 25), yet when they next appear in Scenes 27 and 29 it is prior to the decision to leave their 'refuge'.

Friel employs startling dramatic effects and stark juxtapositions from the start. Aptly in a play dealing with the distortion and debasement of language, *The Freedom of the City* opens wordlessly, relying on visual metaphors to set meanings in motion. The stage is silent and dark, except for a chill blue light on the empty apron, which singles out three broken bodies in a contemporary crucifixion scene.[6] The silence, once established, is intruded upon first by the distant wail of an ambulance siren – too late and too far away to bring relief – and then by two scuttling figures, a photographer and a priest. Like those who will succeed them, both have a considerable stake in the dead, the one commercial, the other ideological. The photographer's eerie white flashes, like the constant blue apron light, drain the dead further, offer an illusion of definition, while the priest's hasty gestures and blurred words seem mild impositions in comparison to those which will occur in the main text.

The introduction of a spotlight, picking out '*the JUDGE high up in the battlements*' (107), draws the eye away from the crouching and stricken shapes, and becomes a signal for the play's 'descent' into language, and the introduction of the tribunal as a dramatic formal device. The placing of the Judge, as Elizabeth Hale Winkler, among others, has noted, is both scenic and symbolic, and alludes to Derry's fortress history.[7] The positioning also establishes a precedent for other characters whose function it is to frame the dead and their narrative. Subsequently, Father Brosnan and Liam O'Kelly, the TV commentator, will be presented sharing these battlements with the Judge and the Brigadier, despite the fact that they embody competing ideological positions and rival discourses to those of the British establishment. By means of this 'speaking picture' (Sidney 101), this geopolitical metaphor, Friel implies 'a similarity in dissimilars' (Aristotle 1478), and enables the audience to imagine a tenuous affinity between their own position and that of the play's lower-placed victims. Thus the staging itself sets Lily, Skinner, and Michael at the mercy of seemingly antithetical political forces, or, as Shakespeare has it, between 'a pair of chaps',

> And throw between them all the food thou hast
> They'll grind the one the other (*Antony and Cleopatra*, 3.5.13-15).

That Friel is concerned with language as a site of conflict in which monologic, authoritarian forces strive to close down meaning and suppress the challenge of dialogic, quickly becomes apparent. The play's opening lines themselves serve as a paradigm for what will follow, as the unnamed Judge – a *'fussy'*, *'testy'* Englishman *'in his early sixties'* (107) – makes a brusque demonstration of his considerable authority. The early exchanges find him forcing an RUC witness to repeat himself, asking leading questions which might well be interpreted as an attempt to justify the Army's shoot-to-kill policy, and dismissing out of hand any reference to the socio-economic circumstances of the victims, since the hearing is not a 'social survey' (108). Despite the Judge's subsequent claims that he is engaged in a search for 'an objective view' (109) of what happened, it soon becomes abundantly clear that this is not the case. The tribunal he is conducting is, he explains with unintended irony, 'in no sense a court of justice' (109). One minute he characterizes the tribunal as 'a fact-finding exercise',[8] unconcerned with 'moral judgements', the next he presents the audience with only two possible readings of events and people both of which fix the Guildhall three as guilty (109-10). Immediately after learning the names, occupations and ages of each of the deceased, he seeks to establish whether they had any previous convictions and whether firearms were found on or near the bodies. When the officer mentions that he had come across Skinner before, the Judge's question, 'As a terrorist?' (109), suggests that he may well be working from preconceptions. Instead of trying to acquire an understanding of the people whose deaths he is investigating or the contexts within which he is working, he appears determined to impose closure, 'to block other narratives from forming and emerging' (Said xiii).

The Judge's later speeches and exchanges confirm these initial impressions. During the course of his next appearance, it emerges that the Judge is 'an old army man' (134), as Lord Chief Justice Widgery was. Again he refers to the three as 'terrorists' as if this were an indisputable fact. Ineffectually, almost apologetically he cross-examines the officer responsible for the killings. Having established that Brigadier Johnson-Hanbury had a massive number of military and police units at his disposal (133), he then fails to press the Brigadier as to how, given this 'rather formidable array', he could be described as in any way 'exposed' or seriously threatened. Like Widgery (Taylor 71), the play's Judge privileges 'sworn testimony' (142) from the security forces over the 'persistent suggestions' (134) of civilian witnesses and counsel for the deceased, preferring to believe eight soldiers and four policemen and dubious forensic evidence rather than the evidence of Father Brosnan's eyes or Mr Montini's 'very lucid' photographs. By the time one encounters Dr. Winbourne, the forensic scientist's references to 'smear marks' (143) on the bodies and hears Professor Cuppley's account of the 'serious mutilation' (162) the three victims suffered, one is fully conscious of the Judge's contribution to the dishonouring of the dead, and mangling of truth. In some perverse way he believes that justice took a hand in their fate, since they had 'defaced' the building, 'despoiled' the furnishings, and 'defiled' its records (149).

In his characterization of the Judge, Friel deploys what Mikhail Bakhtin termed 'parodic stylization'. This method of representation is similarly deployed in depicting other 'types' who seek to 'manage' discourse, including Father Brosnan, the priest, and Liam O'Kelly, the man from RTE. Within the priest's two sermons, Friel reproduces a number of the rhetorical devices traditionally used by Irish clerics to maintain a spirit of sheepish obedience amongst their flock. Although their openings are identical, the politics of each of Brosnan's homilies are radically different. Both of the priest's sermons begin by proffering a ritual channel for the congregation's 'deep and numbing grief' (124, 155), before harping on the efficacy of his ministrations, which, he claims, fortified the victims before they met their Maker. In neither text does he name the truly culpable, or provide a credible answer to his own rhetorical question, 'Why did they die?' (125). The first sermon translates the deaths into a conscious sacrificial choice, and 'naturalizes' the killings by placing them within a traditional Catholic-Nationalist ideological narrative. This process of 'familiarization' – *ostranenie* in reverse – is primarily effected by such means as repetitions in grammatical structures and the use of clichés:

> They died for their beliefs ... for their fellow citizens ... because they could endure no longer the injuries ... injustices and indignities that have been their lot for too many years. They sacrificed their lives so that you and I and thousands like us might be rid of that iniquitous yoke and ... inherit a decent way of life (125).

Whereas the first address ends with rhetorical gesturing towards unspecified forms of political action, the second rejects confrontation with the authorities at Stormont and Westminster in favour of a crusade against evil, poisonous, contaminating influences from within their own community. What were once iniquities and inequities that the priest deplored are subsequently translated as 'imperfections' in a system that was regrettably 'less than equal' (156). His contention is that the Civil Rights Movement has become hopelessly compromised, 'an instrument for corruption' in the hands of godless communists and revolutionaries, whose oratory and persuasiveness threaten his own. As an orthodox Catholic cleric, he distrusts people's democracy, and, like Michael, places his trust in Dignity and Decency as the means by which 'the meek shall inherit the earth' (156). By reverting to the passive, pre-Civil Rights Nationalist Party position, he sidelines himself and the Church, leaving a gap that in the 'real world' outside the text the Provisional IRA were eager to fill.

Through his depiction of the RTE commentator, Liam O'Kelly, Friel continues his withering critique of the culture and politics in the Republic.[9] For him, those inside the Guildhall, whether dead or alive, exist only as 'copy'. Like the priest, at first O'Kelly is prepared to flirt with Republican fervour; like the Judge, he has a criminal disregard for accuracy, and is content to recycle clichés and misinformation. Regardless of whether he has been duped by the Bogside's *usually reliable* spokesmen' (118; emphasis added), or is colluding with them, his irresponsible claim that 'a group of about fifty armed gunmen' have seized the Guildhall serves as a contributing factor in the military's overreaction and in the tragedy that ensues. By repeating the Bogsiders' cocky allusion to the fall of the Bastille in his report, he confirms the apprehensions of the Army hierarchy, who cast themselves, in Burkean fashion, as the Forces of Order confronting a lawless revolutionary mob.[10]

O'Kelly's importance within the play's dialectics can be seen from the fact that he is given *The Freedom of the City*'s penultimate speech. Appropriating the role of voice-of-a-nation's-grief, he describes the funeral of the Guildhall victims. With less excuse than *Faith Healer*'s Frank Hardy, but with equally suspect eloquence, O'Kelly tries to transmute the locus for a brutal, sordid, unnecessary killing into something 'most beautiful, most triumphant' (167). Derry provides him with an opportunity to display his art. A cultural void, a socio-economic black hole, it can only be redeemed by the presence of lords spiritual and temporal, Bach's music, his own metaphors. A complex text he cannot conceptualize, he falls back on stock phrases about the 'bitterly cold' city with its 'narrow ghetto streets' and humble parishes, and uses stock devices like the pathetic fallacy to describe how 'the clouds … can contain themselves no longer' (167). Whereas none of the minor actors in this grand ritual are individualized in his discourse – the possessors of the 'patient drawn faces' or the pious men 'kneeling on the wet pavements' – the Cardinal Primate and the Taoiseach are singled out in obsequious references. Ironically, although he has no problem remembering the name of Colonel Foley (the President's representative), or indeed the number of Bach's *Prelude and Fugue*, he makes a hash of Skinner's name, calling him Adrian Fitzmaurice – not that it matters, of course.

More problematical within the characterization of the play's figures of authority is the case of Professor Dodds. From the outset there is an ambiguity about Dodds's relationship with the other representative figures since at no point is he made to acknowledge their existence. The fact that he is an outsider – an American sociologist – obviously distances him from the three principals and their Derry, and has led several critics to place him amongst those other discredited authorities in the play. His speech-acts – like those of other agents of what Althusser has termed the Ideological State Apparatuses (qtd. in Rice and Waugh 54-62)[11] – are couched in formal register, standard English, professional language, and consist of direct, Brechtian addresses to the audience. Friel's placing of him in the stage directions '*in a small area stage left*' (104) might be interpreted as an indication that he is aligned with the marginalized characters off-stage, such as the Civil Rights protesters, and Michael, Lily, and Skinner who have yet to appear; certainly he is separated geographically from the 'voices of control' (Deane, 'Introduction' 18). However, against that it could simply be argued that it would have been inappropriate to set him on the battlements alongside the British and Irish Catholic establishments.

An interesting case for a re-evaluation of Dodds's role and significance has been made by William Jent, who uses the character to contest readings which impose too neat a symmetry on the play's form and debate, though in the process he overstates the sociologist's centrality by identifying him as 'Friel's proxy' (575). Necessarily for his argument, Jent cites the playwright's assertion to a contemporary interviewer that *The Freedom of the City* is 'not about Bloody Sunday' (Boland 18), but rather 'about poverty' (Jent 575-76). Friel's comment, like some of his others, should perhaps be treated as something of a diversionary ploy on his part to discourage audiences and critics from interpreting the play solely as a one-issue piece, or simply as anti-British polemic. Jent argues that Friel intended us to recognize *Freedom*'s global, internationalist agenda, and how in a sense it is located 'not in Derry as such … but in every city where the poor struggle for political and economic freedom' (579). Such a reading, however, like that of the fictional Dodds, seems to diminish, if not to deny the very particularity of Derry that the play insists upon and which is embodied in Michael, Lily, and Skinner, who are clearly individualized and not simply

members of a homogeneous caste or class. There is more than
a grain of truth in George O'Brien's contention that 'the
seductive fluidity of the professor's confident language does not
disguise the generalizing and impersonalizing tendency in his
approach. Ultimately his language is as suspect as the rest, since
its objective is to assert a model for Lily, Skinner and Michael
to fit' (82).[12]

The first two sections of Dodds's segmented lecture on the
culture of poverty are sandwiched between, and concurrent
with two off-stage 'scenes' depicting a Civil Rights gathering,
addressed by a fiery woman orator, who is heard urging her
supporters to '[s]tand your ground!'[13] Whereas their marginalization in society, ironically mimicked by the staging, is
indisputable, the question as to where Dodds stands is difficult
to determine. His speeches clearly function as a counter-
discourse to the Judge's, since they construct a larger socio-
economic narrative to which the principal characters appear to
conform, but ultimately resist. Dodds's generalized critique
frequently intersects with and, on occasion, usefully illuminates
elements in Michael, Lily, and Skinner's story. One thinks, for
example, of his description of the values and conditions shared
by ghetto-dwellers 'all over the Western world' (111, 133), and
how external 'events', like the campaign led by Martin Luther
King, Jr., for black Civil Rights in America, can induce a sudden
burst into consciousness which 'breaks the pane' (Heaney,
Wintering Out 23)[14] of hopelessness and despair.

In a number of significant respects, however, Dodds's
readings do not describe the Derry characters with much precision, despite Jent's assertions to the contrary.[15] His suggestions that the poor are not 'psychologically geared to take
advantage of changing conditions or increased opportunities'
(110) and are 'present time-orientated' (133) may apply to Lily,
but certainly not to Michael, who, like Butt in Friel's *Volunteers*,
is determined to 'improve myself' (122). Immediately following
Dodds's allusion to 'increased opportunities', the stage directions speak of '*the roar of approaching tanks*' (111), as if to
undermine his urbane discourse. Although Dodds talks about
how economic conditions induce feelings of inferiority, help-

lessness and dependency, in practice Skinner, Lily, and Michael show themselves to be buoyant, unbowed, and often mutually supportive; his assertion that the poor 'often have a hell of a lot more fun than we' (135), though seemingly confirmed by Lily's and Skinner's antics with the mayoral robes, does not take into account the price exacted for their 'fun'. Informed, articulate, logical, sensitive, as Dodds's analysis most definitely is, it cannot tell the whole story any more than a playwright or a single character can, because there is no whole story, only partial narratives.

The Individualized Principals

In sharp contrast to each of these frame narrators, who ascribe a unity of purpose and collective solidarity to the marchers trapped in the Guildhall, the author is at pains to differentiate between them. Through his characterization of the three, Friel demonstrates how, like any other mass membership political grouping, the Northern Ireland Civil Rights Association was an inspirational, but potentially unstable entity, drawing on 'resources of recalcitrance' (Lloyd 2) in people with very diverse opinions and agendas.

These are made apparent during the early flashbacks when the audience became acquainted with Michael, Lily, and Skinner. Even before these, however, Skinner is in a sense marked out from the others by the presence of the ceremonial hat beside his body and, more importantly, by his 'form' (109). His record of petty criminal activity confirms Seamus Deane's account of the disaffected younger generation in the Bogside amongst whom 'the prevailing notion ... was that in a totally corrupt society like theirs, delinquency was an expression of intelligence' ('Bogside' 1a).[16] From his very first entry, Skinner quickly distinguishes himself from his prostrated, disorientated companions, through the speed of his thinking and action. Significantly he has not been blinded by gas, and the verbs describing him – *'races'*, *'looking about frantically'*, *'races'*, *'runs'*, *'discovers'*, *'flings'*, *'glances'*, *'runs'*, *'grabs'*, *'drags'*, *'rushes'*, (112-13) – convey energy, *'lithe efficiency'*, and an ability to adjust quickly to new situations. Observing his brisk man-handling of Lily and

Michael as he leads them to the 'safety' of the Guildhall parlour, inevitably the audience recall the moment a minute earlier when they saw soldiers dragging the same bodies off-stage by the feet.

In the theatre programme or on the page, the juxtaposition of the two names Lily and Skinner – names associated with a popular chain of shoe shops – hints at an affinity, and indeed they soon establish themselves as a comic double act through their brusque manner with each other.[17] Their repartee gives an early sign of the affection and trust that will develop between them:

> **Skinner:** Did you get a dose of the CS gas?
> **Lily:** D'you think I'm playing blind-man's-buff? …
> **Lily:** What got into them … ?
> **Skinner:** … the march was banned?
> **Lily:** I knew the march was banned.
> **Skinner:** Did you expect them to give you tea … ?
> **Lily:** I didn't expect them to drive their tanks through us and shoot gas and rubber bullets into us … . It's a mercy to God if no one's hurted (112-14).[18]

For a sizeable section of their opening encounter (Scene 7), however, Friel has Skinner dropping out of sight, and allows Lily, the forty-three year old mother of eleven, to take centre stage. Her obvious concern for Michael's well-being, her lurid fascination with blood and injuries, and above all her comic anecdotes bring warmth and relief after the austerity, brutality and formality of the previous scenes. Where Dodds offers the audience urbane generalizations about the poor couched in elaborated code, Lily peoples the stage with her working-class acquaintances in animated dialect. Her thumbnail sketches of local characters show her to be a natural born storyteller and humorist; at the same time her anecdotes remind us how violence has become normalized, as common an accessory to life in Derry as a miraculous medal. Friel repeatedly draws the audience's attention to differences between her insistently 'non-standard' linguistic usage[19] and the languages of the better educated, more socially mobile Michael and Skinner, thereby questioning Dodds's construction of the 'poor' as a uniform block of humanity. Some commentators seem to regard Lily as a lovable ignoramus, yet she has heard of Che Guevara and Joe Stalin (115, 121), and though in her posthumous speech she laments that she had never 'isolated, … assessed … articulated' (150) her life's experiences, in conversation with Skinner and Michael she demonstrates considerable social skills.

Such is the economy and skill of Friel's writing that even scenes apparently devoted to comic 'business' are never just that. Subsequently it will emerge that Lily's garrulousness masks a lack of self-esteem, and the fact that like *The Gentle Island*'s Sarah – another solitary female character, half her age – for most of her life she has been subjected to an oppressive domestic patriarchy. The respect she accords to 'the Chairman' is not one that is reciprocated, as we subsequently discover when she confides to Skinner how she had recently been addressed by her husband: 'You're a bone stupid bitch. No wonder the kid's bone stupid, too' (155). Though several times she describes him as the one with 'the brains', she later refers to him sitting round all day reading the children's comics, which gives a rather different twist to his honorary title. From her seemingly innocuous question to Michael about where he was standing, there emerges a telling distinction between the two:

> **Michael:** Beside the platform. … below the speakers.
> **Lily:** I was at the back of the crowd … (114)

Michael's placing of himself highlights the attraction authority holds for him and the respect he affords it. Beneath his commitment to the new spirit of collective action within the community lies a strong measure of self-interest, though it is not something he would like to admit to. Lily's positioning of herself on the margins, by contrast, is indicative of the modest, self-deprecating side of her character, exemplified unconsciously in one of her next comments, 'How would I know where I run. I followed the crowd' (116), and may be understood in the light of her later revelation to Skinner about her secret, private motives for marching; she is doing it for the sake of her mongol son (155).

Significantly it is Skinner who is the first to learn that their place of shelter is the Guildhall, just as later he will be the first to realize the dangers it entails. The extravagance of his response at this discovery – he whoops, rushes maniacally round the room, and somersaults across the table (115) – contrasts markedly with that of his companions. Lily and Michael's initial responses of disbelief, followed by reverential silence, makes a nonsense both of the British soldiers' description of them as 'fucking yobbos' (117)[20] and of the balladeer's mythologizing.[21]

Personal and political differences become more pronounced during the audience's second encounter with the three. Ironically the individual who will receive the most wounds, according to Professor Cuppley (162), and of whose guilt Dr. Winbourne, the forensic specialist, is most convinced (143), is the one who displays the most deference towards the trappings of Unionist power, once inside its temple. At first the Guildhall's splendour and opulence strikes him as almost supra-human – 'Christ Almighty!' 'God, it's very impressive', 'God, it's beautiful . . .' (119) – but soon afterwards Michael strikes a slightly more down-to-earth note as he meticulously itemizes each of the room's features. Friel contrasts his enthusiastic patter with Lily's rapidly cooling response. She soon voices her sense of unease and exclusion, and awareness of the gross disparity between her world and this (119-20).

Clearly here the dialogue serves to underline the play's concern with political, social, and economic injustices, but also to draw attention to a different kind of power struggle which is beginning to be acted out inside the Guildhall, as the two young men vie with each other for Lily's interest and approval. Increasingly irritated by Michael's fawning tone and language, which at this point he chooses not to confront directly, Skinner promotes a counter-discourse, asserting *their* rights of ownership of the Guildhall (120). His prising-open of the display cabinet is on one level merely a piece of exhibitionism intended to impress the maternal Lily; on another level, it is the first of several acts of what David Lloyd terms 'reterritorialization', a 'gesture' of redress comparable to Doalty's shifting of the surveyors' posts in *Translations*, whose purpose is 'to indicate … a presence' long denied (Friel, *Selected* 391).

Keen though he is to hint at future divisions between
Skinner and Michael, it is dramatically necessary for Friel that
his characters develop a rapport that will enable them to divulge
details of their personal lives and thus their motives in marching. The conditions for this are carried forward through the
characterization of Lily. She is the first to name herself, crisply
informing Skinner that she should be properly addressed as
'Mrs Doherty ... Mrs Lily Doherty'.[22] Her suggestions for im-
proving the décor in the Mayor's parlour with a lick of 'nice
pink gloss' (121) help ease tensions further, but also constitutes
a kind of imaginative repossession. Soon after one senses what
seems to be a growing self-assurance when she imitates the
assured formal language of her social 'superiors':

> since this is my first time here and since you (SKINNER) seem
> to be the caretaker, the least you might do is offer a drink to a
> ratepayer. (*She sits – taking possession*) (121).

This constitutes an early contribution towards the
carnivalesque, the holiday role playing in the parlour fostered by
Skinner, which cocks a snook at the authorities waiting in the
wings, and which is central to Friel's dramatic purposes and
technique. Fortified by a glass of port, Lily encourages Michael
to relax – '. . . will you quit creeping about on your toes ... as if
you were doing the stations of the Cross' – and draws him out
on his name, family, and origins. Again the mordant ironies are
not lost on the audience, as they listen to Michael's optimism
about an imagined future in a language which 'lacks the vigour
of the class he wishes to leave, but has none of the confidence
of the one to which he aspires' (Andrews 131): '... my father's
trying to get me into the gas-works ... I'm going to the tech.
four nights a week ... to improve myself (122).

A combination of distaste for 'Mr Hegarty's' social pretensions and sense that he is being sidelined, leads Skinner to
steer the dialogue back towards Lily. As a result, the audience
learn of her previous confinements, of how, at school, she used
to be locked in the cloakroom when an inspection was due, and
of the cramped home, which she shares with eleven children,
and a husband with a dickie chest. Despite her apparent open-

ness about her domestic circumstances, she suppresses the truth about Declan in claiming that all of her brood are 'sound of mind and limb' (123).

Confirmation that Lily primarily sees her role in life as a minister to the needs of others comes when she suddenly begins to busy herself about Skinner's welfare, forcing him to strip off his wet clothes. This act of divestment has three main purposes: it discloses Skinner's poverty, showing that he is without either a vest or socks in early February (124);[23] it prepares the way for Scene 19 when Skinner, dressed in borrowed robes, confers on his disenfranchised fellow citizens the freedom of the city (135-41); and thirdly, it functions as a metonym for the process of exposure and self-exposure – or skinning – within the Guildhall.

Prolepsis is used to undercut the celebratory resolution of this, their second scene together, when in the next a priest announces that a solemn requiem Mass is to be held in their honour. Early in their next appearance cracks open in the impromptu alliance, principally because of Skinner's growing hostility to the self-righteous tone and content of Michael's political pronouncements, but equally perhaps because of his insecurities about his own identity. An enigma to his companions and the audience, Skinner appears to enjoy anonymity, but hungers for approval. His bizarre 'name' is not disclosed until ten pages after Lily has given hers and eight pages after Michael, yet even then it is left unexplained, a further instance of the text's preoccupation with repressions. When Lily does successfully prise a little information from him, he claims to be an orphan and to have been expelled from grammar school,[24] but then deflects possibilities of further probing (132).

His antagonistic attitude to Michael seems partly political, partly personal. The latter embodies a world of sureties he has never known, and of obeisance he could never subscribe to. Despite being galled by Michael's condemnation of 'the hooligan element' and 'strange characters' who have 'knuckled in on' the civil rights act – that is, working-class protestors who do not conform to the turn-the-other-cheek philosophy Michael espouses – he contains himself. However, once Michael starts to replicate the rhetoric of the middle class civil rights leaders (127, 128-29), Skinner breaks ranks. This first takes the form of parodying the blandness and caution of their language ('At this point of time', '. . . taking full cognizance of all relative facts'). Later, however, he lambasts their naive premises and inter-class solidarity as so much 'Shite' (129).

The play's hostility to rhetoric – except its own – is further illustrated in Lily's reaction. Utterly indifferent to Michael's talk of 'a united front' and 'ultimate objectives', she is more concerned with immediate *physical* needs; ('*To* SKINNER: It's hot whiskey you should be drinking' [127].) Lily's interest is only rekindled when Michael alludes to his forthcoming marriage, a detail that intensifies the pathos and adds significant intertextual resonances to the play. Unlike, yet in some ways *like* his equally impassioned, naive namesake in Yeats's *Cathleen ni Houlihan*, who abandons bride and family to follow Mother Ireland, Friel's Michael imagines he can have both political freedom *and* the girl. As they listen to Lily's toast to his Easter wedding, the audience are only too aware of the sacrifice that awaits him because of his engagement with politics.[25]

Friel uses these fleeting allusions to Michael's hopeful future as a device to trigger Lily's memories of her own time as a teenage bride and to deepen Skinner's sense of isolation and exclusion. Let down by this latest surrogate mother who ignores his plaintive appeal – 'Leely, the language I speak a leetle too – yes?' (128) – Skinner's mind reverts to 'Bingo Mistress', and he rings up Jackie, his bookie, to check on how his luck is running.[26]

Once more Skinner's actions are used to foreground differences between the men, and ratchet the tension. Stung by Skinner's repeated jibes, increasingly conscious and disapproving of his feckless behaviour and life-style, Michael begins a counter-attack, insinuating to Lily that Skinner may not be a *bona fide* civil rights supporter; ironically, like the forces ranged against all three, Michael suspects that Skinner is a revolutionary in disguise (132).

Yet the next Guildhall scene finds Skinner and Lily even more firmly bonded together, as they articulate their desire for redress, and the play's carnivalization reaches its climax. Following Shakespearean precedent, Friel employs meta-dramatic devices, deploying changes of costume and speech to comic, subversive effect. Kitted out in mayoral robes, Skinner officiates at a parodic ceremony, conferring on Lily 'the freedom of the city' and on Michael – with an eye to his middle-class pretensions – a life peerage, and the title 'Lord Michael – of Gas' (136). His opening quotation from *King Lear*

> Through tattered clothes small vices do appear;
> Robes and furred gowns hide all (4.6.166-67).

is particularly apposite, and not only in the light of the Brigadier's perjury which the audience has just witnessed. It could almost serve as an epigraph for the entire play, which, like *Lear*, deals with injustice, corruption, murdered innocence, blindness, a vicious abuse of authority by people with 'glass eyes' who 'seem / To see the things thou dost not' (*King Lear* 4.6.172-74).

Witnessing Skinner's confidence at play acts as a liberating experience for Lily. Empowered by drink and his direction, she throws herself into the costume drama. Re-casting herself as Lady Elizabeth, she mimics the talk and – to borrow Yeats's famous phrase – 'the walk of a queen'. Unaware that Crown forces are waiting in the wings, with deadly intent, Lily revels in the part of being a partner again. Freed at last from her in-hibitions, she is even prepared to take a lead at one point, dragging Skinner into a *military* two-step around the parlour floor.

Throughout all this Michael sits aloof, but once the radio is switched off, he swiftly attempts to restore decorum. Hostilities between Skinner and himself are renewed when he again attempts to wrest Lily from Skinner's malign influence (138). Skinner's response once more takes the form of a symbolic gesture when 'very *deliberately he stubs out his cigar on the leather-top desk*' (138). Michael reads this act, as the Judge will later (149), as incontrovertible proof of Skinner's criminality.

And yet surprisingly, after all the animosity, a kind of civility breaks out between the two when Michael makes the decision to leave. In exchange for Michael's thanks for 'pulling him in', Skinner, in a change of role from clown to Fool, warns him of the danger outside. Michael imagines that the law will protect him when he asserts his inalienable right 'to walk straight out of here and across the Square' (140). The ideological and moral divisions and confusions, which paralysed the Civil Rights Movement and would split the Nationalist community from the early 1970s onwards, over what the appropriate response to state violence should be, find voice in these final exchanges:

> **Michael:** Gandhi showed that violence done against peaceful protest helps your cause …
> **Michael:** As long as we don't react violently, as long as we don't allow ourselves to be provoked, ultimately we must win
> …
> **Skinner:** Mr Hegarty is of the belief that if five thousand of us are demonstrating peacefully and they come along and shoot us down, then automatically we … we … (*To MICHAEL*) Sorry, what's the theory again? (140-41)

The play loses momentum in the closing scene of Act 1 (143-47), occupied as it is with Lily's rather embarrassing attempt at a telephone conversation and a re-run of Michael's outrage. What revives dramatic interest and intrigue immediately before the interval are the repercussions of the Brigadier's announcement, 'We know exactly where you are and we know you are armed. … surrender before there is loss of life' (147). Given the insight Skinner displays earlier in the act in pointing out the very real possibility that they might all be shot, it is rather surprising that his only response to the Brigadier's threat is to comment on his accent. It is dramatically necessary for the tragic outcome, of course, that the three underestimate the Establishment reaction.

Closures

The tragic impetus is restored at the beginning of Act 2, with a startling, non-naturalistic stroke on Friel's part. For the first and only time in the play the three enjoy the privilege of addressing the audience directly. In speeches shot through with an under-stated, poignant irony, Michael, Lily, and Skinner convey their thoughts and feelings at the moment of death. Calmly speaking, *'without emotion, in neutral accents'*, each conveys a sense of the terrible wasting of their lives. Characteristically, Michael continues to deny the possibility of the nightmare scenario, even when he hears 'the click of their rifle bolts' (149). As in life, he can only read 'outlines', and as he dies he is trying for a form that eludes him, 'mistake-mistake-mistake'; as an illustration of understatement, it is on a par with the Priest's choice of the word, 'imperfections' (156). For this highly stylized scene, Michael throws off his rather smug, self-righteous *persona*; the exposure of his frustration and disbelief humanizes him.

For Lily, the imminence of death was instantly recognized; its wake brings a 'tidal wave of regret', an epiphany and articulation that arrive too late to be of service. Like a character out of Chekhov, she experiences a sense that 'life had somehow eluded me ... now it had finished; ... had all seeped away' (150).

Given the last word, Skinner leaves life promising to change his ways, regretting how 'unpardonably casual' he had been about the authorities, lamenting his 'defensive flippancy' in the face of injustice. His last words are full of first-person plurals. Instead of reckoning the odds at races, his mind runs philosophically, on the poor and how they are 'always over-charged' (150). The most appropriate means to redress injustice, he speculates, is to seek 'a total dedication, a solemnity as formal as theirs' (150). What this means in *political* terms is unclear: although the speech is that of a fictional character, it is tempting to read it as pointing towards Friel's future artistic and cultural project, Field Day.

The concluding scenes between Lily and Skinner enact a move towards a fuller dialogue, a growing understanding of and trust in each other, and an inching towards self-apprehension. Lily's compassion once more comes to the fore when she learns of Skinner's nomadic existence over the past ten years: 'I can't offer you no bed, Skinner, 'cos there's six in one room and seven in the other. But I could give you a bite to eat most days of the week ... If you're stuck' (152). Profoundly affected by her generosity, Skinner's defensive response is literally to take up arms. His gesture in seizing hold of the medieval Gaelic sword (152) also serves to translate him into a latter-day Quixote, and draws attention again to the impossible odds, the 'sea of troubles' about to engulf them. The sword-play spurs him into questioning the whole civil rights' alliance and its mustering of nationalists from different social classes. Does an affinity of interests really unite 'you and me and him' with doctors, teachers, accountants, or are they all following a fiction? Refusing to be fobbed off with Lily's hesitant explanation as to why she marches, he avers that her real motives are '[b]ecause you live with eleven kids and a sick husband in two rooms which aren't fit for animals ... Because you know your children are caught in the same morass' (154).

His impassioned rhetoric here contains more than a grain of truth, but like Professor Dodds's readings, it is presumptuous. Recognizing that his language is leading him into hazardous political terrain, he retreats into mock political patter. A key outcome of his outburst, however, is Lily's decision to reveal her principal motive for marching; it is for the sake of her despised, rejected, written-off son, who exists in part as a metonym for herself, and perhaps for her class and race.

As the others bustle round the Mayor's parlour in an effort to create an orderly closure, Skinner insists on leaving his mark, their signature. He dissuades Michael from removing the sword thrust into Sir Joshua's portrait, and persuades Lily to sign herself into the Distinguished Visitors' Book. After giving her a parting kiss, he goes out singing as if to maintain the spirit of carnival. Our last sighting of the three, like the first, finds them stretched across the front of the stage (168-69). The difference is that now they are standing, making long shadows. And as a result of the play's duration and Friel's skill in animating illusion, their faces and identities have been illuminated.[27]

Conclusions

In the course of one of his Oxford lectures, 'The Redress of Poetry', Seamus Heaney reflects upon the problematic intersections of literature and politics and their shared concern with 'alternative worlds'. Despite voicing deep reservations about the concept of 'applied art',[28] which sets out to intervene in politics by 'direct action' (2), he acknowledges many examples of writing 'which consciously seeks to promote cultural and political change and yet can still manage to operate with the fullest artistic integrity' (6). Brian Friel's play is one such work. It represents an exemplary and necessary inscription of 'that which is denied voice' (2), attempting as it does to individualize, rather than idealize three members of the northern nationalist community, and to identify the forces – Irish and British – which persistently misread them.[29] Inevitably the picture it presents is partial in both senses; all art is. Nevertheless, *The Freedom of the City* is a skilfully constructed, powerfully written, but neglected work, which deserves to be examined again and judged in the context of Friel's sustained contribution to cultural dialogue in the North, with its changing cast of speakers and cast of changing speakers.[30]

Notes

[1] The DHA bought large properties and then subdivided them into flats. Early in the play, it is established that Lily Doherty lives with her husband and eleven children 'in a condemned property behind the old railway – a warehouse ... converted into eight flats' (108).

[2] During one of these demonstrations, one DHAC member temporarily seized control of the Guildhall council chamber and declared himself Mayor: 'After the mayor abandoned his chair and adjourned one Corporation meeting, Finbar Doherty vaulted from the public gallery into the chamber, installed himself in the mayoral chair, declared himself First Citizen and issued a number of decrees ... there were very few in our area who failed to smile when they heard of the incident' (McCann 28-29). Doherty's action clearly anticipates Skinner's antics in Friel's play.

[3] Ulf Dantanus cites several reviews, which dismiss the play as 'an entertaining piece of unconvincing propaganda' (*Daily Telegraph*), as 'too loaded to encourage much intelligent sympathy' (*Daily Express*), and as exhibiting, according to the *Evening Standard*, 'an over-zealous determination to discredit the means and motives of the English in the present Ulster crisis' (140).

[4] In response to Clive Barnes's charge that Friel's presentation of the tribunal was 'far-fetched, indeed impossible', Christopher Murray

remarks 'A better informed reviewer would have been aware that such a finding had indeed been officially published in the Widgery Report'. See his essay, 'Friel's "Emblems of Adversity" and the Yeatsian Example' in Peacock 71).

5 The text itself does not number the scenes or episodes in the narrative, but I have done so in order to investigate the play's structure. As well as the seventeen characters listed in the *Dramatis Personae* (103), there are three Voices from the Bogside (125-26), two Pressmen (126), and a children's chorus (118-19).

6 It is perhaps not fanciful to suggest that the geopolitics on stage reproduces the political attitudes of the three, with Lily in the centre, Skinner on the Left and Michael on the Right within the Civil Rights Movement. I would concur with Jent's view that Nicholas Grene is far from the mark in describing Skinner, somewhat tautologically, as 'a potential Provo in the making'. Politically Skinner comes closest to Anarchist thinking. (See Jent, and Grene 47, 70.)

7 Winkler draws attention to Derry's pre-twentieth-century history and the significance of its walls. She refers to the famous siege of 1689 when the Catholic forces of King James II failed to take the city, and how, as a consequence, in the words of Conor Cruise O'Brien, 'Derry is more than a city, it is a symbol of Protestant Ulster' (168). Friel alludes to the siege in the text, when, Skinner is seen examining exhibits in the Mayor's parlour (119).

8 These are the very words Widgery used to characterize his inquiry. An article by Eamon McCann and Owen Bowcott, published in *The Guardian* on 10 November 1995, revealed that two days after Bloody Sunday the Lord Chief Justice was sent a confidential memorandum by Downing Street Minister reminding him to bear in mind that 'we were in Northern Ireland fighting not only a military war but a propaganda war' (1).

9 This began in *Philadelphia, Here I Come!* (1965), and was extended in *The Mundy Scheme* (1970) and *The Gentle Island* (1971).

10 O'Kelly may be intended to represent many in both the South and North, who harboured ambivalent feelings towards militant Republicanism. Though his use of the term 'terrorists' might imply condemnation, his delight in the discomfiture of the Unionists and the British suggests approval of their actions.

11 A Marxist reading of *The Freedom of the City* might well begin by focussing on the range of Ideological State Apparatuses (ISAs) represented in the text. ISAs, the systems and structures used to maintain ideological control, are extremely well-represented in the play; there is the religious ISA (represented by the Church), the family ISA (Lily's husband, Michael's family), the communications

ISA (the RTE commentator and the photographer), and the educational/cultural ISA, represented perhaps by Dodds. These ISAs function alongside the Repressive State Apparatus (RSA) to which the judiciary, the Army, and the police belong.

12 In asserting Dodds's objectivity, Jent states that 'as an American, he is neither colonizer nor colonized' (577). This claim ignores both the fate of the Amerindian population, and the United States's involvement in Vietnam at the time Friel was writing the play.

13 One is tempted to 'identify' this orator as Bernadette Devlin, who was present on the platform on 30 January. She was accompanied by other M.P.s, all of whom were 'forced to prostrate themselves while a hail of bullets was fired in their direction' (*Parliamentary Debates: Hansard*, House of Commons Official Report, Session 1971-72: 41). Within Friel's play, this lone female voice, which can only be briefly heard, is drowned out by the noisy responses from her fictional audiences, her supporters, and the Army. Confidently resisting silence, she contrasts with Lily, who, until her confinement with Skinner and involvement in Civil Rights, has been clearly under the thumb of the 'Chairman'.

14 'Gifts of Rain', *Wintering Out*, 23: 'A man wading lost fields / breaks the pane of flood: / a flower of mud – / water blooms up to his reflection'.

15 'Skinner, Michael and Lily literally embody Dodds's ideas about the subculture of poverty and the role of politicization in escaping from it' (Jent 580).

16 Deane in his article, 'Why Bogside?', provides invaluable insights into the thinking of young working class nationalists in Derry, who trod a very different path to his own. 'Delinquency', we are informed, ranged from 'street fighting to cynical detachment to moral and political numbness'. His analysis of the impact of television and pop music bears some affinities to Professor Dodds:

> 'It was a slow shock of awareness ... alienation, inertia, aimlessness were not experiences peculiar to us. They were part of a general climate of disaffection. The minute alienation is seen to be a shared fate, it ceased to be a sad one The next step is towards commitment, brotherhood philosophies like civil rights and socialism ... Thus from the traditional dignity of the older generation to the new commitment of the young alienation was the paradoxical bridge' (1a-2).

> One senses reverberations from this important article in Friel's characterizations in this play.

17 Friel frequently uses comic pairings effectively such as the two Gars (*Philadelphia, Here I Come!*), Shane and Peter (*The Gentle Island*), Keeney

and Pyne (*Volunteers*), Doalty and Bridget, Hugh and Jimmy Jack (*Translations*), Maggie and Michael, Chrissie and Gerry (*Dancing at Lughnasa*).

18 The week before Bloody Sunday, on Saturday, 22 January 1972, civil rights marchers arriving on Magilligan strand, near Derry, were in fact offered tea and buns by Royal Green Jackets. These were declined by the marchers, who, when they proceeded towards the internment camp, were offered different fare. Along with the Royal Green Jackets were men from the First Battalion of the Parachute Regiment. It was they who opened fire on the demonstrators with gas guns and rubber bullets, often at close range, when an attempt was made to outflank the wire. See Bowyer Bell 257.

19 For example, phrases such as 'no thicker than', 'hurted bad', 'bleeding internal', 'I seen', 'I was afeard', and 'breathe shalla'.

20 It is interesting to note how the soldiers initially define themselves through lyrical metaphors. Their code-names 'Blue Star' and 'Eagle' are suggestive of remote beauty, grace, and power. Ironically, they quickly switch to demotic, with one 'fuck' and four 'fuckings', when referring to subjects drawn from similar socio-economic, urban backgrounds to their own.

21 For him they are 'one' with 'Tone, Pearse and Connolly' (118).

22 Lily's surname, *Doherty*, may not have been chosen at random. When the names of the thirteen killed on Bloody Sunday are arranged alphabetically, the list begins with Patrick Joseph Doherty, aged 31. Other well-known Derry Dohertys, who Friel might have had in mind when developing his principal characters, include Paddy 'Bogside' Doherty and Finbar Doherty. Denied a council house by a Londonderry Corporation official, Paddy Doherty responded by buying some land and building his own home. 'One of an energetic group of Derry Catholics who put their faith in self-help' (Bardon 648), he joined Father Anthony Mulvey and John Hume in 1960 in the Credit Union enterprise (White 29-31). Finbar Doherty was a member of Derry Housing Action Committee, who mounted a series of demonstrations in the Guildhall in April & May 1968. See note 2.

23 The stage directions explicitly state '*he is wearing nothing underneath*' his shirt. When '*He takes off the canvas shoes*', we discover that '[*h*]*e is not wearing socks*' (124).

24 Significantly many of Friel's key characters suffer from the loss of one or both parents. Skinner most closely resembles Shane in *The Gentle Island*, who also presents himself as parentless. In other plays, *Philadelphia*'s Gar, *The Gentle Island*'s Philly and Joe, *Living Quarters*'s Ben, *Translations*'s Manus and Owen are all motherless, exacerbating their 'exposure' in their struggles against their fathers. It is also

indicative of the profound sense of discontinuities afflicting their and their creator's worlds.

[25] For an Irish audience the reference to Easter would almost certainly bring to mind the 1916 Rising, a time associated with sacrifice, victimhood, and violence. Padraic Pearse's name and memory had been invoked earlier in the play by the Balladeer (118).

[26] Deane ('Bogside' 7-8) stresses that gambling is endemic within Derry's working classes.

[27] This frozen moment may have been in the mind of Frank McGuinness when he was creating the closing frames of *Observe the Sons of Ulster Marching Towards the Somme*. There the eight principals raise their weapons, and use their voices to create a crescendo of noise.

[28] Such a view of art's political responsibilities resembles that of the Sinn Fein spokesman quoted in Fionnuala O'Connor's *In Search of a State*, who regarded Brian Friel's *Translations* as 'useful', but accuses the playwright since of a failure to 'engage' with 'the conditions of conflict' (361-62).

[29] The emphatically upbeat note Elmer Andrews strikes at the close of his discussion of the play seems wide of the mark to this reader. For him it exhibits 'a faith in the unquenchable human spirit' which is apparently 'memorably and vividly personified in the character of Lily' (138). This is to sentimentalize the play and to separate it from its deeply tragic point of origin, Bloody Sunday.

[30] A new production of the play was staged at the Abbey Theatre in the Spring of 1999. At the time of writing, Bloody Sunday and the Widgery Report continue to make headlines in the British and Irish press as a result of the Saville inquiry set up to look again into the events of 30 January 1972. A clear instance of this coverage can be seen in two articles in *The Guardian*, 7 July 1999: 3, which quote an interview on BBC Radio 4 given on 6 July 1999 by the commanding officer of the 1st Battalion of the Paratroop Regiment on Bloody Sunday, Lieutenant-Colonel Derek Wilford, in which he claims that most Ulster Catholics are 'closet republicans' and that the victims' relatives support group is a 'republican organization'.

Works Cited

Althusser, Louis. 'Ideology and the State'. *Lenin and Philosophy and Other Essays*. Trans. B. Brewster. Rpt. in *Modern Literary Theory*. Ed. Philip Rice and Patricia Waugh. London: Arnold, 1989.

Andrews, Elmer. *The Art of Brian Friel: Neither Reality Nor Dreams*. London: Macmillan, 1995.

Aristotle. *Poetics. Basic Works of Aristotle*. Ed. Richard McKeon. Trans. Ingram Bywater. New York: Random, 1941.

Bakhtin, Mikhail. 'Discourse in the Novel'. *The Dialogic Imagination*. Trans. Caryl Emerson and Michael Holquist. Austin: Texas UP, 1981. 269-73, 295-96, 301-05.

Bardon, Jonathan. *A History of Ulster*. Belfast: Blackstaff, 1992.

Barnes, Clive. 'Brian Friel Writes of Current Troubles'. *New York Times* 18 Feb. 1974: 32.

Bell, J. Bowyer. *The Irish Troubles: A Generation of Violence 1967-1992*. Dublin: Gill, 1993.

Boland, Eavan. 'Brian Friel: Derry's Playwright'. *Hibernia* 16 Feb. 1973: 18.

Boyce, D. George. *Nationalism in Ireland*. London: Routledge, 1991.

Buckland, Patrick. *A History of Northern Ireland*. Dublin: Gill, 1981.

Connolly, Peter, ed. *Literature and the Changing Ireland*. Gerrards Cross: Smythe, 1982.

Dantanus, Ulf. *Brian Friel: A Study*. London: Faber. 1988.

Deane, Seamus. 'Why Bogside?' *The Honest Ulsterman* 27 Jan.-Mar. 1971: 1-6.

--- 'Introduction'. *Selected Plays of Brian Friel*. London: Faber, 1984.

Foster, Roy. *Modern Ireland 1600-1972*. Harmondsworth: Penguin, 1989.

Friel, Brian. *The Gentle Island*. London: Poynter, 1973.

--- 'The Man from God Knows Where'. Interview with Fintan O'Toole. *In Dublin* 14 July 1982: 22.

--- *Selected Plays*. London: Faber, 1984.

--- *Volunteers*. Oldcastle: Gallery, 1989.

Grene, Nicholas. 'Distancing Drama: Sean O'Casey to Brian Friel'. *Irish Writers and the Theatre*. Ed. Masaru Sekine. Gerrards Cross: Smythe, 1987. 47-70.

Hansard: Parliamentary Debates. House of Commons Official Report, Session 1971-72, Fifth Series, Vol. 830. London: Her Majesty's Stationery Office 1972: 32-33.

Heaney, Seamus. *Wintering Out*. London: Faber, 1972.

--- *North*. London: Faber, 1975.

--- *The Redress of Poetry*. London: Faber, 1995.

--- Letter to the author. 30 Oct. 1985.

Jent, William. 'Supranational Civics: Poverty and the Politics of Representation in Brian Friel's *The Freedom of the City*'. *Modern Drama* 37. 4 (1994): 568-87.

Lloyd, David. *Anomalous States: Irish Writing and the Postcolonial Moment*. Dublin: Lilliput, 1993.

Lodge, David. *Modern Criticism and Theory: A Reader*. London: Longman, 1988.

McCann, Eamonn. *War in an Irish Town*. London: Pluto, 1984.

--- McCann, Eamonn, and Owen Boycott. 'Memo Reveals "Propaganda War."' *The Guardian* 10 Nov. 1995: 1, 19.

McGuinness, Frank. *Observe the Sons of Ulster Marching Towards the Somme*. London: Faber, 1986.

Maxwell, D.E.S. *Brian Friel*. Lewisburg: Bucknell, 1973.

--- 'Semantic Scruples: A Rhetoric for Politics in the North'. In Connolly 157-74.

Mullin, John. 'I Was Made the Scapegoat'. *The Guardian* 7 July 1999: 3.

Murray, Christopher. 'Friel's "Emblems of Adversity" and the Yeatsian Example'. In Peacock. 69-90.

O'Brien, Conor Cruise. *States of Ireland*. London: Hutchinson, 1972.

O'Brien, George. *Brian Friel*. Dublin: Gill, 1989.

O'Connor, Fionnuala. *In Search of a State: Catholics in Northern Ireland*. Belfast: Blackstaff, 1993.

Onega, Susana, and Landa José Ángel Garcia, eds. *Narratology*. London: Longman, 1996.

Oxford English Dictionary shorter ed. 1984.

Pallister, David. 'Fury at Bloody Sunday Outburst'. *The Guardian* 7 July 1999: 3.

Peacock, Alan, ed. *The Achievement of Brian Friel*. Gerrards Cross: Colin Smythe, 1992.

Pine, Richard. *Brian Friel and Ireland's Drama*, London: Routledge. 1990.

Rice, Philip, and Patricia Waugh, eds. *Modern Literary Theory: A Reader*. London: Arnold, 1989.

Said, Edward. *Culture and Imperialism*. London: Chatto, 1993.

Sidney, Sir Philip. *An Apology for Poetry*. Ed. Geoffrey Shepherd. London, 1965.

Taylor, Peter. *Families at War: Voices from the Troubles*. London: BBC, 1989.

White, Barry. *John Hume: Statesman of the Troubles*. Belfast: Blackstaff, 1984.

Widgery Report: Summary of Conclusions. HL101/HC 220. London, 1972.

Winkler, Elizabeth Hale. 'Brian Friel's *The Freedom of the City*: Historical Actuality and Dramatic Imagination'. *The Canadian Journal of Irish Studies* 7.1 (1981): 12-31.

15 | An Interview with Richard Pine about Brian Friel's Theatre[1]

Mária Kurdi

The interview was conducted in Dublin in 2002.

Mária Kurdi: What inspired you, what made you first think of writing a book about Friel, and then re-edit, update, and expand it almost ten years later?

Richard Pine: I realized that I wanted – needed – to write a book about Brian Friel[2] while I was attending a performance of *Translations* (1980) at the Abbey in the early 1980s. I was not very familiar with the work of Brian Friel then – I knew about *Philadelphia, Here I Come!* (1964), *Aristocrats* (1979), and *The Freedom of the City* (1973) as almost everyone did, as a matter of course! – but I had read *After Babel* by George Steiner (1975), and during the performance I realized that parts of *After Babel* were being used in the text of *Translations*, the characters were actually speaking sentences from *After Babel*. I found this very exciting intellectually, but I also found that what the playwright was doing with Steiner's text and, as I later discovered with Heidegger also, was something which was emotionally exciting as well. All the books that I have written were written out of an inner need of my own to explore something in myself which is also present in the work, the subject of my book. This is particularly true of the book on Friel and that on Lawrence Durrell.[3] And in this case the initial momentum came from this experience, which was a very real one for me at the time because I was exploring the difficulties of translation and the difficulties of communication, as part of my consultancy work with the Council of Europe on cultural development in a post-imperial society. My book was published in 1990, and therefore when Friel had written several more plays during the following eight years or so, it seemed necessary to produce a new edition which has a very substantial extra chapter on the more recent plays and a much more extensive Introduction.[4] When the book originally came out *Making History* (1988) and *Dancing at Lughnasa* (1990) were still very new, and I did not really have enough time to give due attention to them, so they receive much more attention in the 1999 edition, along with the subsequent plays.

MK: Did you introduce a new viewpoint as well, for instance the postcolonial critical approach?

RP: Although the original edition addressed the postcolonial topic, the appearance of Homi K. Bhabha's *The Location of Culture* in 1994 gave me the encouragement I needed to look more discursively at this theme, and Bhabha's ideas about hybridity and the 'gap', which is so important in *Making History*, were very persuasive in writing the new edition. Also, as I experienced the more recent (post-1990) plays, I became more deeply conscious of the private music within those plays, and I addressed this in the final two parts of the 'Music' section, 'Plays of Beyond' and 'Magic'.

MK: On the back cover of the new edition one reads that you have written it with the full co-operation of the playwright himself. How could you characterize this co-operation?

RP: It is well known that Brian Friel is very reluctant to give interviews or to assist would-be students of his work, and when I started writing the book I was quite certain that I would need to meet him and talk with him and get his confidence if I was going to really understand what was happening in his work. I approached Seamus Deane who is a close associate of his, not least because of their involvement with the Field Day Company, and he recommended to Brian Friel that he should see me. Then I went to Derry where we met, and we had a very long meeting. And since that time I have been very lucky that Brian Friel is always very courteous and honest in answering questions that I may have for him. He has never, as far as I am aware, tried to conceal or hold back anything. I think that as the co-operation is a friendship now (and I would be happy to call it that). It has deepened very considerably over the years as we got to know each other much better and to trust each other, and I think we are very fond of each other on a personal level. On a professional level, I have been very honoured to be asked to write the programme notes for three of his plays including the most recent at the Gate Theatre in March 2002, a two-part production – an adaptation of Chekhov's *The Bear*, and a very important original one-act called *Afterplay*. And besides Deane, another close associate of Friel, Seamus Heaney, wrote an endorsement that appears on both editions of the book, which means a great deal to me because it goes to the heart of my interest in Friel and accords with my personal style as a critic. He said that the book contributed 'to an understanding of how Friels's plays transmit meaning within the acoustic of the Irish cultural and political scene' and that my 'readings' of Friel 'deepen the sense of [his] complexity and modernity'.

MK: The title of this second edition of your monographic study on Friel is *The Diviner*, which is also the title of one of his short stories. Why did you find it appropriate for your book?

RP: In my book I give considerable attention to the characteristic of the diviner, the person who can look down into the ground and see what is hidden there. Seamus Heaney also speaks about this in relation to Friel, and it was the title I originally wanted for the first edition but the publishers of that edition, Routledge, simply refused to allow me to use that title.

It is to me a most important thing that an artist looks at his environment and can see another environment that is its shadow image if you like, it is a buried image. Greeks believe, for example, that for every village there is an identical village down beneath the surface of the earth, somewhere towards the middle of the earth, and they would never think of the one real village on the surface without remembering the buried village. There is a great deal running throughout Friel, as there is throughout Chekhov, of people digging within themselves for their buried selves and to me that seems to be most important. The picture of Friel by Bobbie Hanvey, which appears on the cover of my book and has been used in several other places too, seems to me absolutely symbolic of the diviner in that short story: an extraordinary, priestly figure looking down into a lake, and being able to tell what is there within. It is an extraordinary photograph of clairvoyance, literally.

MK: The main chapters of your book are as follows: 'Private Conversation', 'Public Address', 'Politics', 'Music'. Three of these titles refer to themes and approaches primarily, but the fourth one, 'Music', seems to introduce a different plane. Could you explain this choice?

RP: The original three sections were designed, first of all to distinguish private conversation from public address, to use that very common cliché, to distinguish between the short stories and the radio plays on the one hand and the more open, political approach of the stage plays. It is in public address that Friel later becomes much more outspoken, and outward-speaking about the matters that have been presented on the stage. The third section 'Politics' was intended to show that Friel, if you like, militantly moves with Field Day and *Translations* into an arena, which is not merely public but is political, that it is trying to engage with governments. He says at one point 'why should not writers rule the country'? The final section of the new edition, 'Music' is there because it seems to me that Friel, partly because of his resignation from Field Day, partly or more so because of his moving as a writer into a very much more private sphere, is not writing so much nowadays about public and political matters as he is exploring once again the inner chambers of the heart and the imagination. And he is asking that we respect his privacy in this, and there seems to me to be a much stronger sense, in inverted commas, of 'music' being able to reach or to open up areas where language fails. He says this at the end of *Dancing at Lughnasa*, and he says it in the programme note for his seventieth birthday: 'Music can get to the uncharted areas where most of our lives are lived'. And this musicality seems to me to be the overriding characteristic of what he is writing at the moment. In *Wonderful Tennessee* (1993), in *Give Me Your Answer, Do!* (1997), and in his new rewriting of Chekhov, in *The Yalta Game* (2002) and in *Afterplay*, the musicality of what he writes is very evident. It is not just that he writes musical prose, its important effect is the music that is transmitted, and transferred from the stage to the audience. It may also be the case that 'music', as a powerful medium which, at the end of *Lughnasa*, takes over from language, is the medium needed by people in a postcolonial context where in a sense language has failed them and has failed itself. Friel himself has suggested this, most famously in the concluding lines, or 'bars', of *Lughnasa*, that music can empower a 'ritual', a 'wordless ceremony' which supersedes language and puts us 'in touch with some otherness' (71). He has said that 'music can provide … another way of talking, a language without words. Because it is wordless it can hit straight and unmediated into the vein of deep emotion' (*Essays* 177). So I mean that our modern society, which is more rightly called 'post-imperial', if we are looking at it from the perspective of the western European experience as a whole, has exhausted our traditional strategies of speaking to ourselves, and that some kind of 'music' is necessary, even if only to give language a rest and an opportunity to reformulate itself, to find translations between its ancient cultures and rituals and the new cultures and rituals that are shaping, and being shaped by, the world into which we appear to be entering. But all that is very tentative, of course.

MK: The section 'Music' concerns itself with images of the child, and child characters in Friel's drama. Do you think this element is unique in his work, or can you think of his deploying the child as part of the general importance of the child in Irish drama?

RP: This may sound flippant, but all Irish dramatists, all Irish writers, perhaps all writers everywhere suffered from some kind of impaired childhood. I mean that in the sense that very, very few people have what you could call an idyllic childhood, and people who do not, tend to set out to find a compensation for that in their lives, and are always striving to replace the unhappiness or the neglect or whatever it was that impaired their childhood, with something else: they become business-men, politicians or racing drivers, or something the like. Those who become writers, as Georges Simenon said, often write out of a sense of unhappiness. In Brian Friel's case the short story, the *very* short story *'The Child'*, which he refuses to allow to be reprinted, is very indicative of what may have been his own childhood insecurity. I do not for a moment suggest that he had a very distorted childhood, he speaks very fondly of musical evenings spent with his parents and his two sisters at the piano, and it was obviously not entirely a disturbed childhood. But I cannot believe that when he writes of children as he does in the case of the silent, what I would call an autistic, child in *Give Me Your Answer, Do!* at the beginning and at the very end of the play, that he is not at least able to empathize with that kind of experience, even if he is not drawing on his own experience. A very specific instance which he has talked about is the fishing expedition with his father, becoming an important question in *Philadelphia, Here I Come!*, a kind of experience which I suppose a lot of people would have shared in Ireland, because of the until recently prevailing difficulty of talking about emotions, talking about relationships, inhibitions which are there partly from the school system, partly from the religious environment. People do not open up and talk about things and, therefore, when an audience is presented in a play with an experience with which they can identify, even though they cannot talk about it, they go

home very moved and it will strike chords which many people
cannot talk about. It's something that is familiar to the Irish
Catholic mindset, because it has to do with the 'confessional'
method of communicating and gaining some level of absolution
from that silent experience or exorcizing oneself from it. A
further point that I would mention about this is that the nostalgia play has its roots in the trying to get back inside childhood,
inside the original 'home'. There was an English critic who said
when he heard the words 'when I cast my mind back to that
summer' etc. at the opening of *Dancing at Lughnasa* (1) that his
heart sank, as he thought it was going to be 'yet another nostalgia play'. It is possible that non-Irish audiences, let us say
English audiences, would have less sympathy with this kind of
harking back or casting one's mind back, which suggests that a
vignette of some kind of heaven, some sunny summer's day is
going to be the substance of the play. Friel, Tom Murphy, and
Sebastian Barry are harking back in many of their plays, and we
always have to remember that nostalgia literally means *the pain of
the homeward journey*. And that painful experience of the
homeward journey or the attempted homeward journey is what
a lot of memory is about, it is a journey which asks the audience
to accompany the characters in order to try and tease out some
aspect of childhood, and of growing. In another, much wider
sense, the analogy can be made with postcolonial societies
where the 'old certainties' are no longer reliable, where the
reaching back of our memory into the past is no longer
sufficient to connect with the household gods or the communal
home truths that command our affections and empower our
daily lives and our political actions. In that sense, the need to
'touch base', to undertake the homeward journey, is bedevilled
by that inability to establish adequate lines of communication
between son and father, pupil and teacher, servant and master,
between our blank ignorance of today and the funds of wisdom
that existed *in illo tempore*, and that can be very painful in
situations where parent and child, or junior people and figures
of authority, are at loggerheads. Again, I address this rather
extensively in the new introduction to my book.

MK: Is the question of growing up a seminal issue for Irish writers, as opposed to English ones?

RP: The *Bildungsroman* or, as I call it in the book, *Bildungsdrama* is quite different depending on the context and the wider society in which one did the growing up – or, of course, failed to grow up. Again, Murphy would be very close to Friel in his intentions here. The Irish experience – again, I would stress the confessional aspect to society, which is so closely related to the 'whisper-in-your-ear' of betrayal – is far removed from that of other societies, such as Britain or America, which have been infused with a different kind of religious awareness. It may be that it strikes much stronger chords with societies in which mystery and magic have a greater role, such as those studied by Victor Turner which I refer to quite extensively in my book. Of course, the problem of growing up in Irish society is one that is constantly being revisited by Irish writers both on and off the stage. In many ways it can be seen as parallel to, if not symptomatic of, the wider societal experience of growing a newly emergent state into adulthood, maturity and world stature. A frequent subject for debate in Irish schools for decades was: 'That Emmet's epitaph can now be written' – in other words, that Ireland had taken her place among the nations of the world. And it's the haunting backdrop to Friel's early play *The Mundy Scheme* (1970). It remains a vitally important issue for the Irish writer.

MK: By far the internationally best known contemporary Irish playwright, nevertheless Friel remains a very national author, in accordance with Yeats's one-time claim that great art and nationality are interdependent. The presence of national concerns in his work is fairly obvious, but what aspects of its form and technique qualify as unmistakably Irish?

RP: I think the most straightforward answer to that is that the traditional form of a kitchen is something which is explored over and over again. Of course there was a 'kitchen-sink' phase in British drama in the 1950s and 60s, but there is a much bigger proportion of Irish plays just set in a household and usually in a kitchen. Again, Tom Murphy would be an obvious parallel to Friel in this respect. The play, which has been regarded as the father of modern Irish drama, is Friel's *Philadelphia*, and yet it did not entirely 'break the mould' of Irish playwriting as it was still set in a kitchen. And although there were certain technical novelties, I do not think that they are as important as the fact that what Friel managed to do in that play was to set people in a kitchen and yet transcend the limitations which we had seen in many other plays. When we get to *Translations*, it is ostensibly someone's home, the home of the schoolmaster and his two sons, and yet it obviously is not a home in the sense that most people would expect. There is no comfort in it, and there is, in fact, no focus – there is no hearth in any productions that I have seen. And in *Lughnasa*, again, you have got a household under threat – it is Kate who is trying to hold it together while all other forces seem to be pulling it apart. *Living Quarters* (1977) would be another example. The title is a terrible pun, of course, for it is not a home, it is something provided by the army for its officers to occupy, and yet, as long as they can remember, it has been their home – as for the three sisters in Chekhov's play. In other words, in a large number of his plays Friel has stuck to the traditional venue and forum of Irish drama, and yet he has been providing incisive commentaries, such as the fact that the place is not a home. In *Lughnasa* the whole home is threatened and eventually disintegrates, under the weight partly of modernization, and partly ostracization. I suppose the other thing that is invisible, quite distinct from the question of where he locates his plays, is of course speech. Friel's speech is quite unmistakably Irish. And yet – and this is partly responding to the question of his being an internationally well known author –and yet despite the fact that everyone is quite clearly Irish and is located in Ireland, these plays travel extremely well: you would know that from your experience of Hungarian productions of Brian Friel.[5] *Molly Sweeney* (1994) is currently in the repertory of the Maly Theatre of St. Petersburg. *Translations* because of its appeal to any postcolonial society has played in a vast range of countries including Estonia, Catalonia, Nigeria. This is partly because the emotions that have been expressed find a resonance within the audiences in other countries, and partly because there is an international vogue for the Irish theatre, and it is partly, I think, because the sheer music through the voices of his characters is so emotionally appealing to audiences everywhere.

MK: What are the most important connections of his dramatic work with the international theatre, classical and contemporary both considered?

RP: Apart from what I have just said about postcolonial themes, I am not sure that there are many playwrights with whom his work connects, and I cannot think of many play-wrights with whom you can compare his work. I would be very tempted to say that he is one of the greatest living playwrights: the reason for that is because so few people elsewhere are writing what I would call challenging drama. Athol Fugard and Wole Soyinka would be cognate authors in this respect, and, perhaps, because they are close to the same postcolonial experience to an African reality that accords somewhat to the Irish reality. There are few plays on in the Broadway theatres apart from musicals, or resurrections of old stuff, and no one in England is writing much – Tom Stoppard, for instance, has been relatively silent for a time. Stoppard, I think, is a wonderful writer but he is not quite in the same league as Friel, and if British theatre is applauded because of facile writers like Alan Ayckbourn, then it is a theatre in serious trouble. I think the reason that Friel's importance has not been recognized as widely as it should be is because, in Britain obviously with a much larger market, someone like Stoppard has a success immediately, and because of that success he becomes inter-nationally well known. Whereas it took a very long time for Friel to become known, accepted, recognized, and celebrated outside Ireland. It is a difficulty that Tom Murphy is still experiencing in getting his plays produced outside the British Isles.

MK: *The Yalta Game* is another adaptation of Chekhov after his 1998 version of *Uncle Vanya*, preceded by *Three Sisters* in 1981. Why do you think Chekhov is so important for Friel that he comes back to him the third time?

RP: Friel's new version of *The Bear* and his own 'Russian' play called *Afterplay* are also works that represent this coming back. The basic reason is that Friel empathizes very deeply with, let us call it, the spirit, and the themes of Chekhov and Turgenev that are paradigmatic of the Russian soul or spirit. People who spend their entire lives waiting, hoping for something, people who are quite convinced that real life is elsewhere – these I think Friel recognizes as being also very Irish themes, because of the nineteenth-century experiences of emancipation and of famine, and he loves reading the Russian writers. I think it is easy for him – comes naturally to him – to write versions of Russian plays and stories. I think it has been quite an exciting thing for him to write *Afterplay*, which consists of two characters, one of whom is Sonya Serebrjakova from *Uncle Vanya*, and the other is Andrej Prozorov from *Three Sisters,* because of the challenge he set himself of 'marrying' them into some kind of intimacy which would illuminate both precedent plays while creating new lives in a new play.

MK: What are Friel's main thematic preoccupations?

RP: Questioning the concept of home. He said to me that he resists the concept of community, and is not sure that he can accept the idea of home, and that is a massive preoccupation. Within that preoccupation is the whole question of what constitutes the home. Obviously, it means family. Both within family and outside, in relation to the rest of the society is the question of trust, the question of understanding, the question of faith, not only faith in the religious sense but faith in oneself, faith in others. These obsessions come out for example in *Give Me Your Answer, Do!*, in which two marriages are under very great tension, and a home certainly under very severe threat of collapse (I mean emotional collapse), and while the whole idea

of faith, trust, and understanding is being explored in most
intimate and painful detail, there is also this idea of the miracle
and magic, which is there in *Wonderful Tennessee* together with
storytelling which Friel described as a *Canterbury Tales* type of
play, where reaching out for the invisible island, the Island of
Magic, has the central character Terry so excited, and the rest of
them revolving around him telling their tales. The idea, and the
whole question of storytelling which I think is absolutely fundamental to the Irish theatre, is something which I should add to
what I said about the form and technique of Irish theatre being
present in Friel's plays. Well, not just storytelling in the sense of
spinning out a yarn, but reaching the point at which, during a
play, during one's own life, a story has to be told, which releases
a secret and the telling of the secret releases some emotional
angst. To move briefly away from Friel, the most telling, the
most piercing example of that in my experience, and I was
lucky to see it with Siobhán McKenna in the role, was Tom
Murphy's *Bailegangaire* (1984).

MK: Why is getting nearer to telling the truth through his
characters so important for Friel?

RP: Someone has to tell a story or admit to having told an
untruth. It is going all the way through *Molly Sweeney*, the three
stories being told there – three interrelated stories – and it is in
Afterplay too, where Sonya and Andrey have to keep apologizing
and admitting that what they just said is not quite true, it is a
little bit of fiction. So they are getting nearer and nearer to
telling the truth all the time and, I think, that is a very strong
element running through Friel's plays. Going right back to say
Philadelphia, and to *The Loves of Cass McGuire* (1967) – a play I
have not mentioned yet. Establishing a truth is like providing
oneself with a benchmark that *ought* to have been there for one
from the outset, but which *wasn't* there. If we can find it, or a
satisfactory substitute, even at this late stage, it will assist us in
completing the essential journey which began with this 'outset'
– i.e., the leaving home which has to be fulfilled by the journey
back home, the *nostalgia*.

MK: The portrayal of failure and loss are often mentioned concerning the world of Friel's plays, yet it does not lack comic scenes, and characters either. How do these two features go together?

RP: A case of that of course would be *The Gentle Island* (1971), which is a terribly serious play about the collapse of a community and the stories told within it, but it has some extremely funny lines in it. I think the point is that the telling of a truth is much more piercing and effective when tears are accompanied by laughter. At the end of the first edition of my book, I said something that I actually brought to the front of the second edition, which is my own view that ultimate freedom equals a self-deriding laughter. That is something in which I still believe – that the ultimate freedom is to go wherever I go at my own risk and at my own pace, and under my own direction. The Greek word for freedom, *eleutheria* means literally, etymologically, 'to go where I will'. One's inclination for self-destruction, which we see in Fox in *Crystal and Fox* (1970), is that kind of freedom. I think a black comedy is something that Friel would see happening within a great deal of his own work. Look at Teddy in *Faith Healer* (1979) and his commentary on the world of make-believe with which he has been associated all his life. And look at the extraordinarily funny ways in which he comments on that.

MK: Which of Friel's plays mark artistic turning points in the development of his work?

RP: I already mentioned *Philadelphia*. I wouldn't say just an artistic turn, because I think that what happens in a play in terms of themes, and the way the author deals with them in terms of artistic technique, are interrelated. I would say quite simply that it is the major plays, and I would list those as *Philadelphia, The Freedom of the City*, then we move on to that extraordinary two-year period where he had *Faith Healer, Aristocrats*, and *Translations*, from 1979 to 1980. And those two years or so saw Friel's work moving onto a plane immeasurably higher than it had been before. Then, as we know, there was an extraordinary silence from 1982 to 1988, and that *Making History* has been put down as not a great play is, I think, due to the fact that it did not have a very good first production. It had a quite fantastic production in the late 1990s at the Peacock Theatre with Gerard McSorley as Hugh, and I think that production restored the play's reputation as a very important turning point. Obviously, so was *Dancing at Lughnasa* with its openly autobiographical stance, although I do not give quite as much reverence or admiration to that play as most people do. Then we move on to *Molly Sweeney*, and here I find myself absolutely in awe of what he achieved in that play. Friel himself, jokingly, said that it was like *Faith Healer* – but I do not see that there is any real connection here, because the structure of the later play is quite different. Instead of the monologues of three characters you have monologues which are interspersed so effectively in the course of the play, that it is almost as if, *but not quite*, that they were meeting, and exchanging on stage. I think it is his most transparent play, his most beautiful play, and I think when the time comes to take a look at his entire output, *Molly Sweeney* will rank as one of the few best plays by Brian Friel. As I say, 'but not quite' – that nearness without touching is so potent in emphasizing how very distant they are from each other in terms of being able to understand or even cherish one another.

MK: How far, in your view, did the Field Day connection, in my understanding Friel's taking part in Northern Irish cultural politics, enrich his dramatic art; would it have, perhaps, taken a different route without this connection? What is Friel's 'road not taken'?

RP: In a sense, I do not think Field Day enriched his dramatic art, it diverted his dramatic art into the service of politics, cultural politics perhaps, but politics nonetheless. And Field Day is not only a company producing and travelling their plays, but is a publishing house in which Friel took enormous personal interest, and huge personal commitment travelling frequently from his home into Derry to do office work. Field Day was a very necessary interruption to the way his work was going. What we have seen in the last, say, ten years is the direction, in other words the road not taken *then*, the road he is *now* taking with *Lughnasa, Wonderful Tennessee, Molly Sweeney*. In other words, attending to the inner man, the inner anxiety, the inner strength and weaknesses rather than – let us call it – doing military service in the cause of his (in inverted commas) 'community' – an extremely dangerous term to use but short-hand for what one would understand as an intellectual response to politics in the North of Ireland in the company of people such as John Hume, the politician, and Seamus Deane the intellectual (some people say the ideologue), and Seamus Heaney the poet, and Stephen Rea on the stage side. In another sense, there is always a 'road not taken', in that the chosen road, or the road one is compelled to take, prevents one from travel-ling other roads. In terms of homecoming, the chosen road is the road towards self-discovery, and if that road proves to be the wrong road, then, of course, there are other possible roads that one may regret not having taken. In Friel's case, the world and his wife perceive *Lughnasa* as the right road, the road of homecoming, and I don't argue with that. *Translations*, too, as it has been described as 'a national epic', has a sense of bringing both the playwright and his 'community' home to a certain set of truths – a point of arrival. But at a deeper level I think we can see that Friel has 'come home' in much more profound ways – especially in the sense that *Give Me Your Answer, Do!* is an equally autobiographical play, not about *nostalgia* but about *hindsight* – the 'reckoning' of a seventy-year-old writer. And in *Molly Sweeney* – I don't apologize for coming back to the ex-cellence of that play – there is a definite sense of achievement that says, to me at least, that a homecoming has taken place in the locus that is of most concern to the writer: his own imagination and its connection with the world, both the in-timate world and the more public world. So I would say that if Friel had continued producing plays in the 'Field Day formula' there might well have been a 'road not taken', but the road taken since Field Day has represented a much more satisfying route in the sense that the playwright has found a more effective way home to that personal hearth *and* a new way of communicating with an audience which is a new kind of 'community'.

MK: Would you call Friel an experimental playwright? Which plays qualify as most experimental in the Friel canon?

RP: I do not think he is very experimental, and much less so today than in the earlier plays, when he was still finding his way in the business of stagecraft, because today he is not interested in anything other than getting the voices across from the stage to the audience. And I do not think there is a single play by Friel which is totally original in any experimental way, even in *Philadelphia*, in the Gar divided into Private, and Public: there are instances of previous playwrights dividing a character in one way or another. How he does it is what makes the work so fascinating, by the strategy that he uses which is expressed in the stage directions in front of the play. If I may digress, the writer who has taken what I referred to earlier as the Russian themes of waiting, hope deferred, wasteland, etc., and made them Irish and has done it in a very experimental way was, of course, Samuel Beckett. Athough I understood when I first met Friel that he really did not have much interest in Beckett, he was not terribly excited by Beckett, I found him more recently referring to Beckett, and if he does that there is perhaps some excitement derived from Beckett. Maybe it is Beckett who does hurry forward in a very advanced way some of those – what I called – 'Russian' themes that are so important to Friel.

MK: You call *Molly Sweeney* a 'risky' play in your book. In what sense is it risky? Does it, perhaps, share an aspect of Beckett's late theatre, in that it affects the nerves of the audience, rather than their intellect?

RP: Obviously one would think that there might be some link with Beckett, but it is not that at all. It is the fact that there is such emotional honesty, such transparency in the play. I think it is extremely demanding on the three characters, on the three actors; it is extremely demanding if you believe those actors just actually *are* those three characters; it is extremely risky for them to be coming to us in the same way as *Faith Healer*, and telling us their stories. And it is terribly risky for the audience because there are such huge questions being raised that must make people in the audience look into their own hearts and be very disturbed by what they find there – questions about the accuracy of vision, of memory, the ability to express oneself clearly, to understand what another is saying, to appreciate their standpoint and their perspective.

MK: Memory scenes have such a marked presence in Friel's drama: is this phenomenon related to his interest in the importance of the past as an author from Northern Ireland, and the meaning of the past for various individuals?

RP: Although the North has obviously had a huge presence in his writing life and in his writing consciousness, I think that Friel is just doing what anybody would do who is fascinated with the past, with that business of trying to make the journey home. It is not a Northern fascination, just a human one, which is more evident in Ireland, a country for which the past is so problematic. The whole question of how the Irish came to be a dominated people, and how they began to deal with their freedom when they got it. Of course this is the subject of *The Mundy Scheme*, a play that has only been produced once and I should love to see.

MK: Can you identify character types in Friel's work, who keep on returning in different guises? What establishes the importance of his outsiders, and commentators, for instance?

RP: The fact that in most of his plays there is someone called O'Donnell, it is the O'Donnell family, and they are always living in Ballybeg. In my book I refer to a piece that he wrote, 'A Fair Day at Glenties'. Glenties is the town in the background of *Lughnasa*, his mother's town. And I say that these are the

archetypal people who make up a whole microcosm, which of
course is very Chekhovian, too. And they are the people who
keep cropping up, he lists them and they are all there in his
plays. Let us call them an organic group of people, otherwise
known by that awful word 'family'. When I say 'awful' I do
share with so many people a fear of the term 'family', it is
something that when I am talking to Brendan Kennelly, for
example, we revert to again and again, this problem of intimate
blood relations within that other four letter word 'home'. The
outsiders and commentators are part of his experimentation if
you like, each of them coming from some theoretical source,
like Dodds, the sociologist in *The Freedom of the City*, or Sir in
Living Quarters. These are devices, experiments again, but I do
not think the plays that include them are more important than
the plays that do not have them.

MK: So many books and articles have been produced about
Friel's art so far, that they are likely to fill a smaller library. Do
you notice some main directions in this growing bulk of the
'Friel industry' as one might call it?

RP: Apart from the fact that people write books on Friel to
promote their career, I think people are attracted to his work
for two reasons, which may seem contradictory. One is the
transparency that I already mentioned. When you pick up the
copy of a play, you hold a whole world in your hand. And the
contradictory thing is the difficulty of actually trying to describe
it, it is a tremendous challenge, as I say it is partly what drew me
to Friel in the first place. Most people who have written about
Friel have a very strong reason, inner or personal reason for
doing so. On the other hand, one wonders whether it is really
justifiable to keep on producing books which in many ways
reproduce the same material, I am thinking particularly of
volumes of essays rather than monographs. I do not think that
there are many main directions, not many people have tried to
follow my sense of direction in looking at the spiritual side of
Friel's work, the emotional side, the depth of that work. There
has been more written about him from the political side and

then, of course, there was a book quite recently by F.C. McGrath about Friel as a postcolonial writer,[6] which is typical of so many academics who pick a subject to try and fit it into a thesis rather than trying to make a thesis out of the subject. I have never been persuaded by any kind of -isms. All I know is how I personally describe a subject that I am passionately interested in, and if that fits in with something someone else has written about some other writer, and it can be conveniently labelled with an -ism, then that is fine by me. I had recently a case of it in relation to my work on Lawrence Durrell, where somebody wrote about Durrell's *Avignon Quintet* (1974) with such a weight of ideological luggage that he succeeded in completely reversing my argument and still managed to quote me with approval! It is very frustrating to find this happening but it is entirely due to the way in which literature is taught nowadays in universities, that theory is more important than the plays, which are taken to be illustrative of theory. So as far as the 'Friel industry' is concerned, I hope it stays immune as far as possible from that kind of treatment because it is not the sort of attention that Friel deserves.

MK: *Philadelphia*, an allegedly early masterpiece of Friel's is strangely downgraded in McGrath's post-colonial study of Friel, while *The Loves of Cass McGuire* is highly thought of and is given a very substantial subchapter. How do you see this unusual repositioning of the two works? I also wonder if you have a similar appreciation for a less known play of the author.

RP: There are plays McGrath simply ignores completely, because they do not fit in with his thesis. I felt that although *Wonderful Tennessee* is not in the front line of Friel's plays, it did not deserve, nor did *Give Me Your Answer, Do!*, quite the rejection which it got from the critics and which I think seriously disappointed Friel himself. *Give Me Your Answer, Do!* is autobiographical again, and I think the critics got that all wrong. The essence of that play is faith, understanding, communication, and self-regard, and of course, we can quite rightly say it depicts a writer approaching a certain landmark in his life, the age of seventy, who wants to find out if his work is of any value, meaning, and significance. That is a perfectly reasonable inference to draw and, again, it is a play that has not yet found its right niche. I have already mentioned *The Mundy Scheme* as being a play, I suppose out of just curiosity, that I would like to see. It might need a little bit of rewriting because it is very much of its time and place, but I think it is so relevant. Beginning with the words 'Ladies and Gentlemen, what happens to an emerging country when it has emerged?'(6), which of course is the question mark standing over the entire literature on the issue of postcolonialism.

MK: What were the – for you – most memorable Friel productions that you have seen in or outside Ireland? Can you describe their most gripping effects?

RP: I have mentioned the *Translations* production that sparked off my entire interest in Friel's work. The premiere of *Dancing at Lughnasa* at the Abbey in 1990, the premiere of *Molly Sweeney* at the Gate in 1994, were immensely gripping, exciting, challenging and, of course, Donal McCann in *Faith Healer* during an Abbey revival in the mid-1980s. A production of *Aristocrats* some time in the late mid-1990s with Sean McGinley and Frank McCusker was very exciting. To come to something personal: I saw a student production of *Translations* in Montgomery, Alabama, in which the director had the very interesting device which no one had thought of before, of having Owen speaking in an Irish accent when he spoke to his own people and an English accent when he spoke to the English soldiers. And I told Friel about this, and I think this is why in *Making History* he specifically says it in the stage directions that Hugh is to speak in a Tyrone accent when talking to his own people and in an English accent when talking to Mabel, his wife, and Mary, her sister. I am very pleased, indeed, if I did have any partial responsibility for that. The most gripping effect, when you witness any Friel play, is that it appears that he is directly addressing *you*, and he is engaging your emotional response, he is demanding an emotional response, and he is getting it very easily because he is almost picking you up by the collar, and dragging you on the stage. It is that immediate effect that makes you realize he wrote the play for *you*. And that is what I find extremely moving, emotionally speaking, and also amazingly challenging, stimulating, and obviously very difficult as the emotional charge is like being put in the emotional chair and having fifteen million volts put through you. That is the highest point available to you in a Friel play, and *Molly Sweeney* is probably the play that most had that effect on me.

MK: What is Friel's relationship with the younger Irish playwrights? Do they respond to each other in any meaningful way? Can you see developments in Irish drama that open new paths leading away from the Frielian achievement?

RP: I called Friel the Irish Chekhov – I was astonished a couple of years ago to find someone writing in the English *Sunday Times* 'which is the new Irish Chekhov, Conor McPherson or Martin McDonagh'? Now, I do not want to talk very much about those playwrights except to say that I feel far too much adulation has been directed at them, for far too little in terms of artistic quality. I cannot see any justification at all for writing of people who are so young and untested in many ways, to be regarded as anywhere near the work of Chekhov, or anywhere near the work of the man who has been called the Irish Chekhov – Brian Friel. The premiere of *The Yalta Game* – Friel's version of Chekhov's short story 'Lady with a Lapdog' – was presented in tandem with new plays by Conor McPherson and Neil Jordan. After their plays, and after the interval, the audience was presented with the Friel work, and there was a palpable sense of relief that here was a work of real theatricality – and I intend that oxymoron, of *real* makebelieve – a work so well written, so well conceived, that the other presentations were in a quite definitely lesser league. I don't mean to disparage those other writers, merely to insist that there is very little 'competition' for the laureate position among the newer writers. I do not think that Friel is terribly interested in anybody else's work, I am sure he has read and he may have seen some of McPherson, or McDonagh, or Marina Carr's work, or perhaps Sebastian Barry's. What I do worry about is that I see these younger writers, with few exceptions – and Carr and Barry would be two of these exceptions – that the writing is not of great quality. Carr is a very poetic writer, and I enjoy her work very much, but what I call it is 'the reinvention of the wheel'. We are continually getting the same themes, related to the rural experience, the rural-urban divide, loneliness, faith, and mystery – I write about this in the conclusion of my book. One young writer said that he had written a play that is the first one to have ever depicted young people going mad in the Irish countryside. He is writing out of a very high level of ignorance. He is not aware of Tom Murphy's early work, he is not aware of *Philadelphia*, he is not aware of M.J. Molloy's *The Wood of the Whispering* (1953). There is an extraordinary arrogance in the ability of a young playwright to think that he is writing the most original plays that have ever been written, and on subjects which have never been addressed before. I am afraid 'what goes round comes round', and I would like to see much more new work being done on themes which are not necessarily Irish themes. There was great hope back in the 1980s for the work of Paul Mercier. I went to see a couple of his plays because I was led to believe that they were about the urban situation, and the working classes, and that at last we were getting plays which would address this section of the population – like Heno Magee's *Hatchet* (1972) or Peter Sheridan's and Jean Doyle's *Shades of the Jelly Woman*. And I found that they were all about middle class suburbia and about football teams. This to me is a waste of energy. A middle-aged playwright I have not mentioned so far, Frank McGuinness, is someone with whom Friel does have a relationship in the sense that Frank directed the revival of *The Gentle Island* at the Peacock back in the early or mid 1980s, and there is a certain amount of, I believe, warmth of affection there. Certainly it is not just one-sided, Frank McGuinness acknowledges that seeing *Faith Healer* was the experience which enabled him to become a playwright, it gave him the courage to do that, and that in itself is an extraordinary achievement. And I think Friel likes the work of Frank McGuinness. After all, it was Frank who adapted *Dancing at Lughnasa* for the film screenplay – very sensitively, I thought. It is not from a Frielian perspective that I say this, but I am just very disappointed by the fact that Irish drama does not seem to have a development. The starting-off point is the same all the time, because of this awful urge to go back and examine origins, so you are always standing and waiting at the same bus stop. You never actually let the bus take you to another country – tomorrow you will be back standing at the same bus stop, wondering if the same bus will come.

MK: Do you think Friel will become, or has already become a classic? What makes him one according to your understanding the word?

RP: Yes, in the sense that he is one of the absolutely top writers of plays in the English language in the world today. What makes him a classic is that he has universal appeal, because he writes hugely compelling work and because of the sheer quality of the language that he uses. It is of course Irish, it is not an inflection of Irish, it is Irish through and through, which of course immediately makes people realize that it is not standard English playwriting, but the quality of it is something which has gained him universal recognition. As he himself has made clear, writing about Ireland in the English language is an alien experience with which one cannot be comfortable until one feels at home in the 'new' language, until one has made it 'one's own'. While that may be an arduous and painful journey for the writer, it is an extraordinarily fruitful and rewarding experience for the reader or listener who is meeting an extremely expressive and beautiful form of 'English', which is lyrical or pointed, or abrasive or beguiling by turns, but which has, above all, a strangeness about it that is sometimes mocking, sometimes appealing, sometimes confessional, but comes to you in an oblique voice that *should* be familiar and *should* sound like one's own, but doesn't. This is an attraction that one cannot explain – that's why we keep going back to it.

MK: Which of his work would you like to write about again, because it still mystifies you even after having analysed it in your book?

RP: All of it. That is the answer, all of it.

Notes

[1] Brian Friel does not give interviews any more, but he consented to the idea that an interview be conducted about his work with Richard Pine.

[2] Richard Pine. *Brian Friel and Ireland's Drama*. London: Routledge, 1990.

[3] Richard Pine. *Lawrence Durrell: The Mindscape*. London: Macmillan, 1994. New edition Corfu: Durrell School of Corfu, 2003.

[4] Richard Pine. *The Diviner: The Art of Brian Friel*. Dublin: University College Dublin Press, 1999.

[5] So far *Dancing at Lughnasa*, *Translations*, *Philadelphia, Here I Come!*, *The Communication Cord*, and *Afterplay* have been produced by Hungarian theatres.

[6] F.C. McGrath. *Brian Friel's (Post)colonial Drama: Language, Illusion and Politics*. Syracuse: Syracuse University Press, 1999. Reviewed by Richard Pine in *Irish University Review* 30.2 (Autumn/Winter 2000): 373-76.

Works Cited

Friel, Brian. *Brian Friel: Essays, Diaries, Interviews 1964-1999*. Ed. Christopher Murray. London: Faber, 1999.

--- *Dancing at Lughnasa*. London: Faber, 1990.

--- *The Munday Scheme*. New York: Farrar, Straus and Giroux, 1970.

Contributors

Csilla Bertha, Associate Professor of Irish and English Studies, University of Debrecen, is the author of *A drámairó Yeats* ('Yeats the Playwright', 1988), co-author (with Donald E. Morse) of *Worlds Visible and Invisible, Essays on Irish Literature and Culture* (1994). Co-editor of several volumes of essays including *More Real than Reality: The Fantastic in Irish Literature and the Arts* (1991) and special journal issues on Irish literature, she also edited *Homeland in the Heights*, an anthology of contemporary Hungarian poetry in English translation (2000). Her publications include essays on Irish drama, parallels between Hungarian and Irish literature, and the fantastic in literature and the arts. She is currently a European representative and member of the Executive Board of the International Association for the Study of Irish Literatures (IASIL), member of the Advisory Board of *Irish University Review*, has served on the IASIL Bibliography subcommittee for many years, and in 2003 co-hosted the IASIL conference at the University of Debrecen.

Paulo Eduardo Carvalho, Lecturer at the Department for Anglo-American Studies of the Faculty of Arts of the University of Porto (Portugal) and researcher at the Centre for Theatre Studies, University of Lisbon, and at the Institute for Comparative Studies, University of Porto has special interests in Portuguese and English-speaking drama and theatre and Translation Studies. Having completed an MA on the work of

Brian Friel and the Field Day Theatre Company, he is currently preparing a doctoral dissertation on translation and cultural representation, titled 'Identities, Bodies and Figurations: The Translation of Irish Contemporary Drama into the Portuguese Theatre'. A theatre practitioner, he has translated and assured the dramaturgy of a wide range of contemporary playwrights and has published translations of plays by Brian Friel, Frank McGuinness, Martin Crimp, Caryl Churchill, Harold Pinter, and Wallace Shawn. He currently serves as a member of the board of directors of the Portuguese Association of Theatre Critics and of the Executive Committee of the AICT/IATC.

Richard Allen Cave is Professor of Drama and Theatre Arts at Royal Holloway (University of London). His extensive publications on Anglo-Irish literature include a study of George Moore's novels and editions of Moore's *Hail and Farewell, The Lake* and *The Untilled Field* (forthcoming); editions of plays by T. C. Murray for Colin Smythe, and of plays by both Yeats and Wilde for Penguin Classics; essays on the work of Robert Gregory, Tom Murphy, G.B. Shaw, Wilde, Yeats, Frank McGuinness and on dramatizations of the life of Swift. He is currently completing a study of Yeats and stage design.

Ger FitzGibbon is a Senior Lecturer in the Department of English, University College Cork. He has lectured on Irish drama and theatre in America, England, and Ireland. His current critical writing is in the area of contemporary Irish theatre – especially the work of Brian Friel, Tom Murphy, Frank McGuinness and Sebastian Barry. Recent publications include updating of all the contemporary Irish entries in the current editions of *The Cambridge Guide to Theatre* and *The Concise Cambridge Guide to Theatre*, and contributions to *The Oxford Companion to Irish Literature*. He has written a number of plays, the most successful of which, *The Rock Station*, was premiered by Soho Theatre Company in London in 1992, and later adapted for radio production by BBC. His play, *Sca*, a contemporary adaptation of Sheridan's *The School for Scandal*, was premiered in Cork in October 1999.

Mária Kurdi, Professor and Head of the Department of English Literatures and Cultures at the University of Pécs, Hungary, teaches and does research in modern Irish literature and English-speaking drama. Her publications include a survey of contemporary Irish drama in Hungarian (1999), a volume of essays discussing aspects of identity in contemporary Irish plays (2000), and a collection of interviews made with Irish playwrights in her Hungarian translation (2004). She guest-edited the Brian Friel special issue of the *Hungarian Journal of English and American Studies* in 1999, is author of numerous articles, and editor of an anthology of excerpts from critical material for the study of Irish literature in Hungary. Since 1998 she has been editor of the biennial journal *Focus: Papers in English Literary and Cultural Studies*. She has been a member of the International Association for the Study of Irish Literatures since 1984, and served as president of the Hungarian Society for the Study of English (2001-2004).

Márton Mesterházi has been working with the Drama/Literature Department of the Hungarian Radio since 1964, as script editor responsible for plays and radio-plays translated from English and French, or written in Hungarian. He is the author of two books, *The World of Sean O'Casey* (1983), originally his Ph.D. dissertation, and *The Hungarian Reception of Sean O'Casey 1926-1986* (1993). He has translated the plays of John Arden, Sebastian Barry, Brian Friel, Tom Murphy, and other playwrights.

Donald E. Morse, Emeritus Professor, Oakland University, USA and Visiting Professor, University of Debrecen, has been twice Fulbright Professor and twice Soros Professor at Debrecen. Author or editor of ten books and over one hundred scholarly essays, his most recent book is *The Novels of Kurt Vonnegut: Imagining Being an American* (2003). With Csilla Bertha, he co-edited *More Real than Reality: The Fantastic in Irish Literature and the Arts* (1991), *A Small Nation's Contribution to the World* (1993), co-authored *Worlds Visible and Invisible* (1994), received a Rockefeller Study Fellowship to translate contemporary

Hungarian plays into English, and co-hosted IASIL03. Associate editor and book editor of the *Hungarian Journal of English and American Studies*, he has co-edited special issues on Irish Studies and one on Science Fiction. Since 1984 he has chaired the annual International Conference on the Fantastic in the Arts. Currently he serves on the Hungarian-American Fulbright Commission of which he was the first elected Chairman of the Board. In 1999 the University of Debrecen awarded him an Honorary Doctorate in recognition of his service to Hungarian higher education and his international scholarship.

Christopher Murray, Associate Professor of Drama and Theatre History in the School of English, University College Dublin, is former editor of *Irish University Review* (1986-1997) and chair (2000-03) of the International Association for the Study of Irish Literatures (IASIL). He is author of *Twentieth-Century Irish Drama: Mirror Up to Nation* (1997) and *Sean O'Casey Writer at Work: A Biography* (2004), and has edited *Brian Friel: Essays, Diaries, Interviews 1964-1999* (1999). Currently he is editing *Selected Plays of George Shiels* for Colin Smythe's Irish Plays series.

Ruth Niel studied English and Geography at the University of Wuppertal, where she worked for several years as a postgraduate assistant in the English department. She has written articles on Brian Friel, Seamus Heaney, Tom Murphy, and Iris Murdoch, as well as on contemporary Irish theatre and postcolonial writing from the UK and Caribbean. She has also translated various books on business management and finance, and is currently working for Lufthansa German Airlines.

Michael Parker is Professor of English Literature at the University of Central Lancashire. His books include *Seamus Heaney: The Making of the Poet*, Macmillan (1993), *The Hurt World: Short Fiction Of The Troubles*, Blackstaff (1995), *Contemporary Irish Fiction: Themes, Tropes, Theories* (co-editor with Liam Harte), Macmillan (2000). His latest, most ambitious project to date is

Northern Irish Literature, 1956-2001: The Imprint of History, which explores the drama, fiction, and poetry of the Troubles and the political contexts from which they emerged. It will be published by Macmillan in 2006. He is also responsible for research exchanges involving Charles University Prague, the University of Lodz, and the University of Ulster, where he held a Visiting Fellowship in 2005.

Richard Pine, Director of the Durrell School of Corfu, which he founded in 2001-02, previously worked in broadcasting for twenty-five years, in both music and public affairs of Radio Telefis Eireann. A former secretary of the Irish Writers' Union and chair of the Media Association of Ireland, he is consultant to the Council of Europe on cultural development programmes. His books include *The Diviner: The Art of Brian Friel* (1999), *The Thief of Reason: Oscar Wilde and Modern Ireland* (1995), *Lawrence Durrell: The Mindscape* (1994/2005), and *Music and Broadcasting in Ireland* (2005). In 1998 he edited the Thomas Davis Lectures for RTE Radio on 'Music in Ireland 1848-1998' and co-authored the official history of the Royal Irish Academy of Music, of which he is an honorary Fellow. From 1999 to 2005 he edited the six-volume series 'Broadcasting and Irish Society'. He is currently writing a biography of the Irish music critic Charles Acton and editing a volume of essays on the connection between madness and creativity.

Giovanna Tallone, a graduate in Modern Languages from Università Cattolica del Sacro Cuore, Milan, holds a Ph.D. in English Studies from the University of Florence, and is currently cooperating with the Department of English at Università Cattolica, Milan. She has presented papers at several IASIL conferences and published articles and critical reviews on Brian Friel, James Stephens, Seamus Heaney, Lady Gregory, Mary Lavin, Angela Bourke, and Éilís Ní Dhuibhne. Her main research interests include contemporary Irish drama, Irish women writers, and the remakes of Old Irish legends.

Index

abjection, 184
absence, 17, 73, 75, 150, 151, 152, 156, 159, 161, 169
adaptation, 303, 311
aesthetics, 78f., 83, 89, 112, 143, 194, 254, 256, 258f.
agent, 21f., 24, 173, 231, 234, 274
Albee, Edward, 24
alienation, 241, 271, 296
allegory, 7, 128f., 133, 202
alliteration, 132f., 133
allusion, 155, 158, 240, 280, 282
Almansi, Guido, 53, 59
alter ego, 40, 77
alterity, 231
Althusser, Louis, 281, 298
ambiguity, 29, 31, 53, 184, 185, 190, 192, 280
ambivalence, 63, 125, 243, 274, 295
anachronism, 74
analogy, 150, 165, 172, 178, 224, 307
Andrews, Elmer, 2, 171, 203, 223, 251, 257, 259, 298
Andrews, John, 74, 268
anglicization, 147, 173

anglophone, 174, 255
Apollonian, 89
archetype, 174, 201, 318
Arendt, Hanna, 30
Aristotle, 242, 245, 276, 299
Arnold, Bruce, 59, 65, 72, 138, 298, 300
artist, 7, 9, 13-53, 62, 67, 70-95, 143, 210, 219, 225, 230, 237-63, 292, 294, 304, 313, 321
artistry, 5, 128, 201
assonance, 132f.
atavistic, 83
Auden, W.H., 13, 30, 32
authenticity, 54, 81, 89, 149, 175f.
authoritarian, 9, 255, 277
autobiographical, 84, 154, 177, 188, 314f., 319
Axton, Richard, 131, 137
Ayckbourn, Alan, 310

Bakhtin, Mikhail, 9, 274, 278, 299
Ballybeg, 19, 24, 38, 46, 64, 81, 86, 106, 125, 151, 187, 192, 210f., 223, 237, 264, 268, 317
Bardon, Jonathan, 297, 299
Barnes, Clive, 226, 248f., 273, 294, 299

Barry, Kevin, 74, 268
Barry, Sebastian, 182, 307, 322
Beckett, Samuel, 1, 28, 32, 60,
    89, 182, 196, 232, 247f., 316
Behan, Brendan, 246, 248
Bell, J. Bowyer, 153, 175, 180,
    297, 299
Bennett, Alan, 80, 91
Bertha, Csilla, 1, 2, 3, 7, 8, 59,
    72, 88, 91, 203, 215, 223, 225
Bevington, David, 129, 132,
    134, 137
Bhabha, Homi K., 302
Bildungsroman, 308
bilingual, 98, 109, 113
Birker, Klaus, 241, 248
body, 3, 6, 11, 14, 104, 132, 155,
    168, 181-203, 235, 238, 283
Boland, Eavan, 281, 299
border, 6, 47, 143, 170, 221, 239
Boyce, George D., 272, 299
British, 60, 75, 115, 138, 142,
    208, 224f., 261, 268, 271,
    273, 276, 281, 286, 294f.,
    298, 308, 310
Brown, Terence, 153, 172, 175,
    179
Buckland, Patrick, 272, 299
Burke, Patrick, 49, 56, 57, 59,
    70, 72, 81, 91, 223, 225

Calvino, Italo, 263, 267
canon, 9, 36, 37, 124, 316
Carberry, Sean, 37, 59
caricature, 187, 191, 242
carnival, 9, 274, 290, 293
Carr, Marina, 4, 322
Carson, Clayborne, 240, 248
catastrophe, 15, 117, 209, 223,
    244
catharsis, 58, 90
Catholicism, 78, 88, 97, 101,
    105, 142, 163, 170, 173, 178,

187, 192, 194, 201, 210, 217,
    224, 279, 281, 295, 307
Cave, Richard Allen, 6, 204
Celtic, 13, 83-8, 91, 138, 153,
    189, 192, 199
ceremony, 6, 29, 90, 192, 198,
    290, 305
Chambers, E.K., 128, 137
Chambers, Lilian, 10
characterization, 5, 9, 39, 46,
    147, 174, 234f., 274, 278,
    280, 283, 287
Chekhov, Anton, 94f., 102, 195,
    253, 256f., 264, 268, 292,
    303-305, 309, 311, 321
childhood, 55, 76, 84, 87, 124,
    191, 197, 201, 211, 232, 306
chorus, 103, 199, 295
Christian, 79, 89, 99, 199, 202,
    217
Civil Rights movement, 171
class, 78, 82, 156, 161, 195, 241,
    282-96, 322
classical, 83, 86, 88, 101, 191,
    197, 200, 262, 310
claustrophobic, 126, 142, 172,
    224
cliché, 133, 136, 304
colonialism, 75, 97, 119, 182,
    208, 252, 254, 296, 319, 324
comedy, 28, 44, 64, 81, 89, 96,
    131, 135, 150, 172, 201, 218,
    235, 242, 264, 284, 285, 290,
    296, 313
commitment, 3, 9, 22, 143, 155,
    197, 207, 210, 253, 255f.,
    266, 285, 296, 314
communication, 78, 81, 90, 96,
    99, 146, 202, 206, 220, 264,
    302, 307, 319
community, 13-18, 74f., 78, 80,
    84, 95f., 116, 142, 145, 173,
    177, 184, 187, 197, 208, 213,

257, 271f., 279, 285, 291, 294, 311, 313, 315

conceit, 103

confession, 26, 37, 46, 114, 165, 186, 201, 307f., 323

Conrad, Joseph, 28, 32

conservatism, 148, 188, 259

convention, 4, 6, 103, 133, 135, 182, 190, 194, 222f., 245, 258f.

Corcoran, Neil, 35, 37, 59

Corkery, Daniel, 106, 107

craft, 59, 80, 86, 128, 135, 162, 254, 259, 261

creativity, 5, 15, 18, 20-9, 49, 52, 62, 65, 67, 80, 132, 194, 198, 218f., 245-7, 266

Cronin, Anthony, 21, 32

Cushmann, L W, 137

cynicism, 81, 162, 198, 296

dance, 6, 61, 82-90, 104, 144, 147f., 156, 183, 186-97, 203, 235

Dantanus, Ulf, 2, 37, 59, 114, 121, 251, 267, 272, 294, 299

Davison, Peter, 130, 137

Dean, Joan Fitzgerald, 107

Deane, Seamus, 32, 44, 57, 93f., 137, 171, 179, 181, 204, 213, 223, 225, 254-57, 261f., 265-67, 281, 283, 296, 298f., 303, 315

death, 17, 19, 29, 32, 36, 42, 44, 56, 63, 66, 68f., 80, 95f., 99, 116, 118, 127f., 161, 169, 184, 199, 215, 233, 237, 243, 248, 275, 292

decoding, 113

deconstruction, 264

democracy, 142, 279

demotic, 297

demythologize, 261

desire, 16, 57, 65f., 74, 87, 88, 148, 156, 214, 223, 236, 238, 244, 246, 289

destruction, 14, 18, 28, 36, 38f. 54, 75, 83, 167, 202, 209, 211f., 243

Devine, Kathleen, 217, 225f.

Devlin, Anne, 147, 179, 296

dialect, 110, 114, 121, 284

dialogue, 5, 6, 9, 44, 79, 84, 103, 116, 147, 155, 157, 161, 174, 189f., 200-202, 247, 274, 275, 277, 286f., 292, 294

Dillon, Myles, 125, 130, 137

dindsheanchas, 127

Dionysian, 83, 84, 89

director, 48, 52, 83, 87, 90, 101, 105, 118, 170, 174, 189, 193, 208, 256, 290, 296, 313, 315, 318, 320

disability, 5, 173, 205f., 210, 213, 219, 222, 224, 235

disintegration, 145, 151, 218

dislocation, 82, 213

disruption, 41, 77, 130

diviner, 14f., 303

division, 47, 76, 105, 107, 145, 197, 257

Dowling, P.J., 49, 97, 107, 262

Doyle, Jean, 322

dramatis personae, 74, 205, 208, 220

dramaturgy, 6, 75, 77, 82, 200

dream, 41-5, 54f., 67, 69, 115, 152f., 168, 170, 178, 182

dualism, 87, 206, 208, 213

duplicity, 171

Durrell, Lawrence, 302, 319, 324

Eliot, T.S., 27, 32, 172, 179, 240

elusiveness, 42, 49, 57, 129, 133, 215

emancipation, 311

emblem, 29, 150, 218

embodiment, 18, 65f., 146, 160, 173, 193, 208, 215, 265, 281

emigration, 76, 125, 142, 167, 172, 177

epic, 127, 182, 315

epiphany, 18, 185, 238, 292

episode, 44, 46, 55f., 76, 128, 167, 185f., 190-93, 196, 198, 201, 221, 237, 275

epitome, 129, 132

escapism, 193

Esslin, Martin, 46, 59

ethics, 16, 193f., 246

exhibitionism, 177, 286

exile, 145, 152, 167, 171f., 221, 238, 239

experiment, 8, 9, 94, 124, 258, 264, 316

fable, 90, 109

fairy-tale, 44, 55f.

family, 18, 21-30, 38, 52, 62, 76, 78, 81, 124, 149, 152, 162f., 168, 170f., 188, 190, 197, 206-225, 257, 287, 289, 295, 311, 317

famine, 95f., 311

fantasy, 18, 28, 77, 87, 104, 185, 221, 232, 237f., 314

farce, 39, 95, 110, 111, 264

Farrell, Michael, 142, 179

festival, 1, 85

Fiacc, Padraic, 177-79

fiction, 16, 24, 46-58, 78, 144, 160, 172, 216, 222, 240, 262, 265, 293, 312

Field Day, 9f., 38, 80, 93f., 97, 108, 171, 182, 241, 249, 251-57, 260-69, 292, 303f., 314

Field Day Theatre Company, 9, 80, 94, 108, 182, 251, 253, 261, 267-69

FitzGibbon, Ger, 6, 10

folk drama, 131

folklore, 55, 84

Foster, Roy, 176, 271, 299

Foucault, Michel, 141, 179, 239, 244, 246, 248

fragmentation, 45, 125, 127, 133, 136, 161

Frazer, James G, 85, 88, 91

Friel, Brian
  'The Theatre of Hope and Despair', 179, 268
  A Month in the Country After Turgenev, 1, 267
  Afterplay, 303, 305, 311f., 324
  Aristocrats, 1, 7, 19, 32, 39, 76, 78, 81, 137, 173, 179, 210, 212, 214, 224f., 235, 256-58, 263, 301, 313, 320
  Crystal and Fox, 7, 18, 32, 36-59, 313
  Dancing at Lughnasa, 1, 2, 6, 29, 32, 38, 61, 72, 76, 82-4, 90f., 94, 107, 180-83, 186, 194f., 202-204, 206, 226, 247f., 252f., 258, 263, 269, 297, 302, 305, 307, 314, 320, 323f.
  Faith Healer, 6f., 15-60, 63, 72, 79f., 84, 90, 123-30, 135, 137f., 143f., 179, 181-85, 203, 204, 211-215, 220-26, 235f., 245, 247f., 256, 258, 259, 275, 280, 313, 317, 320, 322
  Freedom of the City, The, 1, 9, 39, 68, 76, 78, 137, 143, 160, 171, 178, 212, 216, 224, 240, 248, 255-62,

271-76, 280f., 294f., 299-301, 313, 318

Gentle Island, The, 8, 39, 59, 84, 141-47, 160, 162, 167-75, 178f., 204, 206, 225f., 256, 285, 295-97, 299, 313, 322

Give Me Your Answer, Do!, 1, 7f., 15-33, 38, 62, 218, 222, 225, 305f., 311, 315, 319

Gold in the Sea, The, 137

Home Place, The, 8

Living Quarters, 1, 39, 137, 179, 214, 224f., 235, 245, 297, 309, 318

Loves of Cass McGuire, The, 37, 214, 226, 312, 319

Making History, 1, 10, 39, 76, 79, 94, 160, 179f, 182, 253f., 265, 266-69, 302, 314, 320

Molly Sweeney, 5f., 14, 32f., 38, 83, 91, 144, 173, 206, 214, 219-48, 309, 312, 314-16, 320

Mundy Scheme, The, 1, 32, 39, 169f., 175, 178f., 295, 308, 317, 320

Performances, 8, 61-5, 70, 72

Philadelphia, Here I Come!, 6, 22, 32, 37, 59, 76, 79, 81, 89, 99, 125, 137, 150, 168, 179, 212, 226, 238f., 256, 258f., 295f., 301, 306, 324

Translations, 4-6, 9, 39, 60, 63, 73-6, 80, 83, 91-99, 102, 105-109, 116f., 120f., 124, 136f., 143, 151, 160, 173, 176, 179, 182, 203, 206, 208, 212, 213, 215f., 224, 226, 241, 249, 252, 254, 256, 259-68, 272, 275,

286, 297f., 301, 304, 309, 313, 315, 320, 324

Volunteers, 39, 76, 179, 255, 274, 282, 297, 299

Wonderful Tennessee, 6, 7, 15, 17f., 20, 28, 32, 38, 61, 71, 82f., 87, 91, 181, 183, 186, 195, 202-204, 214, 225f., 247, 248, 305, 312, 315, 319

Yalta Game, The, 305, 311, 321

Fugard, Athol, 310

Gaelic, 97f., 103f., 112, 124, 142, 147, 153, 164, 173-76, 265, 275, 293

generation, 3, 148, 158, 171, 176, 271, 283, 296

gesture, 31, 35, 70, 90, 94, 99, 103, 157, 196, 201, 286, 290, 293

Gottlieb, Vera, 257, 268

Graham, Martha, 179f., 183, 204

Greek, 75, 88, 103, 233, 313

Grene, Nicholas, 61, 72, 128, 137, 295, 299

grotesque, 129, 159, 187, 191, 274

Gussow, Mel, 260, 268

Hadfield, Paul, 252, 254, 266, 268

Hansard Parliamentary Debates, 296, 299

Hanvey, Bobbie, 304

Happé, Peter, 129, 131, 133, 137f.

Hattaway, Michael, 133, 137

Hawkins, Maureen E., 212, 226

Heaney, Seamus, 14, 17, 32, 35, 59, 93, 100f., 143, 152, 170-80, 209, 213, 226, 238, 248,

260, 265, 268, 273f., 282,
293, 299, 303, 315
hegemony, 173, 176
Heidegger, Martin, 301
Henderson, Lynda, 252, 254,
266, 268
hermeneutics, 6, 263, 265
Hickey, Des, 19, 32, 170, 179,
268
Hillman, James, 183, 204
history, 4, 5, 22, 39, 73-8, 81,
95, 98, 100, 102, 105, 109,
115-27, 131, 136, 146, 159-
61, 171, 195, 197, 198, 211,
213f., 219, 222, 224, 225,
230-39, 243f., 246f., 251-67,
273, 276, 295
history play, 253, 262, 265
Hogan, Robert, 40, 59
home, 10, 19, 23, 56, 58, 70, 76,
86, 96, 110, 120, 135, 145,
148-50, 158, 163, 170, 206,
214, 218-21, 229, 234, 236,
239, 287, 297, 307, 309,
311f., 315, 317f., 323
homosexuality, 166, 175, 207
Howard, Jean E., 131, 137, 248
Hughes, George, 49, 59, 135,
137, 203f., 212, 251, 261, 268
humanism, 120, 223
Hume, John, 178, 272, 297, 300,
315
Hungarian, 2-4, 10, 91, 109,
110-14, 119f., 225f., 309, 324
Hussey, Gemma, 98, 107
Hutcheon, Linda, 241, 248
hypnotism, 61, 124, 128-30

icon, 128, 185f.
identity, 6f., 11, 36, 39, 42, 44f.,
50, 52, 63, 75, 98, 101f., 104,
115, 120, 123, 133, 157, 177,

200, 208f., 221, 224, 231,
233, 235, 253, 265, 288
ideology, 93, 112, 143, 153, 170,
246, 251-53, 258, 274, 276,
279, 291, 295, 319
illegitimacy, 96, 155, 166, 190,
210
illusion, 28, 46, 47, 52f., 80, 90,
153, 158, 162, 208, 246, 258,
276, 293
image, 14, 27, 47, 54f., 67, 82f.,
106, 114, 169, 175, 186, 191,
195, 202, 218, 233, 237, 259,
266, 304
imagination, 5, 11, 27, 52, 62,
65-9, 87, 102, 125, 158, 169,
176, 183, 197, 213, 220, 232,
255, 263, 266, 273, 276, 287,
305, 315
immram, 130, 135
incantation, 45, 124, 130-32,
135f., 189, 203
indeterminacy, 166
individuality, 18, 37, 66f., 74-9,
89, 100, 185, 202, 205f., 212,
220f., 252, 254f., 259, 286
industrialization, 189
inferiority, 282
initiation, 88, 96, 157, 232
innocence, 76, 84, 86, 115, 154,
158f., 161, 165, 183, 193,
217, 232, 290
integrity, 23f., 194, 294
intergeneric, 37, 127
interiority, 74
interlude, 130-36
interpenetration, 6, 76f.,
interpretation, 7, 68, 70, 100,
107, 149, 161, 185, 195, 202,
209, 224f., 229, 247, 253, 265
intertext, 5, 7, 87, 100, 127, 144,
152, 174, 231, 241, 289
intuition, 29, 83, 217

irony, 17, 29, 55, 68, 73, 86f.,
    103, 107, 111, 114, 144, 146,
    159, 162, 177, 209, 224, 237,
    241, 247, 275, 277, 291
irrationality, 18, 22, 89
isolation, 77-9, 89, 125, 146,
    148, 218, 220, 289

Janáček, Leoš, 8, 61-71
Jent, William, 281f., 295f., 299
Jordan, Eamonn, 10
Jordan, Neil, 321
journey, 130, 136, 200f., 307,
    312, 317, 323
juxtaposition, 46, 70, 236, 266,
    284

Kahrl, Stanley J., 133, 137
Kamm, Jürgen, 203f.
Kavanagh, Patrick, 100f., 143,
    161, 173, 179
Kearney, Richard, 49, 59, 144,
    179, 223, 226, 241, 248, 263-
    65, 268
Kenneally, Michael, 36, 45, 57,
    59, 139, 226
Kennelly, Brendan, 101, 318
Kerwin, William, 58f., 137
Kiberd, Declan, 14, 17, 23-6,
    33, 37, 49f., 53, 60, 98, 102,
    106f., 124, 127, 137, 225f.
Killanin, Lord, 173, 179
Kilroy, Thomas, 3, 48, 60, 94,
    102, 126, 138, 254f., 268
Kosok, Heinz, 60, 102, 107,
    138f., 204, 221, 226, 269
Kurdi, Mária, 2, 3, 10, 72

Lancashire, Ian, 134f., 138
Lanters, José, 17, 31, 33, 203f.,
    207, 218f., 223, 226
Lee, J.J., 98, 108, 152
legend, 127, 144, 152, 158, 185

liminality, 52, 69, 87, 107, 274
linearity, 275
Lloyd, David, 283, 286, 299
Lodge, David, 248, 274, 299
Longley, Edna, 105, 108, 159,
    170, 179, 211, 213, 224, 226,
    254, 261, 268
loss, 10, 21f., 71, 74, 83, 85,
    97f., 106, 120, 147, 160, 162,
    169, 178, 194, 201, 208, 216,
    223, 273, 291, 297, 313
love, 8, 18, 19, 24, 37, 38, 40,
    54, 62, 65, 67, 69, 70, 75, 86,
    89, 103-113, 155, 167, 174,
    186, 209, 212, 214, 217-19,
    224, 245, 259, 317
Loyalist, 142
Lyons, Charles R., 262, 268

MacCana, Proinsias, 86, 91,
    136, 138
MacNeill, Máire, 85, 91
madness, 149, 175, 215, 218f.,
    239
Magee, Heno, 322
magic, 13f., 23, 36, 56, 59, 86,
    135, 308, 312
Mahony, Christina, 138
Margeson, J.M.R., 128, 130, 138
marginalization, 281f.
Martin, Graham, 4, 59f., 179-
    80, 240, 248, 282, 321
martyrdom, 185
mask, 47, 85, 154, 168, 191
masquerade, 274
materialism, 148, 155, 189
Maxwell, D.E.S., 2, 39, 42, 60,
    170f., 178, 180, 272f., 300
McCann, Donal, 320
McCann, Eamonn, 272
McCormack, W.J., 113, 251,
    268
McCusker, Frank, 320

McDonagh, Martin, 4, 321
McGinley, Seán, 320
McGrath, F.C., 2, 241, 249, 319, 324
McGuinness, Frank, 4, 9, 16, 29, 33, 60, 94, 102, 182, 267, 298, 300, 322
McKenna, Siobhán, 312
McMullan, Anna, 87, 91, 181, 203, 204
McPherson, Conor, 4, 130, 182, 321
McSorley, Gerard, 314
McVeagh, John, 264, 268
medieval, 7, 101, 123, 128f., 135, 172, 293
melodrama, 36, 46-8, 51, 74, 166
memory, 10f., 39, 44, 56, 67, 76f., 90, 106, 147, 161, 167, 185, 188, 191, 215, 220, 298, 307, 317
Mercier, Paul, 107, 269, 322
mercy, 15, 132, 276, 284
mesmerism, 45, 124, 126, 130, 136
Mesterházi, Márton, 4
metadramatic, 53, 265, 290
metalanguage, 82
metanarrative, 147
metaphor, 8, 14, 38, 48f., 96, 105, 162, 166, 171, 173, 183, 222, 225, 259, 276
metaphysical, 50, 182, 184, 194
metatheatrical, 51
metonymy, 262
microcosm, 318
minstrel, 156
miracle, 7, 11, 14, 58, 80, 123, 165, 184, 221, 284, 312
mise-en-scène, 190
modernist, 46, 230f.
modernity, 96, 209, 303

modernization, 309
Molloy, M.J., 322
monologue, 9, 26, 31, 37, 44-6, 49, 53-8, 63, 125-31, 136, 183, 186, 198, 242, 277
Moore, Brian, 174, 180
morality play, 7, 123, 128, 132f.
Morse, Donald E., 3, 7, 59, 72, 91, 225
Mullin, John, 300
mummer, 35
Murphy, Tom, 3, 5, 116f., 121, 125, 138, 307-312, 322
Murray, Christopher, 2, 5, 7, 9, 14, 33, 72, 91, 117, 121, 124, 137, 203f., 241, 246, 248f., 294, 300, 324
music, 6, 8, 10, 19, 61, 62, 63, 64, 65, 66, 67, 68, 69, 70, 71, 72, 81, 82, 86, 90, 151, 156, 174, 176, 188, 190, 191, 196, 198, 223, 238, 280, 296, 302, 305, 310
musicality, 10, 43
mystery, 14, 18f., 22, 29, 31, 37, 63, 71, 80, 88, 90, 124, 130, 132, 199, 201, 219, 233, 259, 308, 322
myth, 6, 15, 17, 78, 83, 87, 88, 90, 123, 124, 127, 131, 133, 135, 136, 142, 151, 174, 198, 206

narration, 29, 37, 43, 46, 53, 56f., 87, 90, 124, 126f., 136, 145, 147, 159, 162, 165, 168, 188, 198, 245
narrative, 7, 9, 45, 49, 75, 84, 100, 123, 136, 148f., 152, 158f., 162, 164-67, 172, 178, 188, 231f., 243, 258, 271, 274-76, 279, 282, 295

nationalism, 95, 105, 173, 174, 271, 272, 294

naturalism, 7, 9, 38, 195f., 199, 201, 258f., 291

Neuss, Paula, 129, 138

Nicoll, Allardyce, 131, 138

Niel, Ruth, 5, 138, 173, 258, 268

North, 8, 93f., 105, 108, 142f., 160, 169-80, 213, 224, 226, 252-55, 261, 268, 271-73, 283, 294f., 299f., 314-17

nostalgia, 10, 28, 189, 197, 208, 257, 307, 312, 315

Ó hÓgáin, Dáithí, 13f., 33, 86, 91

O'Brien, Conor Cruise, 9, 254, 295

O'Brien, George, 2, 169, 251, 282

objective correlative, 35, 165

obsession, 21, 38, 42-5, 50f., 56, 58, 78, 126f., 130f., 136, 154

Ormsby, Frank, 178, 180

Orr, John, 46, 60

otherness, 29, 61, 90, 194, 204, 305

outsider, 100, 281

oxymoron, 321

pagan, 188f., 193, 217

Paine, Basil, 37, 60

palimpsest, 5, 100-102, 106, 231

Pallister, David, 300

pantomime, 128

parable, 128, 165, 170, 202

paradigm, 135, 277, 311

paradox, 66f., 78, 208, 221, 247

paralysis, 8, 156, 170

Parker, Michael, 8f., 94, 173, 178, 180, 223, 226

parody, 9, 81, 83, 87, 159, 197f., 241f., 246, 274, 278, 290

pastiche, 241

pathos, 103, 106, 289

patriarchy, 144, 152f., 174, 212, 235, 285

Peacock, Alan, 32, 59f., 83, 91, 138, 171f., 180f., 204, 217, 223, 225f., 267-69, 295, 300, 314, 322

peasant play, 259, 262

performance, 5f., 8, 17, 24f., 40-72, 82, 90, 94, 126, 130, 142, 181f., 187, 191-203, 231, 236, 273, 301

performativity, 6, 63

peripeteia, 163

pilgrimage, 87, 100, 199, 201f., 214

Pilkington, Lionel, 224, 226

Pine, Richard, 2, 4, 10, 14, 17, 27, 30-3, 38, 60-5, 72, 78, 80, 91, 138, 220, 223, 226, 240, 249, 251, 257, 269, 272, 300, 301, 324

play-within-a-play, 46, 48

plurality, 274

polemics, 131, 253f., 262, 267

politics, 9, 76, 94, 97, 141f., 162, 171, 231, 253-67, 271, 273, 278f., 289, 293, 296, 314

postcolonialism, 10, 97, 173, 302, 305, 307-310, 319f.

post-independence, 152, 172

postmodern, 5, 7, 127, 230f., 241, 248

post-structuralism, 261

power, 13-17, 23, 29, 36, 42, 45, 47-61, 69, 71, 74, 80, 107, 116, 126, 129-32, 161, 168f., 184, 186, 191f., 199, 211, 212, 224, 238f., 247, 253, 272f., 286, 297

pre-modern, 76
primitive, 116, 119
privacy, 6, 9, 16, 21, 22, 24, 42, 44, 45, 55, 61, 74, 75, 76, 77, 78, 79, 80, 85, 89, 90, 99, 105, 124, 125, 174, 182, 189, 193, 196, 201, 206, 207, 214, 223, 237, 248, 256, 263, 275, 285, 302, 304
profane, 172, 188, 189, 201
prolepsis, 275
Protestant, 131, 152, 295
psychoanalysis, 63, 107, 244
psychological, 7, 20, 37, 45, 63, 105, 126, 144, 149f., 154, 182, 206, 213, 221-23, 233, 259
puritanical, 187, 192

Rea, Stephen, 93, 182, 315
realism, 6, 77, 181, 183, 190, 194, 195
reception, 2, 8, 178, 182, 224
redemption, 18, 30, 88, 164
redress, 273f., 286, 290, 292
religion, 84-99, 128, 159, 166, 186, 201, 223, 295, 306, 308, 311
repossession, 287
representation, 74, 175, 182, 186, 194, 208, 212, 271, 273, 278
repression, 153
Republic (of Ireland), 98, 170, 175, 252, 254f., 279
resistance, 69, 105, 115, 117, 145, 155, 167, 252
responsibility, 11, 13, 17, 80, 128, 160, 169, 251f., 320
reterritorialization, 286
retrospection, 38
revenant, 128
revisionist, 100, 102

rewriting, 7, 101, 127, 254, 263, 265, 305, 320
rhetoric, 78, 125, 162f., 236, 278f., 289, 293
rhythm, 133, 154, 191, 193f., 201, 217
Richtarik, Marilynn J., 97, 108, 253f., 266, 269
Ricoeur, Paul, 9, 266, 274
rite, 6, 17, 29, 46, 84-90, 128, 132, 135, 141, 157f., 181, 183, 186, 189, 192, 199, 201, 203, 214, 223, 278, 280, 305
Robbins, Joan E., 42, 55-7, 60, 124, 138
Robinson, Paul N., 43, 60, 138
Roche, Anthony, 1, 69
Roche, Joseph R., 4, 31, 33, 37, 43, 49, 53f., 60, 69, 72, 127, 129, 135, 138
role-playing, 176, 287
romance, 75
romanticism, 189
rural, 35, 76f., 142, 153, 169, 174, 187, 208, 265, 322
Rushe, Desmond, 37, 60

Sacks, Oliver, 5, 225, 230, 239, 241, 243, 246
sacred, 17, 61, 81, 90, 149, 188, 189, 197, 201
sacrifice, 16, 17, 21, 38, 55, 89, 128, 185, 189, 199, 203, 217, 289, 298
Salgādo, Gāmini, 129, 138
salvation, 166, 215
sardonic, 77, 146, 165
satire, 77, 169, 175
scepticism, 89, 150, 161, 260
schizophrenia, 212
seanchaí, 13
sectarianism, 177, 216
self-deception, 114

self-destruction, 36, 40, 135, 313
self-discovery, 315
self-expressive, 83
self-fulfilment, 16, 42
self-reflexive, 154, 258, 265
self-sacrifice, 16, 20
sensitivity, 18, 24, 63, 196, 215, 238, 283
sentimentality, 67, 71, 106, 168, 189
sex, 8, 141-63, 169, 171, 173, 178, 236
Shakespeare, William, 1, 82, 103f., 108, 137f., 144, 172, 174, 176, 262, 265, 277
shaman, 13, 15, 50, 128
Shaw, George Bernard, 237f., 249
Sheeran, Patrick F., 139
Sheridan, Peter, 322
showman, 39, 51
Sidney, Sir Philip, 276, 300
signified, 124, 150
signifier, 124, 193
silence, 28, 43, 71, 99, 123, 130, 152, 165, 191, 194f., 202, 215, 247, 276, 286, 296, 314
Simenon, Georges, 306
Singleton, Brian, 10
Smith, Gus, 32, 179, 268
Smith, Robert S., 19, 59, 170, 241, 249
socio-economic, 240, 272, 277, 280, 282, 297
soliloquy, 103
South, 8, 138, 142f., 170, 252, 254, 261, 271f., 295
sovereignty, 13
Soyinka, Wole, 310
space, 47, 56, 58, 65, 69, 71, 77, 103, 181, 196, 234, 245
spectator, 131, 202, 205, 213, 272

speech-act, 281
spirit, 15, 19, 30, 66f., 146, 170, 182, 185-88, 194f., 201f., 208, 216, 239, 243, 261, 273, 278, 280, 285, 293, 298, 311, 318
Spivack, Bernard, 129, 138
Steiner, George, 8, 64, 66, 71f., 74, 99, 106, 108, 114, 241, 249, 262, 301
Stoppard, Tom, 240f., 245, 310
storyteller, 39, 56, 284, 312
stranger, 160, 163, 188
stream of consciousness, 37, 127
structure, 7, 9, 36-9, 46, 48, 51, 55, 63, 71, 78, 83, 109, 123, 125, 127, 174, 194, 220, 255, 274, 275, 295, 314
style, 5, 66, 71, 76-9, 88, 100, 109, 111, 114, 117-19, 129, 186, 188, 195, 197, 199, 231, 258, 289, 303
subjectivity, 66, 70, 187, 232
subjugation, 235
sublime, 8, 71
subtext, 124, 136, 153, 176, 186, 196, 202, 236
subvert, 82, 90, 192, 274, 290
supernatural, 13f.
survival, 62, 95, 144, 201
symbolism, 37, 56, 88, 151, 156, 170, 176, 183, 188, 190, 194, 198, 205, 208f., 212-14, 217, 219, 223-25, 230, 276, 290, 295, 304
Synge, John Millington, 4, 37, 97, 107, 110, 152f., 167, 179f., 227, 229f., 246, 248, 255

Tallone, Giovanna, 7
Taylor, Peter, 108, 278, 300

Terada, Rei, 65f., 71f.

theatricality, 3, 6, 8, 51, 53, 63,
77f., 81, 90, 126, 130, 143,
183, 194, 196, 203, 229, 231,
244, 252, 254

Throne, Marilyn, 50, 60, 124,
138, 209, 211, 212, 227

Tolkien, J.R.R., 124, 139

totalitarian, 152

tradition, 7, 13, 35, 40, 56, 62,
69, 77, 85, 96, 98, 101, 119,
123-35, 163, 173f., 181f.,
189-91, 200, 225, 230, 246,
258, 265, 279, 296, 305, 308

tragedy, 14, 21, 26, 30f., 62, 81,
96, 98, 105, 112, 118, 135,
192-94, 199, 232f., 236,
238f., 245, 248, 280, 291, 298

transcendence, 57, 88, 255

transformation, 16, 51, 58, 88,
188

transgressive, 239, 274

translation, 4, 5, 65, 95-100,
102, 104, 106, 109-114,
119f., 172f., 231, 256, 259,
263-65, 302

tribe, 100, 104

trickster, 80

Troubles, 143, 160, 178, 180,
256, 267, 299-300

truth, 39, 41, 43, 45, 54, 58, 67,
85, 102, 120, 129, 133, 144,
149, 160, 198, 202, 207, 214,
220, 245, 278, 282, 288, 293,
312, 313

Turgenev, Ivan, 195, 231, 264,
267, 311

Turner, Victor, 308

Tydeman, William, 130, 139

Unionist, 142, 170, 286

universality, 66, 89, 223, 323

Upton, Carol-Anne, 220, 227

value, 10f., 23f., 67, 69, 107,
124, 154, 217, 220, 243, 247,
320

vernacular, 97

victimhood, 36, 42f., 80, 135,
154, 159f., 163, 173, 199,
201, 236, 274, 298

violence, 38f., 87, 119, 142,
145f., 152, 156, 158, 160,
164, 173, 176, 203, 207, 271,
284, 291, 298

vision, 9, 29, 31, 77, 79f., 88, 95,
128, 151, 152, 159, 169, 170,
185-87, 209, 220, 232, 234,
237, 242, 247, 276, 317

vocation, 20, 28, 50, 80, 128,
185

vulnerability, 96, 156, 165, 198

Wallace, Arminta, 49, 60, 231,
243, 245

Welch, Robert, 30, 33, 78, 91,
125, 139

White, Harry, 31, 81

Wickham, Glynne, 128, 129,
131f., 136, 139

Widgery, Lord, 78, 255, 271,
278, 295, 298, 300

Winkler, Elizabeth Hale, 5, 276,
295, 300

Witoszek, Walentina, 139

Worth, Katherine, 44, 46, 49,
56, 60

Worthen, W.B., 231, 249

Yeats, W.B., 13, 29, 32, 65, 69,
95, 152, 180, 182, 192, 203,
204, 236, 249, 255, 261, 289,
290, 308

CARYSFORT PRESS

The Press aims to produce high quality publications which, though written and/or edited by academics, will be made accessible to a general readership. The organisation would also like to provide a forum for critical thinking in the Arts in Ireland, again keeping the needs and interests of the general public in view.

The company publishes contemporary Irish writing for and about the theatre.

Editorial and publishing inquiries to:

CARYSFORT PRESS Ltd

58 Woodfield, Scholarstown Road,
Rathfarnham, Dublin 16,
Republic of Ireland

T (353 1) 493 7383   F (353 1) 406 9815
e: info@carysfortpress.com
www.carysfortpress.com

Carysfort Press was formed in the summer of 1998. It receives annual funding from the Arts Council.

The directors believe that drama is playing an ever-increasing role in today's society and that enjoyment of the theatre, both professional and amateur, currently plays a central part in Irish culture.

NEW TITLES

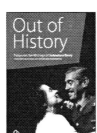

OUT OF HISTORY

ESSAYS ON THE WRITINGS OF SEBASTIAN BARRY
EDITED WITH AN INTRODUCTION BY CHRISTINA
HUNT MAHONY

The essays address Barry's engagement with the contemporary cultural debate in Ireland and also with issues that inform postcolonial criticial theory.The range and selection of contributors has ensured a high level of critical expression and an insightful assessment of Barry and his works.

ISBN 1-904505-18-X
€20

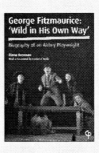

GEORGE FITZMAURICE:
'WILD IN HIS OWN WAY'

BIOGRAPHY OF AN ABBEY PLAYWRIGHT
BY FIONA BRENNAN
WITH A FOREWORD BY FINTAN O'TOOLE

Fiona Brennan's...introduction to his considerable output allows us a much greater appreciation and understanding of Fitzmaurice, the one remaining under-celebrated genius of twentieth-century Irish drama.
Conall Morrison

ISBN 1-904505-16-3
€20

EAST OF EDEN

NEW ROMANIAN PLAYS
EDITED BY ANDREI MARINESCU

Four of the most promising Romanian playwrights, young and very young, are in this collection, each one with a specific way of seeing the Romanian reality, each one with a style of communicating an articulated artistic vision of the society we are living in.
Ion Caramitru, General Director Romanian National Theatre Bucharest

ISBN 1-904505-15-5
€10

SACRED PLAY

SOUL JOURNEYS IN CONTEMPORARY IRISH THEATRE BY ANNE F. O'REILLY

'Theatre as a space or container for sacred play allows audiences to glimpse mystery and to experience transformation. This book charts how Irish playwrights negotiate the labyrinth of the Irish soul and shows how their plays contribute to a poetics of Irish culture that enables a new imagining. Playwrights discussed are: McGuinness, Murphy, Friel, Le Marquand Hartigan, Burke Brogan, Harding, Meehan, Carr, Parker, Devlin, and Barry.'

ISBN 1-904505-07-4
€25

IRISH THEATRE ON TOUR

EDITED BY NICHOLAS GRENE AND CHRIS MORASH

'Touring has been at the strategic heart of Druid's artistic policy since the early eighties. Everyone has the right to see professional theatre in their own communities. Irish theatre on tour is a crucial part of Irish theatre as a whole'. *Garry Hynes*

ISBN 1-904505-13-9
€20

PLAYBOYS OF THE WESTERN WORLD

PRODUCTION HISTORIES
EDITED BY ADRIAN FRAZIER

'Playboys of the Western World is a model of contemporary performance studies.'

The book is remarkably well-focused: half is a series of production histories of Playboy performances through the twentieth century in the UK, Northern Ireland, the USA, and Ireland. The remainder focuses on one contemporary performance, that of Druid Theatre, as directed by Garry Hynes. The various contemporary social issues that are addressed in relation to Synge's play and this performance of it give the volume an additional interest: it shows how the arts matter.' *Kevin Barry*

ISBN 1-904505-06-6
€20

POEMS 2000–2005
BY HUGH MAXTON

Poems 2000-2005 is a transitional collection written while the author – also known to be W. J. Mc Cormack, literary historian – was in the process of moving back from London to settle in rural Ireland.

ISBN 1-904505-12-0
€10

SYNGE: A CELEBRATION
EDITED BY COLM TÓIBÍN

Sebastian Barry , Marina Carr, Anthony Cronin, Roddy Doyle, Anne Enright, Hugo Hamilton, Joseph O'Connor, Mary O'Malley, Fintan O'Toole, Colm Toibin, Vincent Woods.

ISBN 1-904505-14-7
€15 Paperback

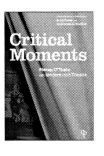

CRITICAL MOMENTS
FINTAN O'TOOLE ON MODERN IRISH THEATRE
EDITED BY JULIA FURAY & REDMOND O'HANLON

This new book on the work of Fintan O'Toole, the internationally acclaimed theatre critic and cultural commentator, offers percussive analyses and assessments of the major plays and playwrights in the canon of modern Irish theatre. Fearless and provocative in his judgements, O'Toole is essential reading for anyone interested in criticism or in the current state of Irish theatre.

ISBN 1-904505-03-1
€20

THE POWER OF LAUGHTER
EDITED BY ERIC WEITZ

The collection draws on a wide range of perspectives and voices including critics, playwrights, directors and performers. The result is a series of fascinating and provocative debates about the myriad functions of comedy in contemporary Irish theatre. *Anna McMullan*

As Stan Laurel said, it takes only an onion to cry. Peel it and weep. Comedy is harder. These essays listen to the power of laughter. They hear the tough heart of Irish theatre – hard and wicked and funny. *Frank McGuinness*

ISBN 1-904505-05-8
€20

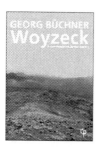

GEORG BÜCHNER: WOYZECK
A NEW TRANSLATION BY DAN FARRELLY

The most up-to-date German scholarship of Thomas Michael Mayer and Burghard Dedner has finally made it possible to establish an authentic sequence of scenes. The widespread view that this play is a prime example of loose, open theatre is no longer sustainable. Directors and teachers are challenged to "read it again".

ISBN 1-904505-02-3
€10

THE THEATRE OF FRANK MCGUINNESS
STAGES OF MUTABILITY
EDITED BY HELEN LOJEK

The first edited collection of essays about internationally renowned Irish playwright Frank McGuinness focuses on both performance and text. Interpreters come to diverse conclusions, creating a vigorous dialogue that enriches understanding and reflects a strong consensus about the value of McGuinness's complex work.

ISBN 1-904505-01-5
€20

GOETHE AND SCHUBERT
ACROSS THE DIVIDE
EDITED BY LORRAINE BYRNE & DAN FARRELLY

Proceedings of the International Conference, 'Goethe and Schubert in Perspective and Performance', Trinity College Dublin, 2003. This volume includes essays by leading scholars – Barkhoff, Boyle, Byrne, Canisius, Dürr, Fischer, Hill, Kramer, Lamport, Lund, Meikle, Newbould, Norman McKay, White, Whitton, Wright, Youens – on Goethe's musicality and his relationship to Schubert; Schubert's contribution to sacred music and the Lied and his setting of Goethe's Singspiel, Claudine. A companion volume of this Singspiel (with piano reduction and English translation) is also available.

ISBN 1-904505-04-X
Goethe and Schubert: Across the Divide. €25

ISBN 0-9544290-0-1
Goethe and Schubert: 'Claudine von Villa Bella'. €14

GOETHE: MUSICAL POET, MUSICAL CATALYST
EDITED BY LORRAINE BYRNE

'Goethe was interested in, and acutely aware of, the place of music in human experience generally - and of its particular role in modern culture. Moreover, his own literary work - especially the poetry and Faust - inspired some of the major composers of the European tradition to produce some of their finest works.' *Martin Swales*

ISBN 1-904505-10-4
€30

THEATRE TALK

VOICES OF IRISH THEATRE PRACTITIONERS
EDITED BY LILIAN CHAMBERS &
GER FITZGIBBON

"This book is the right approach - asking practitioners what they feel."
Sebastian Barry, Playwright

"...an invaluable and informative collection of interviews with those who make and shape the landscape of Irish Theatre."
Ben Barnes, Artistic Director of the Abbey Theatre

ISBN 0-9534-2576-2
€20

THEATRE OF SOUND

RADIO AND THE DRAMATIC IMAGINATION
BY DERMOT RATTIGAN

An innovative study of the challenges that radio drama poses to the creative imagination of the writer, the production team, and the listener.

"A remarkably fine study of radio drama – everywhere informed by the writer's professional experience of such drama in the making...A new theoretical and analytical approach – informative, illuminating and at all times readable." *Richard Allen Cave*

ISBN 0-9534-2575-4
€20

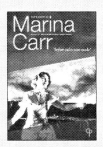

THE THEATRE OF MARINA CARR

"BEFORE RULES WAS MADE" - EDITED BY
ANNA MCMULLAN & CATHY LEENEY

As the first published collection of articles on the theatre of Marina Carr, this volume explores the world of Carr's theatrical imagination, the place of her plays in contemporary theatre in Ireland and abroad and the significance of her highly individual voice.

ISBN 0-9534-2577-0
€20

HAMLET

THE SHAKESPEAREAN DIRECTOR
BY MIKE WILCOCK

"This study of the Shakespearean director as viewed through various interpretations of HAMLET is a welcome addition to our understanding of how essential it is for a director to have a clear vision of a great play. It is an important study from which all of us who love Shakespeare and who understand the importance of continuing contemporary exploration may gain new insights."

From the Foreword, by Joe Dowling, Artistic Director, The Guthrie Theater, Minneapolis, MN

ISBN 1-904505-00-7
€20

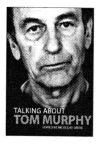

TALKING ABOUT TOM MURPHY
EDITED BY NICHOLAS GRENE

Talking About Tom Murphy is shaped around the six plays in the landmark Abbey Theatre Murphy Season of 2001, assembling some of the best-known commentators on his work: Fintan O'Toole, Chris Morash, Lionel Pilkington, Alexandra Poulain, Shaun Richards, Nicholas Grene and Declan Kiberd.

ISBN 0-9534-2579-7
€15

THE DRUNKARD
TOM MURPHY

'The Drunkard is a wonderfully eloquent play. Murphy's ear is finely attuned to the glories and absurdities of melodramatic exclamation, and even while he is wringing out its ludicrous overstatement, he is also making it sing.'
The Irish Times

ISBN 1-904505-09-0
€10

THE IRISH HARP BOOK
BY SHEILA LARCHET CUTHBERT

This is a facsimile of the edition originally published by Mercier Press in 1993. There is a new preface by Sheila Larchet Cuthbert, and the biographical material has been updated. It is a collection of studies and exercises for the use of teachers and pupils of the Irish harp.

ISBN 1-904505-08-2
€40

THREE CONGREGATIONAL MASSES
BY SEÓIRSE BODLEY, EDITED BY LORRAINE BYRNE

'From the simpler congregational settings in the Mass of Peace and the Mass of Joy to the richer textures of the Mass of Glory, they are immediately attractive and accessible, and with a distinctively Irish melodic quality.' Barra Boydell

ISBN 1-904505-11-2
€15

SEEN AND HEARD (REPRINT)

SIX NEW PLAYS BY IRISH WOMEN
EDITED WITH AN INTRODUCTION
BY CATHY LEENEY

A rich and funny, moving and theatrically exciting collection of plays by Mary Elizabeth Burke-Kennedy, Síofra Campbell, Emma Donoghue, Anne Le Marquand Hartigan, Michelle Read and Dolores Walshe.

ISBN 0-9534-2573-8
€20

UNDER THE CURSE

GOETHE'S "IPHIGENIE AUF TAURIS",
IN A NEW VERSION BY DAN FARRELLY

The Greek myth of Iphigenie grappling with the curse on the house of Atreus is brought vividly to life. This version is currently being used in Johannesburg to explore problems of ancestry, religion, and Black African women's spirituality.

ISBN 0-9534-2572-X
€10

IN SEARCH OF THE SOUTH AFRICAN IPHIGENIE

BY ERIKA VON WIETERSHEIM
AND DAN FARRELLY

Discussions of Goethe's "Iphigenie auf Tauris" (Under the Curse) as relevant to women's issues in modern South Africa: women in family and public life; the force of women's spirituality; experience of personal relationships; attitudes to parents and ancestors; involvement with religion.

ISBN 0-9534-2578-9
€10

THE STARVING AND OCTOBER SONG

TWO CONTEMPORARY IRISH PLAYS
BY ANDREW HINDS

The Starving, set during and after the siege of Derry in 1689, is a moving and engrossing drama of the emotional journey of two men.

October Song, a superbly written family drama set in real time in pre-ceasefire Derry.

ISBN 0-9534-2574-6
€10

THEATRE STUFF (REPRINT)

CRITICAL ESSAYS ON
CONTEMPORARY IRISH THEATRE
EDITED BY EAMONN JORDAN

Best selling essays on the successes and
debates of contemporary Irish theatre at home
and abroad.

Contributors include: Thomas Kilroy, Declan
Hughes, Anna McMullan, Declan Kiberd, Deirdre
Mulrooney, Fintan O'Toole, Christopher Murray,
Caoimhe McAvinchey and Terry Eagleton.

ISBN 0-9534-2571-1
€20

URFAUST

A NEW VERSION OF GOETHE'S
EARLY "FAUST" IN BRECHTIAN MODE
BY DAN FARRELLY

This version is based on Brecht's irreverent and
daring re-interpretation of the German classic.

"Urfaust is a kind of well-spring for German
theatre… The love-story is the most daring and
the most profound in German dramatic
literature." *Brecht*

ISBN 0-9534257-0-3
€10